PHILOSOPHY OF THE NAME

A volume in the NIU Series in Orthodox
Christian Studies

Edited by Roy R. Robson

For a list of books in the series, visit our website at cornellpress.cornell.edu.

PHILOSOPHY OF THE NAME

SERGII BULGAKOV

TRANSLATED, ANNOTATED, AND WITH
AN INTRODUCTION BY THOMAS ALLAN SMITH

NORTHERN ILLINOIS UNIVERSITY PRESS
AN IMPRINT OF CORNELL UNIVERSITY PRESS
Ithaca and London

First published 2022 by Cornell University Press

Library of Congress Cataloging-in-Publication Data

Names: Bulgakov, Sergiĭ, 1871-1944, author. | Smith, T. Allan, translator.
Title: Philosophy of the name / Sergii Bulgakov ; translated, annotated, and with an introduction by Thomas Allan Smith.
Other titles: Filosofiia imeni. English
Description: Ithaca [New York] : Northern Illinois University Press, an imprint of Cornell University Press, 2022. | Series: NIU series in Orthodox Christian studies | Includes bibliographical references and index.
Identifiers: LCCN 2021057528 (print) | LCCN 2021057529 (ebook) | ISBN 9781501765650 (hardcover) | ISBN 9781501765667 (pdf) | ISBN 9781501765674 (epub)
Subjects: LCSH: God (Christianity)—Name. | Word of God (Christian theology) | Logos (Christian theology) | Language and languages—Religious aspects—Christianity.
Classification: LCC BT180.N2 B813 2022 (print) | LCC BT180.N2 (ebook) | DDC 231—dc23/eng/20220126
LC record available at https://lccn.loc.gov/2021057528
LC ebook record available at https://lccn.loc.gov/2021057529

CONTENTS

ACKNOWLEDGMENTS

Translating the writings of Sergii N. Bulgakov is a challenging undertaking. Over a decade ago, I was encouraged to enter the fray by Boris Jakim, whose efforts to produce English versions of dozens of Russian religious philosophical texts is a towering and inspiring achievement. His work and that of another prodigious Bulgakov translator, Constantin Andronikof, have been of great help in sorting out some particularly obscure passages of Bulgakov's prose. I am grateful to Professor Emeritus Joseph Schallert who helped me untangle some Serbian folk sayings that appear in one of Bulgakov's lengthy notes. I owe a special word of thanks to the anonymous readers of my translation and introduction, whose comments have been instrumental in bringing this project to completion. I am most grateful to Amy Farranto and the publishing team at Northern Illinois University Press for their encouragement and assistance at various stages in the publication process. Above all, finally, I thank Bulgakov himself for captivating my mind and inspiring me to rethink so many things about the wonderful, meaningful, and beautiful world in which we all live and the language we use to give voice to its truth.

Abbreviations

Abbreviations for the names of books of the Bible follow those of the New Revised Standard Version.

altn.   Altlatein. i.e., Old Latin
Goth.   Gothic
PG.   *Patrologiae Cursus Completus, Series Graeca.* 161 volumes. Ed. J. P. Migne. Paris, 1857–1866.
Skt.   Sanskrit

A NOTE FROM THE TRANSLATOR

Bulgakov uses a pair of synonyms with subtle semantic differences that are important for this particular text: *sub"ekt / podlezhashchee* for "subject" and *predikat / skazuemoe* for "predicate." I translate *sub"ekt* and *predikat* as "subject" and "predicate" respectively. *Podlezhashchee* typically means "subject of a sentence," and where this meaning needs to be made clear, I have translated it as "grammatical subject." *Skazuemoe* means "predicate of a sentence," but this is always clear from the context and has simply been translated as "predicate." In addition to the pair *predikat / skazuemoe*, Bulgakov also uses the word *skazuemost'* when talking about predicates. Where it seems to indicate an abstraction, I have translated it as "predicative value," otherwise, as "predicate." Another word related to the matter of predicates is *predikativnost'*, which I have translated as "predicativity." The noun *sub"ektivnost'* is usually translated as "subjectivity"; however, on occasion it is clear that Bulgakov is talking about the quality of a grammatical subject, and in those cases I use "subjectival value" as more appropriate. I treat the noun *sub"ektnost'* as a synonym. Translation choices for several other important terms are explained in notes to the text.

Bulgakov uses scriptural references liberally throughout this book, but he is not always accurate. This is particularly true of his use of the Psalms. He sometimes follows the Orthodox numeration, sometimes the Protestant one. For the sake of consistency, I have corrected and renumbered all Psalm references to match the New Revised Standard Version of the Bible.

For the convenience of the reader, I provide a list of the works cited by Bulgakov, with titles translated. For the classical and premodern works, it is not possible to determine which editions Bulgakov used, except in rare cases. For these latter I provide publication information, otherwise only the title. Titles are not translated in the notes. Bulgakov's text is laced with citations in German, French, Greek, and Latin, which I have translated. Some Greek passages have been omitted because Bulgakov himself provided a translation for them; where that is not the case, they have been retained. Insertions in the text are marked with square brackets. Unless otherwise noted, all translations are mine. Occasional textual errors in the original have been corrected.

I follow the Library of Congress system for transliterating Russian and Greek text; however, for the Greek letter upsilon, I use *u* and not *y* and do not use diacritical marks.

PHILOSOPHY OF THE NAME

Introduction

As he moved intellectually and existentially away from his earlier career as a Marxist economist and commentator on contemporary Russian social and cultural issues toward a life as a theologian and priest, Sergei Nikolaevich Bulgakov (1871–1944) made one final formal foray into philosophy, under conditions that were far from optimal.[1] Stripped of his university appointment in Moscow by the Bolsheviks in 1918, he relocated to Crimea, where he taught political economy and theology at the university in Simferopol'. Two years later he lost that position when the city fell to the Red Army, and at the end of December 1922, he was expelled from the Soviet Union, landing first in Constantinople before ending up in Paris in 1925.

During this period of personal and societal upheaval, Bulgakov continued to write. His "At the Feast of the Gods," a dialogue modeled on Soloviev's *Three Conversations*, was included in the collection *Out of the Depths*.[2] His disillusionment with the Russian Orthodox Church found expression in *At the Walls of Chersonesus*, only published in 1991;[3] and his formal farewell to philosophy took shape in *The Tragedy of Philosophy*[4] and *Philosophy of the Name*, which he worked on from 1918 to 1922. While *The Tragedy of Philosophy* attracted some attention during his lifetime, *Philosophy of the Name* remained largely unread and unknown.[5] Neither book appeared in print during Bulgakov's lifetime, though a German translation of *The Tragedy of Philosophy* came out in 1927.[6] *Philosophy of the Name* was only published in 1953, nearly a decade after his death, through the editorial efforts of Lev Zander. As late as 1942, Bulgakov was still making changes to the manuscript, adding a significant postscript dedicated to a sophiological interpretation of naming and the name of Jesus. In the post-Soviet era, the book has been published three times, in 1997, 1999, and 2008.[7] In 1930 the first chapter was published in a German translation as "Was ist das Wort?" The book in its entirety was translated into French in 1991 with the title *La philosophie du verbe et du nom*, and in 2012 an English translation of the final chapter, "The Name of God," appeared in print.[8]

Philosophy of the Name consists of six chapters, a postscript, and some excursuses. In the first five chapters Bulgakov examines in considerable detail the nature of words, parts of speech, the simple sentence comprised of subject-copula-predicate, and the epistemological implications of grammar. The book demonstrates Bulgakov's extensive reading in classical and modern linguistic and philological theories: he cites the works of eleven premodern authors, two English, five French, twenty-two German, and twenty-one Russian authors. Of the modern linguists or philologists, the most important for Bulgakov are Wilhelm von Humboldt (1767–1835) and his continuators, especially Heymann Steinthal (1823–1899)[9] and Aleksandr Potebnia (1835–1891).[10] Other philologists cited are Jan Baudouin de Courtenay (1845–1929),[11] Georg von der Gabelentz (1840–1893), Max Müller (1823–1900), Gustav Gerber (1820–1901), Vikentii Ivanovich Shertzl' (1843–1906), Tadeusz Zieliński (1859–1944), and Michel Bréal (1832–1915).[12] His creative use of these historically important linguists is by itself a notable contribution to the history of modern linguistics.

Buried in the extensive excursus section of the book is Bulgakov's résumé of Plato's incomplete dialogue *Cratylus*, which revolves around the question of whether names are conventional or natural, whether words are arbitrary signs or intrinsically related to the things signified. The three speakers in the dialogue, Hermogenes, Cratylus, and Socrates, each wrestle with the question of the correctness of names, with Hermogenes speaking in favor of the conventional nature of words, Cratylus of the opposing natural view, and Socrates probing the positive and negative aspects of both positions. A significant portion of the dialogue concerns the etymology of the name Hades, as well as the appropriateness of the sounds of certain letters for the formation of words, i.e., the onomatopoeic theory of word formation. Bulgakov, unlike Plato or his own mentor Florenskii, engages with etymology only to a limited degree in *Philosophy of the Name*, perhaps displaying by his reticence a feeling of uncertainty about the actual purpose of that at times comical section of the dialogue. Rather, it is the dialogue's dissection of the natural or conventional nature of words that most resonates with him. Summing up his précis of the dialogue, Bulgakov wrote, "It is remarkable that in his dialogue, Plato touched on all the most important aspects of a philosophy of the word, even if only casually. He is equally concerned with the question of the inner nature of a word, or the word of a word, as he is with the body of a word, i.e., the sound, and he wants to push through the labyrinth of the history of words and of semasiology to the proto-elements of words, letters, i.e., he offers his hand to the mystics of the Cabbala."[13] Bulgakov also briefly discusses Plato's treatment of words in the *Sophist*. What particularly interests him in that dialogue is the examination of grammar as a way to understand the nature of words and meaning more generally.

Bulgakov acknowledged the importance of Leibniz, whom he regarded as the sole modern philosopher to have addressed the problem of language, word, and name. His philosophical foil, however, is Immanuel Kant, who comes in for considerable criticism for failing to pay attention to language and grammar.[14] He continues his debate with Kant that had occupied such a prominent place in *Philosophy of Economy, Unfading Light*, and the contemporaneously written *Tragedy of Philosophy*. Natalia Bonetskaia has demonstrated convincingly the extent of Bulgakov's indebtedness to Pavel Florenskii's thought on the nature of names, especially as they appear in Florenskii's *Imena* [Names], written in the 1920s and included in the incomplete *U vodorazdelov mysli* [At the watersheds of thought].[15] Aleksei Losev, who wrote extensively on the meaning of names, does not seem to have influenced Bulgakov.[16] However, he, Florenskii, and Bulgakov formed a triad of intellectuals who, in the process of examining the name-glorifiers movement, elaborated their own distinctive philosophical and philological studies of words and names from a sophiological perspective.[17]

Bulgakov's first systematic treatment of Sophia and sophiology comes in his *Philosophy of Economy*. There, Sophia is described as the transcendental subject of economy and as the transcendental subject of knowledge.[18] He notes, "Sophia, partaking of the cosmic activity of the Logos, endows the world with divine forces, raises it from chaos to cosmos."[19] As in *Philosophy of Economy* and *Unfading Light*, so in *Philosophy of the Name* Bulgakov describes Sophia as "the Soul of the world, the Wisdom of the world, as the all-perfected organism of ideas, as the Pleroma, the fullness of being. It is the intelligible basis of the world, the world as cosmos. . . . By contrast, our world is this same cosmos in the process of becoming. . . . It is sophian in all its being, but extra-sophian and even anti-sophian in its state."[20] It is in that environment that words appear and naming occurs.

Bulgakov believed that the universe communicates with humankind, and that as part of that communicating reality, human beings are able to receive and interpret the message, to speak for the otherwise mute and voiceless cosmos. The one speaking to them, he thought, was Divine Sophia. "Today I visited Niagara Falls," he wrote in his diary for November 30, 1934. "It is a vision of Divine Sophia in powerful elemental chaos! The Canadian side particularly astounded me. The mist and spray, the chaos, the seething in which the lucid form of the flowing power of the water would open up, and then close under a watery cloud. It was just like the ocean before the first day of creation. . . . This is clear evidence for the existence of Divine Sophia and her power in the world."[21] For Bulgakov it is the human being who receives the ideas of the universe and speaks them in words. Meaning precedes the human being; it is eternally present in God and manifested in the created world, the cosmos, in which humans act as the creative amplifiers for that meaning. The universe and the human being belong to the one same reality, dual in nature, united without confusion, without change, without division, and without separation, sophian in its foundation, imperfectly realized in its state. The ideas, the meaning filling the sophian universe are expressed in human language, or as he prefers, anthropocosmic speech.

Building on his own religious experiences stimulated by the natural world, Bulgakov turns to the prologue to the Gospel of John (Jn 1:1–5) to ground his understanding of an animated universe bursting with points of meaning. In his interpretation he distinguishes "two ideas about the Logos: the Logos in himself as a Divine Hypostasis, as God, and the logos operating in the world, although turned towards God, the energy of the Logos in the world, Sophia." Further, containing life, the Divine Logos imparts life as light to human beings, which empowers them as the microcosm to speak the word of the cosmos and to name. For, Bulgakov says, "the power of thought and the power of speech are one—it is the world logos abiding in human beings as their actualizing essence."[22]

The universe, containing meaning, ideas, does not interpret itself except through one particular component, the human being. According to traditional Christian theology, humans are able to call things by their name, to speak as the microcosm of creation because they are created in the image of the Divine Logos. Bulgakov returns frequently to Adam as the first-created human containing all names in himself in virtue of being created in the image of the Logos. Especially useful for him is the scene in the book of Genesis where Adam names all the living creatures. "So out of the ground the Lord God formed every beast of the field and every bird of the air, and he brought them to Adam to see what he would call them; and whatever Adam called every living creature, that was its name" (Gen 2:19). For Bulgakov this verse suggests not that Adam created names for the creatures, but that they spoke their names to him, names that were latent within Adam as one bearing the image of the Divine Logos, who is the source of all names.

Bulgakov charts a meandering course toward an elucidation of the mystery of names and our capacity for naming, by first considering the nature of a word in general. He focuses on three aspects: the origin, the composition, and the function of words. With respect to their origin, Bulgakov insists that words are not invented; they are not the result of some process, and are definitely not human works, but simply are. He reviews various theories put forward by linguists to explain the origin of words—onomatopoeia, convention, imitation—but rejects them all. He writes, "It remains simply, humbly and devoutly to recognize that it is not we who speak words, but words, sounding in us interiorly, speak themselves. . . . The world speaks in us; the entire universe, not us, sounds its voice. . . . A word is the world, for it is the world that thinks itself and speaks; however, the world is not a word, or rather it is not only a word, for it still has metalogical, nonverbal being. A word is *cosmic* in its nature, but it belongs not to consciousness alone, where it blazes up, but to being, and the human being is the world's arena, the microcosm, for in it and through it the world sounds."[23]

A second feature of a word is its composition. A word is dual in nature, composed of form and content; the form is the sonic body, the sound generated by the speech organs, while the content is the meaning enclosed in the sonic covering. There can be no word without an inner content, or meaning. The two fuse into an inseparable unity, without losing their distinctiveness, analogous to the union of the divine and human natures in the one person of Christ as defined by the Council of Chalcedon. Bulgakov writes, "A word is not merely an instrument of thought, as is often said, but is thought itself, and thought is not only the object or content of a word, but also the word itself. And yet, a thought is not a word, for it abides in itself, and a word is not a thought, for it has its own proper life. Logos has a *double* nature: word and thought, body and meaning, are merged in it without division and without confusion."[24] Further, he notes that every word signifies an idea, so that there are as many words as there are ideas. However, ideas do not exist without being incarnated, just as sounds are not words unless they contain an idea. Later, when he focuses on grammar, he will expand the description of word and speak of the phoneme, morpheme, and sememe, but a word remains twofold. The morpheme and phoneme are together the body, the sememe, the inner content.

Finally, he looks at the function of words. Bulgakov believes that words are necessary for thought; without words, no thought is possible. He calls words "symbols" and "hieroglyphs." In his understanding symbols are not arbitrary, external subjective signs but are naturally connected with the idea they convey. He says, "But it is not their arbitrary and deceptive use that makes symbols into symbols, it is their realism, the fact that symbols are alive and efficacious. They are the bearers of power, condensers and receivers of world energy. And this energism of theirs, divine or cosmic, forms the true nature of a symbol, thanks to which it is no longer an empty husk, but the bearer of energy, a power, life. To say that words are symbols means that in a certain sense they are *alive*." Hieroglyphs seem to be a particular type of symbol, for he calls a word that clothes an idea "the hieroglyph of the world, its verbal microcosm. . . . Words are living and efficacious hieroglyphs of things, in some sense they are themselves things as meanings."[25] But the meaning represented by a hieroglyph is not immediately evident. One must be able to read the hieroglyph correctly, as it does not necessarily correspond to the thing it represents. As an aside, it bears mentioning that he regards the image depicted in an icon as a hieroglyph of a word.[26] One could say that the function of a word is to envelop, embody an idea in some sort of discernible, perceptible, and intelligible covering, but the covering is not identical to the idea it contains.

One other feature of a word that attracts Bulgakov's attention is its magical quality. Words are incarnated meaning, idea, but they are also power, energy. Magic emphasizes the energy and power of words. Spells, incantations, hypnotism are all manifestations of the magical quality of words, in his opinion. He laments the loss of appreciation for the magic of words in modern culture, where words have become merely instruments of communication and not the voice of the world.[27] For Bulgakov only poets and poetry retain a sense of the magical power of words. Poets stand in awe of words that resonate with the voices of the universe. "In poetry a word ceases to be only a sign that it uses for signaling meaning, 'concepts'; here it appears as itself, i.e., as a symbol, and waves ripple away from it as a cosmic surge. It seems that one more moment and the lyre of Orpheus will tame wild animals and move mountains."[28] Poetry captures the magic present in words.

Although a word is the root of cosmic self-expression, were it to stand alone it would cease to be a word and revert to a meaningless sound. The word-symbols of the cosmos are interconnected, like the elements of the cosmos itself. The human articulation of the cosmic word-symbol occurs in speech, language, in the sentence, and it is only in speech that words exist in the true sense. Here the still undefined quality of the cosmic word-symbol acquires definition as a part of speech and a part of a sentence, thanks to the creative work of human beings. We use words, but we do not make words. The very essence of our use of words comes to light in naming. Bulgakov reaches that conclusion through a philosophical analysis of grammar, particularly the simple sentence or judgment.

All sentences consist of a subject and a predicate. The subject is typically a substantive noun, although any part of speech can assume the status of a substantive noun in the function of subject of a sentence. The substantive noun declares that some object exists. Bulgakov defines it as follows: "A substantive noun is an existential judgment, in which the subject is a certain point of being, that which of itself cannot be expressed in a word, but is named, whereas the predicate is a name."[29] He offers another, quite important description of the substantive noun in terms of Kantian language:

> The antinomy of a substantive noun is that what is named is unnamable, is transcendent to the word-idea, which expresses the modus of cosmic being. That which is found *under* the name—*under*-lying, or the *sub-jectum*, *hupo-keimenon*, is the transcendent noumenon, *ousia*, the Kantian "thing in itself." That *by which* it is named, is the predicate, *kategoroumenon*, the phenomenon with respect to this noumenon, its *ergon*, entirely belonging to the world of being and forms, immanent. So then, a substantive noun is something transcendent-immanent, noumenal-phenomenal.[30]

As a particular manifestation of the substantive noun, names will also display this antinomic quality.

Pushing his grammatical analysis further, he concludes that the actual subject of every sentence is the pronoun "I," which is present in all statements, in all words, either explicitly or implicitly, because every human word, every sentence is essentially a judgment made by a thinking subject. To offer an example, the substantive noun "house" actually represents a compressed sentence: "this is a house." That sentence or judgment is uttered by some "I." "I" is in itself empty of meaning; it is not an idea but stands in the place of a substantive noun. The personal pronoun "I" occupies, he writes, "a special position, because it embraces everything and nothing: everything, because it can be introduced into a predicative link with everything, and nothing, because it is itself not anything in the world of ideas, it is not a word-idea but is a word-gesture, a mystical demonstrative gesture."[31]

For Bulgakov, the essence of a word is its capacity for predication. Of themselves, words do not designate objects or concepts; words are only meanings or ideas, but the human being, in the act of naming, transforms those words into predicates, into names. But something must join subject and predicate to form a sentence, and that is carried out by the copula verb "is." Bulgakov repeatedly refers to the copula as the glue that fixes the predicate to the subject. It expresses the *energy* by which the subject is manifested and becomes known in one or another definition.[32] When subject and predicate are joined together in a sentence or judgment, we have naming, a name.

Naming is a human action, and from what he writes about naming, it seems to be the defining quality of humanness. It is a kind of template for any human creative act. In formulating a judgment, we take preestablished words and transform them into names. Without the act of naming, names would remain abstract; they have existence only thanks to the work of the person naming something. Naming is a free action: we can name or not name a given object, and in theory, we are free to name it in multiple ways; however, the freedom of naming is not absolute. The human being must listen to the object being named, because a name is the self-revelation of the object and belongs to the object, not to the one speaking. An object names itself. Bulgakov says, "If words are really the sounds of the world in the human, if they have an anthropocosmic nature, then they must really sound from the world and through the world, and in particular have concrete causes of arising."[33] Words as predicates, as ideas, are rays of the intellective world, which break into our world below. We name earthly objects according to their ideas, their intelligible forms. Continuing this adaptation of Plato, Bulgakov states that naming is actually remembrance: "We name them because *we recognize* in them the idea, slumbering in our very selves, as their ontological fundamental principle. . . . Together with Plato it is possible to say that we *remember*, we perform anamnesis, by naming things, so that in the final analysis, *naming* to which the living mystery of speech-word is reduced, is nothing other than *remembering*."[34]

What then is a "name"? Bulgakov offers many approaches to a definition: a name is a sonic word, the inner form of a word; it is vital; it is the power, potential, and content of the one named. An object's or a person's name is its "idea" in the Platonic sense. Even though it belongs to the very core of individual being, a name only represents the covering of an individual. "A name defines the being of its bearer but only in its state, not in its essence." It is "an expression of the essence of a human being, his essential substance."[35] The bearer of a name participates in the idea that underlies the word-symbol that becomes their name. Using Kantian language Bulgakov equates name and phenomenon and says that name is the revelation of the noumenon. "The noumenon does not 'lie at the foundation' of the phenomenon and is not entirely transcendent to it. . . . The noumenon simply *is* the phenomenon, this 'is' is expressed in its naming."[36] When he turns to the specific question of the Name of God, he says the same thing using Palamite theological language: a name is the energy of the thing named, whose essence remains unknowable for humans. The name is the thing named, but only in its state, not in its essence. A name is immanent-transcendent, an antinomy.

It is customary to distinguish common and proper names, and Bulgakov spends considerable time articulating how the two differ. While we might say that "Sergei" is a proper name, Bulgakov would offer a nuanced disagreement. This is because names, like words themselves, express ideas, and ideas are general, capable of being shared by multiple bearers. "Sergei" is a common name that only becomes proper when it is attached to a specific individual. Every Sergei shares in the quality common to the name, but each particularizes it in accordance with their specific personal histories. The only actual proper name of any human being is the pronoun "I," which remains mysterious and impenetrable. The following example may make his thought clearer. The statement "I am Sergei" would mean that a specific historical human being, who has been given the name Sergei and made it his own, is revealed in the name; however, the actual full truth and reality of that individual is not equal to or exhausted by the name Sergei. The state, not the essence, is expressed. It is similar with God, whose own mysterious essence remains unknowable for creatures, though through the revealed names, God can be known.

Combining his theory that words are spoken in the human being by the object, that is, they are in a certain sense a manifestation of the object's "energy," with the thought expressed in the *Divine Names* by Dionysius the Pseudo-Areopagite that the ineffable and transcendent Divine Essence reveals itself to human beings in its properties, which then become predicates, Bulgakov arrives at his understanding of the Divine Name as an manifestation of Divine Energy by the unknowable Divine Essence. He reviews the many instances in Scripture where God revealed himself, each of which becomes a name for God, but he identifies two instances in particular as supremely significant: the revelation of the name Yahweh to Moses and the revelation of the name Jesus to Mary. Both words-names are God's name, spoken in a human being by God; however, both words-names are also human words-names because it is the human being who articulates them by means of vocal chords and all the other mechanisms of speech. The Divine Names, which in a certain sense are the personal pronoun "I" of God, simultaneously reveal and conceal who God is. They are predicates of the subject; they are both human and divine. This is especially clear with the name Jesus: as Bulgakov points out, it was an ordinary, widely used name among the Jews of Jesus' time and thus is in itself not extraordinary or special. What makes it special in the case of Jesus of Nazareth is that he is both human and divine; in humility he condescended to incarnation in the flesh, parallel to his humble assumption of an ordinary human name by his "I," an act that makes the name Jesus also the name of the Second Person of the Trinity, of the Divine Logos. Like all names, Jesus of Nazareth's name becomes proper to a unique human individual—something made clear by the genealogies included in the gospels of Matthew and Luke. And like all names it is a predicate attached indivisibly to the person bearing it, manifesting some qualities or properties of its bearer but not disclosing its bearer's inner essence, which remains unknowable. At this point, it is important to turn to the original context in which Bulgakov composed his philosophy of language.

Bulgakov wrote *Philosophy of the Name* in response to the Name-glorifying controversy that erupted into Russian public ecclesial consciousness during the first decade of the twentieth century.[37] Its origins are connected with the 1907 publication of *On the Mountains of the Caucasus* by the schema monk Ilarion (Domrachev) (ca. 1845–1916).[38] Elder Ilarion spent his early years as a monk in the Russian monastery of St. Panteleimon on Mt. Athos from 1872 to 1892 before relocating to New Athos monastery in Abkhazia and eventually taking up a peripatetic solitary life.[39] His experiences with the mystical life and his efforts to explain them form the basic content of the book, though the focus is on the Jesus prayer. The aim of the book, he said, was "to express all the need, importance, and necessity of practicing the Jesus Prayer in the matter of eternal salvation for every person."[40] Paul Ladouceur situates the book in the popular devotional literature tradition of Russia and notes that much of the teaching contained therein is in line with expositions of the Jesus Prayer by Ignatii Brianchaninov (1807–1867), Feofan the Recluse (1815–1894), and the *Philokalia*.[41] Ilarion's utterances on the Name of God, however, proved to be quite bold and open to misunderstanding. For example, he claimed that God was present with his whole being and infinite properties in his holy Name, and that the fullness of divinity rests in the holy Name.[42] Because the Name contains Christ himself, the one praying the Jesus Prayer has a direct, transformative experience of him, which in the eyes of some could lead to a downplaying of liturgical prayer and sacraments.[43] Nevertheless, the book enjoyed wide popularity and received financial support for its publication from Grand Duchess Elizaveta Fedorovna, sister-in-law of Tsar Nicholas II.

The Name-glorifying controversy first broke out on Mount Athos after a negative review of the book by the monk Khrisanf of the St. Elijah skete, copies of which were circulated among the Russian monks on the Holy

Mountain. The salient points of this criticism were that by identifying the Name of God with God's person, Ilarion was merging God's essence with something outside his essence, i.e., he was teaching pantheism; he was also accused of attributing too much meaning to the name "Jesus," giving it characteristics that were proper to the divine essence, when the name itself was not divine but human.[44] The subsequent publication of the review in the journal the *Russian Monk* in 1912 brought new life to the controversy, eventually dividing the Russian Athonite community into two camps.[45] While the supporters of Ilarion, the *imiaslavtsy* [Name-glorifiers] believed they were faithful to the traditional prayer discipline of the Orthodox Church, his opponents the *imiabortsy* [Name-fighters] accused them of pantheism, idolatry, blasphemy, and eventually heresy. Disagreement reached such a state that an appeal for a ruling on the matter was made to the Ecumenical Patriarch, Joachim III, within whose jurisdiction the monasteries on Mount Athos stood. He referred the matter to theologians at the Theological School of Halki.[46] Based on their negative report, the patriarch censured the Name-glorifiers, but a significant segment of the Russian monks refused to accept his ruling.[47]

When news of the patriarchal intervention reached Russia, concerns arose about the possible implications for future access to the Holy Mountain for Russian monks if a sizable portion of the Russian Athonite community adhered to a theological position condemned by the Ecumenical Patriarch. This would be a factor in the eventual violent resolution of the Athos period of the controversy. Further complicating the matter was the First Balkan War (October 1912–May 1913), during which Greece wrested control of Mount Athos from the Ottomans. Russia proposed various options for the future status of the territory, including making it a joint protectorate of Russia and other Balkan nations. Its status was only settled after World War I with the recognition of Greek sovereignty over the Holy Mountain.

In Russia the Name-glorifying controversy reached a new level of intensity with the 1913 publication of *A Defense of Faith in the Name of God and in the Name Jesus* written by Hieromonk Antonii Bulatovich to defend Ilarion's work.[48] Antonii had received tonsure on Mt. Athos in 1902 under the influence of John of Kronstadt (1829–1908), an extremely popular, effective, and controversial parish priest active in St. Andrew's cathedral in the Kronstadt naval base near St. Petersburg. In *My Life in Christ* (1894), John of Kronstadt formulated a phrase, "the name of God is God himself," which encapsulates the core belief of the Name-glorifiers movement. Antonii agreed with Ilarion that God is present in his Name but is not identical to the Name. At the same time, the name is inseparable from God. He drew on the doctrine of Gregory

Palamas (1296–1359), who distinguished the divine essence from the divine energies of God. God is unknowable in his essence, but through his external operations or energies, humans can gain true knowledge of God; both essence and energy are truly God. For Antonii, the Name of God was one of God's energies, and thus truly God but not God's essence. He also claimed that the Name of God was superior to icons, for unlike the latter, which merited only veneration, the divine name could be worshipped.[49] Antonii's book attracted as much as or more negative criticism than had Ilarion's.

The Holy Synod of the Russian Orthodox Church appointed Archbishop Antonii (Khrapovitskii) (1863–1936), Archbishop Nikon (Rozhdestvenskii) (1851–1918), and a young lay theologian and canonist S. V. Troitskii (1878–1972), to examine the Name-glorifiers' views and submit separate reports. Archbishop Antonii, although a highly regarded theologian, wrote a polemical report and condemned *imiaslavie* as heretical without seriously engaging with it. Troitskii and Archbishop Nikon took more nuanced though critical approaches. Scott Kenworthy notes that Nikon was known as a defender of monasticism; he did not espouse academic scholastic theology but a more contemplative, experiential, and reasonable theology gained from his lengthy career as a monk before becoming bishop in 1904.[50] Nikon worked diligently to renew monastic life based on contemplative prayer and spiritual eldership. What most disturbed him about Name-glorifying was its central tenet that "the Name of God is God himself" and that the Name-glorifiers claimed the authority to define church dogma. His report refrained from declaring them heretical, though after he met with the Name-glorifiers on Mount Athos he changed his opinion.

In his report Nikon broached the subject of doctrinal authority in the Church, which was not located in a specific person but resided in the church as a whole; Ecumenical Councils had the ultimate authority, but in their absence, the Holy Synod and Ecumenical Patriarch functioned as legitimate representatives of the whole Church.[51] Nikon also focused on a topic that would become extremely important for subsequent evaluations of the Name-glorifying controversy, the role of reason in formulating theology underpinned by a philosophy of language. For him, a name was a conventional sign with no objective reality; that being the case, the Name of God could not logically be identified as God, who is the most real being. He argued that there could be no contradiction between dogma and reason. He examined carefully the Name-glorifiers' claims about the spiritual experience they enjoyed when praying the Jesus Prayer, and without denying the reality of their experience, he spoke of it as an experience of grace rather than of God himself. Nikon accepted that theology rested on spiritual experience of God, but

he argued that theological education was necessary for the correct formulation of theological opinions and doctrine. Kenworthy importantly draws attention to an inadequate grasp of Palamism and the distinction between the
divine essence and divine energies that hobbled both the Name-glorifiers and
their critics as they sought to clarify their respective positions. Nikon believed
that because Ilarion and Antonii Bulatovich had not presented their largely
unobjectionable teaching in a sufficiently clear fashion, the less educated and
the insincere monks could be misled to believe that by merely repeating the
Divine Name they would be saved. As Kenworthy concludes, Nikon objected
to imiaslavie "not out of a lack of sympathy or understanding for asceticism,
but precisely because he believed it would have a detrimental effect upon
ascetical effort."[52]

After receiving the reports, the Holy Synod commissioned Archbishop
Sergei (Stragorodskii) to compose a letter on imiaslavie for the Church at
large.[53] Kenworthy notes that Archbishop Sergei's letter offered a theologi-
cally balanced consideration of Name-glorifying but proposed stringent
measures to deal with it in practice. Name-glorifiers in monastic communi-
ties were ordered to submit to Church authority and cease further involvement; abbots were instructed to remove Name-glorifying literature from
their monasteries and turn over recalcitrant monks to ecclesiastical courts
for trial and possible defrocking. The Holy Synod published the three reports
and the letter in Tserkovnye vedomosti [Church Gazette] on May 18, 1913, and
sent Archbishop Nikon and Troitskii to Mount Athos to bring closure to the
controversy there.[54] They were joined by officials from the Foreign Ministry.
Meeting with considerable opposition from the Name-glorifying faction on
Mount Athos, the delegation took decisive and controversial action: with
the aid of the Russian navy, it forcibly deported over eight hundred Russian
monks for resettlement in Russia, where they were stripped of their monastic rank and returned to their places of origin.[55] These actions earned scath-
ing public criticism. Finally yielding to pressure, in May 1914 the Holy Synod
rescinded its condemnations and referred the matter for a final resolution at
the planned All-Russian Church Council of 1917–1918. The special commission
established by the council to reassess imiaslavie was not able to complete its
work before it adjourned on September 20, 1918, amidst repression by the
Bolshevik government. The result was that the Name-glorifying controversy
remained unresolved. Large numbers of Name-glorifiers took a short-lived
refuge in the Caucasus, for in the newly constituted Soviet Union they were
deemed a subversive clerical group and were systematically eradicated.

While on the surface the Name-glorifying controversy may seem to be
a relatively minor disturbance in the life of the Russian Orthodox Church,

especially given the historical context in which it flourished—World War I and the Bolshevik Revolution and seizure of power—it raised profound questions that continue to vex ecclesiastical authorities and theologians. Perhaps not since the Hundred Chapters Council of 1551 or the reforms of Patriarch Nikon and Tsar Aleksei Mikhailovich in the mid-seventeenth century, and the resulting schism, had the Russian Church been confronted with such an array of theological, doctrinal, disciplinary, and spiritual problems.[56] To claim that "the Name of God is God himself" is to provoke debate on the meaning of names in general and the Name of God in particular, which in turn leads to a general consideration of language and theology. It rouses from dormancy a doctrinal tenet of Orthodoxy about the distinction between the divine essence and the divine energies. Further, the insistence on the centrality of the Jesus prayer as a privileged locus for direct communion with God necessitates a reconsideration of religious experience and of the church's liturgical and sacramental life. More generally, the controversy exposed a vital question for any religious tradition concerning the ability of human language to express experiences of the Divine truthfully and authentically. The fact that Name-glorifying continues to inspire heated debate in the twenty-first century among Orthodox laity and clergy strongly suggests that neither the proponents of Name-glorifying nor their ecclesiastical opponents have managed to provide a fully satisfying resolution to the problems it raised.[57]

Publication of the synod's reports motivated many of Russia's leading religious thinkers to join the debate, including Nikolai Berdiaev,[58] Sergei Bulgakov, Pavel Florenskii,[59] Aleksei Losev[60] and Mikhail Novoselov,[61] who were largely sympathetic to the Name-glorifiers.[62] Bulgakov first addressed the controversy in an article, "The Athos Affair," in 1913.[63] There he explained that the advocates for imiaslavie were attempting to conceive in theological terms the religious experience had by monk-practitioners of the Jesus Prayer. He praised Antonii Bulatovich and the Mount Athos monks for their service to Orthodoxy by raising the question about the meaning of the Name of God. He was far less sympathetic toward the Holy Synod, strongly criticizing the three experts commissioned to write reports on imiaslavie. The article, however, focused more on the possibility of the church to make a dogmatic pronouncement on the matter, which he felt would be premature. He then produced a brief article on Gregory of Nyssa's understanding of names, in response to the book by S. V. Troitskii, *On the Names of God and the Name-divinizers*.[64] Troitskii compared the Name-glorifiers with the fourth-century heretic Eunomius, who had argued that human language was entirely adequate to expressing the mystery of God's essence, so that by naming the

Father "unbegotten" humans knew the Divine essence. He also claimed that Gregory of Nyssa's response to Eunomius showed him to be of the same opinion as the Name-fighters. Bulgakov argued the contrary position. While acknowledging the difficulty of systematizing Gregory of Nyssa's views on language, he asserted that Gregory ultimately would side with the Name-glorifiers, particularly with their religious devotion to the divine names.[65] Bulgakov was subsequently appointed to the subcommission of the All-Russian Church Council to assess *imiaslavie*; it became a question that would occupy his thinking for over two decades.

The Name-glorifying controversy took place at a time in Russian culture where interest in language in general, and the power of words in particular, was high. As Catherine Evtuhov noted, "The artistic and literary elite . . . perceived the name-worshipers as standing for the mystical investment of the Logos with meaning or divine energy. On this theory, language as such has mystical content."[66] Poetry in particular was the medium for the exploration of the mystical power of words, something that Bulgakov refers to frequently in *Philosophy of the Name*. At the same time, however, Bulgakov does not directly engage his contemporaries from the literary and artistic circles that flourished in pre- and postrevolutionary Russia. The only notable literary figure he identifies by name is Andrei Bely (1880–1934), a leading theorist and practitioner of Russian symbolism, with whom Bulgakov was personally acquainted.[67] He does pause briefly on the Russian futurists, showing some appreciation for their focus on the sounds and letters that constitute words but disdaining their attempts to subvert the essential unity of thought and word.[68]

Bulgakov's philosophical exploration of the word appeared at roughly the same time as the linguistic turn in philosophy in Western Europe, but he does not engage directly with this development. Perhaps even more surprising is the absence of Augustine of Hippo, whose treatise *De doctrina christiana* deals explicitly with the question of words and symbols,[69] although N. A. Vaganova has detected echoes of Augustine's Trinitarian thought in Bulgakov's discussion of the "metaphysics of utterance."[70] By 1911 Bulgakov had published a collection of essays on religion, culture, and socialism, *Two Cities*, loosely inspired by Augustine's *City of God*,[71] and Augustine would occupy a significant place in his theological writings to follow, once he settled in Paris.[72] His chief Western interlocutors are representatives of German Idealism, his linguistic sparring partners, the "romantic" philologists indebted largely to Wilhelm von Humboldt. John Milbank has noted, however, that Bulgakov's prescient recognition of the central importance of Fichte for modern European philosophy and his critical reception of some of Fichte's insights has positioned him to be an important countervoice to phenomenology and analytic philosophy, both of which had appeared in western Europe by the time he wrote *Philosophy of the Name*.[73] Gottlob Frege (1848–1925), a professor of mathematics, logic, and philosophy at the University of Jena, is another thinker with whom Bulgakov's ideas on language can be fruitfully contrasted. While working to recast traditional logic, Frege delved into a philosophy of language, focusing on identity statements and the sense of the subject and predicate in a sentence, themes that figure prominently in Bulgakov's book.[74]

Bulgakov reflects at length on words as symbols and signs and insists on a natural connection between a word and the object it refers to, although acknowledging that the current human condition vitiates our ability to hear and accurately voice the object's meaning. His reflections bear some resemblance to ideas developed by two nineteenth-century thinkers whose divergent interpretations of signs and meaning made a lasting impression on twentieth-century linguistics, semiotics, and literary theory, namely Ferdinand de Saussure (1857–1913) and Charles Sanders Peirce (1839–1914).[75] Saussure argued in favor of a dyadic structure for signs, distinguishing the signifier, or the form of the spoken word, from the signified, or the mental concept. His differentiation of *langage* and *parole* may be compared with the distinction Bulgakov makes between language and idiom, that is, between the underlying universal language and its dynamic realization by different peoples. Unlike Bulgakov, however, Saussure held that there was no necessary or natural connection between the signifier and the signified. Peirce shares Bulgakov's belief in a real connection between the sign and the thing it signifies. In his investigations into logic and meaning, he advocated a triadic structure consisting of the sign, the object, and the interpretant. For his part, Bulgakov resorted to a Trinitarian structure—the subject, predicate, and copula—which grounds the connection between a name and the thing or person being named.

No longer enjoying the ready access to Western scholarship that had been possible before the 1917 Revolution, Bulgakov produced a book of fundamental importance for his own future theological development and one that confronts Western philosophies of language with a different, religious appreciation of that most basic element of human communication, the word.

For the question raised by the Name-glorifiers and their opponents, Bulgakov has a simple answer. "The Name of God is God" is a true statement if and only if one understands "is God" as a predicate, the actual function it performs in the sentence. The copula attaches the predicate "God" to the subject, i.e., the Name, so that the sentence could be accurately rendered "the Name of God is divine." The copula is not an equals sign where the elements on either side are interchangeable: it is not possible to reverse the sentence and say, "God is the Name of God," precisely the statement that some overly zealous or incautious Name-glorifiers made and with which the Name-fighters discredited them. Bulgakov's answer is an important modern application of Palamite theology and vindicates both sides in the controversy: yes, the Name-glorifiers know God through his name, through the divine energy, which the name is; no, the name is not God, the divine essence.

There are several other dimensions to Bulgakov's argument concerning the Divine Names. Two prominent themes that he explores are the similarity of name and icon, and of predication and transubstantiation. Both these pairs will find fuller elaboration in special studies: *Evkharisticheskii dogmat* [The Eucharistic Dogma], 1930, and *Ikona i ikonopochitanie* [The Icon and Its Veneration], 1931.[76] A theme that drew his attention, as it did that of linguists, is the fact of linguistic pluralism, the presence of hundreds of different languages used by humans for communication. How is one to account for this? Bulgakov presents the hypothesis of a single original language from which all others somehow derive, but he does not immediately give his assent to it. For him, the crux of the matter concerns words-ideas. As ideas clothed in sounds, conveying the meaning of the cosmos in a sonic verbal bundle, words are the foundation of all languages. They precede language. The idea or meaning that is the core of any word is unchanging, but the covering, the sound in which it is clothed, is variable. Because the inner word is constant, translation into other languages is possible. He comments, "What does it mean to learn another language or to translate into another language? It means to vest one and the same inner word in different clothes, to make it real."[77] He likens the inner word to a Chinese character whose meaning can be understood by people whose spoken Chinese is unintelligible to others whose language uses different sonic registers. In an interesting interpretation of the Tower of Babel episode, he believes that the ability to understand the different dialects or idioms that were used to express the one common language was lost—and not that everyone was using the exact same language, which then degenerated into multiple and various languages unintelligible to any but their speakers. Bulgakov touches briefly on Sophia in his essay on names, but it is only in the postscript, written some twenty years later, that he develops a sophiological interpretation of naming and the Name of God.

In *Philosophy of the Name*, Bulgakov focuses on religious-philosophical cosmology, deriving from his commitment to the doctrine of "all-unity" inherited from Vladimir Soloviev. Despite his own claim that the book was the most philosophical of all his writings, it also betrays a deeply theological purpose. An apt epigraph for the book would be the words of Psalm 19:1–4, "The heavens proclaim the glory of God; and the firmament shows forth the work of his hands. Day unto day takes up the story, and night unto night makes known the message. No speech, no word, no sound is heard, yet their voice extends through all the earth, their words to the utmost bounds of the world." Bulgakov's book is a philosophical-theological explication of how this might be understood in the modern world.

CHAPTER 1

What Is a Word?

Words are the medium for human cognition; thought and word are inseparable; the self-reflection of thought inevitably demands an analysis of what constitutes its primary element or material, i.e., it must begin with an analysis of the word, with an investigation of its essence.

What then is a word? Of course, in this form, the question sounds too inarticulate, for it is multivalent; it can be understood in thousands of different ways, depending on our intention, on our focus, on the concrete target of probing thought. Even within the relatively narrow limits of the scientific study of language, where it has its specific formulation, what most interests us here usually remains unnoticed.[1] Linguistics studies a word from the aspect of structure, phonetics, history, morphology, semasiology, and psychology, in connection with the whole rich content found in the contemporary scientific study of language. However, in this history, physiology, psychology, anatomy, and mechanics of words where the formation of a word and its fate are studied, the genetic investigation generally predominates, resting on an abundance of scientifically studied facts; but in the process, the problem of the word as such is not even noticed in the majority of cases. What makes a word a word, what constitutes its nature, its *eidos* [form], in any set of circumstances, in any language, in any epoch, in any usage? What is that specific sign without which there is no word? What is its ontological description?

This is a question not about genesis or becoming, but about essence, about *to ontos on* [that which truly is] of a word. All questions about the genesis of a word that usually arise here, namely, about the origin of language, about the primordial unity or plurality of idioms and the like, remain outside consideration in this formulation of the question. In fact, it is erroneous to think that, by investigating the genesis, we thereby are able to establish the essence; on the contrary, in a certain sense one must already know it before investigating, otherwise the investigation itself becomes impossible. A conventional investigation dictated by special purposes is not needed here; what is necessary is an intuition of word, a vision of word in its immediate being, in its idea. It is necessary to highlight and establish what *is self-evident* about a word and constitutes its axiom.

It is obvious that this first and fundamental axiom is found at the boundary of linguistics, which knows only concrete words, clothed in flesh and blood; linguistics deals with sounds, with already formed words, and it studies this flesh of the word in various contexts. Meanwhile, this word, clothed in historical flesh and having its definite place in a language and its history, is a stranger from another world; rather, it belongs to two worlds at once. Although it is given into the hands of a linguist for all of his analyses, it is not given to him entirely with this covering, and remaining itself, it does not fit into his research. There is no room for the question of the word in the science of words as such. If linguists consider themselves sometimes called upon to speak on the question of words, they are usually satisfied with obvious evasions and occasionally even with ingenuousness, the very worst sort being the pronouncement by a learned specialist that his own personal metaphysics, and sometimes personal prejudice, without being critiqued, is the scholarly resolution of the problem, not noticing that a preliminary elucidation or analysis is still required. In fact, the question about words is not a question of philology, although of course philology does have an opinion and gives its conclusion in the first instance. Usually philologists are not even properly conscious of it. But it is even more surprising that philosophers too are unaware of it to the same degree. For them language remains, according to the expression of Müller (Lectures on the Science of Language, 19), "like a veil too close to the mental eye of humans, scarcely noticeable." They usually look at a word only as an instrument of thought and not even of thought itself, but only of its statement, as a self-explanatory and self-evident means. In it they see an absolutely transparent medium letting in light, not unlike a window, about which one must be concerned that it is thoroughly washed or, at the very least, that it does not deceive with its colored panes of glass. In this sense they sometimes feared the word, measures were taken to set it in order, venomous tricks were let loose about it, not unlike Mephistopheles':

Denn eben wo Begriffe fehlen, da stellt ein Wort zur rechten Zeit sich ein.[2] [For where concepts are lacking, a word appears at the right time.]

Opinions such as we encounter in the theorist of language, Humboldt, that "die Sprache ist das Bildende Organ der Gedanken [language is the formative organ of thoughts]"[3] and that "es gibt keine Gedanken ohne Sprache, und das menschliche Denken wird erst durch die Sprache [there are no thoughts without language and human thinking happens first through language]" have remained incomprehensible and unheard. All modern philosophy, except Leibniz, passed language by, one can say, without having noticed the problem of the word. Neither Kant, Fichte, nor Hegel noticed language and hence were repeatedly victims of this ignorance. This was repeated in subsequent philosophy where some, the representatives of logic, saw in language only an indifferent means, while others considered the question purely psychologically. Philosophy and philology clung to the question about the meaning of a word for thought even when considering a more complex question, namely, the relation of grammar and logic; however, here this question remained either not considered at all or was handed over to psychology for consideration.

Thus, we repeat once more, our question stands on the boundary where the broad and abundant field of philology lies on one side and from which the obstinate paths of philosophy lead to the other; however, it does not arise as a special problem of either special field of knowledge, but as one of the fundamental, immediate, and primary perceptions of human self-consciousness, as *gnothi seauton* [know yourself]. Humans are thinking and speaking beings; a word-thought, or a thought-word, is found in their possession *prior to* any concrete expression. Humans think in words and speak thought; their reason, *logos*, is inseparably linked with word *logos*. In an untranslatable play on words self-consciousness says to us—*logos* is *logos*.

So then, what is this *logos*—word—thought?

A word is the combination of the sounds of the voice and noises drawn out by our organs of speech, and it can be effectively pronounced or only indicated through a letter or by some other means, for example, by a gesture. This sonic mass is, according to the felicitous expression of the Stoics,[4] the body of a word, *soma*. Without this sonic body there is no word; whether it is pronounced or only schematically indicated, or only arises in our imagination (as notes already contain music regardless of their being played)—it is all the same. How this body of a word can be defined closer and more precisely, into which elements it can be broken up, which elements in it prove to be essential, which derivative, how they arose, etc.—these questions we can here set aside; they comprise the proper field of the scientific study of language. For the time being it is enough for us to establish that *every* word has a sonic body that can really come to be, i.e., be pronounced, or that is only present in an ideal form. Essential in this matter, obviously, is not the physical aspect of sound, the timbre of the voice, its power, and the like, but a definite combination of sounds, a sonic or musical phrase, ultimately, perhaps, a definite correlation of sonic vibrations, expressible by a mathematical formula, even by a number. It makes no difference: even a concrete number expresses a definite rhythm and sound, the structure of the sonic body, and determines the flesh of a word. The body of a word is a form, no matter in what it has been imprinted, or realized, even if in a gesture.[5]

As a form, a word is something incarnate, belonging to the natural, material world, inscribed in it, engraved and engravable in it. Is a word an object of the external world in the same way as this table, this pen, this ink? Is this written word such an object? Obviously, yes. And this printed word? Obviously, also yes. And this pronounced word? Why not? Can it be that the wind, whistling in a pipe or any other sound is not a (sonic) object or a manifestation of this world, is not in general a material object? What about a word that is copied onto a phonographic record, in the form of some grooves or that sounds from a phonographic trumpet as the cylinder turns? Or a word that I read in a book, hear, or feel (in the letters for the blind), or see (in the case of letters for the deaf)? Why not? What of a word that I think or by which I think, although I do not pronounce; which no one knows except me, which remains in the core of my soul? This word may be without sound, but it is not without significance. Indeed, I think in a definite language, not in language in general. Even my interior word is incorporeal, i.e., unformed, although it is stripped of sound; in my organs some sort of rudimentary articulations can occur, and the corresponding work is accomplished in the brain. Briefly put, it is possible for a word not to come to light, not to be revealed, but it nonetheless exists in its flesh, its ideal form is found in the imagination of the subject, where our silent word-thoughts more often than not cross over into thought, hearing, and monologue. Such in general is the origination of any living word, which proceeds from the darkness of silence. But it is already present in it before its pronunciation, as an object in a room emerges from the dark when light is introduced.

When I want to share my thoughts with another, I must make the words, the forms of words, which are only in the imagination, real. By clothing them in the flesh of sounds or signs, oral or written speech, I must thereby attest that my inner forms of the word, my inner speech, are the same word only realized contemplatively, a word of the imagination; and the material for this imagination, the object of memory or phantasy, is also a word in its concreteness. Word-speech, in the address of one person to another, crosses over into word-thought; it constantly appears and disappears from the surface, like a river that disappears under the earth; but where it comes up to the surface, it is carrying not new water, but the very same water that had only been hidden.

If it is still possible to contest the idea that thinking is accomplished by word, and is not only expressed by it (see below), one cannot dispute the fact that the interior word exists in us, clothing thought before speech. We *speak* not only aloud, but also within ourselves, about ourselves, in ourselves; we speak in sleep and awake, in consciousness and oblivion, and different degrees of the realization of a word, diverse means of its psychological experience, do not have a decisive significance for its being or essence. Likewise, it is of no importance whether I listen to a symphony of Beethoven in an orchestral performance or on a piano, whether I read it by following the notes with my eyes, or sing it by memory, whether I hallucinate it, and finally, whether I summon it in my memory in the imagination by an interior act alone, it is all the same: it is a symphony of Beethoven, a musical form having a certain shape, which can be incarnated and, what is more, only exists in the imagination. For form inherently forms, otherwise, it does not exist; in the given case, the very form itself is also the true flesh of this composition.

Of course, when we use the expression of the Stoics that the voice is the body of a word, we must not forget all the uniqueness of this body, which differs from a natural body to the same extent that any work of human art differs from it. The latter is the incarnation of an intention-form. Here the bearer of corporeality is precisely *form*, which however is necessarily realized in something formless until then (*me on, apeiron* [non-being, limitless]), and is clothed in flesh, really taking a body. The form, inherent in a certain image, is energy, power, neither material nor ideal, but inseparable from matter, existing only in it, antinomically conjugate with it, as its negation, overcoming and confirmation. This is idealized matter, illuminated by form, where the ideal and distinctive being of the form is realized precisely in its operation, i.e., in its ability to be incarnated; this is why it is impossible to speak about an incorporeal form abstracted from that which it forms.

The relative independence of the form of a word from the matter of its incarnation is also clear: it is as it were indifferent to whether it is pronounced or written or only realized by the imagination, by some such interior nearly indefinable articulations; it remains true to itself and identical in all of these reincarnations. However, like every form, a word also has *its proper matter*, in which it is incarnated fully and naturally. It chooses its matter and is selected by it, to a certain extent it is even created for it, so that for remaining incarnations matter is constrained, it is not their own, but is transferred. In this sense a symphony of Beethoven is written for an orchestra, the Venus de Milo is sculpted out of marble, and the Paris cathedral of Notre Dame is cut out of stone, and therefore neither a piano transposition nor a print or engravings can replace the original, although, undoubtedly, they reproduce their form, but without its power and sonority, without the fullness of its resonators.

The human word is first of all and principally a sonic word, realized by the organs of speech. Here it is born, here it lives in its fullness, and all other forms of the word can be understood as superstructures, repetitions, copies, works of this word. We think and write by word because by it we speak and learn to speak from hearing, i.e., perceiving the sonic body of a word. A closer inspection of the nature of a word shows us that it is similar to a work of art—or why not say it directly—**it is** a work of art, of course, *sui generis*; in it the substantial distinction belongs namely to *form*, in which the ability to be incarnated is necessarily inherent and which does not exist outside incarnation, and yet, matter has a comparatively secondary significance and in any case is not decisive. The body of a word is its internal form, and for a word it does not matter by what script, by what color, or on what kind of paper it is printed—it is preserved in its being, and by a similar means a given verbal form is reconciled with its various realizations, from internal soundless articulations[6] to a marine megaphone and gramophone.[7]

Of course one needs to bear in mind that *the whole word*, as form, is understood here, and not only the elements, which are called the formal parts of a word in grammar—this grammatical distinction is not relevant here. The essence of form is the relation of parts, a definite rhythm, a schematic. Therefore, a random aggregate of sounds, of those same sounds from which a word is composed (as, for example "water" and "waret") or the disorderly typesetting of letters as they happen to fall into one's hand, is not a word, for it does not realize a given correlation, and thus does not fulfill a definite form, and hence is also not a word-symbol—*logos*. Moreover, in the soul of the one hearing or reading, these combinations awaken at best sonic images of separate letters as such, not forming a word, nor entering into the unity of form. If it were possible to imagine a case of aphasia in which the memory of a word were lost, but the memory for definite sounds and letters were preserved, then the word and speech would be irretrievably lost. But sounds and letters result from the decomposition of a word as much as words result from putting letters together, and if the words were forgotten, then letters would cease to be letters.[8]

So then, a word is a definite form that can be realized in various ways but having as its original material a sound that can be articulated by the organs of speech. A word is a sonic sign—the form of sound. However, this only defines the external covering of a word, the physical body of a word, but this alone is not sufficient at all for obtaining a word. In fact, in nature different sonorities are encountered that have a definite form and even represent the results of the articulation of vocal organs: the cries of animals, the singing of a bird that has a definite melody, even the "talk" of a parrot that has learned to speak. But are these really words? Is this in fact different from a random melody that another bird whistles, having borrowed it from a human being? What of the cries of animals, and finally the cries of a human being in frenzy or pain, in intoxication? Indeed, any musical work is a sonic form, but it is not a word. It is obvious that a word becomes a word not from one sonic form as such, but only in the presence of definite conditions. The condition is that a word has not only form but also content, it has significance, hides *meaning* within. And this meaning is inserted in a sound, is fused with its form—there you have the mystery of a word.

Significance, meaning, is the necessary content of a word, and without this it will cease to be a word; "water" is a word, "waret" is not a word, for it signifies nothing, although formally it could be and perhaps it is one, if it exists in some language. *Every* word has a significance, there are no meaningless words, a word is meaning. Language has auxiliary words as well, the meaning of which is only intelligible in the context of speech. Setting aside for now such words, so as not to complicate the question, we must say that every word signifies *an idea* and there are as many words as there are ideas with their endless nuances and modulations. In order to become aware of this richness, it suffices to pick up a lexicon.

Grammar, clothing words in grammatical form, furnishes them with a supplementary meaning, allots them a certain modality that we here likewise dismiss so as not to complicate the question before its time. For now, we will pause only on the original, root significance, from which are formed different clusters and families of words and grammatical usages. Such a rudimentary word—neither substantive nor verb—is the stump of a word, its trunk, still not fully formed to live a full life, but it has already been born as a word, as meaning, as significance, as idea. Further, we know that one and the same word can have dozens of different meanings in metaphorical use, and one and the same thing can have dozens of words for its expression; this is the phenomenon of ever flowing life. But if we stop (of course, only by the effort of abstracting thought) this torrent of words and single out a definite word in some concrete use, then we will see that without fail it has significance, expresses an idea. The whole difficulty of detecting this process is that speech is always in motion; it is physiology and history, and not anatomy and mechanics, and yet, with the effort of thought we can detain or stop the breathing of a word in any place. I will take the phrase "the sea sparkles blindingly." It consists of three words [*more sverkaet oslepitel'no*] that enter into the totality of one meaning. But they only enter into this sense because separately they are words, each has its own proper meaning, by which it signifies, expresses its idea: the idea of the sea, the idea of sparkling, and the idea of blinding. Moreover, each of them expresses its idea independently of the given use in general, before this or that use of the word in a definite phrase, *irrespectively*. The use of words in speech, the expression of thought, is only possible because each word has its meaning independently, is an element of thought. Thus, in order to get the complex symphony of colors in a painting, with the richest hues and tinges and in the startling complexity and consonance of the whole, one must have separate paint elements, color sounds, just as for a symphony of Beethoven sonic elements are necessary in all the variety of their pitch, length, and timbre. And although in integral speech the significance of a word depends not only on the word itself but also on others entering into the phrase, on its whole meaning, still a word in and of itself, before any context or, rather, in any context, must have and keep its own significance, however it may be nuanced and modified. This is the *prius* of meaning; with words deprived of significance, it is impossible to express anything. If meanings were extinguished and words grew numb and broke loose, falling out of their settings like dead things, it would not be possible to say or to think anything. Here is the first antinomy of a word: a word has meaning only in a context, only in a whole. A word apart, isolated, does not exist. Separate words are abstractions, for in reality only connected speech exists, and yet a word has and must have its own proper independent significance, its own proper coloration. Nothing exists outside the whole, outside the cosmos, and words likewise exist in the verbal generality of the cosmos, and yet the cosmos is not an all-devouring unity, but is concretely polymorphous, in which everything individual is upheld. If we take any word in any form, in its history, in each given case, we will arrive at the conclusion that it is impossible even to define and pick out a separate word from its living context, and yet the fact is that a word is present as meaning, and the idea of it burns in its qualitativeness.

If we want to place a specimen of a word under a mental microscope, striving for an aesthetic vision of its substance, we must take the meaning of a word, its idea, in the idea's unmediated and nonrelational state, independently of that place which grammar and syntax, as well as logic, assign it. Idea, as the meaning of a word, is the pure qualitativeness of meaning, not suffering or permitting any secondary definition or expression through another, out of context. One must perceive it by absolute hearing, as the certain sounding of a definite pitch or timbre. One must liberate it also from its psychological covering, although this is always present (and usually psychologists and linguists fix their attention on it: apperception, association, reflexes, representation, apprehension, understanding, and the like—with all this they make other treatises on linguistics colorful; an example of such psychological porridge is the treatises of Steinthal, who is recognized as an authority for this). The psychological covering only shows how the semantic word germinates, but it cannot explain its very appearance: if there were no word, there would be no language nor would there be a psychology of language. Therefore, in respect to a word as such, as idea or meaning, it is misplaced to inquire if one or another word—water, light, darkness, book—expresses a representation or a concept, the abstract or the concrete. Perhaps this, or something else, or a third thing. It is possible to define and fill this verbal form psychologically one way or another. One can use it differently for both a representation and a concept, as well as for *Wahrnehmung* and *objectiwes Urteil* [perception and objective judgment] (in Kant). But none of this is as yet in the word itself: there is in it only an idea that exists in and of itself, as a single bare quality, outside relation or, more precisely, prior to relation to this or that logical use and the psychological experience connected with it. An idea caught fire and a word was born, that is all. Therefore, the eidetic essence of a word is completely lost, when for the comprehension of its nature one takes instances of the secondary formation of a word, or more precisely, of the new use of an already existing word; for example, terms: "let us call something this." Then the words take on the characteristic of a road post, placed entirely at random and for a definite purpose. Words are born, they are not invented; they arise before one or other use. That is the whole point. Sometimes it seems as if for the sake of convenience, an agreement was reached to invent a word to designate certain objects, but here an unresolved question is introduced into the problem itself, and often the very agreement about words already presumes their presence.

Thus, words, as the proto-element of thought and speech, are bearers of thought, they express an idea, as some quality of being, simple and not further reducible. This is the self-testimony of the cosmos in our spirit, its sounding. Concepts, representations, opinions, all are products of speech and thought, they are already the further results of the use of words; but they are completely inapplicable for qualifying and explaining them. Concepts can be abstract and concrete, general and unique, subjective and objective, etc., but not words. Words are all found equally beyond this distinction, they are pure meanings, qualities of being, ideas, pronounced in the interior word of a human being.[9] True, every word-thought, every idea, exists in speech in a formed shape as its definite element; it occupies a definite place in a sentence and has an etymological face: it is a certain part of speech, taken in a certain form, case, number, time, person, mood, and so on. Nevertheless, they are different concrete verbal captures of one and the same proto-element—of meaning. Thus, light, in light, about light, light, lightly, it lights, it lit, it lights up, etc.—all these are variants or, rather, formations of one thought-word-idea *light*. Wolf, wolves, wolfish, wolfishness, wolf cubs, she-wolves, etc. are variants of the idea *wolf.*

A word-idea can never be shown in its pure guise because all words are formed and drawn into the organism of speech and therefore impart definite nuances of a given meaning, of its usage. The root is, of course, not such a word-meaning, because the root word as such exists; it is not the result only of philological analysis, of abstraction. All the same, it has the one or other semantic nuance thanks to its placement in a sentence, to word order, as in Chinese, and to some extent in French and English. Of course, the core of meaning of a word is connected precisely with the root, as a comparison of words of one meaning but of different nuances shows, where namely the root remains constant and unchanging, or at least, the foundation, i.e., the complicated root. And yet, one cannot say that roots are only abstractions in the sense that they do not exist strictly independently, whereas words or even sentences do exist.[10] Roots exist, no more and no less than the remaining parts of a word and of speech, or words and sentences, for of course parts exist no less than the whole. But fully defined functions are connected with the roots of words, namely, they are bearers of semantic significance, the core of meaning is connected with them, the idea itself, which remains unchanged in all words of a given root and significance, whereas all the remainder has only a formalizing significance and introduces nuances. And just as no word exists that consists of the root alone (even when in a sonic way it is so, context then plays the role of inflection, prefixes, suffixes, and so on), neither does an absolutely isolated word exist that does not enter into the composition of speech and therefore is outside the defining formation and connection. Connection and formation are presumed by the nature of a word in the same measure as meaning—this is impossible to deny, but so too is it impossible to deny the core of a word, the root, with which the significance of a word is connected, the idea, the meaning. The formal elements are general and uniform; the root elements are individual and distinctive. And the meaning is connected with the root.

The most substantial and perhaps one must say fateful question for understanding a word now rises before us. How ought one to understand the significance of a word, the meaning of meaning? What does it mean that words have significance, what is the origin of words-ideas? We scarcely managed to open our mouth for this question when psychology already meets us, and quickly takes into its own hands the matter that naïve linguistics trustingly transferred to it. It diligently explains associations, apperceptions, apprehensions, representations; it shows that path by which a representation is born from demonstrations of feelings, and then for the convenience of designation a certain sign is admixed to this representation—thus does a word arise. Perhaps the cause of the origin of words is in the imitation of sound—the onomatopoetic theory,[11] perhaps the secret of its origin is in involuntary exclamations, interjections—the interjectional theory,[12] perhaps it is in interior gestures,[13]—the psychophysiological theory. However, in any case, consonant with all these theories, a word arises out of the need to have a conventional and abbreviated designation for a certain psychological content, more or less complex. The function of a word is representative, it does not contain meaning but only designates it; it is like paper money in a metal currency, the necessary and useful surrogate, the conventional abbreviation of a psychological complex. It is the result of a psychological technique, directed toward an economy of means; it is the outcome of a kind of economics of the soul.

One way or another a word is invented, contrived by humans for their needs, for the needs of communication and thinking, or it arose according to psychological or psychic laws and hence was perfected along the path of "evolution." The latter, as is well known, can explain the origin of anything from it, which is why it is now the reigning theory, and its point of departure is the notion about *homo alalus*[14] [speechless human], who gradually invents language. This appears to other naïve people no less proven and convincing than the pithecanthropus is for Darwinists. In the process, some do honor to human beings and leave for them a faculty for thought that separates them from animals, sometimes even leaving them a verbal faculty, while others consider thought and word a product of evolution.

The common feature of all these opinions about the psychological genesis of speech for the question at hand is *ignoratio elenchi* [ignorance of proof]: they pass by the content of the question but actually presume it resolved. All that happens in a human being, of course, passes through his psychological milieu, is subject to the action of a psychic mechanism, to psychic becoming. And by halting our attention on this psychic mechanism, we will learn much relating to how these or other functions in the soul run, how it masters, adjusts itself to and subordinates acquired habits, establishes *automatism*. And for understanding the phenomenon of the automatism of language and of the genetic processes of its origin, psychology can yield much. However, in addition to the question of *how* is the question of *what*. In addition to the question about the mechanism of language and psychic automatism, there is the central question about the very being of language, about the nature of a word. For, if there is a word, psychology can outline its patterns for the psychology of speech, just as if there is thought, it can analyze the psychic laws of thinking, and if there is poetry, it can develop the laws of poetic creativity, and if there is science, it can develop the laws of scientific creativity, etc. However, the genesis can track only development but not the phenomenon of what is developing, not the origin, not the generation, for evolution excludes generation, it deals only with what has already been generated and given. If language is given or a word exists, there can be an evolution of language, its psychology, but if it does not exist, then evolution will not help. Psychology, which deals with data already prepared, is without an answer where it is a matter not of the psychological situation in which these data exist and develop but about the data themselves, and it can neither understand nor explain the mystery of a word. In general, fashionable evolution, no matter how it is served up, is absolutely unsuited here and appears only by mistake.

Even less can one be satisfied with the idea of the premeditated invention of language. Who was the genius who came up with language? And how was he able not only to come up with it himself but to communicate it to everyone, to instruct everyone, to convince everyone, for language is universal? When and where did this happen, where are the signs of this? If one refers to the distant past, in which nothing is visible, then surely this is an *asylum ignorantiae* [refuge to ignorance], and one can cram anything into that grey expanse. But if I say that it was Pallas Athena who gave language, as the Greeks thought? Does it not please you? Well, then, say that you are advancing your explanation only because it pleases you, gratifies your prejudices. And indeed, what fantastic work beyond their powers would have been accomplished by those who began to devise language, what precision of thought would have to be displayed, what retentiveness of memory, what inventiveness!

Well, then, surely evolution, especially social development, would have been of assistance in this, would it not? Yes, it works all miracles for us, but here from the beginning you will have to hold everything in one head: first to invent a language, and then to pass it on to another, to others, so that they would be convinced, appropriate it, and understand it. But how do you pass on a language when there is no language? That is the problem. "Thoughts without speech and feelings without name," how is one to pass them on and name them? What is necessary, obviously, is no less than already having language and words, that is to say, what is already assumed must still be explained.

But here an even more important assumption is made, just as inconsistent as the conjectured presence of speech before its invention. This is the assumption of blind and mute thoughts without words. The supposition here is that an inventive *homo alalus*, who of course is still measurably an ape (and this surely so pleases our Darwinists), proposed to his fellow apes that he would express his thoughts and ideas in words so that the thoughts and words would be spliced together, resulting in a word-meaning. There you have the assumption of thoughts without words, of thoughts stripped from words, not incarnated in them and at the same time already generated and known—this is the greatest absurdity, because the indissoluble is torn to pieces. *Thoughts without words do not exist any more than words without thoughts.* We cannot think away a thought from a word or a word from a thought, just as we cannot separate our shadow from ourselves. This is not an actual or psychological impossibility, it is not the absence of skills or mechanism (e.g., how I am unable to play the piano because I do not have the associative mechanism and in general the corresponding automatism)—it is a purely subjective, factual impossibility, which is not present for others, and which I can overcome, at least in principle, if I should want to take lessons. It is not a logical impossibility that is established by contradiction and the destruction of the law of identity, like a round square; for there is no such *logical* contradiction in the idea that words can be separated from thoughts, where on the one hand, thoughts stand bare and not clothed in words, and on the other hand, where words rendered meaningless are already prepared to receive meaning. It is possible to think this because formal logic is essentially powerless to express itself here, because it takes no notice of formal impropriety. But there is here an *ontological* impossibility, lying in the nature of speech and thought themselves and establishing their *indissolubility*. We cannot think away thought from word and word from thought, we cannot tear their connection asunder, just as we cannot merge them, make them identical to the point of complete coalescence, but we are conscious of a thought born in a word and of a word expressing a thought (the bi-unity of *logos*).[15] And this is a final verdict without appeal, which all psychologists who study and interpret the genetic processes must take into consideration and put to use. Here is an axiom that is not proven but shown: all the power of persuasiveness lies only in demonstrativeness, in direct evidence.

But we also think without words, say those who wish to run behind the scenes of thought and observe what is happening there, *behind* a word (it's entirely the same as observing what happens in our room when we are not there). Others are satisfied with noting that a certain effort of thought or even creative intention elapses without words.[16] But surely it is thus a matter no longer of thought but of what precedes its generation, of the effort of the thought being generated, of the pressure of the mental pulse; in a word, it is a matter not of *speech* but of thinking as a voluntary activity, as energy, and perhaps not of consciousness but of what is deeper than that, "the subconscious." Thus this can also be true when applied to thinking as psychic tension, as the generation of thought from that which is not yet a thought, although it also gives birth to a thought. But our judgment refers to a thought already existing, to an uttered word. That *logos* is both thought and word retains here its absolute force. A word is not merely an instrument of thought, as is often said, but is thought itself, and thought is not only the object or content of a word, but also a word itself. And yet, a thought is not a word, for it abides in itself, and a word is not a thought, for it has its own proper life. Logos has a *double* nature: word and thought, body and meaning, are merged in it without division and without confusion. And that which can be expressed about thought and speech, this very same thing must be said also about word-thought. One cannot talk about the genesis of meaning and word in isolation or about their later pasting together or superposition one on the other.

In this sense generally speaking there is not and cannot be a genesis of a word, a word cannot arise in a process. It can be or not be, be present or not present in consciousness, this is a question of fact; already existing, it can have a development, a history, and in this sense a genesis also, but all this will be the history of a word already given and existing. One cannot explain word itself, nor thought; neither word nor thought, in this sense, has a genesis or arises, but simply are. One can explain thought only by thought or by thinking about it, which is clearly a vicious circle; in a similar way, one can explain the origin of a word only through a word, consequently, by presuming the word-creating energy already present, the inner word already having sounded. There is no thought not incarnated in a word, and there is no word not incarnating a thought. And in this sense, to explain the provenance of a word is a false task, a misunderstanding, an inability to think things through. A word is inexplicable; it exists in its miraculous primordial state. Moreover, the most surprising thing in this and at the same time the most essential is that meaning and form, idea and body, cannot be divided or confused in it.

As an idea does not exist without incarnation, so too sounds are not words without an idea.

But is this union of idea and form as indivisible as we assert when confronted by the presence of many languages? Does not the same idea clothe itself in different and numerous forms depending on the language? Does language in general exist or only languages? Is there word or only words? The question is serious and difficult, and at the same time unavoidable. Is there only one true primeval language (for a long time one considered, and many probably even now consider, that it was the Hebrew language), whereas all the remaining ones are variations or surrogates? And if not, then what is one to do with the many hundreds, perhaps, thousands of languages that linguistics currently knows?

Even if one were to accept the first supposition, all the same one would have to accept that for the given state of language all idioms have equality of rights and equivalency and serve the same purpose by different means. To say it another way, their verbal robing in the sounds of a given language becomes only the actual means of realizing the inner, unchanged word, so to say, the meta-word, the thought. Precisely this inner word-thought, idea, makes them all words. What does it mean to learn another language or to translate into another language? It means to vest *one and the same* inner word in different clothes, to make it real. And this realization, language as idiom, is a relative, historical matter. People learn a language, it is something acquired, languages are born, they die, and they are generally subject to history, psychology, to all kinds of genetic investigation. No matter how we understand the nature of a word and the structure of each concrete language, we must say that multilingualism makes a word similar to a Chinese character: each person reads in his own way certain written signs designating entire words, with the inhabitants of different provinces not understanding each other. The inner word-thought is similar to this Chinese character. The very fact of multilingualism, where one and the same word is realized differently in different languages, that is, *a word*, and not a concept, which is usually slipped in here, bears witness that body and idea cannot be confused in a word. If an idea and its incarnation completely merged and penetrated one another (as it is necessary to think with respect to the absolute divine language), then they would be indivisible, whereas now they are only seen one in the other, and at times they fall into decay for each other, they drift quite apart, die one for the other, in general they bear the seal of the contingent and the temporary. As Humboldt stated, "*Language* arises spontaneously only from itself, but languages depend on the nations to which they belong."[17]

So then, the inner word, idea, meaning is the real core of a word, which is contained in its verbal covering. Words of different languages, the different coverings, are threaded into one and the same meaning, and precisely this meaning makes them words. What does "to speak," to pronounce words, mean? It means to stir up in the consciousness meanings through words, as incarnated ideas. One can speak in different ways: first of all, one can speak with oneself, stir up meanings in oneself. I can think and in so doing speak "to myself," or with a pen in the hand, clothing the word in written form. I speak or write in a definite language, i.e., I do not use a word in general, but definite, concrete words. But to speak usually means to have communication in words. This communication likewise is accomplished in a definite language, and it is in principle all the same in which one, here the most important thing happening is that in the soul of the one listening the same inner words resound, the same meanings blaze up that are in the one speaking.

Words exercise the power inherent in them to realize meaning, to awaken an idea in the human consciousness. All the rest—the sonic body of word, the physical and physiological conditions of hearing, its cerebral substratum—all this belongs only to the realization, the incarnation, it is only the wires and the telegraphic apparatus, but not the telegram itself. The essence of speech is the awakening of meanings, it is the life of ideas-words in a human that connect the consciousness of people, and this connection is accomplished through language. This inner word has its own life; before it is incarnated in a word, in consciousness, it is realized in it.

Can one explain the origin of words-ideas by some sort of causes included in the human psyche, by a psychological mechanism? Here we encounter all the doctrines about the origin of a word from associations, apperceptions, reflexes, articulations, but all of this, to a certain extent, explains the psychic *mechanism* of language; at most it can explain only the psychic side of the origin of this or that word, its germination. Of course, none of these psychological explanations can explain the provenance of the core of a word—ideation itself. Why from perceptions, experiences, and connections does this core-idea come out, which possesses distinctive life capable of blazing up in the consciousness of every human being and preserving its vital force longer than grains of wheat found in the tombs of the Pharaohs, for words preserved in the most ancient writing have in no way lost their vitality, their immortality. Between the psychological explanations of the origin of a word and the word itself an inevitable hiatus arises. A word in its essence cannot be interpreted psychologically at all, in psychological terms, although in its incarnation it has its psychological clothing; the problem of the inner word does not even submit to a psychological formulation, it is not grasped with its tongs. One can, and in a certain sense, very likely one must understand any creative piece psychologically: the Venus de Milo, the Ninth Symphony, indeed anything at all—but does the most detailed psychological analysis really explain these things in their eidetic essence? Whatever may be the conclusions of such psychological analysis, the Venus de Milo lives its own proper life independently even of the psychology of the sculptor. More than this, because it could be created, it exists in a certain sense independently from the *means* of realization, or else the psychology of creativity would beget nothing. So too words exist only because they yield to mastering or realization through a psychic mechanism. Similarly, in order to learn a foreign language it is insufficient to have memory and time, but necessary that this very language exists. It is not people who unite themselves with words, by using language as a means of mutual comprehension or an instrument of communication, but words, language, unite people, who use their unity in word as they are able.

Sociality is not the efficient cause here as people now willingly think, but the consequence, result, realization. Language is not created in society but only implemented there, it binds society together and substantiates it. The Babel event, which, according to the biblical account, concerned only the sonic body of language and was conveyed in multilingualism, not yet having abolished the inner language, nevertheless proved to be so ruinous and destructive for human communication. If this event had concerned the inner word too, and if it had been extinguished in humanity, being replaced by various self-fabricated inventions in the manner described by psychologists, then human society would have been destroyed and every human being would be surrounded by the impenetrable wall of his or her own subjectivity. Each would have to discover their language for themselves; each would be born and die with it, and the succession of culture and history would have become impossible. Thus, humanity is connected by that inner word that sounds in a human being, communing with life at every utterance.

In order to be delivered from directly acknowledging this axiom, of which it is clearly sufficient to be aware in order to accept it, different explanations signifying nothing are usually seized upon, the whole advantage of which lies in their complete indeterminateness and paucity of content: heredity, evolution, associations, with a clear *petitio principii* [begging the question]. The ideal essence of a word can in no way be broken into psychological elements; it is not psychological at all, and hence is not even affected by a psychological explanation. *Words exist*, this is the fact with which psychologists must already reckon, but since they exist, there is also language. It is not language that creates words, but words that create language for their vestment, for their realization. Words-ideas are forces, some kind of ideal potencies, which create a body for themselves, and which possess the power of incarnation. It is a mistake to seek the genesis of language in psychology. Language, according to the felicitous expression of Humboldt, is not *ergon* but *energeia* [not *product* but *activity*], and only because of this can it become *ergon*.[18]

But if the inner word does not submit to a psychological reagent, perhaps it is subject to a logical or epistemological reaction and then, decomposed into its components, it will display its proto-elements or braces. Logic and epistemology explain precisely the meaning of a word, by detecting in it a general concept or notion, a concealed judgment, etc. Therefore, we can, as it were, suppose that the laws of logic and epistemology precede word, are the *prius* for it. However, if we scrutinize such arguments more attentively, we will be convinced that in such instances it is not the word itself that is being discussed, but one or other of its uses, i.e., what is already the product of a word, a thought; we are talking about constructions and not about proto-elements, which are not even noticed separately, although they too exist. In order to judge if *human* is a "representation," a "*Wahrnehmung*," an "*Urtheil*," and so on, it is necessary beforehand that the word *human* exist. A word is the proto-element of thought, into which thought decomposes, but a word is itself not further decomposable. We think with words-ideas, and thought is not in a condition to go beyond these limits, i.e., beyond its very self. And everyone puts this truth into practice as soon as they open their mouth for speech or take a pen for writing. We are standing here close to the elements of a thought in its proto-elements, the *cell* of a thought.

It remains simply, humbly, and devoutly to recognize that it is not we who speak words, but words, sounding in us interiorly, speak themselves, and at the same time our spirit is the arena of the self-ideation of the universe, for *everything* can be expressed in a word, and the creation of the world and our psyche enter equally into this word: *sun* and *boring* are equally ideas of the universe, thinking and being aware of itself. Because ideation is inherent to the universe, to the world, the world is also a word (for—"everything came to be through the word and without it nothing would be what it is"). The world speaks in us, the entire universe, not us, sounds its voice. Schelling's idea that the world is the identity of the subjective and objective, of the ideal and the real, or as we must translate this, of the verbal and nonverbal, of the logical and alogical principle; Schopenhauer's similar but distorted idea about the antilogical will and logical ideas; the similar idea of Hartmann about unity in the unconscious of the alogical and thought; the idea of Plato and Plotinus about the world of ideas showing through the dark alogical realm—all these are historical expressions of that axiom that is silently implied about a word: they say of the world that the world itself speaks of itself.

A word is the world, for it is the world that thinks itself and speaks; however, the world is not a word, or rather it is not only a word, for it still has metalogical, nonverbal being. A word is *cosmic* in its nature, but it belongs not to consciousness alone, where it blazes up, but to being, and the human being is the world arena, the microcosm, for in it and through it the world sounds; hence a word is anthropocosmic, or let us speak more precisely, anthropological. And this anthropological power of a word is also the real basis of language and of languages. Idioms are various and multiple, but language is one, word is one, and the world speaks it, but not the human being; it is the world-human that speaks.

Of course, this question about a single language as the real basis of multilingualism has no relationship to the historical question that is discussed by scholars: does a single "primordial language" exist, and can all idioms be traced back to it as to their primary source? Essentially language always was and is one—the language of things themselves, their own ideation. Incidentally, the Babel event therefore becomes intelligible as a phenomenon of the increase of one and the same reality, similar to the refraction of a white ray into the spectrum, as a linguistic increase and complication of *the one* inner language that originally was not distinguished even according to its sonic body. In this sense, we can understand the story from the book of Genesis about how God brought all the animals to Adam in order to see "how he would name them," (Gen 2:19), i.e., to put it differently, how they call themselves through him and in him, for he as a human being, as a microcosm, had them all in himself existentially, as the bearer of the divine Logos, as the image of God. He had in himself the power of the ideation of the world, in him the world's word was born. Which is why there is added: "And as Adam called each living being, so was its name." Here no mistake could occur, for it was not subjectivity: the names of creatures sounded in the human being as their inner words about themselves, as the self-revelations of the things themselves.

Yet this naming was not passive on the part of the human being, who was not just a mirror where objects saw themselves in order to know themselves in an idea, in their name, but it was also the action of the human being, for only the human being possesses speech. Speech is "the Rubicon separating humans from animals" (Müller); in him is the logos of the world, which is why the Divine Logos himself could be incarnated in him. And a certain feat of his humanity, a creative exertion, a manifestation of his power was demanded of the human being. Like every effectual creative act, it can be executed better or worse, more fully or weakly. If in first-created Adam, alien to sin, the ontological essence of his being stood against "psychologisms," then in his descendants, in the human race, the sounding of the world inescapably and regularly changes in the refracted atmosphere of distortion and obscuration. Language is given to humans because in them and through them the whole universe speaks; the human is the logos of the universe, and every word is not only the word of a given subject about something, but also a word of the something itself. Humans here are not free, they are compelled by ontological necessity, they are free to say or not say a word, to summon or not summon an idea, but once it has been summoned in their consciousness they no longer have the authority to change it, but can, at most, distort it in its actualization.

So then, word-ideas are voices of the world, the sounding of the universe, its ideation. Side by side with its alogical being, it acquires an ideal expression in word. With respect to its unuttered and unutterable essence, transcendent for thought and word, logos is expressed by a word. With respect to substance word is what is manifested, said, brought to light from the unuttered depth of being from which the shroud of darkness is removed; in the light, multiplicity, correlations, and individual traits become apparent, the face of being appears, its word and words. Such are the ontological roots of language in the most general and preliminary features, the meaning of meanings, the word of a word.

From the foregoing, an important conclusion about the ontological nature of a word itself results. What does a word represent—*realia* or *signa* [*real things* or *signs*]? The hoary centuries-old question of philosophy. The psychological understanding of words sees in them *signa*: abbreviations of thoughts or of representations, algebraic signs, or even signposts of the process of consciousness, and only in this sense are they *signatura rerum* [signature of things].[19] Arbitrariness, chance, and subjectivism define here the nature of words. We have already said that if it were so, the existence of language with its marvelous regularity instead of a universal shambles would be an incomprehensible riddle. But here more substantial by far is the fundamental idea of psychologists, namely, that it is we who speak, fabricate, and invent words; it is not words themselves that sound in us and are spoken. But in fact words are the self-evidence of "things," of the operation of the world in us, which awaken their corresponding ideas. The energy of the world is contained in words; word-creation is a subjective, individual, psychological process only by form of existence, whereas in essence it is cosmic. The world *all*, refracting, splitting, and sparkling in rays of meanings, reflects these rays, and these are words. Words are not at all galvanized corpses or sonic masks; they are alive, for in them is present the world energy, the world logos. The sun, sailing across the sky, constitutes the true soul of the word "sun," and by its ideal energy it *is present* in it, speaks about itself, more precisely, *speaks itself* in the human being. *Shines* is likewise the idea saturated with the shining power of the cosmos of the idea of luminescence; *storm*—here the cosmic storm speaks of itself; *goes*—the language of the world's expanse speaks, etc.

Briefly put, when a human being speaks, the word belongs to him or her both as microcosm and as human being, an integral part of this world. The cosmos speaks through the microcosm, but at the same time its living organic concreteness speaks through the human being, its definite psychical and historical individuality and its definite language, a definitely structured, individually qualified instrument. Therefore, a word as it exists is a surprising combination of the cosmic word of things themselves and of the human word about them, and besides, such that the one and the other are united in indivisible fusion.

This fusion is something incomprehensible and antinomic: the infinite of a thought is expressed in the finite sculpture of a word, the cosmic in the particular, meaning is joined with what is not meaning—with a sonic covering. That which is not at all a sign, but the essence itself, its energy, its operation, is inseparably connected with that which is only a sign, is a definite word that can be replaced by another sign. This puzzling fusion of the ideal and real (material) and the phenomenal, cosmic, and elemental, difficult for thought and disturbing for the heart, we call *symbol*.

Thus, we have come to the point: *words are symbols*. The nature of a word is symbolic, and the philosophy of the word is introduced thus into the composition of the symbolic worldview. Symbolism is greater than a philosophical doctrine; it is a whole perception of life, experience. Symbol is often understood pejoratively, as a sign that is external, arbitrary, subjective: "mathematical symbol," "verbal symbol." This pejorative understanding has its own objective foundation in the nature of symbol, for its matter—that which is symbolized *in it*—really is imprinted with human subjectivism, "with psychologism," as they now express it; in art it is "indicative" symbolism (Ivanov). But it is not their arbitrary and deceptive use that makes symbols into symbols, it is their realism, the fact that symbols are alive and efficacious. They are the bearers of power, condensers and receivers of world energy. And this energism of theirs, divine or cosmic, forms the true nature of a symbol, thanks to which it is no longer an empty husk, but the bearer of energy, a power, and life. To say that words are symbols means that in a certain sense they are *alive*.

So then, the cosmos speaks itself in words, gives up its ideas, discloses itself. A word is of the world, and not only a human word, it is the ideation of the cosmos. But cosmic meaning or an idea never remains bare and exposed; it is wrapped in a covering, and this covering is a word. In this way, in the generation of a word a double process takes place, going in two opposite directions: thought, its idea is distilled out of the cosmic being, is liberated, but once liberated it is clothed there in words, the hieroglyph of the world, its verbal microcosm. It leads its further existence in the world of thought and word. Words are living and efficacious hieroglyphs of things; in some sense they themselves are things as meanings.

An unavoidable question arises. How then does this incarnation of meaning, its wrapping in a sonic covering, the generation of a word, occur? How does a word arise? This is not the customary question for philology about the provenance of language as the faculty to speak, and about the appearance of words among *homo alalus,* although lately it is a question discarded with vexatious annoyance. Although it is connected with the question that interests us, still it is not concerned so much with the provenance of the faculty of speech, which consists of words, as with the generation of words or the symbolization of meaning. In this case, it can be about particular instances, or separate words, as well as about the propagating of words in general as symbolized meaning.

We distinguish in a word its phonetic aspect, its sonic chord, which is sometimes called a phoneme, and then its formal covering, the morpheme, which defines the *how* of a word, its place and usage, and finally, the signification of a word, its sememe, which however is inseparably connected both with the phoneme and the morpheme. When we inquire about the signification of a word, we may be concerned with the relation of phoneme and morpheme, which in essence are inseparably connected with each other in the sememe. The morpheme clothes the phoneme in the sense that it bestows *on it the formal* elements (flexion, prefixes, infixes, suffixes), that which is repeated in many words; as such it can be isolated separately from what in a given word is not repeated individually in other words, from what characterizes a given sememe as such. In the broad sense, this is *the base,* it is what remains in a word unchanged minus the changing formatives; in a more precise and narrow sense, a word is broken down into a root, made complex or noncomplex by some kind of morphological element. According to the definition of Gabelentz, "Wurzeln sind die letzten erkennbaren bedeutsamen Lautbestandtheile des Wortes [roots are the last recognizable, meaningful phonetic component of a word]."[20] And the question about the provenance of a word in a proximate manner depends on the question about the root elements of words. For us it has no significance whether or not a period of root language existed, as many think,[21] or whether this is only a methodological hypothesis; it is all the same. In either case, the individual significance of a word is connected with the root. Linguistics regards it as sufficiently firmly established that the formative elements of speech—endings in declensions and conjugations, prepositions, adverbs, even particles—were originally independent words, which had their root core. In those cases, when it is impossible to prove or to assume this, they have the significance of a shell or of covers that clothe another word. One way or another, an independent word has its own root core, and at the same time, this core is semantic: the fundamental principle of a word exists in which the fusion of word and meaning-idea has immediate primordial being. In the subsequent life of an already generated word, or of an incarnated word, different events and processes can occur, all augmentations, changes, and complications of meaning; relevant here are tropes like metaphor, metonymy, synecdoche, and what is called "the inner form of a word," etc.

No matter how far we come in our analysis of a word, we all the same necessarily rest on its root proto-elements, proto-words, no longer further broken up. Contemporary linguistics reduces these proto-elements to a comparatively small number of roots,[22] a few hundred for the many thousands and even tens of thousands of words. Each word can be splintered and multiplied, and by way of metaphor and every other contrivance (see the analysis of M. Bréal, *Essai de sémantique*), it can merge with another meaning, thanks to which there is an improper, indirect use of the word, in which the "inner form" of the word differs from its meaning, and the latter looks at itself in another's mirror. However, when the original significance of a word is forgotten or, what is the same, when its inner form, which can be discovered either by comparative linguistics or by linguistic paleontology, is lost, the new birth of an old word, as it were, is essentially possible, the new symbolization or fusion of meaning, not with a new sonic chord that did not sound previously, but with an old one that has begun to sound repeatedly, in a new way. Thus a hermit-crab can take up residence in a shell where a mollusk had been living, long after its disappearance. In a similar way, petrified words can once again be brought to life and filled with other meanings. At that point, one can speak not only of a metaphorical use of an existing, still living word in different figurative meanings but also of repeated or even frequent generation in the sonic covering of an unchanged word, and yet forming according to semantic replenishment a series of new words: *non idem per idem* or *idem per non idem* [the not same through the same or the same through the not same].

In any case, we come close here to the birth of sonic symbols of meaning, and this is the original mystery of a word. How are we to understand it? The question is not only why these or other sounds are selected for the sonic body of a word (with which the theory of "bow-wow" is occupied, and in part the theory of "pooh-pooh"), but namely about the fusion of a definite sonic chord with a definite meaning, about the solidification of meaning. All attempts to resolve this question by the hypothesis of rational invention, i.e., of there being words for expressing definite meanings, whatever they might be, err by the fact that they do away with the question itself and pose it in a false way. Imagine the matter thus. There is a certain meaning, an idea, which is given a verbal covering, for example, there is the idea of "water" and a word is sought to express it: water, moisture, and perhaps, earth, dry land, stone, orange, etc.; or the same thought can be expressed differently, for the idea of *water* one person will say water, another *aqua*, a third *Wasser*, a fourth *hudor*, etc. In so doing a completely inadmissible hypothesis is introduced, radically perverting the whole problem and converting every judgment into an empty phrasing about the nonsubstantial, namely that meaning exists *separately* from a word, and therefore that formerly there was meaning on one side, while on the other there was a word, or more exactly, different words, an entire assortment of words, and that they are selected or adapted. (Here it evidently knocks down "the use of words by analogy" and metaphors, i.e., when by free will a person chooses from *already* existing words certain colors for the nuances of his thought.) We however are trying to find out here the proto-elements of thought and speech, of simple word-thought, which actually is the fusion of two elements. But this is the point—that an idea without words, a meaning without symbolic incarnation, does not exist. We cannot even begin to think this, but as soon as we do begin thinking, we thereby will be speaking, for thoughts are inseparable from words.

Similarly, ready-made words (roots) that could be chosen and selected as empty forms or coverings do not exist at all. Sonic matter, realized by the organs of speech, represents practically an unlimited supply of possibilities for new word formations (although we see that language uses them sparingly and reluctantly, preferring to make do with a limited quantity of verbal themes or roots); but there are no ready-made, empty sonic words, void of meaning in sonic matter. Indeed in principle there cannot be: this would signify reducing the human being to the role of a bird, continually repeating definite sounds, a whole phrase that has no *verbal* meaning (although of course also having its own sort of meaning). But these are not words, and the human being does not have such sounds in stock. Alternatively, such elements can be letters of the alphabet and their various combinations, the number of which can be determined by a mathematical formula of combinations. However, letters are the result of the analysis of a language consisting of already existing words; speech disintegrates into them, but it is not made from them, and hence this hypothesis introduces what is subject to resolution. It turns out that the issue cannot be resolved. In other words, *the process of word generation cannot be observed*. A word is not put together, it is not selected, it is not thought up; it arises simultaneously and along with meaning. Therefore theories of the provenance of words from the imitation of sound or interjections prove to be so unsatisfactory because they are concerned not with the original emergence of words but their external covering. Imitation supposes only an inner sounding of a given word consonant with those external meaningless and dumb sounds that exist in nature and are psychologically connected with the representation of the concrete bearer of a given idea. That a cuckoo sings "cuckoo" does not at all explain *the word* "cuckoo" because between the word and the sound a qualitative difference exists. That in the given case the root corresponds to the singing of the cuckoo explains to a certain extent the choice of the sonic body for the word, but in no way at all does it even touch upon the mystery of how a word-meaning is generated in a human being from the meaningless and nonverbal sound of a bird.

We are forced to come to a conclusion that sounds not only paradoxical, but frankly absurd: *words generate themselves,* an idea itself merges with a sonic symbol, a meaning is incarnated in sounds. And yet, this proposition, *that words speak themselves* (Gerber),[23] sound themselves in a human being, but are not created by a human being, corresponds *to the nature of words,* and it cannot be otherwise.

Here explanations are required in order to remove misunderstandings both positive and negative in character. As was explained above, words are symbols of meaning, concrete, indivisible fusions of meaning and sound; a word in its elements—meaning in sound—*cannot arise in parts,* by being put together from these elements but can only occur immediately and prove itself. Since the content of a word is a cosmic idea, one can say that the cosmos speaks it through *a human being*. Since a human being is a microcosm in which and through which the whole cosmos speaks, realizes, is aware of itself, one can say that this word arises or is spoken in a human being, only not in a psychological but in an anthropological sense: words are being's monograms blazing up in consciousness. And their full weight, cosmicity, symbolic significance is connected with the fact that they are not invented but arise, they are as it were forces of nature that manifest or realize themselves.[24]

But do we not know the genesis of many words, their history? Do we ourselves not create language, fashion new words, and know how this happens?

What a tautology, *idem per idem*, "the explanation of x through y" is supposed here! And yet, here it is necessary to be focused on the central question, not being confused or enticed by secondary and extraneous considerations. In many cases, we actually know the history of words, as we know someone's biography, for example. But do we actually grasp through this his spiritual origins, e.g., that the given person whose biography we are studying, is Goethe or Pushkin? Or do his parents know this, who for their part have brought about what is necessary for his incarnation? But this is a lie and nonsense, because in order to want Goethe's birth, you have to be him yourself, you have to know him beforehand in yourself. But this is completely impossible, not only with respect to a genius but to any individual to whom belongs the mark of unrepeatability. So it turns out that a given human being gives birth to himself (of course, by the will of God), himself is incarnated from a given material. It should not be embarrassing that human volition and action (in particular the sex act) play a decisive role. Of course, without human participation, without the presence of parents, people cannot be born; similarly, words cannot be born outside a human being, but neither does a human being conceive of and invent words, as he also does not conceive of and invent a child, but receives it as it is, as it was born. And if children, as spiritual individuals incarnated in a body, in a certain sense give themselves birth, whereas the parents only provide them with their own flesh, so too words, although they are clothed in sounds corresponding to the whole totality of vocal and sonic possibilities (see below), generate themselves. And then, already arisen and existing words have in actuality a biography and history, but by going into this history regressively, in reverse order, we will arrive without fail sooner or later at the primary type—the root, which can no longer be explained genetically, which is subject only to ascertainment and not explanation.

And it is only about these proto-elements of speech, about the words of words, about a certain initial number of them in each language, perhaps different, that we are speaking. There are not and cannot be sufficient empirical grounds for defining this quantity and even saying whether it is limited or unlimited, whether it submits to a full calculation. The factual presence of such root words, which we are able to establish and which is, let us admit, diverse for different languages, will still not be exhaustive because some words could disappear as a result of their infrequent use or for other causes not sufficiently manifested. Therefore, the hypothesis of a definite complex or pleroma of these proto-words can be proposed, like rainbows of colors in which the sonic colors of the whole world are included; this hypothesis can be supported on common grounds, but for the question that interests us, this problem can and must be set aside. It is enough for us to accept the empirically established fact of the presence of a certain quantity of proto-words or roots in every language, on which the biographies of words rest as on their bedrock and indecomposable fundamental principle. And precisely these words, these elements of speech, are found in every existing language possessing power and vitality; they are properly language in language, and about them all these theories "of the emergence of language" arise: both "bow-wow" and "pooh-pooh," and others. Therefore, against the idea that words give birth to themselves we cannot raise the objection that we continually make words, and that our speech, as also the history of language, is an unceasing word-creation. It is entirely correct to point this out, but in fact, we create from prepared, already existing material. This is the most striking feature in the history and life of every language: a certain initial *givenness* exists in it to which the entire creatively, artistically realizable task corresponds. Language is created by us; it is our artistic product, but at the same time, it is given to us, we have it as a certain primordial endowment. We do not create what we have, but we create from it.

We also assert that these proto-words have spoken themselves. They are living, verbal myths about the cosmos,[25] in them cosmic events are consolidated, a word says something about itself, and primordial word-creation is cosmic myth-creation, the tale of the world about its own self, a cosmic rainbow of meanings, a verbal symbolism. Myth differs from representations, concepts, and their subsequent logical adaptations in that the latter are created by us in conformity with something, they are our hand-made articles; myth is not created and is not fabricated but is given and exists, and apropos of it, concepts arise.

But here we can recall: do we not even now fabricate and invent new words for different needs? All our automobiles, locomotives, carriages, telegraph and others—are they not newly created words? But the point is that these words are not invented but are formed from old already present verbal material, and such precisely is their inner history. They are composed according to a pharmaceutical recipe: so much of this and so much of that. In order to name a moving machine let us suppose that first a word is taken that designates place, for convenience and expressiveness in Latin, and then a word in the same language designating motion, and locomotive is obtained. In this way, in general, scholarly terminology is created: to express a complex of available meanings, concepts, and words, words are fabricated as abbreviations, which in their root meaning have precisely the required sense; hence a term is always an abbreviated verbal description that then receives in usage the form of a verbal monolith. Even more than this, psychologically a term is experienced as an independent, new word, a new verbal birth, and more than this, it is that new word that finds and creates for itself a new meaning. To say it differently, one has to acknowledge that word-creation is possible not only through primordial words that have given themselves birth, word-myths, a living linguistic givenness, but also through these already existing words; thus it is primary and secondary (and tertiary, etc.). This has enormous significance for the life of a language: through the forced windows of proto-words, the elements of meaning, ever new and expanding meaning is continually poured, just as the whole infinity of music develops from a few notes of the scale. Finally, others can still brag that entirely new words "are being forged" now, for example, all those hideous *sovdepy* [council of deputies], *vikzheli* [all-Russian executive committee of railway professional unions], *zemgory* [united committee of rural and urban unions] and the like. But it is obvious that here we have only a particular, more mechanized, and simplified case of the terminological process adapted to written speech, to capital letters, and by way of their so to say algebraic constitution new mannequins of words are formed. However (and mystically this is the most weighty side of this matter), such word-mannequins become vampires, they take their life, their being, and power. A whole cloud of such dead word-larvae, vampires, is formed that suck the blood of language and serve their black magic. Such is the occult meaning of this profanity.

In order to express more vividly our thought about the sense in which words speak themselves, or give themselves birth, let us compare it with some points that seem to be similar to it, but at the same time are profoundly distinct from it. And first of all our thought differs deeply from the crude notion, now scarcely defended by anyone, that God directly deposited in humankind separate words or a whole language in the manner by which a mother teaches her child to speak or how we learn a new, foreign language. This crude anthropomorphism is first of all not anthropological, and thus also not theological, and indeed is not devout at all. In accord with this notion, words or language are reduced to the level of signs of some sort, whereas instruction in speech brings a parrot to mind, with a completely passive, blindly appropriating role ascribed to the human being. Besides, according to the portrayal of the book of Genesis, God brought the animals to Adam to *see* how he would name them or, according to our understanding, how they would name themselves in him, through him. It is not the anthropomorphized God who teaches words to the human being, but the world created by God, the ontological center of which is the human being, to whom are stretched out and in whom sound the strings of the entire universe.[26]

Of course, we too suppose that the aptitude for speech is innate in the human being, and the idea of *homo alalus* goes back to Darwinian ravings, unfortunately holding sway over the souls of many linguists.[27] However, in asserting that the human being is *human* by nature, in the full significance of that word, i.e., a cosmic and at the same time a thinking being, the aptitude for logos as thought and speech is precisely what makes him or her a human being.

However, one must not bend this idea in such a way as to suggest that God inserted a general aptitude for speech into the human being, who then invents separate words himself. Such a viewpoint was sometimes expressed, it is true, in polemical enthusiasm and in patristic literature, in particular, for example, by St. Gregory of Nyssa.[28] Here again the notion creeps in that the human being, on the foundation of a general, indeterminate aptitude for speech, thinks up a language, composes words, evidently being guided by the one or other onomatopoetic criteria. In this way, language is clearly reduced to grammatical, instrumental, utilitarian significance. The originality of words, the kernels of meaning, the symbolism of language thereby is silently negated, for its problem is not noticed. The idea itself has such a vague character (the entirely indeterminate concept of "the aptitude for speech") that it does not even lend itself to criticism. Many representatives of linguistics share this very idea, that language, as a general faculty thanks to which separate words arise according one or other particular motive, is innate in the human being—outside any theological coloration or preconditions. One can name Steinthal,[29] Wundt,[30] and others. More often, this is united with an evolutionary doctrine, and then the whole burden of the question is transferred to the side of evolution, which in general works miracles and leads to completely new and unexpected results. Essentially the ancients—Diodorus and Vitruvius,[31] Lucretius,[32]—already took refuge in evolutionary concepts. The onomatopoetic and interjectional theories, which we already mentioned, are a variety of this—they only indicate particular causes of the natural evolutionary development and origin of language. For some it developed from wild-animal noises, for others from imitation of sounds, but in each case, a word is produced here from what is not in and of itself a word or is not yet a word. In the process, the chief, central, and sole question is not answered here—how does a word arise from a *not-word*, or what is the same, how does the *first* word appear in its originality—but is skirted with reference to the *gradualness* of the transition, as if one can construct a future evolutionary bridge over a precipice. *Ignoratio elenchi*, evasion of the question, self-deception—this is the unavoidable lot of evolutionary theory, here as in other cases. By this we do not at all want to negate the fact of the development of language, but one must know from what it proceeds and where it leads to, one must know its actualizing final cause, which contemporary evolutionists usually do not want to know, and in that bad infinity is the entire pathos of their theory.

However, is not our view also evolutionary? Yes and no. Yes, in the sense that of course language has a regular development corresponding to its nature; no—because this nature itself is not at all determined by development; on the contrary, development arises from the nature of language, and in the final analysis from the nature of humankind. The anthropocosmic nature of a word makes it a symbol, a fusion of word and thought, and precisely because words are not composed, but only brought about, realized by means of language in a human being and through a human being.

But if proto-words are cosmic symbols or myths that announce themselves, then the problem of multilingualism, of a Babel-like confusion of languages, and their existence in the several hundreds, gains particular acuteness. It would seem natural to expect that definite cosmic motives must also have homogeneous if not directly identical sonic expression. However, this is not so. Languages are multiform, and thus far no one has succeeded in reducing their multiplicity to a single ancestral language. If one did succeed, the question about the current multilingualism would remain in full force all the same. On the one hand, only the inner word, the meaning, establishes the one lingual quality of different languages, their inner unity as instruments of word, and creates the possibility of *translation* of a given meaning from one language to another. The confusion of Babel does not extend to the semantic side of a word; otherwise, it would completely annihilate the supreme creation of God—the human being. On the other hand, this multilingualism offers evidence that there is a refractive medium that multiplies the sonic output of a single meaning. The organ of speech, or the organism of language, is not the same among the different races. This difference affects not only the roots but also the entire structure of a language, its whole character or spirit, which yields to definition with such difficulty.[33]

However, here we are speaking for the present about roots. This difference of a sonic word, in the face of the identity or at least unity of the inner word, of meaning, forces one to postulate the equivalence of words in different languages or of these languages themselves. Actually, there are no grounds for extolling one at the expense of another, apart from personal tastes, sympathies, and blood ties. Every language is good in its own way,[34] and one can say everything in any language, perhaps with a different degree of difficulty, but this depends on the degree of development of a language or the skill of the one speaking, on the performer and not on the instrument.

This difficulty confronts us, for example, when translating philosophical or especially scientific ideas from one language to another. However, surely no one will say that the Russian philosophical language is worse than the German, although it is less developed. Probably the translation of Hegel into the Khoisan language will encounter still greater difficulties, but on the other hand, a precise, good translation of certain hunting expressions from Khoisan into German likewise constitutes no fewer difficulties, and if until now no Khoisan Hegel has appeared, one must imagine that this is not because of some obstacle on the part of the language.

If one listens attentively to the inner meaning of the narrative about the tower of Babel, it will become clear that in keeping with God's express intention, there was a single, natural language that apparently was veiled by the multiplicity and unintelligibility of idioms, which however would not have been such as to make instruction in a foreign language and its comprehension impossible. Moreover, reasoning on principle, instruction in any language, indeed in every language, is possible. The actual impossibility does not remove its possibility in principle; in bringing this about, multilingualism would be overcome and unity would be realized. And in the main what is important for us in the narrative of Gen 11:1–9 is that initially and naturally "language was one and speech was one" essentially (1). This unity of language is primary; it lies in the nature of language, in its foundation. Multiplicity is the *condition* of language, its modality, and what's more, it is unhealthy, for it is connected with the condition of the sinful dissociation of people. "The Lord said: see, there is one people, and among them one language for all, and they are beginning to do this, now nothing can prevent them from what they have proposed to do. Come, *let us confuse their language* so that they cannot *understand* each other's *speech*" (6–7). There is no talk here of creating new languages but of understanding the speech of the one language, which thus remains essentially one. If we take into consideration that the event in this narrative took place at a time when three branches of peoples had already formed, the Japhetic, Semitic, and Hamitic, resulting in whole nations that spread over the face of the earth (10:32), it can appear puzzling not that they stopped understanding one another as a result of a multilingualism, but that until this event they had one language and they understood each other completely. Then suddenly it was as if the veil of multilingualism fell and they stopped understanding each other. Linguistics was born at Babel.

If one believes in the divine inspiration of the word of God and attends to the exact content of this story in the general context it becomes clear that language and idioms were there even *before* the tower of Babel was built, and yet the language was *one*, so that everyone understood each other. The linguistic properties of peoples likewise hardly hindered this, just as now the individual features of pronunciation and speech do not hinder this, for speech is always individual, and if one compares words under a sonic microscope, then it will turn out perhaps that the unity of language does not exist even within families. I am no longer speaking about the structure of speech, about that to which the phrase "le style c'est l'homme" refers. So, language differences, whatever they might be, did not overshadow the inner word, and suddenly these panes of glass became opaque, and only with the help of special efforts can the understanding of meaning be achieved. Language, of course, remained unharmed in its foundation, but its inner meaning, which had previously been open, was closed, and there was a painful impressionability to individual features of sonic speech, to the realization of language. Humanity, which used its cosmic unity in word only for the attainment of its human goals, fell into psychologism (and psychologism is human pride), and naturally turned out to be punished by the psychologism of word. For in a certain sense multilingualism is this psychologism, closing off the ontological essence of language.

The reverse conclusion is possible: human beings, integrated and restored to their chasteness, can receive the inner word through a linguistic covering, i.e., defeat multilingualism. One instance of such a restoration of humankind to its normal state with respect to language has been related to us— Pentecost, when after the descent of the Holy Spirit on the apostles they began to speak in new languages as the Savior had promised them after the resurrection (Mk 16:17, cf. 1 Cor 12:10). The great number of peoples who were there heard them with surprise and asked, "Were they not all Galileans" (Acts 2:3–11). Thereafter the gift of tongues is frequently noted as the manifestation of the grace of the Holy Spirit and of a particular inspiration (Cf. Acts 10:46, 19:6; 1 Cor 12:10, 28, 30, 13:1, 14:2).

How should we understand this miraculous gift of tongues from the nature of language itself? It indicates only that its disease has been cured, which consisted in the haziness of meaning, and that its natural, original transparency and the unity that had been proper to it from Adam to the confusion of Babel returned. In consequence, the shroud of multilingualism was lifted. The apostles' sermon before the many nations can be understood in two ways. Either their own native Galilean speech became so distinct and transparent relative to the inner word-meaning that those who had not learned the language felt as if they had learned it, and they understood it as if they knew it, or, let us say, as if they understood some sort of expressive gesticulation without special translation or instruction. Or the reverse proposition is possible, namely, that the apostles received the ability to clothe their inner word in different clothes, in conformity with individual sonic peculiarities, so that the apostles actually spoke in many languages (as was the case in 1 Corinthians which described glossolalia at prayer assemblies, when not everyone understood the languages of the one speaking, and an interpreter was required). Essentially, however, this difference is transitory or ephemeral and both propositions are equally suitable, i.e., the apostles spoke in foreign languages because they all were transparent for them and, the reverse, by speaking in their own language, but with a meaning made transparent, they became intelligible for all the nations, for *language is one*, and only its modes are multiple—its idioms. If that ontological, or rather, anthropological, initial unity of language had not existed, Pentecost would have been an unintelligible absurdity. A miracle is not hocus-pocus, having no roots in being and even negating them, it is always the restoration of nature to health, the disclosure of its authentic nature and in so far an elevation to a higher level. In the miraculous, we identify precisely the true nature of the natural, and in the given case, the primordial unity of language is revealed that is just as primordial as the unity of the human race.

However, the question about the confusion of Babel or the many languages is posed even more sharply. No matter how we might understand the mutual relation of languages, or trace them to some first source—to an ancestral language—or leave them in an irreducible multiplicity (at least that of language families known by contemporary linguistics),[35] the question of multilingualism remains in its acuteness. True, this multilingualism in no way alters the unity of the inner language, otherwise mutual understanding would be impossible, and languages would split humanity itself, abolishing it; there is no plural of language, for language is one; only a multiplicity of idioms exists.

How are we to understand this multiplicity? It is first of all obvious that it does not concern the inner language, its noumenon, but its phenomenal incarnation, its realization, individuality. This is evident, first of all, from the fact that a language in the sense of idiom can be learned, and they are in fact learned; we learn our native language in childhood, and if we were deprived of this instruction, we would hardly invent our language and our people by ourselves. Language in this sense is a social-historical phenomenon and numbers among the garments one puts on and takes off over time, by circumstance, milieu, and society. On the contrary, we *do not learn* the inner language that lies beneath an idiom and at its base, words as ideas that are incarnated in sound or as symbols; rather, they *arise* in us and moreover they do so among us all equally in the measure of our humanness. (It is here understood, of course, that the fundamental, dynamic equality can in fact be realized disparately among different subjects.) The basis of language is cosmic, or anthropological; its investment and realization is a social-historical matter. In addition, language as idiom is a matter of human creativity,[36] art, psychology, history. Languages as idioms arise and die; they differ in age and elaborateness, and have different individual properties. They are prisms that refract and color rays in their own way. Language carries within itself the crystals of history, of national psychology; in general it is always not only an organism, but also a conglomerate that linguistics studies, applying to it different methods.[37] And of course, the one or other quality of the instrument, its properties, workmanship, and condition do not remain without influence not only on the realization of language but also on the very awakening of the inner language, of its energy. Here we have the not infrequent case of mutual, bilateral influence. Here is why it seems to us that an inner language is potentially proper to all people equally, even those who are deprived of an external language, i.e., the deaf, the mute, and the deaf-mute. In a fateful way, their language remains not fully incarnated and inaccessible to us, and yet those successes in language that are achieved by the alphabet for deaf mutes, the training that goes into it, would be impossible if that inner language were absent. This muteness is external, and not internal.

But the previous question about the symbolic nature of a word returns to us here anew. If a word is a symbol of meaning, the fusion of idea with sound, and if this fusion or incarnation of meaning is here a necessary condition, then how is one to understand the multiplicity of idioms? Evidently, one has to postulate some sort of meta-word, its noumenon, which is manifested in a sonic covering. These coverings in their totality form language, and of course, language is not the mechanical combination of words but their organism, so that in each separate word the entire language becomes apparent. Languages are as it were different resonators tuned in a definite manner, which resonate to given waves, and of course their special tuning is different, but at the same time all the remaining sounds resonate differently too.

We can and must speak *about the equivalence* of languages in the sense that each of them in its own way serves its goal—to be the logos of the cosmos and thinking, but at the same time, we must have in mind this difference too. To define, to detect, this difference is incredibly difficult; we do not now even know how to approach it, but immediate feeling bears witness that this difference exists, and the rainbow of language representing the refraction of a white ray, of *natural* language, or the authentic language of the world, has in its spectrum for each language a ray of definite coloration and significance.

All languages are natural, connected with the language of things, but each in its own way and differently. Thus, in the face of the equivalence of languages, we can and must postulate their inequality as well, their hierarchy: just as everything is hierarchic, so too language, although we do not have the means of establishing this hierarchic quality. And the rays of the solar spectrum have their qualification, and consequently a hierarchy, like the sounds of an octave. Perhaps different sounds have their own kind of *language keys* which we neither can nor know how to decipher. (I say this about the main languages and not about dialects that have a sufficient life or historical explanation and relate to the changeable fluid elements of the language.)

Science is now gradually disclosing to us the structure of the organs of hearing and speech. From the identification of these organs, the secret of language and the secret of hearing may ultimately be found. Undoubtedly, these organs are an ontological cryptogram of the world that we do not know how to read. From phonetics, we are coming to know how from definite groups of sounds and movements of the vocal organs sonic groups are obtained—words. What insanely complex and fine, "unconscious" work takes place here! If words are broken down into sounds and noises, i.e., definite vibrations of sound waves, then it is possible to consider the foundation of words as rhythmic motions that arise in the physical milieu, so that words or rather letters, sounds, are definite qualified rhythms. A word is the rhythm of rhythms, but speech is a complex rhythmic organism. In any case, here we are left with listening patiently to the work of descriptive, experimental phonetics and physiology.

What can be considered the proto-element of speech? Here is one of the accursed questions of the philosophy of the word: is it a letter like Cabbala, a syllable, a word? If a letter, then we must not forget that a letter only approximately designates a class of given sounds and their character, but the number of variants of a given sound that are designated by one and the same letter can be very large: it depends on the preceding and following sounds, on its place in a word, even in a phrase. Therefore, we have to speak *in concreto* not about a letter but about a syllable. For this reason, to stylize a letter as such is still a crude method capable of leading to misunderstanding. Steiner's eurythmy[38] apparently falls into it now, where the letters of the German alphabet are taken as symbols of rhythms, in an attempt to grasp the "surrational" meaning of a word,[39] translating it into a language of gesture or movement, which in turn expresses the sought after rhythms with extreme crudeness. In addition, one cannot formally equate all letters in a word as equal, conveying them by movement. The letters of a word are not equivalent: a word has a root base, an inflection, a suffix, etc. And to read all letters in a line without distinction, to make them into gestural eurythmy, is also incorrect. The crudeness of the eurhythmic approach closes rather than opens the nature of a word. As is well known, Cabbala considers the letters of the Hebrew alphabet (consonantal and semiconsonantal sounds) as the proto-elements of language, which also have cosmic significance. On this is based the Cabbalistic method of analysis of a word, of different permutations, the determination of the significance of a verbal number (gematria), etc. What are letters, as a written sign or sound, or more precisely, in a certain way a nuanced class of sounds? Is it only a vocal or linguistic means for composing a word from something? Do different letters exist because our vocal organs, our lungs, vocal chords, lips, palate, mouth, and nose are constructed in a certain way to take part in the production of sounds? Or is it exactly the reverse, are the organs of speech arranged exactly as they are because they are tasked with pronouncing sounds of a definite quality, and in this sense we can say that labial or dental sounds exist before lips and teeth? The organ itself is understood from function and not the reverse. In this sense are not the Cabbalists right by assuming that letters in their defined nature exist independently and even as if outside any relation to speech, being for example those forces from which the world is created?

Of course, it is beyond the powers of science to settle this question, i.e., which has priority, the organ or the function? No matter how valuable and important the successes of experimental phonetics might be, it is all the same unable to resolve this question and an answer to it will be given only on the basis of general considerations. For us it seems completely impossible to allow that the arrangement of the organs of speech and the classification of sounds arising from it happened by chance—this is too incompatible and irreconcilable with the entire surprising refinement of these organs, which must be understood from their functions. The vocal organs are such because letters are such: their task is not the pronunciation of letters in general but of a definite quality of sounds. And just as the eye, the organ of light, exists because there is light, so too the organs of speech and of hearing exist because there is sound as a world energy. Sounds create organs for themselves in the human being, in which the whole universe must be inscribed. Therefore, diverting our attention from phonetics and the physiology of speech, we must consider letters (in the above indicated sense) to have truly independent being, and not only *flatus vocis*.[40] Letters, the sounds of letters, exist in themselves, and only for that reason do they exist in language. Here there is a strong analogy with numerals and numerical values, to which letters confer the same status everywhere, by forming a numerical alphabet. Numerals are not created by arithmetic, rather arithmetic arises for the sake of numerals. We say this in passing.

Returning to letters, we must pose a new question that has not arisen thus far. Up until now, we have considered root words to be the proto-elements of speech that create clusters of meaning and express an idea. Now we acknowledge alongside these, or in addition to them, letters as proto-elements. What correlation is there between words and letters, between roots and the sounds forming them? Are words only the aggregates of letters, which one can therefore transpose, exchange, or are they letter-organisms? Is this connection mechanical or so to say chemical, in which the old disappears and the new is formed? The methods of Cabbala basically negate and annihilate words, for Cabbalists' language consists only of letters, indeed of a definite class (i.e., of consonants, because in Hebrew, vowels are missing and are not included among letters). Nevertheless, leaving these details aside in order not to complicate matters, we can say that this understanding of a word, which affirms the *power* of a word as a world element, destroys its meaning, the idea of a word; here a word is *only a power*, and not a symbol. Meanwhile, it is necessary to keep both aspects of a word. That letters or vocal sounds really express some initial cosmic qualities like colors, rhythms of a definite type like numerals, and perhaps some other quality, like the elements of chemistry, minerals, planets, etc.—of this we may have absolutely no doubt.

We can say by the way that investigations into the instrumentation of verse, into alliterations, in general into the sonic side of speech, except for the inductive-descriptive aspect, of necessity should include a phonetic description of the corresponding sounds, and then also investigations into their so to say general cosmic significance; and the contemporary impressionism of simple "imagination" that is being employed in the disclosure of meaning of this or that group of sounds must yield its place to a more precise description. At the same time, it is necessary to establish the axiom: although words consist of letters, being composed of them or decomposing into them, still letters are not words and words are not only letters. Here we have formations of a different quality: as a painting consists of paints, and yet it is not paints or only paints, but a concrete fusion of form and paints, so a statue is not only a piece of marble but again a certain concrete form. The secret of the birth of a word, the incarnation of meaning, consists in this transfer from one to the other, from letters to words.

Letters are both more and less, higher and lower than a word. Letters are more than words because there are fewer of them than words; one can even say that there is a definite limited quantity of them, whereas there are many words, even root words, and one can even say an indefinite, unlimited quantity. A letter is the expression of the power of nature, its quality, the primary color, from the mixture of which the world was formed. A word is a flash of meaning, of an idea, of which there are many and which have a fluid, modulating being; they express but do not form the cosmos, they symbolize but do not create it. A letter is that prime matter in which and out of which a word, an idea, shapes for itself a body; it is universal, original just like any simple color or number. On the contrary, a word is higher than a letter because it is full of light and thought, precisely the way that a statue is higher than its marble and a painting than its paint. In a word a mysterious rebirth or transfiguration of sound occurs because it becomes symbolic, containing an idea. An idea in a word speaks itself with letters, but thereby the letters already lose themselves, they cease to be themselves, they form a cluster, a sonic crystal. In this sense a word is not put together from letters, does not arise from them, but it breaks up into letters. And therefore, for a word, a letter and even a syllable as such is not a proto-unit, but an organic part of the word, even were it to consist of only one letter; but this letter will no longer belong to itself but is fastened to the word, penetrated by its energies, qualified by them, reborn. And the root of a word which always forms a cluster of letters, a sonic crystal, is a phenomenon *sui generis* that does not disappear because it enters into new combinations; for the combination to be possible, this originality of the combining elements is necessary.

Therefore, the sonic nature of a word preserves its significance within certain limits; it constitutes the nocturnal, subconscious, feminine characteristic of a word, to which the masculine, diurnal, solar meaning is proper. From this springs that which constitutes the instrumentation of verse or speech, i.e., in a given thought the yearning to accompany it with a definite sonic timbre, having without fail also a qualitative meaning, although not fully accessible to the consciousness. And if we sometimes arbitrarily search for expressions and sounds, if we consciously subject words to instrumentation, corresponding to a common purpose—to express the one or other mood—then the word itself, taken as the proto-element of speech, is not indifferent to its letters but in a certain sense subjects itself to instrumentation, by the unconscious or better to say supra-conscious organic selection of sounds, similar to how for a certain artistic objective the corresponding material and paint, etc. are needed. In keeping with the corresponding key of a given language, the selection of sounds is made not for certain words only, but for their entire complex of a given speech. Therefore, it is difficult to detect it and define it precisely in any detail.

Connected to the question about the relation of word and letter is the question about "surrational" language, esteemed by futurists, who attempt to flee beyond word and scrutinize its rear flank, to see it before birth. They want to throw off the burden of a word as incarnated thought, idea, in order to dash into the pitch-dark night of sound, having extinguished the lamp of meaning. They want to speak not with words but with letters. But therein is rooted the chief misunderstandings and the fiasco, for they want to speak all the same, not wanting a word and precipitating it into the preverbal chaos of sounds. The positive significance of this experiment (inasmuch as there is one) is that here the nocturnal proto-element of a word is felt and through this its massiveness is realized, the primeval quality of its matter, of sound, of letter. (In painting, the yearning to be freed from the yoke of a picture's content and reduce it to the singing of colors offers a perfect analogy, just as in futurist verse there is a yearning to reduce verse to the singing of sounds alone.)

The futurists are right: surrational or rather prerational language is like the proto-element of a word, its matter, but this is not language. The transformation of sound into word, its rebirth, took place in one direction; it is an irrevocable fact, as irrevocable as the division of original chaos and darkness. So too surrational language is a sort of bragging about chaos, an inevitable flirtation with it, or—and this is more interesting by far—experimentations in the fields of the instrumentation of a word, of its musical characteristic, which is given more easily if one prescinds from meaning, i.e., if one enters into the surrational.

The method of Cabbala, according to which the weight of a word and of phrases is calculated not by the meaning but by the significance of letters (established in one way or another) and their composition, is likewise the nonsensical in principle and is either folly or an absurdity. Or perhaps it is justified in the presence of one condition alone: that the given language is the absolute language, coinciding in all of its details with the structure of the cosmos, and therefore its *key* is the absolute key coinciding directly with the sounding of the world. Then one can and must allow that this language too in all its parts, in all its structure, even in its matter, i.e., in letters, is transparent for the cosmos; it displays its regularity, is cosmic. Thus, an analysis of the letter structure of words is an investigation of the cosmos. As is well known, the Cabbalists had such a conviction with respect to the Hebrew language, considering it the language that God used in paradise to speak with the primogenitors, i.e., a single, natural language. This language as such hides in itself the nature of things and has immediate power.

Or perhaps another supposition is possible, namely, that it is here not a matter of language but of definite word combinations, in the given case belonging to the word of God and marked by divine inspiration. In such a case, theoretically, every language could appear as material for Cabbalistic investigation; however, the properties of the Hebrew language in particular, its "consonantism," make it the most transparent and suitable for this. If one looks with sufficient seriousness at the ontological nature of a word, and chiefly in an ontological and sacred language, one cannot negate in principle the possibility that words and the letters forming them have, so to say, several dimensions. In particular, not only is their physiology instructive—their word, but so too is their anatomy—letters; and in the skeleton of a word one can read out meaning, not verbal but another kind, equivalent to it, numerical. If numerals, perhaps, are things-numbers just as words are ideas-things, and both are symbols of being, then generally speaking there can be no grounds *on principle* to negate this path, although its utilization remains a *quaestio facti* [question of fact].

And so, to the general question about the *multiplicity* of languages, on the basis of what has been said, we can reply that this multiplicity in no way at all alters the ontological unity of language as the voice of the one world in the one humankind. But at the same time, language is realized individually in correlation to the plural structure of humanity, which manifests unity in multiformity; here the different organs and centers of feelings in a single human organism, the members of different sex and age, of society, of character in one human family is an analogy. But it becomes multilingualism, the turbidity of the limpid depth of sound, a Babel-like confusion, only in connection with the general isolation and disuniting of humanity, its condition in hostility and discord; however, this multilingualism is fundamentally, basically, already overcome by the divine incarnation and by the event of Pentecost. In this sense multilingualism, or rather the mutual impenetrability and unintelligibility of languages (although not unconditional, but only relative), expresses not so much the nature of languages as the state of humanity. As a state having a foundation in what ought not to be—in disunity—it is psychologism. Ontological unity is obscured by psychologism, i.e., by the actual use of language. If we look at how to our eyes dialects and idioms arise by gradual and at first imperceptible alterations and then become a new obstacle, it becomes clear that the possibility of this multilingualism is embedded in the condition of humankind and is psychologism, a blurred pane, a refracting prism.

CHAPTER 2

Speech and Word

I. Parts of Speech (Noun, Verb, Pronoun)

A word never exists in isolation; otherwise, it would cease to be a word and would become an accidental sound. As the cosmic significance of a word, its symbolic foundation is only some point without dimensions in the world *all*; it exists only on the assumption of this *all* and is connected with it as the starting point of infinite world-manifestations (cosmophanies). So too, its language use is conceivable only in *speech*, in a living and continuously running context of words, meanings, utterances. We can say that one color taken by itself and isolated from every color does not exist (for what can absolute green designate if you completely think away and eliminate the whole rainbow of colors?) Likewise, a single note, outside a relation to an octave or in general to an entire pitch and stop, does not exist (for if it exists what does an absolute unrelated *do* mean with respect to all other notes?) In precisely the same way, each word-symbol dies away and is destroyed outside speech, for a word sounds in us not in isolation but in language; words see themselves in other words, are spoken in them or through them, as in a system of mirrors that reflect each other without end. The genius of language captures this multiplicity of the word when it names *as a word* not an individual word or words but the whole life of a word realized in a verbal element. A word is alive, it is a living meaning only in speech; an isolated word simply does not exist, it is an abstraction, but in the same sense in which an isolated heart or lung or the other organs of a living body do not exist as abstractions.

Therefore, although we searched for and found the fundamental principle of speech, its cosmic roots, in symbols-words, still the world *all* never speaks about itself with a separate symbol or fragmented signal, but always with symbols connected among themselves, merging and overflowing in their outbursts. Briefly, it is not a static *all* consisting of a mechanical sum $a+b+c+d = \infty$, that expresses itself, where a separate word-meaning would correspond to each of the items, but always a self-actualizing dynamic *totality* that speaks about itself *by always connected* speech. Therefore, *logos* is not only a word, a thought, but also *a connection* of things. Human speech is this world connection continuously being expressed by verbal symbolism. *Logos*-word is *logos*-thought, is *logos*-speech, as the thought of a human being about the world or the self-thinking of the world in the human being and through the human being in a microcosm.

Speech deprived of thought is not speech any more than an accidental combination of sounds designating nothing is a word. An accidental set of words, although each of them separately is not deprived of meaning, does not form speech. If on the off chance we take a few letters from typographical cases and put them together, we will not get a word, although we could compose one out of these same letters. If we spill composed type and mix up the words, we will not have speech, but its corpse torn to pieces, although it too can be composed out of these words. In this sense, we can say together with Wundt that not only is a root an abstraction, but also separate words are abstractions; only the *sentence* exists, containing in itself connected thought. We can go even further still and affirm that a sentence too is an abstraction, and only the whole of thought, reasoning, exists. We can be convinced of this visually if we mix up the order of phrases in any text. Moreover, an end to this expansion of the concept of speech-thought essentially cannot be imagined, so far as everything is found in an intellective connection and correspondence and must be interwoven into a single context of world thought or the thought of the human being about the world. This is natural, because the basis of speech and its object is the world *all* that has no boundaries and is in this sense bad infinity, which does not have an end in "discursive" reasoning.

In light of this, it is indispensable for us to establish a general schematic of the structure of speech, or of those *relations* in which words stand, of those clothes or envelopes in which they are thereby clothed, in addition to its direct meaning—to understand the nature of words as "parts of speech" of course in the ontological significance of the latter. Words, symbols of meaning, besides their direct significance, can still acquire *an indirect* definition from their place in speech, from the particular meaning received by them not as such, in their own coloration, but also according to the connection of the whole, in the context. To establish this context it is necessary to fix our attention on some such fragment that is sufficiently large so that the functional structure of speech is already designated in it, that it is a complete, living meaning in itself. This is ordinarily a grammatical *sentence* or some completed element of meaning.[1]

In grammar, parts of speech and parts of a sentence are usually differentiated, where the study of the first concerns etymology, and study of the second, syntax. These divisions of course are conventional and "grammatical," and they coincide in many points: knowledge of the parts of speech is indispensable for understanding the structure of a sentence, and the reverse, the definition of parts of speech is not even possible outside a sentence. (Since the section in which we are conducting our analysis does not fully coincide with the customary grammatical division, we must digress from the latter to a certain degree, although essentially it is a question about the same thing.)

So then, first of all, we are faced with understanding and comprehending the nature of "the parts of speech," and notably, the nature of the "substantive" *noun*, in its relation on the one hand to the pronoun that replaces it and is associated with it, and on the other hand in its relation to the "verb" and the adjective (around this the other parts of speech are distributed).

Linguistics supposes[2] that root words originally did not have a definite grammatical coloration, they were amorphous or were a rudimentary underdeveloped sentence, and only subsequently were they defined as verb or noun[3] (for the time being we will set aside the adjective as a transitional rather than an independent form). Be that as it may, whether this suggestion is in fact true or false (it can of course not be proved, it seems doubtful to us and probably rests on a misunderstanding) we will ask ourselves what changes or what happens with a word when it assumes either a nominative or a predicative character. What does it signify if one and the same root in one case becomes a substantive noun, in another, a verb or an attributive word—an adjective?

Of course, here we must digress from the morphology of words, from those semantic units by which a word will be formed in both one and the other case—from prefixes, suffixes, inflections. All these particles only *express* an already transpired change of meaning, they fix its completed definition but do not create it; their role is auxiliary and to see in them the source of this definition would mean the same as to search for the causes of high temperature in the thermometer that shows it. In addition, these particles are different in different languages, and they can be entirely absent as well, as in Chinese, or can be replaced by a preposition, as in English, and in part in French, etc. Briefly put, the etymological robing of a word in relation to our question is secondary and derivative, and we can turn our attention away from it.

So then, what happens when one and the same word—one and the same as a semantic symbol, a meaning, an idea, a significance—is used in one case as a verb or adjective (attribute) (which is here equivalent to the quality of verbs, of predicates), and in another case as a substantive noun? For example, radiance, to radiate, radiantly, radiant; breath, breathe, breathy; relatives and related; writer and to write; creator and to create; hops and hoppy; gold, to gild, golden; deity and deified, etc.

It is obvious that in meaning, in what is said, there is no difference at all; the most attentive analysis will not show one between radiance and radiant, relative and relation, and at the same time, the difference is colossal. Moreover, it lies, evidently, *on the other side of the word*, it is not expressed in the word. A substantive noun signifies not only a quality, an idea *in general*, but the realization of it in particular, its particular case; it expresses not only an idea but also the existence, the objectification of this idea, its being in some object. In addition to its content expressed in a word, it has a silent but expressive mystical gesture, ontological with respect to its meaning: *this is*.

In this ontological gesture is included the nature *of a name*. To some it seems that every word has a general meaning and is a general concept;[4] this by the way led even Hegel astray.[5] Even if one does not lump together the general with the abstract (which is usually done), it is impossible not to acknowledge that words as meanings, as ideas, of course, have a general significance, or rather, they exist in themselves, without reference to any *particular* being, their semantic being is autonomous and self-sufficient, they exist because they exist. But at the same time, in a substantive noun they acquire a concrete character and become a living antinomy. As a *name*, designating an object, as "a substantive noun" the general is the particular, the concrete. Besides, an idea, a word, expresses itself to the end, it is transparent. A substantive noun, on the other hand, although it is expressed in a word, is by no means expressed by it to the end in its being, in its dark unilluminated depth. This being is not exhausted by its name at all; on the contrary, cosmic universality is proper to it, bottomlessness, it can be brought into an attributive connection with the whole world. Therefore every name—whether proper or common (here for now it does not matter)—is an antinomy: an alogical-logical, inexpressible-expressible, word born from the inner core of being.

In contrast, a verb and in general the attributive or predicative use of a word, is completely alien to this antinomian quality, not to mention to these roots in being. This does not mean of course that here too the nature of a word as cosmic meaning in the above-explained sense is repudiated, but this symbolism here has only an abstract although cosmic significance. It must be fastened to the world-being at individual points, which then orientate cognition and verbal expression of the world and thinking about it.

If it were possible to imagine a language consisting only of verbs, of predicates in general, then no judgment could be expressed in it. It would be objectless, disposing only of ideal shadows without flesh and blood. By contrast, if it were possible to imagine a language consisting only of subjects—of names, deprived of all predicativity, this would be a language of mute gestures, powerless and impotent (perhaps we have something similar in the language of deaf mutes, who alone have to create the apparatus of speech with some inner means). Finally, if we imagine a pure root language, then insofar as the necessary definitions would not be born in it from gestures, emphases, word order, etc., it would be found in the uterine state of a fetus, where the heart, the lungs, and all the organs are ready for conscious life, but the breath of the universe has not yet entered them.

The distinction between a noun and a verb, between subject and predicate qualities, is not some invention that could just as well not have existed in a language, or an accidental property or condition that likewise can be changed (as for example the condition of an agglutinative, inflected and root language). No, here the very meaning of language is expressed, which in one form or other cannot but be in language. It flows out of the ontology of speech.

In the preceding description of a word as a symbol of the world, we showed that the word is not formed by a human being but speaks itself in him. This same ontological idea we must apply here as well to the distinction interesting us. If as cosmic entities we say what we know about the world, these utterances have not only a content, a qualitativeness, but also an objectivity. We not only harken to the world's voices and vocalize them, but we experience this world and find ourselves in an inner communion with it that is expressed in a word, although it is not exhausted by this. Our position as beings in the cosmos dooms us to continual encounters with its agents—to its stimuli, its calls, in a word, to every vital actual interaction. It fastens our words into speech, it organizes speech into judgments, gives it a real ground, objectiveness, leads it out of the psychological limitation of impersonal "mood," against which a root language unavoidably stumbles with its "impersonal sentences." In the distinction between substantive noun and verb, subject and predicate, is included the primary act of thinking and knowing, from which a critical epistemology ought to begin its work, i.e., one that strives to keep thought aware and accountable. Here the fundamental and primary act of cognition takes place, from which thought then develops, as from a kernel. (Kant and his school passed this fact by and began their analysis where the whole affair was already concluded.)

A substantive noun speaks by itself, witnesses by its presence that something is not only being spoken, i.e., is a quality, an idea, but also *exists*, whatever this existence may be. Let it be even only verbal, logical, abstract, its fundamental significance is not changed by this. And this act—of conceiving a substantive noun—is completely irreducible and unmediated; we do not make it but it is made in us. We can observe and interpret it, but we are not able to alter or rescind it any more than we can change our heartbeat or in general the activity of the organs of our body. How a word arises in us as an answer to the voice of the world as a symbol of world-being is precisely how a substantive noun is born in us in response to a stimulus from the world, as testimony about some being. It attests in it not only that the world is qualified and hence is thought and spoken in a word, but also that its things *exist* beyond word, on the other side of word. That *about which is spoken exists*. And this general property of the world—that it exists and is not only capable of being conceived and expressed in a word—is attested by that feature of language that every thought, every utterance is timed to the stimuli of being, receives existential character, is expressed about being through a subject—a substantive noun.

The various considerations relating to the psychological genesis of a substantive noun, so admired by contemporary linguistics, are entirely insufficient for explaining what it is. Let us assume that in the history of the substantive noun there are manifested the same features that are proper to a child's thinking, when a child beats a stool and in general does not distinguish between animate and inanimate objects. Let us assume that the myth-making feature of primitive thinking, which populates the world easily and gladly with living beings, was shown here, this feature being confirmed in language by the existence of a substantive noun (we will not pause here on the question of whether this feature constitutes the privilege of primitive thinking, by making it more real and concrete, or is the property of a weak and undisciplined mind). The manuals for linguistics of a psychological tendency are brimming with such illustrations of the genesis of speech.

It is possible to introduce into language itself a living witness about some mythologized world with respect to its universal animation: this is grammatical gender, in which the human distinctions of sex, male and female, are applied to all substantive nouns. In other words, the mythological idea of grammatical gender is that *everything has a sex*. As is well known, this is not an accidental feature, but a view that has been carried deeply and consistently through the whole of grammar and syntax, distinguishing the entire family of Indo-Germanic languages. The category of grammatical gender witnesses to the general massiveness of the logical form, of the substantive noun, if such ponderous definitions as grammatical "gender" can be suspended on it. A prior great solidification of this general idea is necessary so that this secondary and supplementary definition can appear in it. But, however important, this distinction "of gender" belongs not to the essence of language as such but to the comparative history of grammar. The fact is that the category of grammatical gender is not at all universal generally or specifically. First, there are languages in which it is absent, and yet the substantive noun is not absent because of this: an example is Chinese. In different languages grammatical gender exists in different guises, that is, in some cases two genders are distinguished, masculine and feminine (French, Hebrew, etc.); in other cases, there are three—masculine, feminine and "neuter." The neuter gender, properly speaking, is not a gender, but the absence or negation of gender; it is the category of those cases when gender proves to be inapplicable. Ostensibly, this seems to emphasize and deepen the meaning of the sex categories of gender, although grammatical usage prevails, because the designations of living creatures of different sex are found in words of all genders. In general, the category of gender is already a certain *psychologism* in the ontological definition of a substantive noun because this introduces particular features into the general statement of an act in response to an existential impulse. But at the same time, it is also a grammatical category, and in this capacity it refers to the morphology of a word and not its ontology. Already the nonuniversal character of this category frees us from the necessity of imparting to it a universal significance.

Nevertheless, research on the genesis of one or other linguistic phenomenon, on the mechanism of associations and the like, has absolutely no decisive, fundamental significance for the epistemological-ontological argument. No matter how a psychologically given verbal-cognitive act is realized, taken in its existential cross-section, it contains as meaningfulness that which we attribute to a word or words—the property or power to be not only an idea, a meaning, that has only abstract-cosmic significance, but also *a name* that signifies being, points to a concrete place in the world. If in one case, we have a horizontal section of being, in the other we have a vertical one; if there we move along the circumference of a circle, then here we move along its radius to the center. And the word, which receives the significance of a substantive noun, is that point where the horizontal and the vertical, the lines of the arc and the radius, intersect. This basic evidence about meaning and being is no longer subject to any genetic interpretation; it is because it is. In it is manifested our semantic verbal sense and our ontological sense, our existential sense of touch.

One of the important language phenomena that has paramount significance for understanding the nature of "the substantive noun" is the *pronoun*—so to say, the shadow invariably cast by a noun. For us *personal* pronouns are of interest here, together with what are produced from them, i.e., possessive, demonstrative, and to a certain degree relative pronouns. We can define the meaning of pronouns roughly as replacements for substantive nouns—persons and things—or as expressions of qualities, in which case they replace adjectives or verbs (such, such like, with the corresponding adverbs: thus, such, and the like).

The first category holds our attention here—that of personal or substantive pronouns, the functions of which are reduced to the personal pronoun. What then does a personal pronoun express: I, you, he, she, it, we, you [plural], they? It expresses precisely that tacit mystical gesture that is always present in a name: this is A. Any name contains a hidden existential judgment, in which the mystical act of the exit of a subject into the cosmos and the entry of the cosmos into it is noted, the contact of consciousness and being. This is an ontological act, consisting of two indissolubly united and merged parts, in which the depths of being, its ineffability, are revealed, and simultaneously a meaning, an idea, a word flares up, and naming occurs. This act is carried out in its separateness by the personal pronoun. Whatever the origin of words may be that express a pronoun, according to its initial meaning[6] the function of a pronoun, its significance, is precisely this: to express the inexpressible in a word-idea, to transmit a mystical gesture, ontological points of contact. The presence of the pronoun in language, which is one of the earliest and most universal forms of language,[7] is eloquent testimony about the nature of a word, about the ontological meaning of a noun, and the name of pronoun, given to it already by Greek grammarians *antonumia* (*pronomen*) fully expresses the gist of the matter. It exists overtly or covertly in the conjugation of a verb, and to a certain extent, in agreement. It is impossible to separate it from the composition of speech, without fettering it, without tearing out the central core from it. For, if it is still possible with great stretches and difficulties to make do without the demonstrative pronoun of the third person, language cannot make do without the personal pronoun of the first and second persons, as it cannot make do without conjugation. This applies to both synthetic and isolating languages in equal measure, in which the function of the pronoun is realized by the general means of that language.[8]

Of course, of fundamental importance are *personal* pronouns, specifically the first and second person. To this belongs the enigma of **I**. What is **I**? Does it lend itself to any expression by a word, like any "he" or "it," which is certainly something—a name? **I** occupies here a special position, because it embraces everything and nothing: everything, because it can be introduced into a predicative link with everything, and nothing, because it is itself not anything in the world of ideas, it is not a word-idea but is a word-gesture, a mystical demonstrative gesture. **I** is that point from which the one speaking looks at the whole world and expresses it in a word but does not see himself and so cannot express himself as a general symbolic testimony of being. In relation to the "I" placed under the microscope of contemplation and actually spoken, the ontological argument is valid: *essentia involvit existentiam* [essence involves existence][9]—although only a tautological judgment "I is I" can be deduced from this, and perhaps not even a judgment but simply a logical gesture: **I,**—in itself still mute and powerless (so that Descartes's "je pense, donc je suis [I think, therefore I am]," of course goes beyond the limits of what is allowed). Of course, **I** can have a name, but I do not see it or sense it due to the egocentric condition of consciousness in which the one speaking is the subject of speech and cannot simultaneously be its object also. For this it must speak about itself "in the third person," i.e., not about **I**, but about **he**. (When she was a child my daughter resisted using the first-person pronoun for a long time, and she would say, "Maniun'ka want," using her name instead of the usual personal pronoun. The cosmos held her and prevented her from detaching her personal self-consciousness, which was expressed only in the verb "to want" in the first-person singular.)

So, this one-of-a-kind significance of **I** causes it to be characterized at once by opposite features. On the one hand, although **I** absolutely cannot be conceived of in the plural, for every **I** is "singular," unrepeatable, yet it is a common noun just as much as it is a pronoun (i.e., a formal, conventional designation). On the other hand, it is the most proper of proper nouns. Although it is not a name at all, at the same time it is the most intimate and closest thing by which humans name themselves; they sense this vortex deep down in their being. Therefore, the disappearance of our **I** is completely inconceivable and unimaginable for us; it cannot be extinguished any more than it could come into existence: neither beginning nor end can been seen from it. It is an immovable eternal point in relation to which it is a misunderstanding to ask if it can come into being or perish. All human beings are mortal—Caius is a human being, therefore *he* is mortal. This *he* about whom

I am speaking in the third person, mentally withdrawing from myself as if closing my eyes—*he* is mortal, but *I* who am saying this *about him*, I, of course, am outside this conclusion.

Such is the paradox of I that we know I as inherent in all those whom we can call "we" (that is, many **Is**, or **you**, i.e., another I), or plural *you*, but *for me* all these other **Is** have names, I have some say about them, I name them, i.e., in fact I carry out an existential judgment. They are for me first of all substantive nouns, and only then and therefore do they become singular and plural "you," and "they." In the first-person pronoun, I have something unnamable and at the same time absolutely demonstrable.

If one can really speak about the egocentrism of language,[10] then, not in the sense of a fusion of pronouns but in the sense that any and all speech is spoken, constructed, conceived, and experienced by the first person, and this egocentrism is a completely indispensable premise. I, having knowledge and consciousness of its being, looks at itself in the mirrors of the world and everywhere that it sees points of being—in one sense or other—it speaks about them with substantive nouns but also with pronouns. It is just as impossible to free language from both egocentrism and anthropocentrism as it is for a person to see their own back.

"I" cannot be defined by anything; it does not allow any expression by means of some other thing: it is the eye through which we see the world. Can what sees be defined by what is seen? It is the light in which we distinguish everything, and how can light be defined by what can be seen only in it?

What Kant called the transcendental unity of consciousness he considered motionless in I in contrast to the subjective, psychological I, i.e., its separate states. Let it be so. But this does not end the conversation, something best of all attested by the history of philosophy beginning with Fichte. He unexpectedly continued the conversation about what I signifies. Is it a level point or does it have depth, is it an essence (*ousia*)? And of course it was impossible to be satisfied with Kant's reply, owing to its vagueness and lack of content. Fichte attempted to measure the depth of I by directing the mirror of the world at it; he wanted to define the eye through what was seen by it, to reach I through not-I. (Or, what is the same, to define the world through I, for, of course, the positive content of the negative concept of not-I is connected exclusively with I.) But the fact is that even this project out of which the whole of Fichteanism was born, was false, for it is impossible to translate I into the language of the world; it is transcendent to it, and the whole enterprise was reduced to dialectical conjuring and the human-divine voluntarism of every "practical" I. There can be no bridge between I and the cosmos because on the one hand they are separated by the logical gap between the one who is aware and what he is aware of, and on the other hand because there is no need to unite them, for they are as inseparable as eye and sight. If Fichte had wanted to understand I in its *verbal* nature, in the spirit of language, in the thought included in it, his *Ich-Philosophie* would have disappeared of its own accord, but like all his confreres he did not want to do this, and he paid for it with false reasoning.

As a pronoun with a definite task in language—to bring to light the ontological basis of a word—I is an ontological gesture that, however, has a paramount and fundamental significance. In it the ontological reality of a word comes to light. Language gropes after its own proper ground, and from I and through I it passes over to any "you" and "he," etc., knowing by inner experience that words are points of being, that they are not sketched out only with sounds but in actual fact sound in the world or from the world. In a certain sense I is the root of language, the real surrational word, in which there is no idea, no word, except the simple witness of being, its ontological passport. Besides, this happens not in a speculative system (that comes later) but is the self-witness of the world's logos in language; through I the world bears witness about itself, that *it* is, but, as a result, that *everything* also is. I, the language pronoun I, proves to be the ontological frame in which all being can be accommodated, but in particular the being of this very I, inasmuch as it enters into the cosmos, is named, is called. I itself is the naming of the absolutely unnamable, it is *ousia* itself being laid bare in phenomena as primiparous energy.[11] I is simultaneously phenomenality and noumenality, the transcendent-immanent.

I is the orienting point of being, thought and word. From I directions are counted, and distances are measured by it. All personal pronouns are variants of I, its mirror reflection: *"you"*—this is another I, *"we"*—are many Is, *"he"* and *"they"* are those who have the nature of I: not its consciousness and not its "animation" (these are secondary definitions or states of I), but its being. For every I both "you" and "he" can be said, although not the reverse, not every "he" can be turned into "you" and I. Evidently, the meaning of a personal pronoun and its fundamental principle I is broader than only the expression of personal self-consciousness, "animation." It is also the expression of being, an ontological gesture that also makes the pronoun of the third person intelligible in its special quality: the genius of language, the logos unmistakably bears witness, and we must listen to this witness.

So then, a pronoun does not express any particular idea about *quality*, but it is the verbal witness about *essence* to which being and all its qualities belong. It expresses itself as *ousia* with respect to which any being, any utterance, is the revelation of energy, of energetic phenomena. This is the first hypostasis of being in which the second is born—a word. By recognizing its connection with this verbal expression, and seeing itself and its revelation in it, it realizes its third hypostasis as a function of its predicative power. It is natural that this eternal generation of the world, the seal of trihypostaticity that lies on the whole world, determines also the nature of speech, and the basis of thought. The pronoun is the symbol of *ousia*, of the inexpressible depth of super-being, of proto-hypostaticity. Therefore in comparison with a word a pronoun signifies nothing, contains no nuance of being, and yet it can signify everything, in its faceless, colorless depth. A pronoun is a symbol of noumenality, a gesture in word. One can of course interpret it psychologically, genetically, there is even nothing easier, but this will give no answer to the question about the *meaning* of a pronoun. It should be noted that the nature of a pronoun as a word differs in a radical way from the nature of a word in general, as was disclosed above. We defined a word as a concrete symbol, as evidence of being, its operation; in this sense we said that word is born and speaks itself, that it is reality, etc., and we rejected indicative symbolism, reducing words merely to conventional designations and converting meanings into signs or even little marks resembling algebra. We must now say that a pronoun is just such an indicative symbol; it is not the world that speaks it in us, but we who speak it, by designating certain points of departure, positions: I, you, he. That is why a pronoun is also a mystical gesture, in conformity with the spirit of language clothed in a word, not having its own proper content. If we were to apply Kantian expressions, then we could say that pronouns are transcendental categories of language that do not have any other content and designation than to be a form: all worldly being is **I** or not-**I** (of course, not the Fichtean), in particular "you" and "he" ("you" [plural], "they"). And outside these categories being is not given. But if a pronoun is a category of language containing everything in itself, then of course it does not have content, it is only a form, and the word that designates it is a symbol. Of course, this does not mean that this symbol was only a *flatus vocis*: its indicative nature, its muteness, which converts it into a sonorous gesture, does not make it something empty and composed, ready for any use. This only signifies that it is a word about what is neither verbal nor uttered and yet is the basis of a word. Such a word only can be a symbol. All words in speech are massive, they have weight, flesh and blood; pronominal symbols are shadows from the world beyond the grave, in general from the other side. They are transparent, permeable, they fill up no space; similar to the shades of the *Odyssey* they must be slaked with blood in order to receive the gift of word, but then, having taken their place in speech, they become its central foci around which a series of words is arranged.

It is evident, incidentally, that the nature of algebraic symbols and of any indicative symbols in general is defined by the nature of a pronoun, where a concrete name-word is replaced by a demonstrative pronoun, a gesture. This gesture, in view of the complexity of reasoning, receives its designations—by letters or signs that themselves, however, do not have meaning, but express relations. Inasmuch as it is a matter of different relations and categories, the pronominal function works as an indicative symbol to simplify and abbreviate. However, it is based all the same on the invariable supposition that each symbol can be understood only as a pronoun. On top of this there can be several degrees of the pronominal: for example, when people are counted by numbers (in prisons), by drill units (regiments), or simply by letters instead of by personal names—all of these are more or less decisive for the purpose of replacing word-names by a category.

Of course, this concerns only the personal pronoun and what is connected with it, namely, demonstrative and possessive pronouns, etc., but not qualitative pronouns, where the function is purely algebraic—to really replace a word—and is caused by the economy of language, by the urge to abbreviate and simplify.

Because of this value, a personal pronoun is obviously the ontological *prius* of a name. Using a crude expression, it is the ontological hook on which a name is hung, a concrete, living word. Only thanks to this hook does a word change from a grammatically amorphous and radical state, an idea-meaning, into a *substantive* noun. Every naming contains implicitly or explicitly a judgment of the type: this (or it, he, you, etc.) is X. Learning a language manifests this genesis. A child sees an object and names it, a representation is formed and it receives a name. Both the representation and the name are second, not first. They hide the first, which is a pronominal gesture: he, you, I (this is why, where it exists in a language, all objects have gender, borrowing it from pronouns). Thus, a substantive noun is an existential judgment, in which the subject is a certain point of being, that which of itself cannot be expressed in a word, but is named, whereas the predicate is a name.

It is the property of a substantive noun to be part of a sentence, in which words-ideas are united with it. A subject has a predicate, and all the existential power lies on it, while predicativity constitutes its photosphere. A subject that at the same time is a judgment in its simplest form, A *is* B (what the Germans call a simple, bare sentence having no secondary parts), is only a continuation and extension of that naming that is contained already in a substantive noun. Here you have something, a *he* that is A and in addition there is also B. A and B differ by the degree of their proximity to this *he*; one constitutes its inner core, the other its outer coverings, but in principle—and the history of language bears witness to this—each predicate can coalesce and become a name. What makes a subject, and at the same time a substantive noun, is not this or that content of a word but precisely its grammatical and logical function, connected with a pronoun, with an ontological accent. A snake is an animal; this animal is a snake. Moscow is (the third) Rome; Rome is ancient Moscow, etc. Grammatically the predicate preserves here the form of a substantive noun (although this is only in inflected languages, and not in isolating ones), but in fact it does not have all the force of a substantive here, it is taken only as an adjective, as a word, an idea in isolation from its pronominal foundation. The original connection that is concealed in the name—*this is* A—here is burst asunder, and then only the predicative A remains, although according to form it can remain a substantive.

A substantive noun as the subject of predicativity receives its grammatical expression in the nominative case, which either does not exist at all and is simply an amorphous word, or has the task of expressing the substantiality of language; it is the inflected expression of the ontological significance of a given word.[12] A variant of the nominative case is the vocative, usually identical to it.[13] It differs from the nominative only by volitional, psychological accentuation. In both cases, in a theoretical statement as well as in an invocation, something is affirmed as a being, although of course in a direct and not a figurative sense; the vocative case can be formed only relative to "animate objects" (for psychological reasons).

However, the substantive noun is not limited to the nominative case alone, remaining only in the role of the grammatical subject or the subject of a judgment. In a certain sense, insofar as it preserves itself, and does not become an adjective or verb, it is always a hieroglyph of a nominative judgment, in which the pronoun is the subject and the noun the predicate; hence, where we can sense a pronoun, there we also have a substantive noun. Where it evaporates, the latter also disappears. For this reason although grammatically and logically the normal extended sentence has one subject that is its point of orientation, at the same time it can have several ontological centers, several substantive nouns, and they can be joined with various important concrete relations. By the genius of language these relations are reduced to typical ones, which etymology takes under its authority and manufactures the formal elements for their expression, the semantic units. Here we have, as it were, an algebra of language, for which it is necessary to supply concrete values. This is the declension: cases,[14] i.e., the typical instances of interaction of nouns, number, and preposition (we must treat this below). Cases can express different causal, local, and temporal relations between nouns. Ontologically there are as many sub-jects in a sentence as substantive nouns, because it is characteristic for the latter to be subjects; however, they differ in degree to their centrality. "The tsar sent his general an order." What is being spoken about here? The tsar? But also the general and the order. These ontological points are brought into mutual relation, and one of them is made central (at least grammati-cally); but this does not nullify their multiplicity, and the latter almost al-ways is assumed in a sentence-judgment, provided it does not consist only of verbs and adjectival words.

Although the distinction between a verb and an adjective is grammati-cally very significant, ontologically it is insignificant and is even entirely absent. The point is that an adjective with its copula in a predicative role is no different from a verb, just as verb forms often have the grammati-cal nature of an adjective. Besides this, where an adjective is a definition and agrees with what is being defined, it is an abbreviated expression of a predicate with a copula. The important thing is that both the adjective and the verb, in contrast to a substantive noun, express qualities or states, ideas but not essences. They necessarily must be attached to, or to express this grammatically, be in agreement with the substantive noun, they must lean against it, and therefore they have the nature of predicativity. The most remarkable characteristic of a verb conjugation, given all the wealth of its other meanings, is the pronominal character, which penetrates it through and through; its forms presume a pronominal definition, they are person and number. Where this is lost, verbality is essentially lost, as for example, in the infinitive mood, which is half substantive, and in participles, which are half adjectives, etc. Even in the absence of a subject, the understood pronoun replaces it. Therefore, the area of the dominance of the pronoun as the basis of the substantive noun and subject is immeasurably broader than is possible to judge only by its external prevalence. The hidden pro-noun reigns in language through conjugation. Verbality in essence is com-pletely equivalent to a copula that combines a subject and predicate, the substantive noun and the predicate: what in a verb is "action," passivity, reciprocity, influence or other shades of action, is only the expression of the link between some pronominal sign-name and different properties, as in a judgment brought about by a copula. The type and meaning of these judgments is that the words associated with pronouns, with essences, and that have an ontological meaning, are combined in them with words ex-pressing an idea, the colors of the world. On the thread of being are strung its beads, such is the essence of the sentence-judgment as an elementary linguistic and at the same time cognitive act.[15]

II. The Substantive Noun

Thus, the pronoun is the trunk of the substantive noun, and naming, its clothing. The first is the grammatical subject, the second, the grammatical predicate, the first—the subject of a judgment, the second—the predicate. A name is a latent judgment, an undeveloped sentence. This is something that signals about itself as existing; in so doing, it poses a question about itself and responds to it at the same time. Therefore, it names itself and is named—*by a word*. Word-meaning-idea, as we have tried to explain, is not yet the expression of concrete being; it exists in general but not in particular, as cosmic potentiality. The significance of a word in and of itself is never as an object; it is pure meaning, *gilt* [counts for] but not *ist* [is], it has meaningfulness but not existence. It acquires real significance and is objectified only when it says something about itself—This is A. Every something can have an undefined multitude of verbal covers and can be expressed by a corresponding quantity of words: human, animal, anthropomorphic ape, biped, king of creation, thinking being, political being, being inventing machines, etc., etc. Each of these words can cross from a predicative sentence in relation to a human being over to a nominative sentence, and the possibility of such a change or transition all the more obviously confirms *that a name is initially a predicate*; it is obtained as a result of a latent judgment. This is why, according to our understanding, there cannot be words that according to their nature or original meaning were substantive nouns *as distinct from* verbs and adjectives. On the contrary, *predicative value precedes nominative value:* the value of snake, and not the snake, which is what carries the value of snake; the value of human, and not the human; the value of tree, and not the tree, etc. In a word, it is not the idea-word that is generated or singled out by its carrier, but the reverse, an idea clothes itself, makes real and possesses a particular instance in the one or other fact of being.

Ideas are *verbal forms* of being, names are their *realization*. This must be valid even in those cases when a given word-idea arises for the first time precisely apropos of a given concrete being. Let us suppose that the idea of snakeness, of snake, is the expression of the property or impression of an actual snake. Let us even admit that such is precisely the provenance of word-roots, that all of them have concrete causes. It is even necessary to admit this not only in consideration of the psychological genesis or the concrete history of a word in general (which does not interest us here) but also of the ontology of a word. If words are really the sounds of the world in the human being, if they have an anthropocosmic nature, then they must really sound from the world and through the world, and in particular have concrete causes of arising. However, this is not what is important, it is rather that from every such cause, the pure meaning or the idea in *a word* comes off in layers, having a general, self-sufficient significance. Initially, words have the nature of predicates or verbs: seeing a snake and calling it a snake, the human being essentially invests with meaning a mute being that is outside meaning, and says, "This is snakeness, a snake."[16] Our self-consciousness of speech attests that this is the case, when at every step we continually transfer meaning from the general to the particular, from a verbal quality to a substantive.

But the nature of a word is unchanged, we cannot allow that something is possible for us now that was not possible earlier and vice versa. It is rightly said that the nature of language is comprehended from a single act.[17] It is true that with respect to many words, we now do not feel the predicative function of a name at all; it sounds to us like a monolith, and it seems that it arose precisely as a name (e.g., stone, water, iron, wolf, etc.). But such a feeling can have a purely psychological explanation (in the notorious mechanism of associations) or it results from forgetting the initial meaning of the word; in general the durability of an associative fusion is not evidence that it is primordial.[18] On the contrary, the naming that takes place before our eyes leaves no doubt that it arose from a judgment, that it is a predicate, which became a subject, twined around a mystical trunk where it received the coefficient of concreteness.

Therefore, *the copula, "is"* plays the most substantial role in naming. It is unseen, implied, frequently forgotten and buried by history, but in other places, it comes to light and rises to the surface. Naming is a copula, however not of the usual, weak content but of a special power, intimacy, and exclusivity. The copula expresses in general *the energy (energeia)* by which the subject is manifested and comes to light in one or other definition, but in particular in a verbal one. In relation to the subject, to the substance (*hupokeimenon*) of this definition, it is its *ergon*. The word in which a name is expressed, is joined by the copula to its nameless and unnamable carrier, it is a verbal action, the self-revelation of this carrier. It appropriates to itself, binds itself with a certain word-idea. Here the concrete is expressed by the general (although not the abstract: one need not mix the general and the abstract, and by the way this mixing, which violates the best traditions of Platonism, is the particular sin of contemporary philosophy). A fusion takes place, a substantive noun arises. Regarding unknown things we customarily ask what it is called ("what is this?" is the question of my little son). This question expresses a function that usually remains outside of consciousness, thanks to the psychological automatism of language that here covers exactly the most important processes.

Based on what has been said, the usual distinction between proper and common names loses its significance. Every name is a concrete application of a general idea, and a predicate, latent in a name, is by its nature an idea that has universal meaningfulness (or in general, it means nothing, is deprived of meaning). Here too proper and common names are not differentiated in any way. Sergei is as much a *general* idea as is human being; it can be more complex or obscure, but no less general (or it is not a word at all, but an algebraic sign, a *flatus vocis*). A name in a calendar is an idea, but when it is given to a definite person, it is a name. (And even Europe, Asia, etc. is a general idea which becomes a name: for there is Europeanism, European climate, etc.; in short, Europe can be an adjective or a verb, and this convertibility of a name into a non-name best of all attests that *initially* an idea existed here and not a name.) And vice versa, a word of general connotation can receive a completely unexpected and wholly colorful application as a proper name: "whites," "redskins," "son of heaven" for the Chinese emperor, etc. In proper and common names the *conceptual extent*, which corresponds to given substantive nouns, or their logical capacity is usually confused with the nature of the *idea-word*, and the secondary and derivative differentiation of this capacity, without grounds in language, is transferred to the nature of the idea-word. Besides, the semantic universality outside a concrete sentence is the very nature of the idea-word, and *names* are neither proper nor common, but rather, if one permits the expression, all are proper-common, concretely universal: the copula makes them proper, the name-meaning, common.

But a copula can have a different force as it is used in distinct instances. One and the same thing can receive x number of designations, it can be A, B, C, D, E, F. . ., where all these words will be suspended on the copula *is*, and are radiations of its energy. However, the energy of this self-definition, its intensiveness, is the difference and makes some designations more "proper," and others less so. And at the same time, obviously, *absolutely "proper"* names do not exist in the sense that a given fusion of the subject with the predicate belongs to it alone and cannot be used in any other "figurative" sense: the copula *is* does not possess such durability and exclusivity; it is, as we have already stated, *energeia* and not *ergon*. If a name really were some *ergon*, i.e., if it were not a predicate, then such absoluteness would be unavoidable. Then words would sit motionless on their settings, all substantive nouns would be proper, unique names, and then there would be no sort of logical and verbal copula, neither thought nor speech would be possible. The sole form of logical and grammatical relation admissible in such a sentence would be through the conjunction **and**, i.e., an external union of that which does not lend itself to any other more internal connection: the mutual impenetrability of these atoms of meaning and speech would be such that the world of thought and word would disintegrate into these atoms, which have no windows for one another.

However, in the limit of anthropocosmic thinking, this *"is"* is never absolute, it is an intensive quantity allowing for infinite differences in strength, density, and intensity. As a result, different ideas can serve as internal or external covers for one and the same essence, and inversely, one and the same essence can merge with different ideas, expressed through newer and newer designations which, by incarnating acquire the significance of names, at first common and then proper. This, by the way, is the basis for the possibility of *co-* and *re-* designation, in both the narrow and the broad sense (i.e., the application of metaphors, about which below). Every judgment is a designation *in nuce*, an investing with meaning. Different, infinite *"is"*es curl the petals of meaning, where some of them occupy an internal place, others are outward coverings. But in essence the knowledge that is expressed in judgments is also a process of designation, whereas names as "parts of speech" are semantic masses or crystals.

The most basic facts of the life of a language, disclosed by linguistics but also derived from our everyday experience, bear witness that the stated idea faithfully reports the nature of things. There is, on the one hand, a very limited quantity of initial semantic roots from which the whole multitude of words of a modern language arise, and on the other hand, an "improper" use of words, that is, metaphors and tropes, in general.

Like everything limited, where the wisdom of nature and not human reason operates, language observes the greatest economy of means. If for each substantive a separate word were required, the quantity of words would increase immeasurably, and such a word-creativity would attest not to the wealth but to the weakness of a language, its helplessness, as is sometimes observed in certain barbarian idioms. On the contrary, the rule for a developed, elaborated language is to reach the maximum result with minimal means. We have already recalled that the rich English lexicon, reckoned at up to 100,000 words (excluding foreign ones) is derived from 461 roots; likewise the 40,000 words of Chinese come from forty sound groups, with different accents giving up to 1200 basic words. Hebrew is reduced to approximately 500 roots. Sanskrit grammarians reduced the whole wealth of their language to 1,706 roots, etc.[19] By the way, if one took even only the twenty-four letters of an alphabet, the possible number of two- or three-lettered roots would be 14,400: so far is language from making use of its sonic resources.[20] And of course, the possibility to be limited to so few is connected precisely with the fact that all basic meanings, all root words, have a *general* significance; they express ideas, but are not at all proper names, they are signs that represent things, like the cards or numbers in a catalogue. These words can be used in different combinations and nuances, a fact that is connected on the one hand with their etymological and syntactical equipment and on the other hand with their semasiological significance, with their predicative value. For a great expert who is a genius of language, expressing not personal wisdom but the wisdom of the world, anthropocosmic wisdom, a limited number of colors suffices in order to extract everything necessary from the palette.

Connected with this limited number of linguistic colors is also the multiple usage of the same root word. Its combinations with a given content, as we have already said, are neither durable nor definitive: newer and newer combinations of the same word are possible. Such a multiplicity of words' significance is the basic and elementary fact of language but equally too the so-called tropes. If we take a dictionary, we will find for every given word a series of meanings: *kosa* (hairs), *kosa* (scythe), *kosa* (spit, a geographical term); *golova* [head] (physical), *golova* ([loaf] of sugar), etc. What does this mean? It means that with the same color, with the same word a different thing is named, of course, in a similar sense. In this way the earlier, original meaning and the later, given one are established. The first meaning, in relation to the second, is a means and loses independent significance. Sometimes it is called *the inner form of a word.*[21]

Obviously, a latent idea, a comparison, an identification are already contained in this process of designation; a judgment is generally pronounced. As M. Müller puts it, "A language has its own fossilized philosophy," and in its own way Jacobi's remark is correct: "I do not know a better means of exploring the truth philosophically than to investigate the roots of words" (W. W. III, 550).[22]

This inner form of a word is usually forgotten with the flow of time, and in this way the original shade of meaning is lost, that intuition that is deposited in a given word. Besides, if it is correct that language reflects the soul and character of a people, and word-creation is more ancient than other products of popular genius (like the folk song, the epic, etc.), then how can one not listen to this work by which language-creation happens? The diverse usage of words is, as it were, a system of semantic equalizations; it gives the possibility of gazing into the laboratory of thought where its instrument is forged, where it trickles like raindrops, grows like grass. In the one or other naming, where a single one is selected from a large and essentially indefinite multitude of signs and possibilities, an idea, a stylization, an outline is included that enters into the canvas of the world.

In consequence of naming being judgment, it is possible, even unavoidable that there can be several, even many of these judgments that have naming as a *result* (but potentially this possibility is contained in *every* judgment). From this, the possibility of not only the multi-meaning of one word (polysemy) but also of a plurality of monosemous or one-item words, i.e., synonyms, becomes theoretically understandable. "In the customary Sanskrit dictionaries, according to the testimony of M. Müller (293) are found five names for hand, 11 for light, 16 for cloud, 26 for snake, 33 for murder, 35 for fire, 37 for sun."

Of course, in every living language, this synonymy constantly grows and this battle for existence between synonyms, which leads to the preference or victory of some over others, to the establishment of different nuances, is likewise full of meaning. It shows how thinking, how the perception of the world, changes; it is the insensible sketching of insensible changes, a kind of chronicle of the spiritual world.

Even more instructive are *tropes* (metaphor, metonymy, synecdoche), thanks to which a given word is applied with knowing artfulness in an "improper" sense not belonging to it, or is used as a colorful means or manner for the expression of thought. Usually tropes are considered signs of poetic language (they most of all characterize precisely what is usually called in a writer "language"), they are even set forth thus in textbooks on the theory of literature. Besides, they in fact form "the rigid inventory" of language without which speech could not take a single step. The limitation of linguistic means (both relative and absolute) in the face of the (virtual) limitlessness of the tasks that are put to language compels us to use words in the freest manner, to sketch with words. Words normally do not cover their object; they are now narrower, now wider than it is.[23] Language unwaveringly lops off what protrudes or stretches what is too short in the Procrustean bed of a clumsy word.

The simplest everyday speech teems with tropes and is in this sense uninterrupted stylization, but it is not poetry.[24] Comparisons and images are not the property of poets alone. The difference consists only in the character of these images, their hackneyed state or freshness, colorfulness or dryness, etc. Language always *depicts*. It is always poetic creativity, a portrait of the world made in word. It is not a dead mirror but a living copy. The demand for *precision* that can be raised for a language has its meaning only in application to this property, but it therefore also has its insuperable limits. Pedants often consider dry and impoverished language more precise and scientific (probably for this reason scientific style is so awkward). But language could be freed from figurativeness and reduced to full precision, at least from the lexical side (setting aside the grammatical) only in the case where for each new meaning and its every subtle nuance a new word were at its disposal, i.e., if the quantity of words were limitless.[25] But we know that language would drown and choke on this abundance of words, memory would be overstrained and, what is most important, *the connection* of things and the connection of ideas would not be realized in the face of this victory of centrifugal forces.

Alternatively, this precision would be achieved at the price of removing any colorfulness of speech, of verbal symbolism, of concrete meanings, and it would be reduced to the relations of symbols, of signs of meaning, but not of meanings. In such speech, only relations rich in meaning would be left. Such is mathematics and any mathematical science; the ultra-language of mathematics, the devitalization of living words and their covering with the cerements of mathematical symbols, evidently, is the dream of contemporary language fighters. But one must not forget that the simplicity and precision of mathematics is purchased with the price of a definite stylization or judgment of the sphere of its field: it knows only relations *in abstracto*.

However, the most curious thing here is that from the point of view of language, the symbolism of mathematics is solid tropes, founded on a conscious and deliberate replacement of concrete words by abstract signs. And the usual beginning of any mathematical discussion: let us call the given value "a," etc. is the beginning of a lengthy chain of tropes of a definite style. (The same operation is produced also in so-called logistics and generally in any schematization.)

Incidentally, it is possible to say that the so-called onomatopoetic theory can also be understood on the basis of the properties of tropes, according to which words arise from the imitation of sounds. Indisputably, such sound-imitative words exist (cuckoo, bow-wow); especially in children's language, there are many of them, but it is just as indisputable that they occupy a defined and very limited place in the composition of words, and up until now no one has succeeded in extending them to all words. Therefore, onomatopoeia, the imitation of sounds, characterizes some words, where these sounds, which in themselves have no meaning, were converted into words by way of their tropological use. A given combination of sounds could be employed as a metaphor (in a certain sense similar to how in algebra a value is replaced by a letter) for the designation of a certain object, which thereby could also have other names. The way that onomatopoetic word-creation differs from the usual way is its conscious, reflective character, namely, forcing one to see here a trope, i.e., a premeditated use, a convergence, an abbreviation.

Here the most recent word-creation adorning the Russian language rather unexpectedly invites comparison: *sovdep* [council of deputies], *sovnarkom* [council of people's commissars], and the like. Here we also have a sort of algebraic metaphor that arises from the visual contemplation of the capital letters of given institutions. What is *obviously* not a word (just as caw-caw, coo-coo are obviously not words) begins to be used consciously as a word on the basis of this mathematical-metaphorical designation.

In a similar way, one can also understand the origin of words from involuntary semiarticulate sounds (the interjection theory), which likewise cannot be denied for a certain category of words. Here something similar happens as with onomatopoeia or the algebraization of words: certain *sounds*, by association connected with a given experience and reflexively accompanying it *consciously*, are turned into a word so that they are joined in a certain sense to the subject, they become its designation (a child calls the bench on which he bruised himself *a bobo*). Once this transformation is completed, once certain sounds have acquired the meaning of a root, all possible formations arise for it corresponding to the general equipment of a language. But, of course, it is not language and its roots that are explained from onomatopoetic or interjectional formations by means of the sorcery of "evolution," which changes precisely where an explanation is required and where the center of the problem is, but the reverse: words that have sound-imitative roots arise thanks to the reflective, premeditated, conscious, and completely free conversion of them into words, thanks to the combination of predicative meaning with them, and their conversion initially into a predicate as an element of naming. A similar thing happens even now, when we consciously form a new word out of sounds of some sort, turning them into roots.

The principal significance of tropes for understanding the substantive noun is that here the nature of naming comes to light. The subject of a name is a pronominal gesture, always deeper than any predicate, for by means of its roots it departs into being. In virtue of its universal connection, it can be said in an endless number of ways (about this below). Therefore, no naming knowingly exhausts the essence, but it expresses something in it. If naming happens before our eyes, or is performed by us, then the idea of naming is clear and needs no explanation. But if it happened in time immemorial and its meaning has been lost, its internal form forgotten and become unintelligible, then a word ossifies and acquires the character of a nickname; what is more, as it no longer says anything about an object except as a general indication, it merges with the pronominal gesture and becomes that hook on which all predicates are then suspended.

The majority of our words of ancient provenance are like that: their meaning can be revealed only by the historical study of language, but it is not those words that rise again before our eyes. Unless they are borrowings from a foreign language, they are transparent for us in their significance and of course are tropes. According to their usual classification, the following are tropes: synecdoche, metonymy, and metaphor. Synecdoche is connected with a broadening or narrowing of the connotation of a concept,[26] but we have it in any naming. Metonymy "takes the sign for the designation, the property for the carrier, the cause for the effect and vice versa. Almost any naming has a basis in metonymy."[27] Finally, metaphor, which is the transferal of the name of one object or concept onto another having with it a common point (*tertium comparationis*), rests on comparison, approximation, or contrast.[28] On this is based the possibility of polysemy and synonymy, the use of different colors and different nuances for the expression of a given idea.

The application of tropes in substantive nouns is of particular interest for identifying their nature. Here it is particularly clear that naming is a judgment in which the implied subject is the predicate, which is connected by the implied copula *is*. Thanks to this predicate value, those words that have the character of substantive nouns also become, as it were, adjectives or verbs, playing the role of predicate in a nominative judgment. They are taken down from their pronominal settings and by becoming free meanings lacking objects, verbal ideas, they gain a foothold in new settings and thus get that change of meaning that we have with a tropological use of words in substantive nouns. Hence it follows that the link-copula, which can be equivalent both to a verb form and agreement in an adjective, is the glue or "agglutinating" nature thanks to which a noun adheres to an object, and an idea is added to a pronoun. With a different understanding of the nature of a substantive noun, its "improper" or "figurative" meaning becomes an unsolvable riddle. Therefore, a word in its essence is a judgment, a word is a thought.[29]

So then, two fundamental questions arise in the philosophy of the substantive noun. What does a copula signify? What does naming, the choice of one or other verbal idea to be joined to a given object of speech, mean? Let us begin with the latter.

Joining one or other predicate, or naming, is in any case the *action* of a human being, considered as a separate subject or as a generic entity (the "transcendental" subject), and every action is accomplished with the participation *of the will*; consequently, it supposes the manifestation of freedom. For the will and freedom are inseparably linked in the human being (the dispute over the freedom or slavery of the will is the fruit of a misunderstanding). I can name or not name a given thing that looks at me and, as it were, raises a question about itself; this does not happen without my assent. Besides, I can name it—and practically I do name it—in a thousand different ways. Generally speaking, I can name it *this way or otherwise*, and then the freedom of choice always remains with me and constitutes the very essence of language, which never is a passive mirror but a living, creatively realized process.[30] At the same time, undoubtedly, the human being is not free in naming; he cannot give any designation that comes into his head, unless he suffers from some pathology of coordination. He must *listen* to the thing, attend to its self-revelation, pay heed to what it will tell him. (Speaking of attention, we do not at all have in mind psychological states, and in general, we entirely remove the psychological point of view as irrelevant, for it treats only the mechanism but not the essence, not the *what* but the *how*. We understand "attention" as "intention.") This intentionality can be directed or established in a different manner, in other words, a different question can be posed about a thing and correspondingly a different answer obtained, but the answer itself belongs to the thing. It cannot be devised, although it can be heard poorly or incorrectly. A name is the self-revelation of a thing, it belongs to the thing, and not to the one speaking. In this sense, a thing names itself.

Therefore, here we have, as it were, an irreconcilable contradiction between freedom and necessity. In fact, it is the antinomy of *coincidentia oppositorum*, and we have it in every act of human creativity that is free and naturally determined. An artist must be obedient to the material and the idea of the work: the more fully he yields to it, the more polished, the more artistic is the act of creation. He must reach the full dissolution of his personal I, the full blending with his creative intention, the extinction of the personal and subjective—"of psychologism"; he must let the idea's regularity triumph. At the same time, this is the pinnacle of his personal creative tension, because only by an act of freedom is it possible to complete this creative effort of self-surrender. Creativity is anthroposophical, and freedom lies in the human being, regularity in the sophianity of creativity. The less a human names a thing and the more it names itself, the deeper, more substantial, and more penetrating is the naming. However, a thing can be named only through a human being, in a human being, by a human being. In the human being the names of all things are concealed, he is the microcosm, that being from which substantive nouns are set.

The antinomy of a substantive noun is that what is named is unnamable, is transcendent to the word-idea, which expresses the modus of cosmic being. That which is found *under* the name—*under*-lying, or the *sub-jectum*, *hupo-keimenon*, is the transcendent noumenon, *ousia*, the Kantian "thing in itself." That *by which* it is named, is the predicate, *kategoroumenon*, the phenomenon with respect to this noumenon, its *ergon*, entirely belonging to the world of being and forms, immanent. So then, a substantive noun is something transcendent-immanent, noumenal-phenomenal.

After measuring with his epistemological ruler, Kant here declares a rupture of this cohesion, he crosses out the dash expressing a copula. For him the transcendent remains transcendent, the phenomenal world remains self-determined and closed in itself; between them is alleged a great abyss that cannot be crossed over from either side. Through this juxtaposition the Kantian system dissolves and the whole Kantian heresy sets in with its persistent striving to deepen this abyss and to make knowledge immanent. Kant did not notice that despite his system, in each naming his question is already resolved and the imaginary abyss is overcome, although it is not overcome rationally, i.e., statically, but antinomically, or dynamically, more precisely, actively. A name, a phenomenon, is the revelation of a thing, of a noumenon because here its effectiveness, its *energeia* is manifested. A thing comes out of itself and already becomes a cosmic thing. In the process, a name is known not in isolation and juxtaposition but in combination and unity, in its diurnal and nocturnal, external and internal essence. It is not so that the noumenon existed separately, expressing a name only by a pronoun, by a mystical gesture, and separately, arbitrarily given as a sign or nickname. No, the concrete substantive noun exists that despite its antinomic character, is a unity. Briefly put, the bridge over the abyss, the glue uniting the noumenon and the phenomenon, is the implied copula *is*, this ontological agglutination.

Is, the grammatical copula—there you have a sufficient answer to the skeptical questioning of Kant about the thing in itself, in its transcendence, the answer of a living word and living thought which he did not hear or notice, although he desired or said that he desired to go as far as the fundamental elements of cognition and thought. Kant did not notice and did not appreciate the *copula* at all, but it held the answer to his question. The noumenon does not "lie at the foundation" of the phenomenon and is not entirely transcendent to it (so that it becomes a mystery how, in what sense and for what purpose it is to be imagined). The noumenon simply *is* the phenomenon, this "*is*" is expressed in its naming.

The transcendent-actual (the first hypostasis of being) beholds itself in immanent being, separated and broken down by ideas, by a word (the second hypostasis of being), and it is recognized effectively (*tei energeiai*) and asserts itself by naming; in the copula it recognizes the unity of the transcendent and immanent (the third hypostasis). Naming, which is expressed in the copula, has the deepest philosophical and mystical significance, for here the Gordian knot of Kantianism is cut, and the malicious intent against God's world is overcome—the attempt to make the noumenon deaf and blind, and the phenomenon empty, dead, and spectral. Thanks to the substantive noun, the original *realism* of thinking is established, which at the same time is also idealism, for in the substantive the agglutination of *res* and *idea* is established by the copula. Thus the inescapable Kantian solipsism, which is the accusation against "transcendental idealism," is overcome.

The copula both in its pure form and immediate grammatical expression of the auxiliary verb *is*, and also in its disguised form, plays a paramount role in the ontology of language and is its very foundation, that cementing glue without which there would be no language or speech; there would be at most, atoms of speech, its elements—separate words, root-ideas, without meaningfulness and correlations. Every correlation or binding together of words, a gestating thought, a judgment, is reduced to the type "A is B," where lexically "is" can even be entirely lacking, replaced with a punctuation mark (or dash) and by word order, as in isolating languages. This type is found in Russian in a sentence with an implied copula, where the character of predicate and definition is learned according to position: the man is good, a good man; the day is fine, a fine day; man is the enemy, the enemy man, etc. It is much more important that the function of semantic agglutination, the copula, is in reality not absent in a single phrase expressing a thought. Every judgment, i.e., every thought, is reduced to the utterance of the unutterable, i.e., to naming, and is grounded by a copula; but it can be given not in the bare form, but included and thus concealed in the verbal form. The point is that a copula is concealed in conjugation (and even in declension): the ending, the flexion of the conjugation expresses exactly the joining of a verb predicate to a subject, although in a specific form—of the expression of motion. A personal verb form can be expressed as a participle, plus copula. And whatever may have been the historical relation between them, the semantic relation indisputably remains precisely such: the conjugation includes the copula as that glue with which it is attached to the subject and becomes a name from an idea. For a verb also names by predicating. This will be discussed below.

What then does a copula express, on what is it grounded? That we give nicknames and stick on different labels and little words is not an expression of our psychologism. Such an understanding would destroy language as the faculty for speech and thought. The universal psychological explanation of their association is of no use here at all, because association is actually the glue of memory, the automatism of speech but does not at all explain its content, that which later is enveloped by habit. A copula must have objective, cosmic meaning if it has meaning's language as the carrier of thought.

In other words, *a copula expresses the world link of all with all*, the cosmic communism of being and the altruism of each of its moments, i.e., the capability of being expressed through the other. Three axioms, or more precisely, one axiom in three forms, are assumed by the copula: 1) everything (as modality or diversity) is everything (as totality)—of course in the broadest sense of the universal connection, which is always concrete, individual, and special; 2) each something is (potentially) everything, connected with everything; 3) everything (as totality) is something, the universal connection of being is expressed in each mode.

On this basis, every judgment with an innocuous, plausible *is* includes an antinomy and bridges the gap between phenomenon and noumenon that Kant had declared insurmountable. The antinomy is that here the law of identity is destroyed. The judgment "A is B" consists of two members, A and B. Each of them has its sphere and is limited by it, is closed in self-identity: A is A, B is B, and from this self-identity there can be no exit (as Antisthenes and Stilpo also said).[31] In that case, by virtue of the law of identity neither a judgment nor a grammatical sentence that would realize it is possible. It is necessary to break its fetters, to destroy the imaginary "law," which we indeed literally do in each step, in each judgment, assuring that A is not-A, and this not-A is B, but at the same time it is also A. The result is that A is A and not-A, and it does not fall apart because of this outrage not only against the law of identity, but even more the dread law of contradiction, and it peacefully marches along an even more forbidden path "of the excluded third."

Naming does all of this, the heart of which is the copula. The copula expresses the ability of things to come out of themselves and to be in the other, and therefore also to be expressed through the other. But since the cosmic universal connection of being is expressed in this being of all in all and through all, in this universal wholeness, in cosmicity, then it remains only to bow to the fact that it does not obey the dictates of school logic and does not accept its axioms. Here too it brings about the threefold image, the trihypostaticity of being: one being predicated through the other, the conversion of this other into the word of the first and the recognition of this conversion in the copula, through which the first knows itself in the second as itself, and together their connection and unity is perceived. It knows itself not only in its immobile self-identity, but also in the dynamic antinomism of self-negation; it is expressed through the other, and consequently a separate, enriched self-identity is affirmed.

Until now, we have been considering the implied but grammatically nonexistent copula in the substantive noun, present in a sentence and absent in a verb. In so doing, we put in parentheses some very different grammatical phenomena, which we must now distinguish.

If every substantive noun represents a latent judgment or a sentence in which the underlying or the subject is a pronoun—a mystical gesture, whereas that which is predicated or the predicate is a word, an idea, then *naming* is in general the elementary primary act of both language and thinking. Naming expresses the essence of speech, and it also expresses the essence of cognition (as the original meaning of the word *name* bears witness).[32]

We speak in sentences, but we think in judgments. The content of the one and the other is an expanded naming, a joining of idea-predicate—of the predicate with the copula *is*. It is erroneous to think that words in their grammatical and logical nature are born or arise already as substantive nouns, or as verbs and adjectives. Of course, a language already prepared and elaborated has ready-made forms for the expression of these "parts of speech"; it elaborates typical flexions or other "semantic units" corresponding to them (as for example the order of words in a sentence). But these forms exist for the expression of diverse functions that can fall to the lot of the same words but do not characterize the words themselves. To be a substantive noun or a verb is the *function* of a word as a meaning, but not its essence. One needs to see the essence of a word in its universal *predicative value*, corresponding to the universal, cosmic meaning of the copula *is*. Thanks to this, both the emergence of substantive nouns through the joining of a noun to a pronominal gesture, and the subsequent development of naming through the joining of a name or names already to a substantive noun, sometimes to a proper noun, is possible. Therefore, no words can exist that directly designate "objects" or "concepts" summoned into existence for them or by them. All words are only meanings, ideas, which can become predicates, names, but in the life of a word this naming is carried out by the human being in the human being, as his operation: here too is the anthropocosmic principle, the microcosm, here too psychology with its psychologisms. Naming is primary and elementary cognition, the recognition in things of their meaning, their idea, and the consolidation of this recognition in a name.

A substantive noun is not only a grammatical form that appeared in answer to a definite requirement of a verbal thought but is also a meaning, a gesture. It is entirely possible that the grammatical *form* remains unfulfilled by its mystical or ontological content and in fact does not have its own meaning. We have in a word a crystal of language development, a congealed and not always transparent cluster, a fact of the *history* of language. But it uses living speech in its own way, directing its rays onto it. When it receives the property of a predicate, a substantive noun in form ceases to be one in essence. It expresses only an idea, a quality, but not being. A horse is an animal, and vice versa. A black person is a human being (or vice versa, so and so is a black person), etc. It is evident that even the very same word, depending on its syntactical position, loses its full weight and becomes now something named, now something naming, equivalent to a verb.

As we have seen, the use of words in "an improper meaning," or tropes, is based on this. All predicativity is based on this, where one thing is defined by another, is named by it. In this case not only simple, prototypical, and transparent words expressing qualities fall into this position but also words that are complex in meaning and express voluminous concepts and even terms. Usually every such noun implies the fusion of concepts and ideas, connected more or less closely with it. It is equivalent to their complex or conglomerate, it is a complex color reduced however firmly or flimsily to a certain unit; therefore such a name is a substitute for this whole fusion. In the formula of the simplest judgment—the sentence "A is B" or, what is the same, A makes (= is making), endures (= is found in) B, the first member, A, is a substantive noun that has its support in real although mute being. The second member is the idea of being, the quality, but it does not have support in being and is doomed to ideal existence in the sphere of meaningfulness. Finally, in a mysterious and incomprehensible way, the copula combines mute being with eloquent meaningfulness, performs the disclosure or cognition of meaning—a naming.

To what did not have a name or had only one or a few names, newer and newer names are added: A is B, is C, is D . . . is N. By parodying Kant's famous formula that "thoughts without content are empty," whereas "intuitions without concepts are blind,"[33] we can say here that a subject-pronoun without a name is blind, but a name-predicate without a subject is empty, and their union gives cognition—naming, which is both the principle of speech, and the principle of any knowing and thinking. In the mystery of naming, which is also the mystery of language, the creative *let there be* is contained: "Let there be light" and "there was light." This divine *let there be* resounds in the world with infinite echoes, being repeated in every judgment.

Every judgment is reduced to a subject and a predicate, to an ontological point and an idea-word-meaning. There are as many names, or rather, as many predicates as there are ideas. And vice versa, one and the same idea can be a predicate for many subjects, as Plato taught: "When a number of individuals have a common name, we assume that they also have a corresponding idea or form. There are many beds and tables everywhere but there are only two ideas or forms of them, one the idea of a bed, the other of a table" (*Republic*, X. 596). Where words do not exist, ideas do not exist: "For these reasons, the varieties [of smells] are nameless, not being from many or simple forms" (*Timaeus*, 67).[34] An idea can be expressed about many things not because it is abstract but because as a concept it can be applied to everything that is included in its scope. The latter is only a particular instance, the realization of what is given in a predicate as such. But this property of an idea is connected not with abstraction or capacity but with predicative value, which always and essentially contains an idea. And that very substantive noun (grammatical), which was concrete only as a subject, by being converted into a predicate, an idea, assumes the character of universality: for example, *wolf*. Ideas are not abstract or concrete (as are concepts, the logical preparations of ideas); they are always pure meanings without scope.

A most difficult question arises: is every word, which can be a predicate and a subject (as essentially *every* word can, and the number of words created by the genius of language is practically unlimited), is every word an idea? If not, the word loses its quality, and instead of a meaning, it becomes an absurdity, an empty sound. If it can, then not only are words created but also ideas. Can such arbitrariness or even outrage be permitted in "the intelligible place," *topos noetos*? This question stood in all its sharpness even before Plato, although with him it did not have a special predicative formulation; it arose not in the analysis of a word but in a general analysis of ideas. He had to ask himself, does everything have its own idea? (This question is practically equivalent to ours.) Does the idea of hair, of dirty, sick, few, etc., exist? (See our excursus on Plato.) Plato had to reply to this question affirmatively, although he knew how difficult it was to unite this with the teaching about the kingdom of abiding ideas, about the intelligible place (*Phaedra*, etc.). This question can be answered only on general religious-metaphysical grounds. Words exist only because there is the Word, and there are ideas-meanings only because the Idea-Meaning exists. There is Sophia, the Soul of the world, the Wisdom of the world, as the all-perfected organism of ideas, as the Pleroma, the fullness of being. It is the intelligible basis of the world, the world as cosmos. Here ideas are seen one in the other, are reflected one in the other, here the communism of being really reigns, here the closed number, the fullness of ideas, exists.

By contrast, our world is this same cosmos in the process of becoming, of melting into non-being; it is sophian in all its being, but extra-sophian and even anti-sophian in its state. Here shadows and confusion are everywhere, the colors dirty and mixed. Strictly speaking, here ideas are never admissible in the pure form and one can speak only about the ideal quality of ideas, in the sense of their validity in authentic pure ideas. Therefore, predicates, words, meanings, ideas, which are always parts of a whole process of meaning-speech, both are ideas and are not ideas, but they have without fail a *basis* in ideas; they are ideal in their positive core, even though this ideal content is diluted, mixed, and grown muddied. They always have a positive content, but at the same time, they are pragmatic, accidental in their form. For they are taken from a discursive, logical associative process and not from their ontologically hierarchical correlation. Discursiveness i.e., the *passage* from one to another, causes ideas-meanings to be connected among themselves, they reflect one another on themselves. But this connection is in any case only a modality, and it does not express the essence. The logical connection distributes ideas according to the rubrics of logical categories, i.e., of concepts, but this distribution also takes into account the constructive needs of formal logic, with its negative, prohibitive norms, with its thought police, but it does not take into account the content of ideas. Finally, associative connections have to do with psychologisms of every kind, i.e., with the accidental or automatic side of consciousness.

So then, of course, words are ideas, predicates are pure meanings. But there are two realms of ideas: the world above and the world below. And all these difficult correlations, which are subjected to so much imprecise definition, the Achilles' heel of Plato (*methexis, koinonia,* etc.), are felt here. Plato says that the demiurge creates the world on the model of the ideas, and we create by looking at an idea. "We are accustomed to say that the demiurge of either of the vessels, gazing at the idea makes in the one case couches, in the other case tables that we use" (Republic, X, 596). Words-predicates likewise are created by gazing at the creative proto-words, which shine through their coverings in a system of mirrors, being refracted, dimmed, distorted, but all the same reflected such that without them there would be no words.

It is evident that words differ among themselves both according to their so to say ontological satiety, ideality (there are formal words, fluid words, and resonant, full-fledged words), and according to the ontology of their connection, by the force of their predicativity. A copula can unite everything, and naming can express the inner connections and apply only to the surface layers. The force of such a predicate will be different. Finally, a hierarchy exists in the very kingdom of ideas, the fundamental principles whose reflections are meanings. For us this domain, which Plato characterized by negation, apophatically, remains beyond the limit, transcendent. Undoubtedly, ideas are interconnected in an organic all-unity, but this connection is not a logical correlation of concepts but their dynamic, energetic conjugacy, an ontological hierarchy, where the superior contains everything inferior dynamically (and not logically in the sense of capacity) but is itself not encompassed by it, with the result that its content increases together with its capacity, but not vice versa, as in a system of logical concepts (Vladimir Soloviev pointed to this long ago).

On this basis, the grammatical treatment of a word, its framing by inflections and semantic signs, gets its place without which a word would not exist. This framing belongs to that refracting means that is created for a word by language. A word never exists in isolation in a language. (It can be considered under the guise of logical abstraction, but then it ceases to be itself, i.e., a verbal meaning.) It always exists in a phrase, in a sentence, a judgment, i.e., it is brought into correlation with other words-meanings; it is pronounced in a certain key or timbre. In speech, we do not have ideas in their unity and isolation but always mixtures or conglomerates of ideas. For this reason, judgments like that of Wundt are possible, that being can apply only to substantive nouns, meaningfulness only to predicates. One cannot say about white that it exists; there are only white objects. Whiteness is an idea that has *ideal* being. However, this ideal being is not at all some sort of deficiency or defect of being but only its other sphere.

Words as predicates, as ideas, are rays of the noetic world that break through the cloudy atmosphere. They flow from the fullness of a different being that is not here below, where ideas have all the force of existence. Thus, they shine even though they are not grafted onto the trunk of our earthly being, although they are ready to be grafted, to reflect their ray in a corresponding point. For this reason, the two Platonic worlds are bound together in predicativity, in a judgment-sentence, that is a constant testimony about the multiple levels of being, such that what has force of being in the higher world receives through this the force of meaningfulness (i.e., extra-temporal and extra-spatial, ideal being) for the world here below. Therefore, the copula *is*, or in general the function of predicativity, is the ladder between the two worlds, and it is erroneous to think that words arise or are invented apropos of earthly things, as their mental reflections; on the contrary, earthly things are named according to their ideas, their intelligible forms. We name them because *we recognize* in them the idea, slumbering in our very selves, as their ontological fundamental principle. In this is also that unfreedom, that necessity in virtue of which we name, obedient to a certain command of the thing itself, which is revealed to us. Together with Plato it is possible to say that we *remember*, we perform anamnesis, by naming things, so that in the final analysis, *naming*, to which the living mystery of speech-word is reduced, is nothing other than *remembering*.

III. The Grammatical Sentence: "Parts of Speech" and "Parts of a Sentence"

The substantive noun, having its correlate in the subject of a sentence or the subject of a judgment, and the predicate in a verb or copula, determines the content of speech, forms its backbone. Its development consists in the elaboration of these two themes: subjectivity and predicativity, in expanding them and making them more complex. The process of this elaboration is manifested and secured in grammatical forms; its separate features are crystallized in parts of speech, and then in the composition of an already complicated grammar they look like proto-elements of speech, just as original and independent as these two elements. As "parts of speech," they are the substantive noun, adjective, numeral, pronoun, verb, adverb, preposition, conjunction, and interjection. As "parts of a sentence," they are the subject, predicate, attribute, and adverbial modifier (of place, manner of action). The first, i.e., the parts of speech, are only different modes of subject value or predicativity; the second, i.e., the parts of a sentence, are their expansion and complication.

The substantive noun is the universal form of speech and thought: it expresses the existential accent, the bond of idea and being. A substantive noun has its grammatical form (and in this sense it is a "part of speech") in the vesture of which certain words are used precisely with the significance of substantives. However, the category of substantive noun (not only in thinking but also in language)—not only in judgment but also in a sentence—is wider but also narrower than this grammatical form. An ideal form of a substantive noun exists with which any word is invested provided it is considered in itself and as itself (as a subject) and becomes the content of an intention. Then it can be expressed externally-grammatically either by an article, if the given language has the article (*to, das, le, the*) or only by its position in a phrase, i.e., by syntactic means (in isolating languages or even in both agglutinative and inflected languages, like Russian). *Any* word can be made a subject—in the one or other sense (examples: *or* is a conjunction; *in town* is an adverbial modifier; *to go* is an infinitive; *to write* is difficult; *the good* are loved; *good* means gladly; *alas!* was involuntarily uttered by him, etc.).

Of course, to place words that have an entirely different significance under the guise of a substantive noun, although specially justified each time, is always to do grammatical violence to the "parts of speech," but at the same time, this shows the auxiliary and derivative significance of "parts of speech." The latter are only grammatical auxiliary means of speech that in effect could not exist or at least there could be more or less of them. Given the purely root character of language, as it is postulated for earlier histori-cal epochs, they would not have existed at all,[35] whereas the functions of subject and predicate always constituted an element of speech. If a sentence-judgment had always preserved its simplest elementary form A is B, there would have been no place for the development of grammatical parts of speech, at least in their current wealth and variety. But this pattern always becomes complicated, both on the side of A as on the side of B, which is why intermediate parts of speech arise, adjoining the one or other side, filling in the subject or the predicate.

Three parts of speech or states of words are least in need of an explana-tion: the substantive noun, the adjective, and the verb, where all three parts of speech, being full-fledged, entirely independent words, change their roles and functions. The same root word can freely change its significance, assum-ing the character of a substantive, an adjective or a verb. However, an adjec-tive and a verb are only two different forms of predicativity. In the first case this is expressed with the help of a copula present or implied, as a property in general, irrespective of space and time, aspect and "person"; in the second case, however, the same property is taken from an aspect of time as action. Sometimes this grammatical difference is almost indifferent for the mean-ing (*gora bela—gora beleet, nebo sine—nebo sineet* [the mountain is white—the mountain looks white, the sky is blue—the sky looks blue]), though more of-ten it has shades of meaning that define more concretely the connections of subject with predicate. In general, all three of these parts of speech condition the basic function of speech—naming, which in accord with what was said above is a judgment, and they mutually reflect one on the other, depending on the place of each. We repeat: these are full-fledged words, essential ele-ments of speech that are not created by grammar but are only formed by it. They exist, if it can be thus expressed, *earlier than* grammar, putting to it their demands, which flow out of the nature of words themselves.

It is similar for pronouns. *The personal* pronoun, representing the mystery of a noun as being a hidden basis for it, has already been explained above in its meaning. It is a necessary shadow, delineated by opaque, ontologically filled words.[36] Pronouns have a much more derivative and hence more for-mally grammatical meaning, replacing adjectives and used in fact instead of a noun, as a verbal gesture or an abbreviated, simplified naming. Such are demonstrative and relative pronouns; possessive pronouns, which corre-spond to personal pronouns and replace them grammatically, occupy a spe-cial place: your house, that is, the house belonging to you, etc. The so-called relative pronouns correspond to an already sufficiently developed and hence later stage of syntax: in different Indo-European languages they appear much later or sometimes are even entirely absent.[37] Their role of binding clauses and replacing substantive nouns or adjectives is grammatically auxiliary; it can be understood from the historical development of grammar, with its ways and means, but not from the basic functions of speech. In some sense, it is a grammatical luxury, an object not of necessity but of convenience, which one can make do without, if necessary, just as speech can make do without long and complex periods and consist of principal clauses only.

"The names for numbers" are customarily considered a special part of speech in grammars. It is clear that the category of words of a known content, namely those that designate number, is allocated to a special part of speech for grammatically utilitarian considerations and in a suitably scholastic fashion, and in any case the independence of this grammatical category can in effect be challenged. The initial numbers—one, two, and more, i.e., an indeterminate great number—are given in language not by part of speech but by inflection: the singular, dual (where it exists), and plural number always speak of quantity. On the other hand, there are languages, very poor in numerical words, that do not even have words for expressing a number greater than four and already designate larger numbers as indeterminate sets. In general, names for numbers represent a great diversity in different languages, according to quantity and character. But even in languages with developed numeration, words with number roots are either nouns (*in potentia*)—cardinal numbers, or adjectives—ordinals, or adverbs (about which below). In any case, the distinctiveness of this grammatical category is not in its function but only in its signification.[38]

The adverb, which at the present time is indisputably an independent part of speech and a grammatical category, appears rather late in its historical origin. It arose because a given word lost its independent significance in a phrase and the fullness of its meaning, and because it fused, as a supplementary meaning or semitone, with one of the words entering a sentence. Adverbs are formed either from adjectives, which play the role of attribute, or from verbal adjectives—participles, which are replaced by adverbial participial forms.[39] Their significance can be understood only from their link with that word or meaning to which they are united, and they do not have another independent nature. Therefore, from the point of view of the distinction interesting us, adverbs express the modality of a predicate and hence enter into the general category of predicativity, being a means for it.

The preposition has a similar significance, having become isolated into a special part of speech later than the adverb. The preposition arises from an adverb that loses its full significance and is employed only in a definite verbal combination. Although it is now sharply impressed in our thought as something demanding a definite form (case) after it, originally, as the history of language shows,[40] the preposition had the independent significance of an adverb; therefore, in its meaning it merges with it and departs into the general broad category of the predicate and its means.

The conjunction also has a similar origin; originally an independent word, it then loses independent significance and plays a purely syntactical role in the structure of complex sentences. This role can be understood only from the purely grammatical functions of an already complex and developed language; having purely auxiliary significance, it can be entirely removed from a language without any detriment to the meaning. It is a matter of syntactical ease.

Sometimes interjections are treated as parts of speech, i.e., exclamations that do not have the character of words as meanings but of emotionally charged sounds. They stand on the very border *of speech* in the precise sense: on the one hand they are already "onomatopoeic," "interjected" words; on the other hand they are sonic gestures found already outside words, as for example, cries from pain, from terror, etc. Interjections are only embryos of speech and strictly speaking, they cannot occupy a place alongside actual parts of speech.

This brief survey, which of course could be expanded, is sufficient to show that the grammatical classification of parts of speech and the complex organization corresponding to them essentially do not rescind or even limit our fundamental idea that speech consists of predication or naming, and parts of speech either directly serve this task or play an auxiliary role. They represent organized and dissected predicativity, which is inseparably linked with subjectivity. The so-called parts of a sentence also have this meaning; in addition to the subject and predicate, they include the attribute, the object, and adverbial modifiers of place, time, and manner.

Let us establish first of all that although naming supposes as a minimum a relation between one subject and one predicate, there can also be several relations on either side. With a plurality of grammatical subjects, our judgment is riveted to being in *several* points-nouns, and their connection with ideas-predicates receives a more complex, patterned design. Any plural number offers the simplest example of this: "we are waiting"—or the so-called fused sentence: "we, I, you (he and I, and NN, etc.) are going." Grammar permits liberties here, which have enormous fundamental significance, namely it sometimes expresses the grammatical subject not by the classic nominative case but "by an indirect object."[41] It is exactly the same for a predicate: "He and I both are good people." This simple example demonstrates that although established and crystallized forms of grammar and syntax offer, so to say, the simplest, normal patterns of naming, still we cannot be guided exclusively by them when investigating the question of its ontological roots. We have to broaden the customary grammatical definitions. A subject is usually considered to be what is spoken about in a sentence, where it stands in the nominative case, if it is declinable, and is a substantive noun according to form or, at least, according to meaning.[42] We will leave aside that this definition is not suitable for many cases[43] and fix our attention on this duality in the definition of grammatical subject.

First, the formal requirement of sentence structure that a subject must stand in the nominative case can be fulfilled of course only insofar as a given word is declinable or has a case; otherwise it assumes a quasi-nominative case (examples: "in the distance a hurrah burst forth," "to study is difficult," "*perom*" is the instrumental case of "*pero*," etc.) The second requirement, that the subject be a substantive noun invested with a grammatical form, while generally corresponding to the majority of cases, has no grammatical meaning at all but only a semantic one. It signifies that the subject is not only an idea-meaning, but also a real-life center, "substantive," therefore not only according to form, but also according to significance.

All parts of speech can fall under the category of substantive noun as subject: a verb, an adjective, even all the rest. And vice versa, as we already know, an authentic substantive noun, although in the nominative case, ceases to be a substantive noun according to meaning if it plays the role of the predicate: "hurrah—is a shout of joy." Here "hurrah" is a substantive noun, "shout" in essence is an adjective as predicate. Therefore, when grammar makes its demand about the "substantival value" of the subject, it is clear that here in formal and clumsily imprecise language it is a matter of distributing ontological accents and demarcating the spheres of subject value from predicativity. On the subject's side, apart from a general verbal meaning, there is still an opaque core of being, while on the predicate's side there are pure meanings, ideas, deprived of this core, although according to form relevant to the substantive. In the distribution of these ontological accents, we have to take into consideration not only the grammatical form but also the semantic meaning, and we will have to broaden the category of subject significantly beyond the limits of a formal subject in the nominative case.

As an example, let us take the simplest case first: *a boy* broke a cane. This "active" turn of phrase can be conveyed in "the passive" almost without any change of meaning: a cane is broken by a boy. Where is the subject and the predicate here? What is being spoken of here and what is being said? Formally and grammatically, in the first case, it is said about *a boy* that he *broke a cane*; in the second case,—about *a cane*, that it *was broken by a boy*. But, obviously, neither the one nor the other definition satisfies the real content of this sentence and the judgment contained in it, because in reality it is speaking not only about a cane and not only about a boy, but about a cane and a boy. Both the one and the other represent the subject, and they stand under the ontological accent where their bond is predicated by the idea of breaking. Here of course it is not a matter of the grammatical form of a substantive noun but precisely of the semantic accent.

Compare two more such examples: "learned meets indigent." Here both "learned" and "indigent" are adjectives that have the significance of a subject, but they already lose it in a combination such as "the learned investigator met an indigent elder." Here the accent shifts to *investigator* and *elder*, and this can happen not only with an adjective but also with a substantive: "the Thunderer sent his Perun." "Zeus the Thunderer sent his arrow-Perun." Both nominative cases and the substantive nouns cease to be the subject only because they come out from under the ontological accent; though remaining substantive in form, in meaning they have a predicative significance—verbal or adjectival.

We arrive at the conclusion that the actual, semantic subject of a sentence, that "about which it speaks" is not at all only the grammatical subject but is also the object, whether direct or indirect is of no import, as long as it stands under the ontological accent; it is a full-fledged substantive noun, not only in form but also in meaning. The subject of a sentence can be plural and complex; the link between them is predicated not using a direct pattern of naming—agglutination, but a complex one. A predicate speaks about all subjects taken in their concrete correlation. A sentence has several centers, one of which—the formal subject—is of paramount significance; to it the whole phrase is oriented, it is the sun around which the whole planetary system orbits.

So then, an object, both direct and indirect, can have to do with a grammatical subject, it enters into the sphere of the subject *being discussed*. However, we cannot say this about *every* object, even if it satisfied all requirements, i.e., it was a substantive noun. As we know, not every substantive noun in grammatical form is a substantive in meaning, and only full-fledged nouns belong to the subject's sphere. Here are some examples: 1) *he* went with *his father*—he went with a drooping head. 2) *He* has **a book**—he feels joy (= is joyful). 3) *He* carries his head high—*he* raised *his head*. 4) He moved *his hand*—*he* walked by a pathway—*he* went *by road* to Kiev. 5) They cut *the forest* with an axe—*what is written* with a pen you will not fell with an axe, etc., etc. We cannot always detect the ontological accent easily and precisely. The verbal criterion here is whether or not a substantive noun can be converted into an adjective or verb and whether or not it can be replaced by a pronoun. But one thing is clear, that in fact the subject of a sentence is broader than a formal grammatical subject, and the subjectivity *always* is connected with substantival value, semantic and not only formal. A subject is someone or something and answers the question "who?" or "what?" Whereas a predicate, although it too is a substantive noun in form, answers the question "how?" and "what kind?"

In a similar manner, the sphere of predicativity is broader than a proper predicate. The predicative value opens up and envelops the subject from different sides, overflowing its bounds. Let us examine the parts of a sentence from this point of view except, of course, the grammatical subject.

Let us begin with the attribute. It is not difficult to see that an attribute, no matter to what it might be joined, in particular to a grammatical subject, is on the one hand an abbreviated or underdeveloped predicate, into which it can be converted, and on the other hand, a part of the name of the grammatical subject, an extra verbal petal or cover. An example: "*a good* man is loved by all." The emphasized word can be turned into an independent phrase: "(this) man is good," or a relative clause: "who is good." At the same time, *good* here is the name of the subject, sometimes more substantial than a substantive noun. In the expression "good man," man can be omitted without detriment, and a predicate is left as an independent noun, which then falls under the ontological accent and becomes a subject.

The role of this underdeveloped predicate can be played equally by a verb form—a participle, both adjectival and substantive, of course losing its ontological quality and being used as an adjective. Examples: "Ivan the fool travelled on the Little Humpbacked Horse." "The dread tsar commanded to punish." "The conquerors flaming with rage destroyed the town." "A donkey with long ears and short tail hobbled along the road," etc. Complementary predicativity is introduced by an attribute referring to the grammatical subject, and it can have a more or less concrete significance depending on the extent to which it is fused with the noun and composes with it a single name (Ivan the Terrible, Vasilii the Dark, rosy-fingered dawn, the flaring-nosed Achaeans, etc.) or really contains a fused sentence, an additional predicate (the good tsar spared the town; father, having arrived, was met by everyone, etc.)

An attribute referring to the grammatical subject is found of course in the closest relation to the predicate and even more fills it in and competes with it. But in principle the role of an attribute does not change even when it concerns the secondary parts of a sentence, enveloping them with predicative value and thus introducing it to general predicative value: "he grasped the big cane with his long hands" and the like. Attributes are like the blending of colors on a palette, thanks to which each member of the sentence enters into a common connection in a complicated and somewhat modified form. Of course, in practice it is entirely conceivable that an attribute in some little corner of a sentence contains the main thought or at least the central communication for which the sentence is put together. An example: "father's sickness, developing and repeating through lengthy intervals of time, having recurred on the occasion of a severe cold which was brought on by excessive fatigue, led to his fatal end after all." Whatever "is being spoken about" in this phrase, its semantic center, is contained in the attribute of the supplemental attribute *fatal*: it is the central point of the predicate around which all of its remaining nuances are arranged.

Be that as it may, the one important thing is that the attribute, as a part of the sentence, does not have its own independent semantic field but refers entirely to the sphere of the predicative value. One can consider a sentence with many attributes as an organization of several sentences that have fused into one and are thereby mutually subordinated one to the other. The degree of this connectivity and its character—from the external mechanical union of simple sentences up to an organic fusion in complex periods—is by no means grasped sufficiently in existing grammatical categories, which detect only external grammatical signs. However, if we regard the whole field of speech, i.e., the sentence as the correlation of two spheres—subject and predicate, substantive and verb—then it is clear that an attribute stands wholly on the side of the latter. Every attribute is an element of a predicate.[44]

Other parts of a sentence must also be treated, such as the object and "adverbial modifiers." As for objects, they refer either to the subject, and constitute an extended subject, or to the predicate, and form an extension of the predicate. "An object is any oblique case of a substantive noun with a preposition or without a preposition, whatever it may refer to" (Kudriavskii, 116). Thus does linguistics define it. As is well known, school grammar distinguishes between a direct object in the accusative case and an indirect object in all the remaining cases (except, of course, the vocative and nominative), with and without a preposition. This distinction does not have a fundamental significance for us, but we will make use of it for the sake of convenience, pausing on the direct object. Let us take two examples: "I see Chatyr-dag," "I see scenery," and "I love father," "I love work." Formally there is no difference between these sentences, and yet it exists and will be felt only if we translate them into passive turns of phrase. For the first example (Chatyr-dag is seen by me, father is loved by me) there will be no difference except a slight nuance of meaning, a shift of logical stress; the second sounds contrary to nature (work is loved by me, scenery is regarded by me). The point is that in the first case we have an ontological accent on the object: according to its meaning it is also the grammatical subject; here there are two ontological centers, two substantive nouns in the proper sense of the word. Inversely, in the second example, the object is deprived of this ontological accent and is essentially a complementary color of the grammatical subject (like grey-yellow, blue-red, etc.): I love-work, I see-scenery. This is the concretization of a verb, a particular meaning of a general concept, and it is felt in that roughness of meaning that is felt in the grammatically irreproachable change of the phrase into a passive one. It is always possible to make such a distinction, although with different clarity, in a direct object: it refers either to the subject or to the predicate. Sometimes this ontological accent is connected not with a word but with a meaning, imparted by an indicative gesture: *I love work* can signify in one case: I am industrious (predicate), but in the second: I love my own work ("my multi-year work is finished"). A substantive noun with predicative meaning, being a substantive in *form*, has practically the significance of an adjective or verb, as was the case with an attribute. Here the idea, the meaning of a given word has force, but not its ontological significance.

We can say the same thing regarding an indirect object—a fundamental difference between direct and indirect does not exist. Let us take two very simple examples: I went with father (= father and I went), I went with distraction (= distractedly), I walked through the forest, I walked through this forest; I went at night, at two o'clock, in pensiveness, etc. It is similar for verbal words with complements: worshipping idols (= idol-worship), worshipping these very idols in a given shrine; love for humankind (philanthropy), love for this human, etc. Any object, not always with sufficient clarity, can be tested with respect to its substantival, verbal, or adjectival value and then attributed to subject value or predicativity. We can establish the general rule that if an object does not have the ontological accent on itself ("about what it is said"), then it is part of a predicate, and the general duality of the spheres of grammatical subject and predicate is not destroyed by this.

Let us select for an example the first prose poem of I. S. Turgenev that falls into our hands, *Necessitas—Vis—Libertas* [Necessity—Force—Liberty]. The title, despite the grammatical form of the substantive nouns, is undoubtedly predicative, or rather, corresponds to the indeterminateness of the root language. (The ontological accents, corresponding to the substantive noun and entrance into the field of the grammatical subject are marked in italics.) "The tall, gaunt *old woman* [*starukha*] with a rigid face and fixed-vacant look walks with great strides and with her hand dry as a stick pushes another *woman* [*zhenshchina*] before her." (In this long phrase, abounding in substantives, only two really have this significance: *old woman* [*starukha*] and *woman* [*zhenshchina*], all the rest can be replaced with adjectives or adverbs, i.e., they are verbal attributes.) This *woman* is of enormous size, mighty, buxom, with muscles like Hercules', with a tiny little head on a bull neck—and blind—in her turn pushes a small, slender *girl* [*devochka*]. (In this phrase too, with an abundance of grammatically substantive nouns, only two are such: *zhenshchina* and *devochka*, and all the rest are adjectives or adverbs.)

Only this *girl* has sighted eyes; she is resting, she turns back, raises her delicate, pretty hands; her animated face expresses impatience and courage . . . (Again, with a very significant accumulation of substantive nouns, full weight belongs only to two: *girl* and *face*, and the pronoun **she**. It is typical that a direct object, which can be converted formally into a grammatical subject, although this will be a deformation of meaning, does not have the meaning of a substantive noun, but of a verbal color: she raises her delicate, pretty hands—this can be combined into one verb.) *She* does not want to listen, she does not want to go where they are pushing **her**. . . . And all the same, she must submit and go. *Necessitas, vis, libertas.* Let *whomever* it pleases translate." In this fortuitous example, we can see how essentially small the number of cases are when the grammatical forms of substantive nouns are taken in all their fullness, not just being a means of description, colorful strokes that have meaning only in the ensemble.

In addition to the indirect object, grammar singles out as a special part of the sentence "the adverbial modifier" of place, time and manner, cause and purpose; and we have an analogue of these "adverbial modifiers" in certain grammatical cases (see above). Only the adverb is an indisputable "adverbial modifier,"[45] and the adverbial participle is a verbal adverb. All the remaining adverbial modifiers can also be considered indirect objects according to meaning. However, this grammatical distinction, like its disputability, has no significance for the question at hand. There is no doubt that everything that has force with regard to an indirect object applies also to an adverbial modifier, consisting of a substantive noun in an oblique case with or without a preposition. The ontological accent can be absent or present, and here a substantive noun can be full-fledged or even a semantic allocation. Let us take some very simple examples. A) *Adverbial modifier of place: a tailor* from Moscow works cheaply; from *Moscow* I moved to *Tver'*. I passed the field—I came *to our field*. Go the road of honor—go along the Moscow *highway*, etc. (ontological accents are indicated in italics). B) Adverbial modifiers of *time*: In the 1919th year after Christ's Birth, **I** am writing these lines; on the *night* of Christ's Birth *a star* appeared in the east. During *a solar eclipse* there is general *anxiety*—during the very *eclipse* of the sun *an old man* arrived, etc.

C) *Adverbial modifiers of action*: **I** shouted a shout—with my *shout* I gathered the people; by a deliberate manner of action I reached my *goal*—precisely with this *method* scientific *results* are achieved. D) *Adverbial modifiers of cause*: Because of illness, I had to leave *school*—thanks to the death of my father **I** had to leave *school*, etc. As for adverbs, their belonging to the verbal and predicative category is not in doubt. But all adverbial modifiers either contain an ontological core, perceptible in one way or another, whether thanks to the construction of the phrase, the logical stress, or the content, in which case as in an indirect object we have here the field of the subject, an extended grammatical subject; or they are extended adverbs and in fact are frequently reduced to and replaced by them.

In this way, the whole syntax of a simple sentence reduces to the distinction and taking apart of two functions—subject and predicate. Complex sentences, a principal and a subordinate clause with its different aspects corresponding to the parts of a sentence (object, relation, and adverbial modifier) do not introduce anything new here. On the contrary, their articulation concerns only the syntax of a sentence, i.e., the structure of speech in relation to its already organized parts, which is what sentences are. Of course, special cases are possible, as when an attribute decomposes into a relative clause, is converted into it, and the character of the predicative value of attribute and adjective emerge in total clarity. For example, a good man = a man who is good; having done this = the one who did this, etc. In a different way, in "object" clauses the specific gravity of separate elements of an object come forward more distinctly: I see the goodness of this *man* (the ontological accent is on the grammatical subject and the attribute of the object) = **I** see that this *man* is good; I heard about the killing of N.N. by a soldier = **I** heard that N.N. was killed *by a soldier* = that *a soldier* killed N. N. Similarly, adverbial clauses: during the singing *of the hymn, we* entered the town = when we began singing *the hymn,* we entered the town, etc.

In other cases, subordinate clauses are only a method for uniting separate and completely independent thoughts that have various semantic links among them; hence, they can be united at different points and by different methods. They can also stand as completely independent sentences, united by conjunctions, but also entirely without them. In a similar manner, any period essentially can be broken into separate parts, and a vast canvas divided into several separate studies. It is a question rather of style, of artistic modeling in which words and parts of speech or clauses no longer play the role of colors but whole phrases and thoughts with their modulations and nuances. No matter what may be the nature of this art of the word (about which below), for our current question it adds nothing in particular. Our general point of view remains in force—that speech consists of a substantive and a predicate; it reduces to the simplest form A is B, an exact pronominal something is B. In other words, speech is reduced to *naming*, which is realized in complex, dissected, and richly organized forms, but all of this wealth and splendor of decoration does not darken and does not abolish the unity of function, and this function is, we repeat, *NAMING*.

CHAPTER 3

Toward a Philosophy of Grammar

The greatest one-sidedness in all of Kant's epistemological constructions is that he ignored language and paid no attention at all to grammar.[1] At the same time, of course, he did not free himself from dependence on it. He stands on the ground of grammar all the time and actually uses it; however, he does so unconsciously, blindly, and thus dogmatically. Kant's critical knife did not reach that deepest level of thought that language is; he revealed only the external, superficial, and derivative levels. It is impossible to free oneself from the power of language and the influence of grammar. It would mean making thought free from language, transcendent to words. But this is impossible, for thought is born in words and is inseparable from them; wordless thought does not exist. Here it is possible to say, parodying Locke and the sensualists: *nihil est in intellectu, quod non fuerit . . . in verbo* [nothing is in the intellect that was not . . . in a word], just as vice versa: *nihil est in verbo, quod non potest esse in intellectu* [nothing is in a word that cannot be in the intellect].[2]

Indeed this very opposition or distinction of *verbum* and *intellectus* can only be in the abstract, for the force of a word, of speech, is also the force of thought. That which can be established by epistemological or logical analysis relative to the conditions or content of thought must be found and shown in the realization of thought in a word, in language. Language in effect brings about by its own means the tasks of logic and epistemology. It is these latter in action, *in actu*. As thinking, because of its very nature, exists prior to any analysis or self-analysis of thought, prior to logic, epistemology, and philosophy, and is for it a *prius* and basis, so also in language we ought to find all these elements of thought in actual realization, *in concreto*. Indeed, logic, epistemology, and philosophy already rest on language, use grammar, and look through its window panes for their own purposes—and not only for the exposition of thought, but more importantly, at its birth.

It was this refractive, although transparent and at the same time peculiar medium that Kant did not notice when he began searching for the proto-elements of thought, its roots, when he began striving to overcome all premises to reach *voraussetzungsloser Gedanke* [unconditional thought], like a beacon to which he led all neo-Kantianism. While exposing and removing the veils of thought he did not notice what had necessarily grown together with it and clothes thought from all sides—language, grammar. Historically Kant's fault has many mitigating circumstances: comparative linguistics of his day had only just been born, and the opportunity given by it to see this veil of language was lacking then. (Hegel, however, no longer has these miti-gating circumstances, nor especially does the whole of modern and contem-porary neo-Kantianism, which in its pursuit of *Voraussetzungslosigkeit* [state without presuppositions] is frankly obliged to give an account before the elements of language, for without this, it finds itself in dogmatic captivity to language.) The absence "of a critique of language" in *The Critique of Pure Reason* makes it entirely impotent. It would be possible to create a grammati-cal commentary for the works of Kant and clearly show his actual depen-dence on language and the vagueness of his thought thanks to the absence of this analysis.[3] We make this observation for future Kantians.

So then, with its means language accomplishes the needs of thought, and in this sense grammar—in both of its conventionally distinguishable parts, etymology and syntax—is concrete epistemology and concrete logic. Episte-mological and logical demands are invariable and universal; this corresponds to their formal nature as it is realized by us in abstraction. Conversely, lan-guage is multiform, and its grammatical properties, both in grammar and in syntax, are changeable and diverse. An isolating language, which does not have inflected declension and conjugation, makes do by one means, and an inflected language by other means. But here too within inflected idioms, great differences exist in declension (by gender and the number of cases), and in conjugation (by the number of forms, times, and aspects), and ac-cording to "parts of speech." This difference is due partly to the different ages and elaboration of a language, partly to its natural properties, subject or not subject to further clarification, but in any case assuming their mutual equivalency. In other words, different languages, each with their own means, satisfy the tasks that are set before them by thought; they accommodate the same epistemological schema and give place to the same requirements of logic. *The Critique of Pure Reason* can be translated into different languages.

For our task, it is entirely unnecessary to sort out these individual properties of languages, but it suffices to indicate the general connection between the inquiries of epistemology and the answers of grammar, to look at grammar as concrete epistemology.[4] Our guides will be the properties of Greco-Latin grammar, which some of the modern European languages (like Russian and the Slavic languages in general, Italian, or German) approximate more or less, or from which others (French or English) are more or less distant, as from their prototype.

Let us begin with what Kant designated as the "transcendental aesthetic," which investigates time and space as forms of experience and "pure intuition" (*reine Anschauung*). It is entirely possible not to share the general philosophical views of Kant at all, on time and space in particular, and nevertheless to acknowledge together with him that no matter what their natures in and of themselves might be, one and the other constitute the universal form of our sense experience and inner comprehension. Spatiality is the general property of all sense experience, of our "external" (with respect to the inner processes of consciousness) world; temporality is the same property of the whole world not only external but also internal. This is an inalienable quality of everything knowable by us.

From the point of view of language, as is shown above, knowledge of what occurs in judgments is reduced to naming. The latter adheres ontologically to the logical copula *is*, present or implied, or concealed in the verb: as such, it has only one meaning, "gilt [is valid]" *outside* the relation to space and time—a leaf is green, the sea roars, etc. Kant distinguishes here the judgment of perception (*Wahrnehmungsurtheil*) from the judgment of experience (*Erfahrungsurtheil*). Both the one and the other[5] have empirical character, come from experience, but the first is a purely subjective statement of a given state of the senses, whereas the second has the universal obligatory character of necessity; the subject is linked to the predicate by a concept *a priori*, by a causal connection. In this initial distinction, which has decisive significance for Kant, his negligence regarding language is told in a fatal manner. The judgment "here it is hot," or "the room is warm," even simply "it is boring," "it is merry"—for him they have a completely subjective nature (*Wahrnehmungsurtheile*). However, even for him the question ought to have arisen about how the subjective can become objective, i.e., universal, universally known through language. While I am experiencing boredom, it remains my subjective state, a psychologism. But once I have pronounced or written "I am bored" publicly, my subjective state receives the force of a fact; it unavoidably enters into all consciousness and becomes its ideal content. Kant sees the decisive sign in the category *a priori*, in particular in the category of causality. But the difficulty of the question lies elsewhere. Why is "I feel sad" a *Wahrnehmungsurtheil*, whereas "I feel sad because I love you," which raises this subjectivity to the second power, is an *Erfahrungsurtheil*, possessing *Allgemeingiltigkeit* [generality] in contrast to the first? Obviously, the difference in which Kant sees the decisive sign of objectivity, namely the connection of necessity, the category of causality, already concerns the particularities of content and can be established by a critique of this judgment on the part of *content* but not by formal criteria, not epistemologically. The epistemological question here might not be where Kant sees it, i.e., in the difference of judgments according to content, but in the very possibility of *Wahrnehmungsurtheile*, for, as *Urtheile*, they nevertheless differ by some sort of objectivity, they can be communicated and become the content of universal consciousness no less than the "experimental judgment" of science.

Here it turns out that Kant sees the proto-element of thought not at all where it must be. He looks for it in a category, and the enormous, indeterminate quantity of judgments or thoughts remains *outside* his categories and therefore also outside thinking; however, the difficulty of the question is contained in the possibility of any judgment at all, no matter what may be its scientific value. Kant poses as the *first* question *"wie ist die Erfahrung möglich"* [how is experience possible], and he applies to it a complex, debatable, imprecise definition where each element raises both doubts and the question: "how are synthetic judgments possible *a priori?"* Whereas he ought to have asked himself "how *is any judgment possible*? What does the power of judgment consist in?" And the same for a sentence, which lies at the basis of all knowledge as a ready-made judgment already comprehensible without further analysis. What does the power of a judgment or of a grammatical sentence consist in? What is the naming that takes place in every judgment?

Kant ignored this fundamental and decisive question, without noticing the problems here, and as a result of this, all of his subsequent agenda took on a distorted character. In particular, this concerns the opposition of *Wahrnehmungs-* and *Erfahrungsurtheile*. Here Kant was carried away by the different content of judgments from which one judgment speaks about state, the other about things, but he did not take into account that every state, even the most subjective, expressed in words and clothed in a judgment, is already a thought, meaningfulness, in its own way as rock-hard as any *Erfahrungsurtheil*. Knowledge, the *Allgemeingiltigkeit* for thought, does not at all consist in a category *a priori*, which Kant extends into anything at all, but in a **word**. For a word possesses meaningfulness, it is not a "concept" higher than which Kant does not know, but that which is higher, because more real than a concept—an *idea*. I say, "It is boring." In this way I bring about an act of thought-knowledge in a judgment-sentence, for *in reality* I am saying "I am the one being bored." Between the ontological point **I**, than which nothing can be more firm for thought (even for Kant), is established the immutable connection *is*, which agglutinates to this subject the idea of *boredom*. In the judgment "it is boring," however poor or pitiful in content it might be (this is another question), immutable connections are implemented, the same power of thought, of judgment, of naming is revealed as in the judgment containing the laws of Newton. *Kant does not notice this and does not accept it*, and therefore he must search for the objective foundations of thought in its ulterior and derivative qualifications, which are categories. And so, in judgment[6] there is an element not only extra-temporal and extra-spatial but also in general representing pure conceivability. This is the copula *is*, predicativity; and there is an unconditionally concrete and objective element—the subject, the ontological center. In contrast, there is in the predicate a place for concretization in the sense of Kant's "transcendental aesthetic."

Spatiality and temporality are the most general attributes of being, but space and time are our contemplations that color all our thought and cognition. And we cannot doubt that we will find the reworked and developed form for the expression of the one and the other in a language that realizes our concrete thought. Actually, language has the richest means for the expression of spatiality and temporality in their different nuances. As the basic means for this, it has declension and conjugation; to this are added as auxiliaries still different parts of speech: the preposition, that verbal sorcery that imposes the seal of place and time on both substantive and verb, the adverb, and the adjective. The means of language, in general, are here twofold. On the one hand, it disposes of more or less extensive stores of words, which according to their meaning express space and time in different senses, but on the other hand, it has formal means in the form of inflections or "semantic units," with which it is generally able to give to any variable word the characteristic of space or temporality, and this presents a particular interest of fundamental principle. Declension and conjugation fulfill just such a role with their own tones.

It needs to be stipulated beforehand that their epistemological functions, which will be partially explained below, are still broader than what has been indicated, but among others, they also serve these necessities of a "transcendental aesthetic." Through them, spatiality and temporality permeate all of our speech consciously or unconsciously, so much so that we cannot think them away, we cannot be freed from them even if we wish, because language is mightier than our efforts of abstraction. Where we wish to remove every concreteness and to achieve the greatest "purity," language laughs at us (and of course deservedly).

Case (*casus, ptosis*) according to the usual definition indicates the relation of an object to action, to another object, and so on. This formal definition, which of course says nothing, only bears witness to the complexity, vastness, and at the same time unusual richness of content and meaningfulness of the intellectual and verbal wealth, sometimes the outright splendor that we have in this whole regular declension that was still pretty bothersome on the school bench. As a result of its regularity we stopped noticing what a miracle of thought we have here with respect to subtlety and richness. Among these nuances, we have a special *locative* case, though in truth not in all languages in an isolated form. In an earlier state of the Indo-Germanic languages it even developed into an entire series of locative cases: casus *ablativus, elativus, illativus, adessivus, superessivus, inessivus, pro*-secutivus. These cases are not present in all languages, but then they are replaced by locative prepositions, which in combination with a substantive in the corresponding case, can express any nuance of spatiality. Any being that is expressed in a substantive noun can be projected on the screen of spatiality in all sorts of combinations. Of course, in fact not all languages are equally elaborated and flexible for this purpose and use equally simple means. However, in general one can say that with the help of case inflection and preposition, all possible nuances of spatiality can be expressed. Thought becomes spatial.

With a genial fidelity to instinct, language resolves in declension that for which Kant invented clumsy and extremely dubious "schemas of pure understanding" for which he pleaded with his "schematism." For even the use of the locative and other prepositions refers to declension in the broad sense—and in fact in "analytic" languages or ones that are declined according to this type, like French and English, the inflectional declension is replaced by the use of prepositions or, what is the same thing, the preposition plays the role of inflection. One can consider prepositions to be irregular inflections that only differ from the usual ones in that in addition to this they have independent although entirely incomplete existence. Prepositions add different nuances of spatiality not only to substantives or adjectives, in general, to declined parts of speech, but also to verbs—as prefixes. Here the role of prepositions for the expression of spatiality is in its own way as great as in declension. It would be unusually instructive to subject to such an epistemologically grammatical analysis the means for expressing "an adverbial modifier of place" or of spatiality, at least for any one language. What wonderful riches would be revealed to the intellectual gaze! What is most important is that this wealth is such a thunderous testimony relative to the spatial coloration of our thought (which of course has been noticed since ancient times) that we only need to decipher skillfully these demonstrations of concrete epistemology—of grammar.

Alongside the spatiality of grammar, temporality in its various nuances is expressed no less fully. Here again, as in the foregoing cases, except for words of a special meaning that express different concepts of time, language disposes of typical semantic means in the same declension and particularly conjugation. As regards the first, although here there is no special temporal case like the locative, still for the expression of "an adverbial modifier of time" almost all oblique cases can be employed, corresponding to circumstance, both without and especially with a preposition. The role of the preposition with the assistance of cases for expressing temporality is no less important than for expressing spatiality, if not greater. To a significant extent, spatiality and temporality are equated and merged as measures of magnitude of one, two, or three dimensions. However, the greatest original means for the expression of temporality, which saturates all our speech and thought, is verbal conjugation with its "tenses" or "aspects." In different tenses, the one and the other are equivalent among themselves. In a definite relation, "aspects" express nuances of temporality just as successfully as "tenses" in the proper sense of the word. It is known that conjugation represents the greatest difference in the various languages, both with respect to the abundance of temporal and aspectual forms, as to the wealth of nuance and to the method of their grammatical expression—through inflection, auxiliary verb, alteration of vocalization, and various morphological signs. It is sufficient here to compare, for example, the wealth of forms of the Greek verb and the efficient paucity of English; or Latin conjugation in all the tenses and Hebrew with its rich aspects, etc.

But this variety, which could constitute the worthy theme of a philosophical monograph, does not alter the basic fact of fundamental significance: through verbal conjugation a word realizes the temporality that is introduced interiorly and inalienably into the predicate. Any predicate, expressed through a verb, is already colored by tense, qualified by temporality. Similar to any copula, the "auxiliary" verb, whatever it may be, is in this respect a verb, i.e., it is conjugated and consequently receives without fail some kind of tense or aspectual form. For here a very important conclusion results: the predicate always has the quality of temporality, is oriented to time. True, sometimes this qualification is neutralized—most often for this neutralization the "present" tense is used, which designates not only time but also the absence of thought about time (just as the nominative case designates not only a definite case but also the absence of case.) Such for example are all definitions: "a straight line is the shortest distance between two points"; "God is the creator of the world," etc.

However, grammatically here too we have the form of a tense, which is, as it were, suspended, weakened in its operation, but can always be introduced. This difference suggests a very important idea, which we already ran across in the foregoing investigation, namely about the nature of the *copula* "is." The fact is that being grammatically a verb and sharing its fates and all its forms, the copula *is* also has a tense. Meanwhile the function of naming, of connection, of agglutination that is expressed in it is not subject to the qualification of time, it *gilt*, it has meaningfulness, in a certain sense it is timeless and extra-temporal, as is I. If I say to myself, "I am, I was, I will be," in the sense of nuances of time, then in essence I say about myself "I am the one who was, who is, who will be." That is, the temporal states are as it were separated from it, are its peripheral definitions, which do not intrude into its core: I is supra-temporal. In a similar way, the copula *is*, which constitutes the glue for any predicate—both a verb and a non-verb—does not in itself contain time, and temporality must be entirely attributed to the predicate. Therefore, *I was* means "I am the one who was"; *I will be* means "I am the one who will be"; I made means "I am the one who made," etc. Hence such expressions as "God is good," etc. do not have in their copula the qualification of time, unless it is directly and definitively expressed in the predicate.

Therefore, the limits of temporality, not only its extent but also its boundaries in language, must be defined more precisely. It is remarkable that Kant, having made the transcendental aesthetic the foundation of his whole epistemology and having crammed all the cognitive categories into the schemas of space and time, and primarily the latter, completely overlooks that he ignores the very fundamental principles of cognition from which he himself set out, namely, *judgments*, or sentences. In general alien to the analysis of a word, he gives his critique an extremely dogmatic outfit. For his initial question—how are synthetic judgments *a priori* possible—this question, in which there are three complete unknowns—the synthetic X, the judgments Y and the *a priori* Z—is considered to be composed of definite elements. But Kant's fundamental question, as of any epistemology, should be: *how are judgments possible?* Or translated into the language of our investigation, how are a sentence and naming possible? This weak side of Kant was noticed in his school (in the transcendental normativity of Windelband and Rikkert),[7] but the mistake was not corrected. Instead of investigating in what kind of relation to this fundamental function of judgment all further doctrine about cognition is found, Kant forgets his initial principle and crams all categories into temporality, using for this "the schematism of pure reason." In the final analysis, all the categories turn out to be a function of time: quantity, quality, relation, modality. Kant wanted to define all types of judgment and formally to exhaust the whole field of experience.

Obviously, into the very core of judgment from which, we repeat, he set out but did not investigate, he quietly introduced the pure contemplation of time and space, i.e., by his definition, the forms of sensibility. In the same way, in contending with sensationalism, Kant is the purest sensualist in cognition—but in the most subtle and of course poisonous sense, not through the content of sense experience but through its form. He aspires to let all thinking pass through the forms of sensibility and obtains a universal phenomenalism or malignant positivism as the result, whereas in actuality thought and speech (which are one and the same) contain temporality and in general sensibility by giving place to it, but it is not encompassed or exhausted by it and therefore is not defined. As this was welcome to "the legislation of reason," Kant illegitimately took for his critique the whole power of judgment—naming, and then he phenomenalized it.

Besides—and this is the whole point—the initial, fundamental, exhaustive form of our thought—judgment-sentence-naming—free from both spatiality and temporality, is an extra-temporal and extra-sensible act, reproducing in an infinite reflection the eternal birth of the Word and words. With this, Kant's whole epistemology is crossed out in his own work: the forms of the "transcendental aesthetic" themselves only receive a place in consciousness and judgment but do not determine it. And in this exclusive penetration of all knowledge by the forms of pure opinion, on which all the categories of cognition are constructed and from which they are deduced, is the whole essence of Kant's doctrine. All of his effort, all of his energy, comes down to binding with one knot all the categories of knowledge and tying them to the forms of space and time, "subjective" categories. And thereby he makes them subjective and relative. Terrible is the dream (it is in fact nightmarish), but merciful is God. Naming-judgment—the copula *is*—is not subject to time, and that is precisely why it can receive the predicate of temporality, why it enters into time.

So then, returning to the question about the nature of the copula, we must still emphasize that although like any form it too has a temporal *form*, still this form does not express time. This comes out with full clarity in individual cases when the copula is left out. For example, "twice two—four." Where time really is introduced into a judgment, it belongs not to the copula but to the predicate, although by virtue of the economy of means in language, it merges with the copula, so that its extra-temporal, purely agglutinative character shields itself with the concrete properties of a predicate. Therefore, temporality is introduced into a predicate and has a limited character; it is completely the same for spatiality. Of this there is no doubt because the content of a judgment can have a completely extra-spatial character.

The most important consequence from this is that a judgment in its core, i.e., in the very naming, in the combination of subject and predicate, *is free* of time, although we can set it in temporality and consider it from that angle as well. From this comes a twofold scrutiny: eidetic and psychological. The very same can be added with respect to a subject, either a substantive or a pronoun. As was pointed out, even though it contains a mystical gesture, pointing to the being of an object in the world, in its mystical space, this does not imply empirical spatiality at all. Even if it designates a precise location, e.g., Moscow, the special content connected with place, with spatiality, belongs to the initial predicate that has entered into and been identified with the name. However, Moscow, as a substantive noun and subject, is first of all something that exists in the world, irrespective of place and time, and thereafter already receives this qualification. As in a predicate the extra-temporal element is expressed in a pure copula, so too in a subject the extra-temporal and extra-spatial element is expressed in its pure substantive quality, connected with a pronoun, with that indicative gesture.

Thus, in language, in speech and thought, spatiality and temporality are expressed in the predicative function, as a certain coloration or quality. They therefore have their boundary, they are a *special case* of this predicativity, of its qualification, but they do not constitute a universal form of cognition, the frame for any thought. Kant is not right about language, just as he is not right about thought and cognition. If he listened to the evidence of thought-word itself, he would not take the intuition of time and space as the point of departure for his construction, as the *universal* form itself of cognition, for it is not at all universal; rather, he would take the analysis of predicativity or a sentence, naming. Then he would have been liberated from a whole series of problems and difficulties that arise on his path.

Thanks to the idealistic sensualism of Kant, who put the transcendental aesthetic at the basis of a theory of knowledge, an original problem entirely typical for him arose, the resolution of which he sees in the "schematism of pure understanding." The question is that for Kant cognition on the one hand is accomplished by the application of the categories of understanding (purely intellectual syntheses and logical acts), but on the other hand, all of it is permeated by pure intuition, by spatiality and temporality. Therefore, it is necessary to bridge the gap between understanding and pure intuition, to bind them firmly so that the act of cognition is possible. Kant solves the task in his "schematism" with the method of the repeated inclusion: at first he inserts space into time, and then he inserts rational categories into time; the semblance of addition is obtained. This part of Kant's doctrine is the most important, and one must say, decisive because if the operation of inserting does not succeed, the whole thing will fall to pieces. But it is also the weakest part of his argument, where it's all a stretch. To connect sensibility and reason he invented "schemas" for which time serves as the material. In it is distinguished duration, i.e., (?!) number; content, i.e., (?!) quality; and order, i.e., (!) relation. Here possibility, reality, and necessity are squeezed in under the sauce of time. In this manner all necessary categories are accommodated and "transcendental idealism" triumphs. Reason turns up as the legislator of nature, whereas the critique of pure reason is the law for the legislator. Here everything is strained and arbitrary: for example, one could invert this argument by placing not time but space at the base of the schemas. Perhaps it would not be as convenient, but it is no less convincing.

These schemas are, of course, a self-deception; they themselves need an explanation. Even if they are described with genuine truth, it is not by them that cognition is substantiated as Kant means; rather cognition is only expressed and realized in them, the synthetic unity of which remains a problem as before. Meanwhile it is maliciously denied by Kant, who is fully satisfied with his little schemas and then declares the sum of these little schemas to be the legislation of reason and nature. But the synthetic unity of cognition, in which different possibilities are deposited and given, especially for the Kantian schemas, which do not have such irrefutable and indisputable meaning at all, is established by naming, predication, and proposition. On top of this, predication itself is free from spatiality, temporality and all categories and yet is so flexible and capacious that it makes room for all of them. The Kantian problem of schematism as sensualism of whatever sort simply disappears because time and space, for all their importance in the field of sense experience, are for thought only categories alongside others, for which language makes room.

It is not hard to be convinced of the extent to which language provides for all Kantian categories, and how the legislator of reason in fact followed grammar, "a critique" of which, as the actual instrument of thought, he ought to have given, if only critical fervor had really taken hold of him. Kant distinguishes four forms of judgment, which are expressed in the predicate (here unbeknownst to him he immediately crosses over into the field of grammar). The first case is when the predicate expresses the *scope* of the subject, where the latter can be under the predicate either as a single exemplar, or as a part of a genus (?), or as a whole genus, whence the three categories of quantity: unity, multiplicity, and universality. It is completely clear that the second category, being utterly vague, didn't make it, as they say, and only muddles the third, which for some reason received for its share universality as the measure of scope (?!). In fact, here it is a matter of singular and plural number (to which one could also add the dual, and with the generosity peculiar to Kant, attribute to it the category of duality).

The genius of language places in *number* in effect the *general* category of unity or multiplicity in a subject. A special inflection, a semantic unit, expresses this category of quantity applied not only to a subject with respect to a predicate, but also to any part of a sentence. Everything has number, whereby it is sometimes passive, and then the singular (but in individual instances the plural number also) designates only the absence of the application of this category, its neutrality, although not its impotence. Between the singular and the plural number, there exists no opposition and exclusivity; on the contrary, the singular number can express something known to be multiple (people, crowd, multitude), and the plural more often than not expresses a unit (glasses, pants,[8] etc.) Between the singular and the plural number in grammar, there exist complex relations, where the one passes over into the other, and sometimes is entirely lacking. The plural number can have a double meaning: first, a bad multitude, obtained by adding **and** (fused sentence), and second, an organized multitude, an aggregate and a whole. The grammatical plural number expresses the one and the other. Thus, for example, in a fused sentence all of its members stand in the plural number: both brothers, Peter-Andrew, good children, etc. However, this usually does not signify "many things" but "multiplicity," where thanks to the flexibility of language, the dual character of this multiplicity—one in many or many in one—moving differently from one number to another, shows through in a surprising way. This subject deserves some philosophical probing.

Returning to Kant, one can say that here he only said what is contained in formal grammar, and he added nothing except the appearance of profundity. Meanwhile here it is quite interesting how the category of number *enlivens*. It is necessary to add that this category belongs to predicativity—here Kant somehow got it right. This obviously contradicts the fact that all changeable parts of a sentence have number, beginning with the subject that governs it and establishes agreement. However, this means nothing for solving the problem: as we have established, the subject already contains the predicate in its name, and in it and with it, number is given.

The grammatical category of number must be sufficiently flexible and transparent not to obscure anything, when it is in fact not a question of number and number is recalled only for the sake of order. In other words, although grammatically the form of number, at least in inflecting verbs, is invariably present (however no less expressive is its absence in isolating verbs, where it thus has a special expression), one can say that a judgment-sentence, i.e., naming, only *makes room* for the category of number, for the predicate of number or quantity but is not in any way connected with it, is not permeated by it, is free from it just as from the forms of pure intuition, among which in the intellectual field number can also be counted. The nuance of number can be or not be in naming, which as a universal and basic form does not depend on this for anything. And it goes without saying that the "schema of pure understanding" that Kant adds here is of no use at all.

The following distinction, introduced here by Kant in the footsteps of scholastic logic, refers to the content of a judgment, which can be affirmed, denied, or limited (in the so-called infinite judgment: A is not-B); whence the categories of "reality" (?!), negation, and limitation. (One wonders what reality has to do with it and what Kant understands by this name.) It is obvious that this differentiation too has essentially no relation to "the schematism of pure understanding," but it has a direct relation to a judgment and a sentence. Our epistemology ought to have begun from their analysis, instead of pursuing a utilitarian and particular result—the apotheosis of Newton and mathematics through the establishment "of synthetic judgments *a priori*." It is evident that negation, limitation, and affirmation belong to the sphere of predicativity. It should be noted that affirmative sentences, to which corresponds the imaginary category of reality invented for this purpose by Kant, do not exist at all as a special type; this is simply a copula, the predicate, a function of predicativity and naming. They are always positive and cannot be otherwise, and negation or limitation is only a particular instance of affirmation. A purely negative judgment would already be impossible because it would tear the copula asunder and demolish naming; it would destroy the essence of judgment and lead it to its absence. In this sense, every negation is limitation, delimitation, the qualification of judgment, in general realizable only in a positive context, in connection with and against the background of positive judgments. Negations have different nuances according to meaning, which are expressed either by the general system of a phrase or by separate words (as in Greek—*me, ou, a*). In any case negation proceeds from a preceding or implied positive judgment, it is ostensibly its crossing-out. It is therefore a function of a positive judgment, its variant, or a particular case (just as an "infinite" judgment in the form of its indefiniteness and incompleteness

fulfills a transitional or auxiliary role). Language makes room for the negative or restrictive function, localizing negation in definite points of thought
to which it precisely refers: negative pronouns serve for this alongside negation. Of course, negation always concerns a predicate, lies in the sphere of
the predicate. To apply negation to the subject would signify the crossing out
of the very subject of speech and make judgment impossible. Meanwhile,
according to Kant, affirmation and negation turn out to be in the "schema"
of quality, viz., filled time is the schema of affirmation; empty time is the
schema of negation. One ought to say, first of all, that "empty time" is a
contradictio in adjecto [contradiction in itself], for as form all time is empty,
whereas as content, negation is just as full as is affirmation. But the important thing, obviously, is that in themselves both affirmation and negation
have no sort of relation to time.

   The following group of categories is connected with the relation between
subject and predicate, which is assimilated to the first either unconditionally
or conditionally, or indeed hypothetically (disjunctively). Corresponding to
this we distinguish unconditional judgments, either indicative (categorical),
conditional (hypothetical), or disjunctive. The categories that correspond to
them are substance, cause, reciprocity. In the "schematism of pure understanding," the "schemas of relation" correspond to this, which ensue from
the *order* of phenomena (such that their content is drawn only by a hair
toward the relation of order). These relations are reduced to this: either one
phenomenon remains, and the others pass on (substance and accident), or
one follows the other (cause and effect), or they all exist at one time (interaction or generality). This key group of categories, to which in fact they are all
reduced, is striking in its vapidity, and the betrayal of the philosophical spirit
of grammar here is punished most cruelly. Kant chooses the function of a
judgment, i.e., an ordinary sentence, containing naming, connecting subject
and predicate, and declares this connection a substance, but in the "schemas"
substance and accident. This naming applied to a copula, for this is strictly
speaking what the question is about, is fatuous and lacking clear thought; a
copula is the glue that agglutinates the noun to what is being named. Kant
ought to have said directly that any subject is a substance, whereas any predicate is an accident, which he does not say; on the contrary, he looks for
substantiality in the character *of the relation* between subject and predicate,
i.e., in the copula. Further, to consider the predicate as an accident with respect to the subject, and the latter as a substance once again senselessly and
radically perverts the very essence of judgment. From the point of view of
logical appraisal, the predicate includes permanent, essential, and accidental
signs, but the difference between substance and accident here is for all that

not given. Kant, in going deeper into the twisting side streets of the *Critique*, ignores the most essential question.

Here things go no better than with the deduction of the previous "schemas" of relation, where their threefold distinction has been established. When one phenomenon remains, the others slip by—this is the schema of substances and accidents; one follows the other—this is the schema of cause and effect; all exist at one time—this is the schema of interaction or generality. These schemas go to pieces and fit nowhere, from the viewpoint of Kant himself. Does the relation of substance and accident really consist in the distinction of the duration of the existence of signs and is an accidental sign unable to be of long duration? Is the relation of causality really a simple succession, *post hoc ergo propter hoc* [after this, therefore because of this] against which logic cautions us? Is simultaneous being really in that way interaction, and indeed what does it signify? This little house of cards of schemas does not withstand the touch of criticism.

In a similar way Kant obtains the fourth and final group of categories—modality. Depending on whether the copula of a given judgment signifies that A *can* be B, or *is* B, or finally, *ought* to be B, the judgments are problematic, assertive, and apodictic, to which correspond the three categories of modality: possibility, reality, necessity. Corresponding to this in the "schematism of pure understanding" are either the phenomenon in time exists at some time (schema of possibility), or at a definite moment (schema of reality), or at all times (schema of necessity). These schemas run most unfavorably, even from the viewpoint of Kant himself: how does the first category—possibility—differ from the second—reality? Is "at some time," if this is in fact a moment of time, really not the same moment of time as a definite point of time? From the viewpoint of time as such, one cannot detect the difference. In a similar way, "subsistence at all times" (apart from the whole problematic aspect of this idea) does not at all characterize necessity, which can be equally inherent in only one moment of time (Kant himself adduces as a classical example of regularity a lunar eclipse, which by no means exists at all times but only at a definite moment of time).

As in the previous schemas, Kant mistakenly relates modality to the copula, whereas a copula is neutral toward any coloration of categories, which is precisely why is it able to receive it. Modality likewise refers entirely to predicative value and is expressed by verbality. Grammatically, modality crosses over into a copula and merges with it, as in the case when an auxiliary verb is conjugated and also when the verb predicate receives the corresponding form. (Kant does not notice the latter at all and speaks only about the copula in which, consequently, he apparently sees the main source of modal variability, whereas the copula, which is in its essence outside categories, here becomes the victim precisely of its verbal quality and in virtue of some verbal attraction receives the forms of a conjugated verb.)

The predicate makes room in itself for the quality of category, just as it does for spatiality and temporality; it is enveloped by it but is not swallowed up by it or merged with it; it is not repeated in it but preserves its distinctive character of semantic, verbal agglutination just as it preserves its independence from spatiality and temporality. All Kantian categories are simply qualities of the predicate, its second and not its first definitions, whereas "schemas" are the fruit of an unfortunate Kantian misunderstanding, in virtue of which he has to cram whatsoever it may be of them into the forms of space and time—the consequence of his "idealistic sensationalism." They have decisive significance for all further constructions of Kantian philosophy, whose fates do not now concern us, but they represent an annoying hindrance in the investigation of our question about the epistemological content of grammar. In view of this, we have simply to cross them out. Of course, one can classify the categories in a different way, which is of no interest for us here. It is much more important to bring the epistemological presence of grammar to light as fully as possible and to see by which means it copes with these needs. One can then investigate the succession of their emergence in a language, which is equivalent to investigating the history of forms. In this respect, one can compare the grammars of different languages for, according to the correct expression of Gabelentz, "Die Grammatik eines Volkes ist die büntigste Darstellung seiner Denkgewohnheiten" [the grammar of a people is the most colorful presentation of its habits of thought].[9] The most current forms, in any case those proper to both ancient languages and to the majority of modern European languages, are the object of our attention.

Let us begin with the category of substance as the enduring and invariable foundation for different predicates. Its philosophical meaning fluctuates from the concept of ultimate essence, the *Ding an sich*, or *ousia*, which is knowable only through phenomena, to the concept of a stable center, which endures in the midst of what changes. Both one and the other, both the widest and the narrowest, the deepest and the most superficial meaning can be inserted into that means that, as we already know, instinct or the genius of language has at its disposal, into the substantive noun, and then into the subject. It is not at all in a copula or in an attribute that one ought to search for substantiality, but in a substantive, as distinct from any signifying word, from any idea as a possible predicate. The existence of a substantive noun, as evidence of the natural philosophy of language, makes possible precisely the problem of substance and *ousia*, of stable constancy and deep foundation.

However, in itself this category could not be realized without having been developed in a sentence, without having been converted in it into the category of subject. The subject is a substantive noun, a substance, *en energeia*, in action. By conforming to the Kantian distinction between categories and schemas as abstract possibilities and concrete forms, one can say that a sentence or rather, the bond of a subject with a predicate, gives substance a *schema*. We already know that this schema, like everything living and concrete, is not simple. On the one hand, grammatically substantive nouns exist that according to their real meaning and their role in a sentence are not really substantives but are adjectives; and on the other hand, parts of a sentence exist that are not grammatical subjects but in reality are such. But this refers to particulars and details. Important is the fundamental relation that consists in the fact that a sentence reveals the schema of a substance. On top of this, what stands in opposition to substance from the side of predicate is no accident at all, as Kant's schema would have it, but any disclosure of essence that is established by the predicate, i.e., energy or phenomenal being. In this field of the phenomenal, we further distinguish the constant and stable from the transitory and accidental, *essentialia* and *accidentalia*. That any sentence is a judgment, at least, about two ontological dimensions, the vertical and the horizontal, is the foundation but also the schema for any philosophy in which for the predicate—the phenomenal world, a subject is sought—substance—*ousia*. Every philosophical system is in this sense a sentence, of course more or less developed, or a system of sentences.

Thus, we are convinced that the *Critique of Pure Reason* according to its essential content turns out to be an epistemological commentary on grammar against the will and knowledge of its author. This could not be otherwise, in view of the fact that thought is indivisible from word and everything that one can find in thought one ought to search for in word too; all its forms are found here in grammar. Kant arrived late with his claim to the legislation of reason in thought, for the place was already occupied: legislation in thought belongs to grammar. Kant wanted to peek at the birth of thought so that from being its obstetrician he could become its legislator, but he did not notice that he had arrived late: thought was born already long ago and is breathing with the air of the present world—in a sentence, in grammar. This correlation between different competing fields can be expressed in a diagram:

Lexicology
ideology (root word, morphology, semasiology)
Grammar
etymology, syntax

| Concrete thinking | Psychology |

Concrete thinking   Psychology
Epistemology, logic (Kant and others)   Psychology (Wundt and the psychologists)

We have omitted from our comparative characterization of Kantian categories the most important and fundamental doctrine of "the transcendental
unity of consciousness," of the epistemological I, fastening and connecting
the elements of cognition and establishing the unity of object and unity of
knowledge. Without this unity the categories and schemas would crumble,
they would fall from their settings and a Bedlam of categories would be established, an epistemological delirium. This most important point of Kantian
epistemology, its center, we also find in language. Here it occupies a fitting
central place, from where Kant borrowed this idea. This is, of course, the
pronoun of the first person, I, around which is oriented speech and thought,
around which it rotates as around its axis. If a transcendental subject of
cognition exists, then even earlier a transcendental subject of speech exists,
i.e., the one speaking, who is also the one thinking, with respect to whom
every utterance is in a certain sense a predicate; he is the subject of all speech.
As a result of the predicate accommodating in itself, or more precisely, taking
onto itself every coloration of category, I as subject is the center or master
for all categories, it reigns over them, even when it remains invisible. All
speech is interiorly oriented toward the I of the one speaking, even if he does
not name himself. It suffices to do an experiment. If we remove the I from
speech and thought, we will see that everything falls to the ground, and we
end up with a madhouse.

The ontological sense of I as the existential center that reveals to each
person in their inner experience the unconditional nature of their being
and consciousness is explained above (its problem is posed in the different
metaphysical systems of the Fichtean type). With the help of I, the inner
topography of thought and knowledge is defined, its geometry, "transcendental aesthetic." In language, I not only reigns over thought, by expanding
its authority and influence onto all its twists and turns, but it also has its
place as a point on the surface. It is not only the subject of speech, the one
speaking, but also the first person singular, as *one* of the persons, as a particular linguistic form, operating simultaneously in breadth and in depth,
horizontally and vertically. If this were not so, if the transcendental I did not
have a correlate—a verbal and grammatical expression in the first person

singular—Kant could not have reasoned it out or described it, and his episte-mological arrogance would have been given a painful lesson. But fortunately the imaginary legislator of reason had to be subordinated to the laws of his own thought and speech, and we clearly see that the transcendental unity of consciousness is a function of what in grammar is expressed in the form of the first person singular. The *Critique of Pure Reason* remains a philosophical commentary on grammar in a given particular case. It goes without saying that no matter how languages differ among themselves in their structure, the given form of the first person singular cannot be absent, in no matter what kind of verbal equivalents it is expressed. It would be instructive to have a look at the results of a comparative study of the first person singular in different languages.

A general peculiarity of the critique of cognition in Kant is the sharp con-trasting of *a priori* and *a posteriori*, which distinction sometimes merges with the contrasting of sensibility and reason. In the process Kant insufficiently differentiates the intuitive side of the soul, the material of cognition, as life in all its fullness and diversity appears, and thinking and knowledge, which properly interests him. "By its origination our cognition is indebted to two aspects of the soul: first, to its faculty for perceiving representation (percep-tion in impressions), second, to its faculty of knowing objects by means of representations (the independent activity of concepts). By means of the first an object is given to us in general (?); by means of the second, it is conceived in conformity with the given representation (as the simple state of the soul) (?). Representations and concepts, consequently, are constitutive parts of our cognition, such that neither concepts without the representation cor-responding to them, nor representations without concepts are able to form cognition. . . . If we call the receptivity of our soul, which forms representa-tions according to the measure of how it experiences external influences, sensibility, then the faculty of independently forming representations or in general the independent activity must be called understanding."[10]

Kant's fundamental and extremely vague distinction between "sensibility" or "representations" (i.e., of an already completed elementary cognitive act, but of which kind, we find no answer) and "understanding" or "concepts" has a foundational meaning for Kant's doctrine. By dissecting the field of knowledge and thinking into two floors, that of representation and that of concept, he ends up having to search for their connections: the inclusion of raw "representations" standing beyond the threshold of cognition in the empty forms of "concepts." To that end, he tries to pack all cognition into "schemas of pure understanding," which he manufactures in the required quantity.

However, this whole structure is insufficient because he poses in a general way and not in a concrete form the question of the processing of the given sensed material itself and the concept. (An example: I receive impressions— of form, colors, touch, etc.; they "are synthesized" into a spatial form, which Kant packs into a temporal form, but how precisely *house* and not *tower* or *hillock* is obtained here, to this the schemas do not reply.) Attracted by his formal analysis, by the differentiation of *a priori* and *a posteriori* (of both synthetic and analytic judgments), Kant completely failed to notice the question about the *concrete* content of thinking, the question about how cognition is possible or how judgment is possible. How is any judgment whatsoever that has general meaningfulness, "objectivity," obtained from a raw "subjective" (in Kant's terminology) psychological mass "of sensibility." "How is nature possible?" This question, posed by him only from the vantage point of forms, can be posed also from the vantage point of content. Every judgment consists of distinct generally meaningful words and not of "representations" corresponding to "subjective" and hence ineffable, inexpressible states; it is a judgment. "I feel bored." What can be more subjective than this state? But when I speak, I already express it in generally meaningful words-ideas, I clothe it in generally human garments. And my cognitive act expressed in this way, reporting an occurrence or state in my psyche, has in its own manner just as much generally cosmic meaning as "the whole solar system rushes in the direction of the star alpha-Vega." (Kant could allude to the fact that here there is no category of causality, but it too can be added: "I feel sad because I love you.")

As in his whole analysis, Kant *did not notice here* that between "representation" or "sensibility" and a "concept" of reason or cognition *stands a word* and its nature. Consequently, the critique of cognition should have been focused on the analysis of this means of thought (if it can be expressed thus), which only builds a bridge over the gulf between sensual representations and categorical concepts. Kant wanted to overcome the latter with his cardboard "schema." Inside cognition, according to Kant's portrayal, there is a rupture; "pure reason" collapses because sensibility and categories are of a different nature. "Reason" becomes impossible; it is doomed to remain with empty categories, like a mill without grist.

In fact, only a word can build a bridge between thought and "sensibility" understood in the most general sense, i.e., the whole mass of what can be experienced. The elevated, ideal, thinkable content of experience is isolated and crystallized in a word. Everything is known, is thought, only when it can be said in a word. The concepts of reason are words, as are representations, and a verbal connection can be established between words. It is only because there are words that thought is possible and that "reason" is not left idle. Kant noticed none of this. How could the passage from a subjective state to objective cognition, to judgment, be possible if it were not expressed in words, if the most sensible materials proved to be unthinkable as ideas? For surely all cognition and judgment is continuous ideation, and this is why thinking, the enveloping of words in categories, is possible, and it is *only because of this* and not at all thanks to the telescopic boxes of Kant's writing table or those schemas of his.

In other words, logic and epistemology are possible only because there is grammar. If one rereads Kant's fundamental definitions from this perspective, it is impossible not to be struck by his blindness toward the word. Experience consists of intuitions that belong to sensibility and of judgments that are exclusively a matter for the understanding. But such judgments, which the understanding constructs out of sensible intuitions alone, are still a long way from experiential judgments. They connect perceptions only as they are given in sensible intuition, whereas experiential judgments express the content of experience in general and not of simple perception, the meaning of which is subjective. Consequently, experiential judgment still must add something to sensual intuition and its logical connection (after it has become universal through comparison) that defines synthetic judgment as necessary and through this as universal. . . . The sum of this is that it is the business of the senses to contemplate, that of the understanding to think. To think, then, means to connect representations in consciousness. This joining happens either concerning a subject or in general, and then it is necessarily objective. The joining of representations in consciousness is judgment. Consequently, thinking is the same as judging or is related to judgments in general. Therefore, judgments either are only subjective, when representations only concern the consciousness of one subject and are connected in it; or they are objective, when representations are connected in consciousness in general, i.e., necessarily.[11]

This distinction, of the highest importance for Kant, exposes the whole impotence and emptiness of his critique. On the one hand are representations, on the other—understanding; on the one hand "combinations of representations" relative to the subject, on the other—"in general" (relative to the object).

Even without mentioning that the questions "what is a subject?" and "what is an object?" are in their very posing unsolvable, an unavoidable question arises: "how is thinking possible?" If thinking is "the connecting of representations in consciousness" (is this an association of representations?), then how does it differ from raw sensibility, which also does not flow past consciousness, does it? And if "the connecting of representations in consciousness is thinking," then again, how does it differ from non-judgment, from sensibility? What, finally, is judgment both logically and grammatically, formally and verbally? These basic, initial and decisive determinations tell how little Kant was aware of the very instrument of thought—language; wholly consumed by the spirit of mathematical natural science with its silent and unqualified symbolism, he ignored the question: "how is judgment possible"? If he had taken as the basis of epistemology the theory of ideas-words, then obviously its entire inner orientation would have been different, and the "schematism of pure understanding" simply would not have been necessary; it would have been replaced by the epistemological analysis of grammar. Kant, and after him Cohen,[12] is consumed by a profound materialism of quantity (cf. the doctrine of the latter on the "pure emergence out of the infinitely small" *meden* [nothing], the yearning to extinguish being in meonality).[13]

A sentence can have a twofold aspiration: an active-energetic one, in which the copula assumes a dynamic character, and a contemplative-idealistic one, in which a static meaning is imparted to the copula. This finds expression in predicative quality of two kinds: verbal or adjectival. Once again using the expression of Kant, one can say that in the first case the *schema* for a dynamic-energetic relation is the verb, a verbal predicate, conjugation, and in the second case an adjective, agreement, declension. A verbal predicate differs from every other one precisely in that the phenomenal revelation of substance appears in it as *its activity*, not as passive being, as its spontaneous radiation but as the will for being. In this case the appearance of *modality* is inescapable and entirely consistent, which represents not the property of a copula in general, as Kant proposes, but precisely that of a verbal predicate. In grammar, voice and in part aspect, and chiefly the moods with all their auxiliary particles, correspond to this. In fact, what else do the indicative, subjunctive, optative, and imperative moods nuanced by aspects and tenses express with all the rigor and sophistication of the syntax of a compound sentence, as we find in classical languages? It goes without saying that the nuances of modality do not belong to the rigid inventory of language; therefore, they admit the greatest variations in the different languages, where in one case the primary means for its expression are moods, in another, aspects, tenses, or syntax.

Likewise it is not only the interests of the verb itself that are mixed in with its need for modality, but also those of the other parts of a sentence: the direct and indirect object, different "adverbial modifiers"; for the sake of the closest connection with all this the verb is colored in one way or another. All the same, one relation remains the most important: in conjugation, alongside temporality, but sometimes also spatiality, are included the categories of modality that are absent in declension and agreement, where only a direct connection of a subject with a predicate is established. A verb includes not only a dynamic predicate, because it is inevitably colored in modality (for action is inconceivable without this determinability), but also the category of causality, and not in the static sense of temporal sequence, but in a dynamic, energetic sense. Every verb in the active voice is such a *causation*, and it establishes causality; in the passive voice, it establishes the state of being caused or the object of causation. Therefore, if it really is possible to search somewhere for "the schematism of pure understanding," i.e., the point of conjoining the transcendental forms of pure intuition on the one hand with the categories on the other, then it is possible to see these schemas all the more naturally in a verb, which unites in its forms quantity, quality, temporality, modality, relation, causality, and with the help of a modifier of place, spatiality. Kant could have deduced almost the whole of his table of categories from conjugation, although here they are arranged differently than they are in his exposition, for the living "rhapsody" of language (according to the expression he applied to the table of categories from Aristotle)[14] does not coincide with their formal and seriously contested arrangement in Kant.

Kant attributed all categories to the copula, outside of which he knows no application of them. Language, which does not take Kant's prohibitions into consideration, accommodates the categories not only in conjugation but also in declension. What in fact does number represent if not the category of quantity (and besides in its three Kantian forms: singular, plural, and universal or integral)? What does the instrumental case represent if not the category of causality, and the other cases—in certain combinations the genitive (partitive), dative, prepositional—what do they represent but reciprocity? As we already know, the nominative represents substance. In combination with prepositions, particles, or words different cases are capable of conveying the nuances of different categories, by appearing as the so-called adverbial modifiers or indirect objects and by defining place, time, and manner of action. Subordinate clauses, which express different circumstances, also have such a significance, i.e., place, time, cause, manner of action, and likewise modality—conditional clauses. In the life of thought and speech, categories represent a multibranched tree interlaced with roots and branches that contains different combinations of categories in their free and intricate rhapsody, little reckoning with the procrustean bed of the Kantian table.

There is, by the way, in this "rhapsody" one category that is completely lacking in both Aristotle's and Kant's table of categories; Kant no doubt would have rejected it, not finding a place for it. This is the category of *gender*, present to some extent in the majority of languages and penetrating by way of agreement the whole structure of a language. In the category of gender, sex is introduced into this class, i.e., a sign not of logical universality but of factual state. The spreading of the category of gender to all substantive nouns, i.e., both animate and inanimate, is an operation by analogy and, indisputably, a certain abuse. The creation of a third gender (third sex?) in several languages is just such an abuse; the neuter, which corresponds to the category of "etc." or "and so on," means nouns that are not accommodated in the two genders. Not to mention the fact that the formal category of gender more often than not is not sustained even in relation to animate nouns; there is an indefinite quantity of inanimate nouns assigned not to the neuter gender but to the two remaining ones, whereas the neuter captures animate nouns also.

Grammatical gender, being a well-known luxury in language, onerous for it as is every luxury, in its emergence attests to that time when everything for the human being was animated and had a sex or gender. As a category, gender is actually a certain psychologism, the transference of empirical content into formal categories; in this it differs from number, time, and other categories, and one should not take offence at Kant for ignoring this category. Indeed, some languages that do not have gender or have it only in a limited degree also operate in this way.

This example shows that the relationship between epistemology and grammar is not so transparent and simple that one could take each grammatical category for an epistemological one. What hinders this is not only their intertwining, because of which they must be disentangled and laid out, if not in a strict table, then in a free "rhapsody," but also because grammar as concrete epistemology has in its concreteness nondecomposable aggregates of the historical or factual states of language with the general postulates of epistemology. On the one hand, epistemology determines grammar, setting well-known requirements for it; it subordinates it, by forcing it to serve its own goals, for as we know, thought is speech and speech is thought. On the other hand, however, epistemology has before it a sometimes tenacious, historically and psychologically overly saturated element, that must be overcome so that with its means epistemology can achieve its goals. We know that one method of laying is used for brick, another for stone, one for laying on cement, another for clay, etc. Therefore, it in fact becomes clear that a single epistemology, the same formal postulates of thought, are carried out in various ways in different grammars of diverse languages. For we know that grammars are different—etymologies and even more so, it seems, syntaxes differ. Therefore, it would be a mistake to take any grammar directly and convert it into epistemology.

Apart from everything else, the grammatical elements—declension and conjugation, parts of speech, parts of a sentence and so on—are not considered formal epistemological categories at all; they do not correspond to them, they intertwine and entangle them. This happens because language has its proper historical flesh: in it, as in a human organism, all organs must be present, unless they are some sort of abnormalities, but at the same time, they remain individual. Kant, who treated language with such neglect and completely ignored the epistemological problem of grammar, at the same time let drop this remark in passing. "It supposes . . . little reflection and understanding . . . to track down in a given language the rules for the real use of words in general and in this way to summarize the elements of grammar, without having to provide, however, the grounds for why each language has precisely this formal system and not another, and even less, why precisely so many formal definitions of language exist—no more and no less."[15] This offhanded thought, evidently, includes the supposition that an *a priori* (or philosophical) grammar can exist that can be thoroughly rationalized so that each grammatical category and form must have a formal justification. With this understanding, the tasks of epistemology and grammar (as Kant observes here, though in different expressions) would coincide to the point of completely merging, their whole structure made completely transparent, not only in their functions but also in their forms. This would also signify incidentally that there could only be one grammar for all languages, and from this point of view, the actual variety of grammar becomes both nonsense and an enigma.

If several people are sent to a definite place and with a definite goal, each of them will of course go their own way and, without repeating each other in all of their movements, they nevertheless do the exact same thing. You see that only in this sense is it possible to speak about the unity of *function* or tasks that epistemology sets for grammar, or, more precisely, that thought resolves by means of a given language. In its concrete forms, however, grammar is not *a priori*, although it is constructed out of the most transparent material—the word, yet not even in the sense of words having concrete content, but in the sense of forms of words. In this concreteness, it is empirically conditioned by the whole history of language, by the psychology of language, by the age of a language, etc. Insofar as one can speak about *the autonomy of grammar with respect to epistemology*, it is not in the sense of their mutual independence, for that kind of independence does not and cannot exist, but in the sense of the special character of this dependence. It is a functional dependence, teleological, in which the unity of the task allows for variety in the ways and means, as well as difference in the perfection of their resolution. Here both the spirit of a language and the genius of a people can manifest themselves.

In this sense, the grammar of ancient languages represents the unattainable summit of epistemological transparency to which some of the modern languages only draw near in various respects. When investigating a problem, it is correct to take it where it poses itself most acutely and transparently. This is why, when speaking about the epistemological nature of grammar and grammars, we spontaneously in fact have in mind especially this most perfect and refined instrument of thought and word—the Latino-Greek language and not the Khoisan. It is understandable and correct because both of these languages made room for the thought of Plato and Aristotle, but we still have not heard of a Khoisan Kant, and it is even permissible to doubt that a translation of his treatises can be made into that language. Of course, development of this language is possible in the case when there is an inner force and need.

At the same time, even with this concreteness, nontransparency, and massiveness of grammar, its fundamental categories and forms are so necessary for any expression of thought and for epistemology, that they are more or less general. Such are, first of all, the differences between substantive and verb, on the one hand, and subject and predicate on the other: thought and speech cannot do without these elements. Almost as universal are the basic forms of framing and equipment of the sentence: declension and conjugation, numbers and pronouns. In general, we can take many things out of brackets and set them as the common coefficient, simultaneously epistemological and grammatical, for all grammars, their *a priori*. This is the common part in which they are mutually connected and penetrate each other (although it is not easy actually to perform this extraction); remaining inside the brackets is the area of the autonomy of grammar, its "a-posteriority." Nevertheless, although grammar is not entirely transparent for epistemology, an epistemological analysis of it is indispensable and valuable precisely for the goals of epistemology, because here we see before us the function of living thought, an organic process, and not a lab specimen. The comparative neglect of this aspect of grammar, entirely understandable from its general direction, bears witness to its blindness.

It is extremely odd and instructive that the question about the correlation of grammar and epistemology in all its breadth was not once posed either in philosophical or linguistic literature. Here another question became popular and much discussed—concerning the relation of grammar to logic, where it is difficult to imagine greater vagueness, ambiguity, and polysemy than was displayed in the discussion. It suffices to become acquainted with the arguments of Steinthal, verbose and remarkable in their elementary quality, which were fated to become decisive in this question. First of all, what is the question: about what logic and about what grammar? Sometimes different school subjects are understood here, each of which defends its "autonomy." Grammar does not agree to turn into logic, or the latter into grammar. A calming resolution of the question is suggested: that one is on its own and this one is on its own. Steinthal's wisdom reduces to this.[16] However, it is of course least of all a question about school subjects, whose fate a faculty program decides, but about the essence of the correlations of the tasks of logic and the demands of language.

We have already considered in a more general form the question about the relation of the nature of thought and word, and we shall consider it again. Here, the question before us is narrower: about the correlation of the demands of logic and grammar. A significant part of the argument on this theme concerns not logic but epistemology. As for formal logic, the question stands very much simpler and clearer. The point is that formal logic examines different forms of judgment, of deduction, and by analyzing them, establishes their types or immanent norms, so far as they are normative. In so doing, the "laws" of logic, those implacable demands that it imposes on every thought, on pain of its interiorly decomposing from contradiction and under whose unlimited authority grammar so fears to fall, have a negative and prohibiting character, not a positive one. Logic is similar in this respect to the Socratic demon[17] that always and only prohibits but never commands, or in a more folksy comparison, to the police who intervene only in the case of a violation of public decorum, otherwise letting everyone live according to their own will. When people talk about the "laws" of logic, they thereby imagine that it teaches them how to think and express their thoughts in words, whereas it only keeps order and removes only the obvious violations. The teaching of logic about syllogisms essentially is reduced to this; it is nothing more than a chain of judgments or designations, their collating and bringing together in a positive or negative sense. The theory of syllogisms is also the analytically inferred rules of conclusions. However, due to the evidence about its autonomy, language can hardly ignore the demands of logic to such a degree, as this is allowed in some unsuccessful examples. Likewise, in the name of autonomy logic does not permit itself to show language to grammar (other than by sincere illiteracy, i.e., by nonmastery of language, by the impotence or feebleness of a word) as this is assumed in those same arguments. In general, the question about the relationship of logic and grammar does not at all have that sharpness that is usually ascribed to it because in fact a quite complex and difficult question about the epistemological content of grammar is introduced here. The question about logic and grammar does not even have a content independent of it; it is resolved in the sense that it is a general question. If grammar is concrete epistemology, then it is just as much concrete logic. By means of a given language determined by all its historical, psychological, and cultural status, it must fulfill the function of expressing thought but consequently also the demands of logic, positive as well as prohibiting, and especially the latter. Logic is the internal norm for thought, i.e., for what is the content of speech, with which it is inseparably intertwined.

At the same time these very demands, especially the negative ones, are not such as to prescribe an imperative form of action, dictate rules of speech, i.e., become grammar. For logic does not teach thinking, as others naively think but only warns against *formal* errors. It is powerless to give positive instructions, just as epistemology is. Grammar in this sense is unavoidably found under the control of logic, just as is the content of thought; in the name of autonomy grammatical senselessness or illogical combination cannot be admitted, and only abstractly, in the name of that same phantom of independence can one defend the rights of grammar to absurdity. By formally using the forms of a grammatical sentence, it is possible to say, for example, "This grilled ice is hot." This will be a sentence according *to form*, but it is not a sentence because the latter is not only form but also content, and here the form knowingly belongs to a madhouse or the inventory of a profound philosophizing linguist.[18] And autonomy does not at all consist in this imaginary independence of form from content, which in fact does not exist at all, and indeed must not exist, but in the original nature of grammatical means, which, however, are connected internally by the unity of function and hence cannot contradict the goal. If logic were connected with grammar, a mistake would be impossible, for all judgments would be at the same time logical. In reality, the examples of round squares invented by the same Steinthal would be impossible. But precisely because language, and consequently grammar as the totality of its forms, is a free element, it can fall on false paths, which in fact logic is called to recognize, and not grammar.[19]

With the unity of functions and the same prohibitory norms, the same logic has power over all grammar, for here the nature of thought legislates its laws, which are its immanent norms. At the same time, that diversity and variegation of grammatical styles and norms that we possess is possible and intelligible. Therefore, of course, to state with a simple, crude formula lacking content that grammar is autonomous from logic means simply to tear asunder a delicate fabric, and not to separate its threads. The task of philosophical or logical grammar, which arose in history, can be understood only in the sense that it wants to detach the logical skeleton, the irremovable logical fundament of grammar, from which it cannot come away. But one can no more equate anatomy with a general doctrine about the human body than one can reject it on the sole grounds that bones in the body are covered with muscles and skin. The relationship of logic and grammar is completely specific, flowing out of the nature of reciprocity of thought and word. Critically, however, the demands of logic with respect to grammar are so elementary and, one can say, self-evident that grammar in its scientific work can forget about them, not in order to ignore and violate them intentionally but in order to investigate that which is in itself not understandable but belongs to the historically changing parts of grammar.

In practice, the saturation of grammar by logic and epistemology, springing from the indissoluble connection of thought and speech, is so great that we learn the one and the other from grammar, especially those of us who passed through the intellectually more fully elaborated and, in this sense, more perfect grammars of the ancient languages. In the given instance, of course, we mean primarily their syntax that is almost pure logic, no matter how much they say about the autonomy of syntax from logic. What is even more important and significant, this is not at all intentional or contrived but is due to the inner connection of thought and speech. If the very idea of a philosophical grammar had appeared, it of course was inspired by antiquity or directly connected with it historically. Conversely, in the age of comparative linguistics, when science has been enriched by the diversity of grammatical forms present in different languages, it became impossible not to notice it, and this championing of the independence of grammar was the fruit of an exaggerated linguistic resignation. The comparative study of grammar must open before us not only the diversity of its forms, but also *grammatical equivalents*, etymological and syntactical, for the expression of the same semantic functions and, in particular, logical ones.

In practice, these equivalents are felt perfectly well and sought out in any translation from one language into another, and this is the more instructive, the further removed the languages are from each other, so far as it is a question of a translation and not a transposition or retelling of thought. For example, one would like to know if it is conceivable to translate in full, i.e., with all the nuances of meaning, a dialogue of Plato into Chinese. The champions of independence by the way can be consoled with the fact that every translation is to a certain degree such a retelling, for only such a transmission can be called a *translation* where phrases are transmitted step by step, form by form. But such a literal translation is not only monstrous or even impossible but lacks all precision, for *si duo dicunt idem, non est idem* [if two say the same thing, it is not the same]—and this expression has a literal application for language. It is clear that in translation, actually, a thought is removed from one word in order to be dressed in another; it is reincarnated, although not for a single instant (despite Schopenhauer) does it remain bare. The lexical and grammatical ontogenesis of thought, by which equivalents of all those linguistic means given in the original are born anew, is repeated in the mind of the translator. This unity of content, the independence of thought from different forms, *the problem of translation* (is translation possible? And how is translation possible?) is a topic for reflection that is unnoticed by linguists.

One of the consequences that clearly follows from this is that if we are already talking about the autonomy of grammar and logic, then we need to talk not about grammar but about grammars (so, too, not about language in its general properties but about languages). Grammar with its "laws" is an illegitimate extract from grammars, with respect to which these latter will likewise assert their autonomy, and this desire for independence becomes destructive for science. Whether the champions of independence want it or not, the very possibility of discussing general grammatical problems, even of posing a question about the parts of a sentence and then comparing the data for different languages, involves the putting of some general grammatical categories outside the brackets. The categories cannot be minted by means of a single grammar but suppose the active participation of logic and epistemology. In general, these scholastic questions would not have existed if they had been considered with the topic itself and its properties, rather than with the chairs and disciplines that manage the topic. Then it would be clear that with regard to language and, in particular, grammar, we can only talk about different sides of the problem but not about the autonomy that kills its very essence.[20]

CHAPTER 4

Language and Thought

What are the foundations of experiential cognition, and what is the nature of empirical cognition in which general, formal elements combine with concrete elements? For Kant this problem is resolved by language in the sense that every experience aims to express itself in word by breaking into segments, and the words themselves take the form of judgments that are formed by the categories, including spatiality and temporality. Words-ideas are detached from what they express by a mysterious, ineffable act. Words are born in the innermost depths of human consciousness as the voices of things themselves, proclaiming themselves; by no means "subjective" (although they can be subjectively colored), they are generally valid, and therefore can be communicated; they possess the quality of general intelligibility. The last element of consciousness, on which Kant's analysis rests, is mute, "subjective" sensibility, which by unknown means takes root in consciousness, there constituting a heavy, indissoluble, alogical burden. Hegel and Cohen subsequently aimed to shake off this burden, each in his own way. The last element of cognition, on which our analysis rests, is the birth of word and idea from that which is **not** word-idea (although it is also not odious "sensibility"), from that which is "being" *before* word.

Truly, in each elementary act of cognition, of naming, we are present at the great and sacred mystery of the creation of the human being in the image of trihypostaticity. From the innermost depths of being, a word is born, and this word is recognized not as an invented word brought in from without but generated by the thing itself, expressing it. Therefore, the distinction that accompanies the birth of a word is followed by the synthetic consciousness of what it in fact is: naming, judgment, cognition. What is cognoscible remains undiminished in its being, though it enters our consciousness by its logos, which enlightens and recognizes it from within, illuminating it, and bringing into it its difference and reason as such. Cognition, from the elementary to the most complex, contains a triune act: that of the muffled voice of being, the sounding of a word, and in the act of cognition the union of this stimulus and this word—in naming.

Here since the time of Kant and essentially even before Kant, in every age, the question about the transcendence or immanence of the being of thought inevitably arises, and in the answer to this question all the paths of philosophical thought are outlined. Being is transcendent to thought, the latter is a "superstructure," its epiphenomenon; this is what materialism of different shades says, even metaphysical materialism such as Schopenhauer's with its blind, mute, and alogical will. Strictly speaking, from this point of view, it is impossible even to speak about cognition; it is possible to speak only about functional adaptation. Thought is an "emanation," a means in the struggle for existence, empirical (the Darwinists) or metaphysical (Schopenhauer). The problem of cognition is essentially unresolved. Kant, too, arrives essentially at the same disconsolate conclusion with his "transcendentalism," which is only a mask and an instrument of agnosticism; the object of knowledge, "the thing in itself," is transcendent to knowledge, and all experiential knowledge is not only conditioned by "pure reason" but also hermetically separated by it from the object of knowledge. Hence, the question inevitably arises: "what then is the world that we know? Is it not a dream and 'a representation'" (Schopenhauer)? Therefore, it is natural that in Kant's school in its struggle with the emptiness of knowledge, the idea appeared that "the object of knowledge" is absolute "ought" (Rikkert) i.e., a copula, voluntaristically construed. This is a variation of the cognitive skepticism and nihilism of the ancient Sophists; the object of knowledge here has completely melted like a piece of ice in lukewarm water. In its own way this is the consistent development of Kantian phenomenalism (in one direction), his "transcendental transcendentalism," in the area of cognition. Instead of saying like honest sincere empiricism that the object of cognition is given by experience and includes the whole world, a skeptical and agnostic outcome proves to be inevitable, and this is owing to the fact that the word-meaning, standing between the "sensibility" of experience and the ideality of cognition, is not noticed. Experience as being really remains transcendent to thought, but

experience as ideas is entirely immanent to it, such that the truth of immanentism and the truth of transcendentalism are affirmed.

This was the epistemological theory of Platonic idealism: cognition is
"remembrance," the realization of ideas in experience. The raw mass of experience gives back to thought the gold of its ideal content because "the
Demiurge created the world by gazing at ideas" (*Timaeus*). According to
Christian theosophy, there is a sphere of pure ideas, divine Sophia, and it
is the ideal foundation of creation. But as thoughts, these ideas are words,
logos, as rays of the Divine Logos. And in the human being, who himself is
the logos of the world, created in the image of God, "co-participation" in this
Logos makes cognition possible both in its separate acts and in the whole.

The problem of epistemological monism, i.e., self-enclosed and self-
generated cognition, the very postulate of such a monism, is intellectual
pride, Luciferian pretension. Thought does not exist alone in itself, logos
must be reflected by what is not logical (although this does not mean non-
logical, extra-logical, or anti-logical: on the contrary, being remains in an
indivisible conjunction with logos). This thought is given in a chased metaphysical form by Plato, in a confused form by Schelling in his doctrine of the
identity of the ideal and the real, and in a distorted form by Hartmann in his
idea of two principles in "the unconscious"—the logical and the alogical. In
contrast, logical monism wants to produce being from itself. It is guided by a
muffled presentiment that words are actually forces and realities of a special
order and are ideal. But the Luciferian quality of this pretension is that in
the name of diurnal light, it does away with the creative night of gestating
cognition. For the light "of the unfading light" is in the world, but this light
shines in the darkness, which contains everything potentially, the darkness of
chaos from which being was extracted by the word of God.

Two minds suffer Luciferian blinding: the one in titanic inebriation, the
other in the petty, creeping self-conceit of a hack: Hegel and Cohen. Hegel
absorbs the whole force of being in the thought-idea-concept-meaning-sig-
nificance of a word. (True, he lacks precisely this definition of idea through
word, to his disadvantage.) For him, *Begriff*—concept—begets the object of
being.[1] Instead of a doctrine of trihypostaticity, Hegel propounds the one
hypostaticity of the logos.[2] More precisely, one must say that Hegel admits in
the spirit of Sabellianism a trihypostaticity, not as three hypostases of equal
dignity, but as three modes, positions, or moments in a logical principle. Still
more precisely one must say that for Hegel the second hypostasis, the Logos,
appears in the place of the first, the hypostasis of the Father. It begets nature
as its moment, "releases" it as its otherness, as something extra-logical in
order to encounter it and to absorb it again into itself in the third hypostasis,

in synthesis. Hegel overcomes the natural correlation of thought and being in *Phenomenology of Spirit*, where having attained abstract, "pure" thought, he begins his logical cosmology and anthropology. Of course, this attempt to rearrange the relation of the hypostases, to make the Son into the Father, and the Father into the Son, being heretical, at the same time also leads to conceptual deformities and absurdities. Hegel was compelled to deduce being, the empyrean, logically, and of course, on this he broke his neck and fell from the scaffolding.

That materialist reaction, which Hegelianism provoked, was characterized by the same spiritual blindness; but justified by the latter it is nevertheless an attempt to return things to their place, "having stood Hegel on his head." The fact that being or thought is a function of the brain like the bile of the liver, and other materialistic formulae, still gives a rough outline of the direct relation of the hypostases and not the inverted relation as in Hegel. In other words, against Hegel, the materialists are right in *this*, in the order of correlation, although they are not right in their one hypostaticity, which they share with Hegel, monism: for Hegel it is a logical monism, for them a materialistic one.

Cohen devised transcendental monism, "panmethodism." Since for him the object of thought is the method of "generation," or the rule of synthesis, logically transparent through and through, he would wish that the world, the support of knowledge and only in this sense its object, were likewise only transcendent. A similar intention characterized the Luciferian approach of Fichte. But as the latter could not make do without an irrational *"äusserer Anstoss* [external impulse]" in **not-I**, which begets objects, so too the former had to invent *"reiner Ursprung* [pure origin]" where being, reduced to a pure quantity in the unquantified quantity "of the infinitesimally small," is *me on*, the salutary *Brett* [plank] for cognition. But—alas!—no matter how one transcendentalizes *meon*, philosophy knows firmly that it is all the same *on*, a variety of being, and hence the intention of Cohen does not succeed either. In contrast to Hegel, who aspired to concrete idealism, i.e., to the logical hypostasis of the world, Cohen is satisfied with formal, transcendental idealism, supposing that in having the form he has everything. But did Cohen not think about the fact that besides *meon* his thought makes use of words (and makes use, one must say, rather freely) at the same time not giving the slightest hint about the right and meaning of this use? Of course, it is possible to show whatever legerdemains one pleases if the devices are prepared for them in advance, but you cannot lay claim to a supernatural "purity" of thought and not notice that you are letting it pass through the vividly colored stained glass of words.

From our point of view, the problem of transcendental and metaphysical monism is the problem of word-meaning, or what is the same here, of judgment and sentence, without which thought can neither begin nor be realized, and which therefore is subject to the analysis of the *Critiques* in the first place. Owing to this very reason, a hopeless dualism also arises that decomposes cognition, i.e., the Kantian theory of experience. How is one to put alogical-sensible content into logical forms of thought and what kind of "schemas" must one think up for the production of those critical networks? Kant unites without any differentiation the whole complex of experience and of its logical consciousness and expression. His epistemology wants to accommodate simultaneously both psychology and the logic of consciousness; he merges the act of perception, intuition, and sensation, generally speaking, concrete experience, and the act of consciousness, thinking, and judgment about this experience, whereas they are quite different, nonconfluent aspects of a single concrete consciousness. What is boring to me as a concrete state and my judgment "I feel bored," are entirely different moments, likewise my impression of a mountain, in all its concreteness, and a verbal, semantic judgment: "in the distance a mountain is visible." The difference between them is that in the first case there was a mountain in me, or I experienced a mountain as an entity; in the second case I concretize ideal being, I pronounce a thoroughly transparent judgment in which spatiality is only the definition of a predicate. Hence, the special question about how to accommodate sensibility in logical forms does not arise because sensibility as such does not enter into it but only the idea about it, just as transparent as logical forms. Kant psychologizes cognition by basing it on "representation." The latter is a form arising psychologically, as it were, an abbreviated and schematized reproduction of something given in experience. The representation adapts the form to cognition but is itself not yet the form.

The proto-element of cognition is not at all representation and not sensation, but idea, judgment, naming. That which Kant and the Kantians call an object, in which they search for a transcendental rule or method, all this is realized already by a word, is fulfilled by ideation, and hence the fundamental question of cognition is all the same about word-meaning, about the ideality of the real, about its conceivability and nameability. An impression is mute, a thought is always verbal, and so this generation of a word also contains the mystery and enigma of thought, but all the rest are features and applications. This question is not at all transcendental, although it comes forward with special distinctness during transcendental analysis; it is ontological or metaphysical or even "transcendent," if it pleases Kant to call it thus. However, he invariably places at the center of his transcendental searches the ontology of cognition, the question of the generation of words-ideas, i.e., the question about the generation of thought itself not as form but as content. Indeed the transcendental question, i.e., the question about form, is likewise a question about content, which is why it cannot free itself from it. Is word generated from being or is being generated by word, Plato or Hegel? There can be no other alternative here. The problem of thought is a problem not of the transcendental, "pure begetting of it" but of the concrete and formed content.

Here too, predestined by the immanent analysis of thought itself, we approach the word of revelation, in which the words of the Gospel about the Logos, as if cut with a diamond chisel and miraculous in their measureless depth and conciseness, burn: "In the beginning was the word, and the word was toward God and the word was God. . . . All things came to be through him and without him not one thing came to be which has come to be."[3]

All the age-old perplexities and questions of thought about thought and the world, about the conceivability of thought and the conceivability of the world, are resolved in this eagle's flight. Conversely, they always revert to it in exhausted doubt before the domination of the world's nonsense, or in revolt against the logos and in malice against it, conscious or unconscious. Such are Faust and Fichte, who crossed out the word of God and instead of it, put the word of human pride: "Im Anfang war die Tat [in the beginning was the deed]." Actually, is not this hypostatization and metaphysical magnification of the word the ultimate Hellenism, seemingly alien for us and philosophically already obsolete? Why **words**? Are not words an empty or conditional sign? "Das Wort kann ich so hoch unmöglich schätzen, ich muss es anders übersetzen" [I cannot value the word so highly, I must translate it another way]" (Faust).[4]

"I will write that reason was in the beginning," writes Faust-Kant-Hegel, crossing out logos. And in actual fact: is it not an accident, a historical whim of Alexandrian Judaism in the person of Philo, to whom the unknown author of the prologue to the Gospel of John submitted here? Without a deliberate explanation, it is difficult even to understand why he did not directly put the *nous* or *idea* [mind or form] of Plato, well known to Greek speculation, or *noesis* [thought] or if you will, even the *noesis tes noeseos* [thought of thought] of Aristotle, instead of the dark, ambiguous, Alexandrian or Stoic *logos*.

In the beginning was the word—in the beginning of the world's being, in the cosmic *arche*, in the meonal primal matter of being, in its potential yearning was the word that fulfills it, that brings light, and in which everything received its name, its distinctiveness. The *apeiron* [boundless] was formed, everything rose toward being for itself and for the other, as word-thought. This word of the world and in the world, the cosmic logos, is the direct operation of the Divine Logos: "and the word was toward God." This turning of the world logos towards God is expressed by the preposition *pros* which, in our view, textually excludes the identification of *word* in its first two uses in Jn 1:1 with the *Word*-God ("and the Word was God" Jn 1:2), although this identification is seemingly decided beforehand both in the Russian synodal translation of the Bible and in the English translation, with the same transcription in capital letters. In our reading, we get this transcription: "in the beginning was the word, and the word was toward God and God was the Word." And so, the world's word is here lifted up toward its source—the Divine Hypostasis of the Logos, which shines into the world logos and gives it all the power of world-creative differentiation: "everything came to be through Him, and apart from Him nothing arose from that which arose" (Jn 1:3).

The root of the world logos is in the Divine Logos who dwells in the premundane glory of inner-Trinitarian being but who shines into the world and forms the noetic sphere of words-ideas, divine Sophia, as the ideal foundation of the world. This means that **everything** in its differentiation and harmony, the multiunity or monoplurality of the creature, the aspects of being, were called forth in primal matter, in "the beginning," through a word. Everything was created already in *arche* and not from non-being; everything was called to meonality from the darkness of non-being, *ouk on*, but still not raised to distinct being, to its light; everything abides in chaotic boundlessness—*apeiron*. This potential being was named, marked by thought-word. This same idea is also contained in the narrative of Genesis, where with His word God summons the whole creation to life in six days, and until this creative word "the world was formless and void, and darkness was over the abyss" (Gen 1:2), everything was in the darkness of indistinctness, inconceivability, inexpressibility. "And God *said* let there be light, and there was light. And God *called* the light day, and the darkness night" (Gen 1:3). "And God *said* let there be a firmament. And God *called* the firmament heaven" (Gen 1:6, 8). "And God *said* let the water be gathered . . . and dry land appear. And God *called* the dry land earth, and the gathering of waters the sea" (Gen 1:9, 10) etc. That which God says one must understand in the light of the New Testament revelation, in the spirit of the prologue of John's Gospel: all was through him, and without him, there was nothing that came to be. *Naming* by God must be understood as the ontological basis of thought and knowledge, which lies at the basis of human speech and thought, but by no means in the sense of an empty giving of a nickname.

Thus, in the prologue of the Gospel of John we must distinguish two ideas about the Logos: the Logos in himself as a Divine Hypostasis, as God, and the logos operating in the world, although turned toward God, the energy of the Logos in the world, Sophia. This Logos in creation has a presence and a focus in the human being as image and likeness of God: "in Him (the Logos) was life and life was the light of humans" (Jn 1:4). This light, abiding in the human being as bearer of the world logos, according to the image of the Divine Logos, is the basis for why dominion, the central place in the world, belongs to the human being as microcosm. Therefore, God can bring animals and birds to this human being, "in order to see how he will name them, and whatever the human being calls each living soul, so would its name be." We already know what this naming means: God only wants to see how the power of the logos unfolds in him. But this world, the human, anthropocosmic logos, is plunged into the darkness of meonal semi-being, of becoming, of development: "and the light shines in the darkness and the darkness did not envelop it" (Jn 1:5).

As in the doctrine of the logos of the world, so too here the mystic evangelist clearly distinguishes two aspects of the light of the world: in the human being, the light produced by Divine energy, and the Unfading Light, Christ. "He (John) was not the light but he testifies about the light. The true light was there, enlightening every human being who comes into the world" (Jn 1:9). "And the word became flesh and dwelt among us" (Jn 1:14).

The world logos made room for the incarnated hypostatic Divine Logos, by which was laid the foundation for the divinization of the whole creation in the human being.

So, then, one must distinguish the human logos, more precisely, the anthropocosmic logos from the hypostatic Divine Logos. The first is the logos in the world, Wisdom, Sophia, the world mirror of the Logos, the second is the premundane Godhead which by a miracle of humiliation is incarnated in the world.

The power of thought and the power of speech are one—it is the world logos, abiding in human beings as their actualizing essence, which ascends from the somnolent semi-being of potentiality toward energetic manifestation in the world's development. The basis of thought and speech is included in this primordial unity of thought, speech, and being; by force of that unity everything existing is in principle conceivable and expressible by the word, and the connection of things is at the same time a connection logically conceivable in words. Otherwise, the correlation of thought, word, and being would represent not only incomprehensibility but at the same time strange, unintelligible chance. Words would seem made up and composed, as a signal for thought; thought would remain bare of words, and finally, the triple correspondence of thought, word, and being, i.e., all knowledge scientific and philosophical, would fall apart and become an enigma.

There is only one outcome from all of this, only one answer can be given to this question, the very same that is contained in the miraculous verses of the prologue of the Gospel of John: *in the beginning was the word.* If the connection between word and thought were to be broken, it could not be restored by any kind of instrumentalism. Word could not be devised as an instrument for thought, thought would remain unborn and non-incarnated, unpresentable to the intellect and incommunicable from one human being to another. A word, *before* its adaptation for thought, would have to be an empty, senseless sound and not a word—and how could it have arisen? But this connection is so indissoluble that its elimination is inconceivable. If one is really to search for epistemological axioms (which can be vested in the form of Kant's beloved synthetic judgments *a priori*), then it is precisely the axiom of the logos-nature[5] of being and word—of the conceivability of being and the expressibility of thought in word. In expressing thought in its form and content, a word as the thought of being and about being is thus exposed as the essence of being.

However, the higher we raise the hierarchical meaning of a word, the more difficult and enigmatic its actual meaning becomes. It is entirely evident that empirical reality does not fully correspond to the postulates of word and thought. Instead of words saturated and full weight, it knows words diluted and emptied, lightweight—the problem of empty talk and idle talk arises. Instead of truth expressible in word, we drown in nonsense, in lies, mistakes and errors—the problem of the emptiness of thought, of lie, mistake, and error arises. Both of these problems demand an examination.

Cognition is naming, the act of cognition happens in judgment, in a sentence, in the joining of subject with predicate, which is naming in its static state. Thinking is the joining of judgments, by different means and in various directions, and is naming in its dynamic state. The joining of sentences is speech; the joining of judgments is thinking; the one and the other together are speech, lecture, treatise, book, and this book is being written always and endlessly in different directions. The danger of empty talk and idle talk exists for us in cognition, in utterance; the danger of error, in the joining of words and thoughts. The one and the other danger, or more precisely the sickness of speech and thought, is completely incurable in the given state of humankind, it must be understood in its ontological conditions and elucidated as not contradicting the axiom of the logos-nature of being, speech, and thought. Obviously, these problems do not lie in the field of formal logic or particular branches of linguistics, which as such do not even accommodate them; they are questions of the general metaphysics of the word.

First of all, empty talk. Words that come out of the depths of being, spoken in us by the things themselves, possess the whole fullness of cosmic power: a pronounced word sounds in the whole world, for logos is the universal connection, and everything finds itself in everything. If our language consisted of such cosmic words, it would be the language of the cosmos itself, and the problem of empty talk would be completely absent. But this would be possible only so far as the human being was a human being in all his glory, i.e., a microcosm, the king, master, and heart of the world. But the human being in the person of Adam had not yet succeeded in becoming this and, due to his minority, had not entered into the power prepared for him at the creation of the world when sin already upset the balance in him and in all nature and damaged the organs of cosmic speech, both hearing and the tongue. The voices of things started to be heard muffled and incorrectly, their sounds were refracted through various prisms of human subjectivity, psychologism burst into speech with all its devastating effects. The human being started to listen and lend an ear more to himself in his subjectivity, his isolation from the cosmos, than to this latter. His speech began to sound all the more false and fragmented. Clouds of idle talk obscured the word, and now the only type of speech that is simple and clear for us is idle talk, empty talk: words, words, words.

Meanwhile, of course, a word is not a synonym of either emptiness or thoughtlessness or impotence. The primordial words, the language of things, are meaning and power. In expressing the root of things, they give, or rather they exercise power over things, might belongs to them, they perform magic and spells and have the power to command. Folk wisdom preserves a faithful memory of this, knowing the sorcery of the word, its white and black magic, its blessing and curse, exorcism and witchcraft. It knows what "to know the word" means. With his childlike, deep wisdom, the poet also knows this; he sees that

There are speeches—their meaning
dark or insignificant;
but it is impossible to listen to them
without emotion.

A word begotten
from flame and light
will not meet with an answer
amidst the world's noise.

But in a temple, in the midst of a battle,
wherever I may be,
when I have heard it
I will know it everywhere.[6]

Inherent in words are wisdom and power, natural witchcraft and sorcery: this comes directly from the ontology of a word. The surprise is not that knowledge of this is stored in folk memory but to what extent it has been lost. Words have ceased to be words; they have weakened and wilted, passing through all the mists of non-being and shrouds of subjectivism or psychologism. Now a word is only an instrument of communication, "a tongue" and not the voice of the world. The imperative mood (or exclamatory judgment) is applied only from human to human: now only a human hears a word and obeys (or does not obey) it. This only shows how deep is the sickness of the word together with the sickness of being itself, which has become visible only in reflections, schemas, and caricatures. Where once there were full-weight grains, now a husk is left, swept away by the wind.

Yet even this husk would be impossible and incomprehensible without the ear. Words would be impossible and incomprehensible even in our present pitiful and mongrel state, if light from above were not reflected on them. Words are not *logoi*, forming the kingdom of the Logos, but all the same they are logos-like (or, what is the same in the given instance, sophian) in their foundation. As all the world's being is the mixing of being and non-being, the illuminating of creative light in meonal darkness, so too words in their sphere are the same mixing of the *logoi* of things and "language" in that empirical sense in which praxis knows it and linguistics studies it. Speaking on principle, pure words, the *logoi*, do not and cannot exist in "language," just as there are no sinless people. However, the positive power of the human being is health, chastity, and natural holiness, whereas sin is disease, non-being, and damage. So too the positive foundation of language is nevertheless the primordial word as essence and language as might, as the logos-like (in the sense of *logos* and *logoi*) authority of the human over the world. The infirmity and debility of the word, its utilitarianism and pragmatism (the change of words into terms or sonic signaling), finally, every adaptation (and dilution) of a word by grammatical forms, semantic adaptations, and nuances, all of this makes the logos-nature only the foundation of speech, but not its state. Speech can be thinner or more condensed, the weathering, dilution, and destruction of words can advance more or less. It represents not a tincture but a mixture in which the blends, surrogates, and *aqua destillata* [distilled water] play such a large role that sometimes the taste and smell of authentic essences become hardly discernible. The condensing of word and thought is possible not only, so to say, in a quantitative sense (more or less density) but also in a qualitative sense, in the sense of the intensity of a word. If the Lord ascribes to faith such power that with a word one can send a mountain from its place into the sea, then this means that this effective and imperative power is inherent in a word as such. A miracle happens above nature but not in spite of nature, or rather, it *releases* the natural forces, in the given case, the natural power of a word from its putrefactive, low-power state, if faith gives it the strength of support in the other world.

From what has been said it follows that empty talk is a general disease of the word, and at the same time, unconditional empty talk cannot exist: words have their root in being, and they partake of the cosmos. Therefore—strange to say—they are not completely powerless in any condition. Words are never only "words, words, words"; they are always power, reality, essence. Like clouds, they swirl and cluster together, hiding the intellect's sun, freshening or poisoning the atmosphere. A certain magical force (or witchcraft) is inherent in a word; words have power, they are action. With an evil or unpremeditated word, but for some reason powerful, one can kill or painfully strike a human being. Words always are actions, at least in the same degree as the external actions and deeds of a human being. It is necessary to monitor a word just as attentively as a deed. In a word humans are given a power, an energy constantly flowing out of it, like electricity, and they must master it. Hence one can understand the meaning that religious asceticism ascribes to a word: both to "empty talk" and malignant gossip, both to naming one's neighbor "a fool" and to "silence." Also intelligible from this are all witchcraft by word, exorcisms, and incantations: in a special case, they may be powerless due to "ignorance of the word," but in principle it is possible "to know the word," although it is another question whether one ought to aspire to such knowledge by *any* means.

Seeing that the energy of a word is most effective, penetrating as far as the ontological root of things, the danger in misusing a word is greater than in working with dynamite, which can blow up only the external covering but not the inner core of being. Such, by the way, is the meaning of an anathema, a verbal instrument most terrible and lethal if it has power in it like that of the church over its members and fathers over their children (in close contact). Such is the meaning of a "word of honor" that cripples, disfigures the person who violates it, and especially of a religious oath that draws upon its violator an anathema, such as that which befell Russia for betraying the tsar, and perhaps on the tsar for renouncing the throne. Such too is the incantatory power of a word; by possessing it, a sorcerer can induce withering or love-sickness or shortness of breath, or can obtain power. This is now called hypnotism or the subconscious state, but however it may be called, the energy of the word is preserved in all its force: the hypnotist acts like a sorcerer with the magic of a word, and scientific terminology does not change anything in essence. It is strange that precisely phenomena of hypnotic suggestion did not prompt us to turn our attention again to words as the instrument of suggestion, i.e., as power, energy. Hypnotism is the magic of the word, which is as dangerous as any magic.

So then, the problem of empty talk (and correlatively of pithiness) is resolved this way. Although things themselves speak words in us, and this is their cosmic power, their sophian nature, their participation in the whole and in the wisdom of the whole, their chasteness, and ultimately their *truth*, at the same time words are spoken by us. Or rather, their ontological core is realized by us, like a song sung from a voice, and insofar as they plunge into the abyss of our subjectivity, psychology, history, relativity, impotence, and ultimately, falsehood. Therefore, participation in the truth of the world (the Platonic *methexis*), and remembrance of it (*anamnesis*), are inherent in words, but words are born and live in a darkened milieu that is alienated from the truth. They are characterized by *truthfulness* (together with untruth) in its greater or lesser proximity to or remove from the truth. In its words, in the proto-elements of speech, our speech already carries in itself a source of error, of moving away from truth, but it also contains participation in the truth.

At the same time, a word is most susceptible to corruption, vulgarity, and idle talk. The faculty of speech is in our hands, and there is nothing easier for us than to convert it from an instrument of thought, influence, and power into merely an instrument of communication lacking an objective basis. Then speech degenerates psychologically as jabber, talk, prattle, cursing, in a word, any psychological friction between people. All human debilities and sins show through like a verbal rash, and in the atmosphere of this collapse of the word, a contemptuous attitude toward it crops up. Those sharing it are in any case compromised as people blind with respect to the word, since they only see it as a scabies of the tongue. They are like those who see in the Lupanar[7] the sole possible and complete expression of sexual life and thereby give evidence of their own depravity and blindness. A similar blindness is characteristic of people who do not see the proper nature of words because they use them in a utilitarian and pragmatic way. They only see a term or a verbal sign, like those occupied with the chemistry of colors and scents, who no longer notice them in nature and generally consider everything organic as a particular case or an absence of the mechanical. Of course, terms are also words, although tepid, weak, and sick. Language becomes impoverished and weak to the extent that it becomes primarily terminological (contrary to the taste of other linguists), but the power of language enlivens even the most clumsy verbal articles, like grass pushing through city pavement, and they remain words all the same.

We have often likened verbal elements to colors, and here we have to say that the creativity or life of words, as well as their use, can best of all be likened to the mixing of colors for different shades on a palette, according to various purposes. The quantity of root words, as well as the different possibilities of adding to them these or other hues and mixing them, significantly increases the quantity of colors. As is known, pure colors are used in painting extremely rarely, and those used are mixed already on the canvas in such a way that they are colored by the tones of all the paints applied side by side. In other words, not a single color exists by itself, separate from others; it is their harmony and combination that are operative. In a similar way, there are no separate words in speech, but there is the whole power of a word that is realized in their combinations, and this combining can intensify, deepen, as well as paralyze separate words. Therefore, all observations that can be made about a separate word must be modified in relation to its use. Nevertheless, the idea that there are not words but speech, not *logoi* but *logos,* of course in no way changes the general ruling: words as such possess truthfulness, but not the truth.

So then, words are only participatory in *the word* but they are not its pure images; they are turbid and submerged in psychologism. Statically and dynamically, they are not adequate to their objects; they reveal them as much as they conceal them, *they lie* about them, and deceive. Their deceptiveness is one of the sources of the limitation, relativity, and inaccuracy of knowledge, and also of its bad infinity. Mephistopheles[8] declares sarcastically that *ars longa, vita brevis est* [art is long, life is short]. The followers of Kant or champions of contemporary theories of progress say breathlessly that science and progress are infinite, thinking to speak praise but in reality bearing witness to powerlessness. Science and progress are infinite not in the actual positive sense of removing and overcoming every limitation but in the bad sense of their inability and powerlessness ever to reach the end, i.e., integral, complete, and unified knowledge. It is as if we had a sphere, but instead of understanding each point in its relation to the center, connecting and subordinating it to the center, and thus coordinating all the points, we moved in all possible directions along the surface, joining its points to each other and then boasted of the infinity of such progress. In order to overcome this infinity, we must obviously change in relation to the world, take possession of the word of things, and move along the vertical or toward its center instead of along the horizontal or the surface of the sphere.

It is obvious, reasoning fundamentally, that there can be different degrees or states in the quality of a word or in the power of speech. It is possible to have a sudden revelation of feelings, to hear a word, to perceive the voice of things ("And my dark gaze brightened—and my ear since then hears what for others is elusive," etc.).[9] That state of a word in which science takes it, knowing the word only as a term, an instrument, is distinguished by pragmatism, and although the most pragmatic thinking is nevertheless basically sophian, still this pragmatism is, at the same time, also psychologism, the subordination to a particular, preconceived goal, to the fundamental problem of a given science. Science is incurably sick with psychologism, although it fights with it bitterly, sweeping aside all subjectivism. Scientific terminology is an unconscious antagonism to the ontology of the word; it is pragmatism in the name of *regulated* psychologism. You cannot invent meaningful words, meanings, but you can adapt them, and terms are such fabrications of words, adaptations to a given particular interest.

Therefore, the terms of various sciences are different, and all sciences are enclosed by the high paling of their terminology, outside of which they go to pieces. The seal of the conventional character of scientific knowledge lies on its specialized terminology, as does the major and fateful difficulty of the interrelation of the sciences: science presents the picture of Babel's confusion of tongues, where people speak with different languages about the very same world. In addition, that synthesis of scientific knowledge, the thought of which clearly contradicts its very essence, would above all signify the overcoming of terminology together with its multiple artificiality and a return to a natural language. Science has a sick word, and this sickness of its word is the main source and at the same time symptom of its weakness because it dooms all scientific knowledge to relativity, i.e., to notorious half-truth.

There cannot be another knowledge in the given state of human beings and their words, and scientific knowledge is, in reality, regulated psychologism that is borne to shore and set within definite bounds. Compared with the chaotic chance of elemental psychologism this is already a victory. However, Kant and all epistemologists wrongly attribute this to science. The illusion happens only because they turn their attention to the formal elements of speech and thought alone, only to categories, and do not want to see what is held in them, i.e., the concrete content that even in the framework of categories remains steeped in the same psychologism. The only thing required of the pragmatism of terminology is fidelity and consistency in the accepted attitude of thought and task, but this subordination of the word to a special task is itself psychologism.

Thus, science is objective psychologism in its verbal, informative proto-elements. It speaks about the world and knows it always through a definite prism. With faithfulness and precision of word usage, this can give in its own way a content-rich image of being. However, except for naming and primary judgments, knowledge and thinking consist of a combination of judgments, their chains. And in their coupling and combining there are also the possibilities for mistakes.

Cognition as naming-judgment is a synthetic act, in which a bond is established between several objects (substantives) and ideas (predicates). If one were to express this bond by proceeding from a grammatical subject, one could say that it discloses itself, its content, in a predicate or predicates. From the point of view of a predicate, one can say that the subject is placed under the predicate, whose scope, i.e., the possibility of predicative combination, of course, never is exhausted by the given subject. It was explained above that from each point of being one can on principle suppose connections to any cosmic being, and hence *one* predicate only begins but never exhausts or terminates the path of cognition. Likewise, any predicate, an idea, in virtue of the universal bond of being, can be brought into a connection with an infinite series of points of being and not with only one subject. Therefore, judgment does not represent something closed and finished either from the side of a subject or from the side of a predicate. One can enter and exit these doors and broaden a judgment by adjoining it to new ones or developing its availability.

Synthesis and analysis are two opposing logical operations. In formal logic, induction or the expansion of the field of knowledge, and deduction and syllogism, which puts in good order, correlates, and explains what exists, correspond to them. Syllogism executes an analysis of the content of judgments, and formal logic indicates the formal and analytically established rules and warns against errors in this analysis. Inductive logic points out several rules, in part experienced, in part analytically deduced, by the synthetic combination of judgments; and likewise, it warns against formal, "logical" errors. The danger of crude formal errors, of logical mistakes, always exists, and naturally they distort the course of the discussion, they more or less decrease the degree of its truthfulness.

However, according to its content, cognition is completely independent of logic. Knowledge is begotten by knowledge, i.e., by the power of knowledge, as thought is by thinking, by the power of thought, as too speech is by word, by the power of a word. In other words, all knowledge is a new synthesis, a combination (or separation) of a given object and a given predicate, a content.

Thought is limitless, as word is limitless. Any cognition, i.e., a word about the world, is the awakening of an idea for combining with a subject. It is a demonic act (in the ancient, Socratic sense of the word), i.e., the intuition of an idea, inspiration by the world, an act not of a logical machine but of *ingenii*, of the genius living in us. Cognition is creation, not of course creation out of nothing and in nothing, but it is the voices of the world, the revelations of nature in the consciousness of the human being, as far as he is able to hear them.

However low we might estimate the fateful pragmatism and relativity of scientific knowledge, nevertheless in this knowledge the world knows itself in a human being—the world-human and not human beings in their psychological isolation. Word-thought is the thinking of the world itself; here humans make real their central place in the world. The world too is a human being, the universe is its body, and the word of a human being—it is necessary, finally, to grasp this once and for all—is not empty gossip but the word of the world itself that was created by God's word keeping in itself this word and revealing it to the human being.

Thinking is the combination of judgments in all possible directions, both from the side of the subject as also from the side of the predicate. The accumulation of predicates around a given subject gives a *definition*, fixed by a term, and names, which likewise have their own predicates or signs, are brought under a concept given by a definition. In this way concepts are classified, grouped, and regulated through combination and subordination, i.e., what results will appear as a scientific or philosophical *system*, i.e., a system of concepts.

Science as a product, as a manual, strives to take on the finished form of a system; scientific inquiry, on the contrary, shuns system and prefers to keep open all its wounds, for in this it draws the source of life and development. In this verbal-logical treatment of a given synthesis of scientific knowledge a special verbal energy is developed, in which words-terms or concepts (those very *Begriffe* that Mephistopheles mocks), instead of a grammatical auxiliary significance, receive as it were independent being. In this way scientific prattle arises, the husk of words that from time to time must be swept out in the interests of science itself. However, its origin is itself indicative of scientific reserve, with which it builds a world of words-concepts in its own field. There in this non-universality of scientific concepts-words is the limitation of science.

In our world, scientific cognition is that which most approximates to truthfulness and overcomes subjectivism, and yet the method of overcoming it is clearly untrue. As soon as science begins to lay claims beyond the limits of its field—and it does this constantly—it turns into a monstrous lie and slander against the universe, which is all colored in one color or a mixture of a few colors. The synthesis of the sciences (as far as this is possible and does not contradict the very essence of science) is prepared in some "synthetic philosophy" à la Spencer or Auguste Comte[10] and is an unstylish and tasteless concoction in which the proper flavor of each science will disappear.

So, then, even when its logical operations are irreproachable and logical mistakes absent, the moving of scientific knowledge away from the truth, its falseness, is caused by the general direction of a given scientific point of view in its specialization; but it can also lie in the way this task is discharged, both through the violation of immanent norms of thought when judgments are combined and in the content itself.

In our understanding of it as naming-judgment, cognition remains thoroughly empirical. There are no longer any grounds for limiting the field of experience through "sensibility" by excluding from it the intellectual, spiritual, and mystical sphere, in general, everything that is experienced and enters into consciousness. To please his preconception Kant, by striving to include the whole of cognition in schemas of phenomenalism, recognized as "experience" only sensibility in order to drive it into transcendental schemas of pure understanding. In fulfilling this malice (you cannot call it anything else), he arranged all his watertight partitions that fall by themselves once the foundation, transcendental aesthetics, is rejected.

Naming has to do with the subject—a substantive—and the predicate— an idea; being, substantiality is a general quality of every subject whatever it might be from its first, approximate grasping by thought to its complete capture or concept. The so-called abstract concepts (unity, quality, good, mind, property, nature, beauty, distance, magnitude, etc.) nevertheless have this quality of being; they are taken as existing in the existing, as a facet of being. And in this sense they do not fundamentally differ from any concrete substantives, except by content (and without noticing it, Kant himself uses words indifferently that are equally concrete and abstract as he expounds his transcendental aesthetics, i.e., as he realizes a series of ideas that deny the equal legitimacy of these and other concepts, i.e., substantive nouns).

The critique of the word proves to be the best reagent for the critique of reason. We must break Kant's whole structure and mix up all his cards after recognizing that *all* of our concepts and judgments are fundamentally identical and equivalent: they can be true and untrue, but they do not belong to different drawers of a writing desk. There are only two "categories" of thought-word in the precise sense of the word: subject and predicate, substantive and adjective-verb—idea. Kant was too clever by half but at the same time not clever enough: because of his artificial schematism, word's simple wisdom, lying on the surface, remained alien to him. The application of the one or other qualifications of a predicate: adverbial modifier of place and time, modality, adverbial modifier of cause, mode of action, everything that epistemology and formal logic calculate, on the one hand, and grammar on the other hand, all of this is indicated by *experience*, has an experiential provenance, describes or produces experience.

At the same time, however, experience is not a passive reflection, it is a product, a creative act, realized by a subject, i.e., psychologically caused and psychologically limited. Therefore, experience can have a different quality, degree, or depth; it can be true or untrue, precise or imprecise in its realization. Here is the whole difference between everyday chaotic experience and precise systematic methodological argumentation, which—and this is the most important thing—imparts to experience a collective, or rather communal[11] character, freeing it from the narrow borders of solitary observation and anchoring it in a written and oral word, a book, a lecture. *A book* is a mysterious and enigmatic scroll of meaning that like everything habitual has become unnoticed and is taken for granted, and knowledge is first of all books, a library.

Nevertheless, experience, knowledge, naming can have not only a different depth, but also diverse directions: the nodes of knowledge can arise in all possible points. Judgments can be vital, meaningful, and in this sense true, but they can also be fortuitous, trifling, and in this sense without content and foolish (as in ordinary prattle and gossip). The copula **is**, generally speaking, is so elastic that it accommodates everything in itself, but it can remain unfilled.

Where is the criterion? There are two: the practical is in the utility of the knowledge in question, its pragmatism; the theoretical, as far as it concerns *content* and not formal errors, is lacking. It is contained in knowledge itself, in experience itself. The criterion of science is in science itself, and if it is something general, then in the aesthetics of thought, in its beauty, which, indisputably, is inherent in all the great constructs of the intellect. Mathematics, which knows beautiful problems and elegant solutions, is beautiful; every science is beautiful as far as it brings about cognition, masters experience, and gives to it a coherent and finished form in the process.

This striving for the beauty of thought, for its harmonious composition, is a constant inner impulse of development—of the perfecting of knowledge, an impulse purely theoretical, existing in the human being apart from the practical. Knowledge is not only useful but also beautiful. Mathematics is a poem for the true mathematician. The beauty of self-sufficient thought is also in a certain sense its criterion.

This leads us to a question about the beauty of a word. It is well known from immediate observation that a people, an epoch, an estate, and individuals have their own particular features in language, their own style. It is likewise well known that different branches of knowledge, of science, necessarily appropriate to themselves certain specific features in language through terminology, through the symbolism of signs, so that it is possible to speak of a language of mathematics, physics, biology, sociology, philosophy, etc. Idiosyncrasies of language are also proper to separate actors in the area of knowledge, to scholars and thinkers, shaping the personal and intimate in their work; as Buffon says, "le style c'est l'homme." Of course, it is not the grammar or morphological elements of language, or generally speaking the rigid inventory constituting the totality of technical means and grammatical possibilities, that create this personal style but rather how it materializes by these means in these possibilities.

This is clear from everything that has been said about the nature of a word and the logic incarnated in it. Naming is not only the voice of things and of the world itself but also our creative act, our response to the question of thought thinking itself. A word is not generated mechanically—that automatism of speech with which we make do in everyday life represents a word that has become pale, worn out, and weather-beaten. Any automatism, including words, supposes either that we do not control the given functions for one reason or other (the work of our inner organs) or that having once controlled them, we put them afterwards in an automatic depot. Everything entering there has at one time passed through conscious mastery, even if from a very distant time, for example, childhood, when the grammatical structure of language is picked up (this is repeated consciously in any study of a new language). Automatism is the result of the psychological mechanism of speech with its powerful means of associative coupling, lying at the foundation of habit. Of course, it limits the individual or creative field in language, its style, and creates for it ready-made boundaries. However, only mindless chatter can manage with this automatism, and every thought being generated seeks a form for itself and thereby punches a breach in automatism.

From the nature of speech—of naming—it follows that every verbal appellation is already an act of choosing *one* designation from an infinite series of possible designations. Being fixed it can depart into the automatism of language, but it can also be completely new for the given object of thought. This choice inevitably expresses an act not only of conceptual but also verbal creativity. It would be completely incorrect and distort the essence of speech and thought to imagine that someone thinking and clothing their thoughts in words should see in front of them a series of things and objects with inscriptions on them, verbal labels, and that merely by stooping down they should read and write down these inscriptions, their creativity being expressed only in the preference for some objects over others, for one sequence of records over another. As a matter of fact, such ready inscriptions do not exist; the thinker-speaker learns them by reading, by getting used to the objects, or by taking them into himself and merging with them.

Simultaneously with thought a word is generated that expresses the thought as a certain form. Form is inherent in word and thought, but it contains the logic of form, the law of form, and its demands. And the chief property of any form, both existing in the world and arising in a word, is that it is not indifferent to beauty, that it has its own aesthetic criterion, just as the content of thought has a logical criterion and the structure of a word has a grammatical criterion. All human speech has a form, is form, and thus on principle allows an aesthetic evaluation of itself. Here for the moment we abstract ourselves completely from that difference that is conventionally designated as poetry and prose and has an analogy in the difference between economy and art. However profound this difference might be, as between mercenary, utilitarian and unmercenary, aesthetic activity, between forced labor in the sweat of the brow and the free creativity of an artist, everything that a person does, they do as a freely rational, spiritually actual being and not an automaton. The person's freedom and creativity are realized in everything, and hence an aesthetic evaluation can be applied. A table is a household furnishing that serves a certain need by certain means, and it cannot retreat from or violate this correspondence of means to purpose, the utilitarian connection of form, its pragmatism. But at the same time a table has its own form, and this form is diverse, responding to different tastes, styles, and aesthetic requirements. One can also say this about all economic labor and its products: as incarnated human acts, they have a form and, for all its connectedness, they are not indifferent to the demands of the form.

Applied to words, one can say that even the most prosaic, business-like verbal compositions—a simple letter, a juridical act, a fluent speech—inevitably have their own form and style, different, of course, in each case. It is enough to compare works of this kind from various times and among different peoples. It is not chance or a whim of history, but it is generated by necessity, for all speech has a form, and the form is only concrete, not as a form in general, which is a pattern or shadow of a form, a contour of a form, an unfinished form, but as a given, defined form and consequently different from all others. However, this form can be poor and simple, approximating to a pattern, a cliché, if such is the content. But the more complex the content grows, and the more intensely and tangibly the creative human element is manifested, the more individual, concrete, and autonomous is the form, depending on its immanent laws, serving its own nature. However, the nature of every form is beauty, and there is one criterion for every form as form, the aesthetic criterion. What is subject to a utilitarian purpose, however, has a twofold criterion, both utilitarian and aesthetic. The second does not negate, complicate, or obscure the first but is rather its realization and declaration. Formed, artistic speech best serves its direct purpose, which is to generate and bring thought to light, but a languidly and confusedly expressed thought is a premature thought. The coining of words is at the same time the coining of thought. Every conceptual work is necessarily also a verbal work; science is the creation of the word and not only of the thinking intellect. And to that extent any thought is a verbal work of art, no matter how inartistically executed its works may be.

However, here there is no need to be narrow and to apply clichés of beauty where it is a question of the adequacy of form and content. A foggy autumn day or foul bogs can seem to us to be the height of beauty's deficiency, and yet in their own way, in their distinctiveness, the one and the other can be an aesthetically perfect form, fully adequate to its content. In a similar way, a page from a chemistry textbook or algebra treatise can appear to someone as the height of linguistic ugliness, and yet this is completely undeserved, for it can be a lofty model of its style, a form containing and thus generating its content. One need only recall that frightful chemical names, as well as algebraic signs, are not read on chemical or algebraic labels but are the results of the act of naming. In them the cosmos is made algebraic and chemical, and hence chemistry and algebra arise, and not the reverse; their lexicon is not created from the algebra and chemistry of the world. Moreover, one has to say this about any branch of thought and knowledge. Here a frequent obstacle to understanding is the special scientific terminology, which was dealt with above. Terms are tools of a handicraft, implements, whose instrumentalism is already imprinted with their origination, their very structure, their intentionality. Further, they constitute the habitual content of speech of a given science, already assimilated by the mechanism of associative automatism and made shiny from frequent use, so that by deliberately simplifying one can say that scientific speech consists of terms and grammatical forms necessary only to set them in motion. If this were indeed so, it would not alter our general opinion in the least that any thought clothed in a word (and no other exists) is also the verbal form of a definite style. But no kind of scientific terminology can be liberated from the aesthetic criterion of form. When the form behind the content is not noticed, it usually means they are the most stereotyped products, worn down and reduced to the level of the greatest verbal automatism, like textbooks, for example. But those works, in which the very birth of thought is realized, cannot be freed from the tasks of the form that they generate in the difficult creative act of fighting the disobedient element of the word.

Usually a form stands before us in a hardened guise, covering its object, and we therefore do not see its own generation, just as on a finished statue we do not see the sweat, labor, and torment of creativity that generated it. The temptation to believe in the automatism of form is especially great because the very masters of this form—scientists—have a very confused and weak awareness of themselves in such a role, although it is what they are in reality. Every work of the word, including every scientific composition, is also an artistic work. This does not mean here an aesthetic achievement, its success or failure, but the very property of this creativity, its nature. It is simply impossible otherwise to do science, and every scientist hews sparks of cognition from the world's granite and clothes them in the refractory form of a word that gradually becomes transparent. The beholding of a thought is necessarily also the birth of a word. That is why one can so violate and wear down a word—because it generally does not permit an indifferent mechanical relationship to itself but only an artistic one, positive or negative. Just as banality constantly fights with poetry, and spectacle and entertainment fight with contemplation, so too a word can suffer, be ill, become dirty, and fall into senility and old age precisely because it is alive and because form and beauty are inherent in it. One *can* therefore poison it, which is impossible with dead objects.

In essence, speech is always art, but this does not mean that every human being is an artist and behaves like an artist, although it does mean that to a certain degree or in a certain field (whatever it might be and whatever it might concern), every human being can be an artist. A nation that creates its language with its verbal means, grammar and syntax, a miraculous artistic work in its own way, is also an artist. Scientific creativity is not copying from nature; rather, it is authentic creativity in which both form and content are hewn.

This means, further, that on the part of its form, scientific cognition can be performed both better and worse, *by different* means; therefore, there is not a single generally obligatory form for science, although there are generally accepted ones. Form is created simultaneously with content. The content arises as form, and hence it can never be indifferent to form. If scientists turn out to be indifferent to form, it is a manifestation of an excessive imbalance, of professional utilitarianism that stops seeing the meaning of form out of practical expediency. But an artistic form (if it can be stated thus about works that are not artistic) also possesses a higher practical expediency because thought achieves clarity and minting only when it is clothed in a transparent and flexible form. In its own way, a scientific treatise must likewise be an artistic work with its own style.

From the nature of the logos as an indivisible and unconfused unity of form and content, of word and idea, it follows that the unconditional adequacy but also artistry of a work of the word and thought (whatever it might be and whatever it might concern) is possible where their unconditional balance and harmony exist. Thought ought not to outstrip a word or be borne above it and in front of it, leaving the word to tramp along already laid out tracks. Word ought not to outstrip thought, breaking loose from it and being carried away along the trodden paths of associative connections or habits (in similar cases we say of someone that a word or a phrase got the better of him). How is it possible and is it really possible, if word and meaning exist indivisible and unconfused in the logos, on which we so insist as the very foundational axiom of philosophical language? Ontologically this is impossible, and no sort of misuse, no sort of corruption of a word can deprive it of meaning, otherwise it has already ceased being a word. However, every subsequent use of a word, its concrete meaning in a phrase, in speech, is subject to misuse, because the formal, instrumental elements of language—grammar, which exists to glue it together from a mosaic of words, phrases, and thoughts—can operate as if automatically, working for nothing, replying to momentary psychological outbursts and moods. How many there are who constantly use a word and do not participate in the logos! This is revealed by their speech, which is colorless and empty, displaying an associativity of the lowest, most elementary order—by an association of contiguity. This is manifested with particular clarity in certain psychic diseases, where the centers of consciousness become weak but likewise in many cases of "having the gift of the gab." In a similar way a series of psychological states, be they certain forms, representations, impressions, moods, mental sketches, or observations—can press upon thought with such power that thought appears in the world as immature or premature. The load of content is not overcome in form, and the result is the heavy-as-lead, inert, careless, and often simply semiliterate style of our scholarly treatises. This too is psychologism, although of a different type than the first: the seeming abundance of content, which can even give rise to the illusion that thought is independent of word and only finds expression in it, is in actual fact an insufficient mastery of it.

Taking possession of its object, thought strives to present it for itself in a suitable artistic form, which is why certain artistic demands are inherent to any work of the word or thought. The structure of speech, based on naming, presupposes "tropes," i.e., convergences and comparisons, new and unexpected, and it is impossible not to agree that an artistic intuition is the basis of any original, i.e., really newborn, word, so that prose in the proper sense does not exist in language at all.[12]

What, then, is prose and poetry (*poiesis*-creation) in language? Here we are speaking for the time being not about poetry in the narrow sense, i.e., about verses in contrast to prose, but about the art of the word, or about the word as an object of art in general. The difference in the *use* of the word in the one or other case, irrespective of the results achieved, is that in poetry a word is material for beauty, admiration; the aim here is the form itself as in any art, whereas in prose a utilitarian aim predominates, the heteronomy of word. In defining poetry as the autonomy of word and form, we in no way wish to separate it from and oppose it to content: quite to the contrary, here the balance of the one and the other is achieved, *logos* triumphs—hence the truthfulness, depth, and meaningfulness of works of art completely independently of their particular content or subject. Here the *logos* sounds in all its power and emotion—the sounding of a single string at a single point causes the remaining consonant strings to vibrate, imparting thereby the breadth of the diapason. This is the nature of an artistic symbol, through which the depths of being are revealed and the harmony of the world is heard.

The content in pure poetry too is defined not by its utility—otherwise we have didacticism and tendentiousness, which for poetry, of course, is the same kind of death as any other utilitarianism. Poetry is amoral, or rather *supra*-moral, on the other side of good and evil; it is naïve and disinterested like a child. It arises and is conceived as form. This does not mean the subordination of content to form, which is taken only as a pretext or a theme for aesthetical exercises, because this is the same kind of utilitarianism as any other. Properly speaking, the nature of the word as logos, i.e., the harmonic union of word-meaning, is manifested most clearly in poetry: the psychological film breaks and the word sounds as the world logos, as a sophian word. But precisely for that reason it is clothed in beauty, characteristic of creation in its Sophianity.

There is a state when your consciousness expands, in sleep or awake, when it seems that you are hearing some sort of world rhapsody. You hear how it sounds in you or through you, and it seems that you will pass with it into the world and you will merge with the world; you grow and there is nothing sweeter than these sounds, pleasing without end. This logos of the world is also the poetry of the world, the poetry of the word. Because, by the way, it seems that a real work of verbal art has neither beginning nor end; it lives by continuing in both aspects, radiating energy from itself, for any perfect form has symbolic nature, power, and depth. It speaks about another relationship of the human being to the world, which is neither utilitarian nor servile but free; it bears witness to the humanness of the world, the anthropocosmos, to the one logos in humanity and in the world. Everything in a human being is recognized cosmically, integrally, chastely, it is the beauty of all in all.

The difference of the art of the word from other arts is in the particular material of this art—the word. This material is so original and exclusive that it demands special attention. A word is efficacious by nature—it is form and meaning, sound and significance. As form, a word has its aroma, its aura seen by the clairvoyant word of a poet. And not only an individual word but also a combination of words, a phrase, has such a sonic aura around it, it gives off an aroma; it is impossible to transpose or change a single sound in it without disturbing the beauty and enchantment of the whole. Here the means of sound, image, and meaning unite into one thing, the most complex, subtle, and tender combination: all other arts deal with mute material, which they force to become transparent for the image, to speak its idea. Only the art of the word deals with material that has its particular qualities as material but that above this possesses a meaning that speaks and is not mute, and it is necessary to combine these meanings into a chord of meaning that would merge indivisibly with the chord of form. Such complexity and subtlety of task arises in no other art. (One can perhaps say that in singing it is repeated to a certain degree, but only to a certain degree, because in singing, a word is given in an already set form and enters as a given and not as a pliable material.)

Such a task is possible only because not a single material possesses us interiorly and intimately to such a degree as does word, which sounds in us and through us. But at the same time—and this is the whole point—with our psychologisms, experiences and caprices, **we are not** this word that lives in us; a word is not even experience, but the life of the world, and suprapersonal. Therefore, a poet must be obedient to the commands of the muse, forget about himself, by surrendering to inspiration, and strive to cross beyond the barrier of personal limitation. Different types of the art of word or of poetry have a basis in the phonetic nature of word, on the one hand, and the semantic, on the other. Word is a certain musical material, which can be worked rhythmically into corresponding musical forms, in conformity with the properties of a given language. In this way, poetry or verse arises in the narrow sense of the word. Human speech in general has its rhythm, clear or unclear, correct or incorrect, but it therefore contains the possibility of versification. (In this sense, Molière's bourgeois gentleman could add to his discovery that he is speaking in prose that he in fact is speaking in verse, though very incomplete and shabby.)

Besides the inexhaustible variety of forms there is also the rhythm of meaning in verse, there is colorful beauty and the expressiveness of images, there is the clarity and sincerity of content. There, this combination of forms, sound, rhythm, meaning, and image make a poem the form of forms. They instill in it the exceptional power of beauty, give to the art of the word a regal place in the midst of the arts like the art of the logos itself (although, of course, one should not tear the other arts away from the logos. Nevertheless, their material is alogical, and their meaning wordless). Only in the art of the word is there a synthesis of logos, of word (as a phonetic value), of meaning, of form. This is given in a brief and concentrated manner in a poem. For that reason, it is considered poetry par excellence, although the other arts of the word are not thereby denied.

The same power of the form, the same principle operates there: the content of a work of art is its form, which is found in an indissoluble fusion with the image, but the purity of poetry, its power, is usually diluted and weakens with the scope. For the vastness of the scope indicates either the weakness of the form or its bulkiness. At the same time the tasks of the form can be absent or can be modified, as for example in artistic prose the tasks of the form, the rhythmics of the word, are absent. However, this does not at all liberate prose from its rhythm: the form of prose in the indefiniteness and irregularity of its rhythm can prove to be no less refractory and unmalleable as verse, as masters of the word attest. But here different combinations are possible in the task of form: the content can involve the form, although it does not coerce it but also does not allow it to develop. That is how it is in a novel, usually too content-rich; it fascinates more by the form of its content, of its development, than by the form of its word, so that here we again get the utilitarianism of a higher, artistic goal. Such are the great novels of the nineteenth century by Hugo, Dickens, Turgenev, and Dostoevsky. But here too on the heights, form prevails in this way and to such an extent that it is completely monolithic and stands before us as a work of nature. (Compare in this sense the completely different but equally perfect pages of the epilogue of Turgenev's *A Nest of Gentlefolk* and perhaps "Cana of Galilee" from Dostoevsky's *Brothers Karamazov*: here we truly have "poems in prose," which you cannot lengthen or shorten.)

Of course, definite quantitative proportions keep in line with any concept, and the dimensions of the canvas for a battle scene are different from those for an intimate landscape. However, no matter what the dimensions, the form must be coherent and thoroughly transparent, and if the scale is vast, the task becomes commensurately complicated and perhaps even grows indistinct. In artistic prose of a miniature type (Chekhov or Maupassant) the form's task is so compressed and transparent that here "a poem in prose" must really be given, which is what the best works of the given authors are. In general, the domain of verse is not at all limited to a poem and perhaps our blindness and inability to notice the characteristic twists of form is the reason why for a long time verse was taken to be the correct alternation of rhymes. The expansion of the field of free verse attests to the insufficiency of such an understanding.

You can ask yourself if poetic science or science as poetry is possible. In other words, can a relationship between poetry and cognition be established that is more intimate, more substantial? Yet another way: can poetry become the rhapsody of the world, be liberated from its reverie, and can science renounce its prosaicism? An important difference between the word in poetry and the word in prose is that in poetry, the life of the word itself is felt; it is born and carries the immediate freshness of its cosmic birth within. What happened at the dawn of the birth of language when words spoke themselves in the soul and arose in it with elemental power, as the voice of nature, when they were felt in their might, originality, and beauty, when they had melodiousness and incantatory power, is now preserved only in poetry, although to a weak degree. The poet himself, a real poet and not an aesthete putting on airs, coached in various verbal tricks, contemplates with sacred amazement the word being born in him (like a savage in the positive sense of the word, or like a child, or like the first human), and his images sound completely new for us, different from all words. They take possession and subjugate us, and independently of the direct meaning, with its descants and accompanying sounds, in them, or rather with them, the voices of the universe sound for us, the sounding of the cosmos is audible. In poetry a word ceases to be only a sign that it uses for signaling meaning, "concepts"; here it appears as itself, i.e., as a symbol, and waves ripple away from it as a cosmic surge. It seems that one more moment and the lyre of Orpheus will tame wild animals and move mountains—the word will receive its efficacy, for it touches the root of being. Poetry immediately borders on the magic of a word; it is to a certain degree already magic in the sense that every powerful word is magical.

So, then, only in poetry is the word itself an end and not a means, as it is in prose. In any community, there is a generally accepted language with its supply of words and forms. They are habitual and customary, they *are used* for expressing thoughts, and they are kept by the memory as is any foreign language we have learned. These words are not born in our soul but suggested by obliging memory, by the mechanism of associations, as required, like ready signs for expressing concepts. Lacquered and made slick from use, obliterated dead words have their own convenience for those purposes for which they are used. The nature of the word is so far from being felt by students of the word that only in these necrotic signs do they see true words and openly prefer them to living words.[13] Language becomes algebraic, from *phusei* [by nature] words become all the more *thesei* [by setting], new words arise only as terms, i.e., also *thesei* and the mystery of word is completely forgotten under the cover of this verbal husk. A word loses its taste, smell, color, just as it loses its algebraic sign. Of course, all of this has its limits; even the most prosaic speech remains nevertheless a creation and cannot be entirely converted into algebra, as even the very partisans of such a conversion recognize with regret.[14] The roots of words still remain and feed on underground moisture. Sometimes whether a word has these roots makes itself felt. For example, we can know a foreign language well, have command of it within the limits of ordinary speech, but to create something in words, even the most modest of works, is possible only in our native language. Such a work demands the birth of a word, it concerns the roots of language, whereas a foreign language that we have learned does not have these roots. It does not have the character of signs, which must not necessarily be words; but even gestures (the language of the deaf mutes) or speech in a foreign language will be poor and limited as to the number of forms or words. This is not because of an insufficient knowledge of the language, which can indeed be quite thorough; rather, it is due to the fact that each human being has only one *native* language, there is a correspondingly established apparatus.

All foreign languages can be learned only through the medium of one's native language. Even people who are exceptionally gifted linguistically, who have interiorly mastered a foreign language, do not constitute an exception to this rule because for all that, history has not yet seen a significant writer in several languages at once, and merely mastering them has nothing to say here. Although we have to learn each language, including our native language,[15] the difference between a native language, what I would call an inner, deep language having roots in the soul, and a foreign language that has only been learned, remains great. For this reason, the art of the word, poetry, is in essence also possible in a real way only in one's native language; only then do words have all their power and depth, they are actually symbols and not only verbal signs. There is a difference between understanding the words and thoughts of a poetic work and feeling the beauty of its language. One can grow accustomed to this foreign speech and its poetry to a different degree, but its magic does not have all its power.

This brings us back again to the problem of translation; either it is only a retelling of content, which is entirely sufficient for prose works, or it is an artistic translation and a new birth of the word. If translation into another language is not a simple repetition of thought, but a new understanding of it, then this should be said to an exceptional degree about artistic translation.

Poetry realizes not only the life of a word but also its limitation. A real poetic work is at the same time a natural word existing in the original state, which a natural scientist can in some sense study. Such a study can touch upon various aspects, for example, phonetics, the body of a word. In Russian literature, on the initiative of Andrei Bely, studies are being undertaken in this area, in particular concerning the "instrumentation" of verse, i.e., that phonetic coloring given by the predominance of these or other vowels or by the accumulation of consonants, in accordance with the content of the work. Of course, this instrumentation is produced, or rather, is not produced but happens unconsciously and unpremeditatedly (otherwise, it would lose all value and interest). It is rooted, evidently, in the deepest rhythms of a language, in its most subtle vibrations. Here the veils are lifted from the inner organs of a word, the link is felt that exists between a feeling and a separate sound, letter, or element of a word. Word-thought and word-sound see themselves in each other and they deliver up their cherished mysteries. For the mystery of the word is the mystery of letters and their combination in a word as a body of meaning.

In prose speech, language is no longer dealing simply with generated words but also with the finished products of words, where their nature is veiled by psychologism and utilitarianism; a unit of speech is not a word but a semantic sign, and what kind of sign is of no interest so long as it satisfies its purpose. There, evidently, it is not possible to discern the fabric of a word, just as one cannot discern the threads of linen in a linen shroud. In poetry, words grow in a free state, but of course, to study this microscopes are required—appropriate methods of observation.

By scrutinizing the organic combinations of words that give poetry to us, we penetrate deeper into the symbolic nature of words, into precisely that which makes a word a symbol. The art of words gives material for this, similar to how material for the science about art, its theory, is given by works of art. That material that linguistics has for its observations is all the same the results of vivisection and specimens. It is not at all so easy to get a living word bearing the warmth of life, even from a living human being, because he too often uses necrotic words. Therefore, poetry offers the material, alone in its class and irreplaceable for our epoch, for the comprehension not only of a word's covering, its anatomy, its embryology, but also the very life of a word, its mysticism and magic.

A word has a symbolic nature, and it is manifested in poetry, for a word comes forward here as an independent essence and power. Poetry borders on word's magic; its tradition, now already lost, is preserved in folk beliefs in sorcery, incantations, in the force of a word in general. Here one can discuss this question only by posing it in principle: Is the magic of a word possible? Or, does a word have force besides its direct meaning? The answer to this question can be given only as a deduction from a general judgment. What is a word: symbol or signum, root of being or sign? Contemporary rationalism, knowing word only in the latter sense, as a real *thesei*, a conditional sign, can see in the idea of magic only superstition, and besides even for it the question remains, where precisely did this superstition arise? On the contrary, for the symbolic understanding of a word the conclusion follows with compulsion that words can have power, being so to say the force of nature, but not every word and not always, i.e., not in every combination.

The magical use of a word, of course, is other than semantic or logical because the guiding aim here is not to express a thought but to unleash energy, to manifest the nocturnal, underground, concealed energy of a word. Of course, it too is indivisible from the meaning of a word, from its sense, but here words do not express thought but unleash power. From the point of view of diurnal, logical consciousness, of the direct semantic use of a word, its magical use can be considered even an abuse; but it is not an abuse so long as it has a basis in the nature of word, in its elemental force. Why should the use of cotton for wrapping be considered the precise purpose of cotton but its use in dynamite an abuse?

An incantatory formula represents, so to say, a specimen of a word, a deployed word framed by a corresponding form. In terms of meaning, this formula must be executed with the same precision as any chemical formula because here too the forces of nature operate, although not on the phenomenal surface but in the underground depth. Fundamentally, there is nothing supernatural in verbal magic, no more than there is, for example, in the action of explosives, which are not found in nature in a free form but must be extracted from it. A wizard or mage is first of all a sage, one who knows, who possesses the science of the word. How this knowledge fell to his lot and what he uses it for is another matter; we will not speak about it here.

It is completely incongruous and incredible that all those methods that are now being studied as primitive magic (including the magic of the word) should be only superstition and not have for themselves any foundation and justification. If anywhere, then here one should have recalled that favorite formula: *ex nihilo nihil fit*. Generally speaking, why not allow *a different* layer of relationships with nature, a natural science different from our own—so to say, symbolic and not phenomenal? In that case, this magic and wizardry would be an ancient tradition, having preserved itself since the days when humans were very much one with nature inwardly and needed quite other means of influencing it: the human being was one thing, nature a different thing.

But contemporary positivism in its haughtiness does not want to make such an assumption. According to the meaning of what has been said, in a *word* as an incantatory formula a cosmic force operates that becomes palpable through the medium of the word, so in a certain sense transcendent with respect to the phenomenal world and a word in the usual meaning. A symbol is the transcendent-immanent action of some essence, the expression of energy, and here there is nothing incomprehensible because as symbol a word has roots in the same depth from which reality also proceeds, not only "reason," but also "sensibility," i.e., all experience in general. It is no more and at the same time no less clear what one can do both with gunpowder and with a word. Why precisely is one or other combination of words, one or other formula, required for a given purpose? Why is a formula required at all? "How is a formula possible?" An answer to these questions in a general and rational form cannot be given, because here we have a concrete operation that has the force of fact: *it is so* and that is all. In fact, if you ask a poet why he chooses these or other combinations of words, will he tell? Or in this sense try to question the poetic word itself why this word is used here and not another word and expression. Is it impossible to replace it, etc.? *It is so*; it will answer with the very fact of its existence in its fragrant beauty. The poetic combination of words or, if it can be expressed thus, the poetic formula, is a phenomenon of nature, in its own way just as indisputable as Niagara Falls, and it is just as out of place to ask why it is as it is as it is to ask Pushkin's "I remember a wonderful moment."[16] The poet should be the first to reject this question, provided he really is a poet and was present at the birth of this poem and did not make it up. In some sense, he is not even its author—it has composed itself. Objective beauty is the exception of premeditation and rational expediency; it does not know our "why" but only the imperative "*it is so.*" Evidently, we must take the next step in this discussion, having recognized that **it is so** is independent of the phenomenon of the world. It is possible for objective beauty, which encompasses all its rays and aspects, not to be revealed in precisely these aspects; they can remain in potential and not pierce the veil of our reality. Creativity, however, is discovery, showing to the world these supertemporally existing rays and aspects. You see, we think in a similar manner regarding the forces and laws of nature that we grasp: the law of gravity (of course, if such a thing in fact exists) has been operating in nature not since the time of its revelation by Newton but completely independently of him, as have all the forces of nature.

Returning to the incantatory formulas, provided we allow on principle the effective force of a word, we must apply to them everything that was said above about the connection of the form of an artistic work and about the laws of nature. This formula is only revealed by a magician and is brought into action or transmitted as an occult tradition (and again not in virtue of some secrecy but in virtue of the essence of the matter: either according to the conditions of the efficaciousness of the formula itself or for other considerations connected with caution, etc.). Between words as keys to the powers of nature, there exists a certain *natural* correlation and link; from this too flows the necessity of the one or other formula, which also can constitute the object of knowledge and of the occult tradition of the hoary past, when people better knew the language of things. That Eden-like undamaged state in which our ancestors were found before the fall, when they conversed with God, when Adam was able to give names to animals and to understand their language, in general, when they abided in a closeness to nature that is now unattainable for us—this was accompanied by an intensification of powers and faculties, including, of course, the most subtle, now called the occult. This state casts reflected light on the first times of human history, and after the fall, the rays of Eden go out only gradually, according to the distance from it. Incomprehensible traditions, which seem to be meaningless superstitions, are perhaps the forgotten traditions of Eden. This is why the seal of antiquity, the grey hair of time, speaks unwillingly about mystery and wisdom. Since for us there are no grounds at all for denying the possibility of such traditions as knowledge of words and formulas, even though with the flow of time their application becomes frequently obscure, magic becomes black and the wizard-sage becomes an exceptionally malicious being, not using his power for good ends.

If it is correct that words have a certain power inherent in them in their own way, even irrespective of the one speaking, one has to conclude that pronouncing words, so to say, the liberation of their energy, is not at all an indifferent matter. Words do not disappear without a trace after they are pronounced, but they live their proper life, lasting or brief; it depends of course on the words themselves and on the one who uttered them. Words fill the atmosphere in a different way but in the same sense as dust, smells, and the various bacteria that are inaccessible to the eye. They huddle together in clouds, bump into one another, and form an environment having its own properties. Why think that a room needs airing out after tobacco but not after words? One who believes in the power of a prayed word and blessing can in no way take up this position, but even apart from this—anyone who sees in a word something more than only a means of communication, but also the very thing being communicated, must become pensive. Does not an uttered word, and consequently, an atmosphere of words, in actual fact exist as such?

To accept that a word like a physical phenomenon, like a sound or color (painted) abides and remains in the world, its action being indestructible—anyone can and must do this who confesses the "law" of the conservation of energy. But a physical understanding of this "law" is here obviously insufficient because although a word is a sound, it is by no means only a sound, and the difference between words as powers depends not at all on the sound (although connected with it) but on the meaning. With a word one can strike and kill a human being, the meaning of a word here bursts into the forces of nature and mixes up the cards of a purely materialistic, physical understanding of the world. Similar to how a word as an ideal meaning is also a physical force (it appears as such as a means of communicating knowledge, for example, communicating the formula of explosives), so too a word itself has being, its "mental" body. These bodies have their own activity although we do not have the means to measure it, and for this the usual measuring methods are unsuitable. But a spiritually sensitive person, on entering a hall, feels the dirtiness and mustiness of the atmosphere, and conversely, a particular lightness makes itself felt under the roof of a righteous man.

Therefore, it is impossible to treat as absurdities and superstitions only the use of a word as such, in its objective being. For example, incantatory or sacred words, like other symbols both positive and negative, as well as nonverbal ones, such as the sign of a cross or a pentagram, when traced on a wall or threshold have power, of course in a different sense than articulated words. People feel this instinctively even when the connection with nature and the comprehension of the word has been lost. Various political parties, for example, by obeying an unaccountable and unclear need to give power to certain words, hang out their slogans not only for the purposes of propaganda but also to trigger their action. If this is applicable to the dead and pitiful slogans of today's parties, then how immeasurably more so to the various prayer, sacred, and occult inscriptions and signs both in homes and in temples. People have always felt their power and significance without words and have expressed this in the varied use of inscriptions. (In general, we should reflect more on the instinctive and unaccountable actions of people.) It follows that the incantatory power of separate prayers or utterances, *mantras*, on principle ought not to be subjected to doubt.

In general, one always ought to treat a word seriously and carefully: although the commandment speaks to us only about using the Name of God in vain, still it has to be understood in a broad sense, at least for our question; indeed, it concerns every sacred thing, all sacred formulae, and further all words in general. Not a single word lets itself be used in vain with impunity; thus, the question of our responsibility for a word and before a word must be persistent.

What has been said about the *power* of a word that is inherent to it as a symbol of cosmic essence leads us to a question about its *divine inspiration*, and from a somewhat special aspect. Since the exegesis of the school of Alexandria,[17] it has been customary to discern three levels of meaning in the Word of God: the literal, the metaphorical, and the spiritual. The first relates to the concrete content of the word in its most immediate aspect, in which the language, epoch, and personality of the author is reflected. Inspiration is the highest degree of spiritual actuality, and therefore it implies not the extinction of human individuality, but its greatest tension. The Holy Spirit inspires the divinely inspired writer, but by no means does he convert him into a passive tool or instrument. Therefore, works recognized by the church as divinely inspired do not thereby cease to be monuments of written language bearing the seal of their historical epoch with all its limitation and properties. Already the fact that they are written in a definite language that belongs to a certain epoch makes them monuments of that language, subject to philological study. Further, they also represent a certain literary form proper to the person, epoch, and given genre of the works. Finally, they can contain indications of purely human creativity, poetic inspiration, and artistic talent proper to a given writer (for example, the vividness and beauty of the style of the prophet Isaiah, the unusual power of Jeremiah, the colorfulness of the prophet Ezekiel, etc.—all these are their personal qualities). Therefore, even without the quality of divine inspiration they will take their place in the history of human thought, even for nonbelievers, for whom these universal human and literary properties exist. For example, for us this is the significance of the Vedas, the sacred books of Buddhism, the Koran, and others, and for educated society this is also the significance of the Bible as a monument of written language.

It is necessary, however, to add that human virtuosity and literary significance are in no way a necessary condition for divine inspiration. Works in a sacred written language can be completely mediocre from a literary perspective, simply workmanlike: for example, the legislation of Moses and the so-called historical books, mediocrely rational, as the proverbs of Solomon and Jesus ben Sirach, and even folkish and barbaric, as some New Testament writings are judged by Greek literary style. There are not the slightest grounds for denying this or closing one's eyes to it, because this would mean crossing out the individuality of the person and epoch to which this work belongs. Either one would have to think that the Spirit of God does not blow where it wills but is found in connection with a certain literary style or that the Spirit demands special human gifts, whereas these latter do not play a decisive role in any case in divine inspiration.

Whatever may be the case, a divinely inspired work has its human content and covering. However, this content, according to the determination of the church, which introduces it into the canon of sacred books, contains *the truth* and is found in direct relation to it. The human content here is, on the one hand, free from errors, and on the other hand, participates positively in the truth; according to the belief of the church, this is due to the inspiring operation of the Spirit of God. The truth is all-embracing; in its particular content, for example, individual articles of the ritual law, and historical narratives, what belongs to its realm is able not to betray its belonging; but this connection can be disclosed under the special influence of the Spirit of God. The Word of God as separate books, as well as the whole Bible, have in this sense a symbolic nature; it is a divinely inspired symbol and has infinite depth, which like the starry vault becomes all the deeper when one looks at it closely. The significance of a symbol is that it is never limited by its immediate being; in it, through it, and beyond it, the depths of being are revealed.

In this sense the depth of the content of the Word of God is immeasurable— any thinking person who lives with the Bible and turns to it at various times of his life is convinced of this. The doctrine of the spiritual meaning of Sacred Scripture also speaks of this, and this spiritual meaning, according to the doctrine of the church, is disclosed likewise under the particular guidance of the Spirit of God in spirit-bearing men. The Bible is a book that is never fully read through; it is a symbol always being disclosed, and in such critical epochs as our own, this is felt with particular force. Is it not said directly of Christ that He "opened their mind" for the comprehension of the writings and prophets?[18] Therefore, the Bible is an eternal potential of divine inspiration, like a window into another world from which the rays and sounds of the Kingdom of God burst through. This is why it cannot simply be read through like any book but must be eternally read. In this sense, in the church the Bible is not a book but a sacrament, and communion in the word occurs. Under the guise of given, historically arising words the faithful receive spirit and life. The word as symbol, the unity of the transcendent-immanent in the Bible, is transubstantiated by the Holy Spirit; it no longer has only a cosmic, immanent nature but a supernatural and divine one.

All this represents an idea that is perhaps unusual in expression but in essence is generally held. It is the basis of the church's teaching about the divine inspiration of Sacred Scripture. It is necessary to add the following. A word, whether separate or in definite combinations, as a verbal formula, in accord with the church's practice, contains a special power; it is a vessel of grace. Obviously, this refers to the words of the sign of the cross, to all the official services, in general to the church's liturgy as a whole, which is regarded by the church as divinely inspired. Apart from their content and that frame of mind put in by worshippers, prayers have force, and this is manifested, by the way, in the fact that some select prayers are repeated many times, evidently without a particular relationship to the content but in some sacred numeration: three, twelve, forty (Lord have mercy). This refers likewise to the repetition of definite groups of prayers at almost every liturgy (the so-called Introductory Prayers).[19]

Finally, one cannot help but notice that the Psalter occupies in general such an exceptional place in private and public liturgy and certain psalms in particular. It is of course impossible to exaggerate the significance of this undying source of prayerful inspiration, always watering the church's field, and yet it is necessary to say that the meaning of the Psalter in practice is even greater than follows from this appraisal. The Psalter is repeated in church and at home, like no single group of prayers; from it is constituted the "rule" of monastics, it is that verbal air by which they breathe in the heights of ascetic struggle and contemplation; the lips of the monk are constantly sanctified by it as is the very atmosphere of his cell. At the same time one cannot say that the Psalter only rarely carries a sharply expressed impress of a people, an epoch, and its composers; with respect to content some, indeed many, psalms have ostensibly only historical significance for us. Yet the church, without pausing over this, prescribes in the "rule" of ecclesiastical and home prayer *the entire* Psalter, ostensibly even being little interested in the content of individual psalms, at the same time seeing in the Psalter an irreplaceable unique method of prayerful exercise.

Individual psalms, corresponding to content, are selected and set in their place in the liturgy as are other prayers, but alongside these runs the reading of the Psalter as a whole. The testimony of ascetics regarding the exceptional, unique role of the Psalter, and also the command of the church, compel us to believe that a special power inheres in the Psalter. Only thanks to this can we understand that the use of the Psalter as required by the church *is possible*, that on the spiritual heights it does not bore and make weary but gladdens and warms. Indeed, spiritual growth and maturity can be determined by one's attitude toward the Psalter, by one's sensitivity toward it.

However, we can and must approach an understanding of its natural foundation, which we also see in the symbolic nature of the very word and in its capacity for saturation with power. A word is or rather can be a condenser of power, cosmic or gracious; the sacred formulas of sacraments are such condensers of power. But this power in no way is determined only by the meaning or content of the formula, which would have at most the significance of a wish, thought, or mood but would not have power. This power is given thanks to the word being not only meaning but also a receptacle of energy, an instrument, a conductor. Protestantism only hit upon the ministry of the word as meaning, but the church knows yet another ministry of the word—as power—and this ministry forms the basis of its sacramental life.

CHAPTER 5

The "Proper" Name

Every act of cognition is naming, and a predicate, an idea, in fusing with a subject, with a grammatical subject, gives a name. Such in general is the origin of all acts of naming and names. As well, the fusion can be closer and more permanent, or temporary and passing; depending on this, we distinguish so-called proper and common names. Every name in its genesis is common as something arising from appellation (naming), but it is without fail also proper if it adheres to its bearer as its permanent predicate, so that its bearer is named with this predicate.

Every name is a proper name in the sense that in it *one* predicate is chosen from an infinite series of others that can be applied to it; this selection is naming in the narrow sense, like long-standing names. When we call a given object a table, the analysis of this word shows that we pick out for its name the sign *to spread* [stlat'], the predicate of spreading, of laying, of a fitted surface; from all other signs that may be connected with table, we select only this one. In a similar way, we name a concave, hollow space *coelum, koilos,* heaven, leaving all other signs aside. In its subsequent existence, this name in its meaning can have its own fate: it can be expanded, narrowed, or become specialized; in general, it has its own history, but at the moment of its origination the difference between a proper and a common name is still not felt.[1]

Every naming is a judgment; in other words, every name has meaning, and this constitutes the so-called inner form of a name. However, with the passage of time, if a given name is destined for stability, it can become pallid in its meaning and will begin sounding like a sobriquet, a nickname, a "proper name." Such is the fate of many names and place-names, which originally were semantic designations, names through predicates, but afterwards they became simply nicknames that had lost their meaning and forgotten their inner form.[2] The majority of place-names but also human sobriquets are like this.[3] In that case, the difference of a "proper name" is its meaninglessness, lack of inner form, and so to say, algebraic character. But this very name will immediately become "common" if we fill it with content, give it an inner form borrowed from its bearer ("that the Russian land can beget its own Platos and swift-minded Newtons,"[4] etc.; Khlestakov and *khlestakovism*).[5] The word-mass melts down and remelts, and it receives a new life.

This question about the distinction of proper and common names has paramount significance for a philosophy of the name. It breaks down into two questions: about the nature of a name itself and about the nature of its bearer. As for the first, we have tried to show that every name in its origination is a word, i.e., a meaning, idea, content: names without meaning or content in their genesis do not exist. Those meaningless nicknames with which names are sometimes equated simply could not arise other than by an onomatopoetic path, i.e., in its own way semantic (see above). This assumption was undoubtedly due to the fact that a special class of words with no other meaning than to be names for definite objects and persons, individual nicknames, appeared with the development of language at a definite period in the history of the word. In this way, the history of the word from its noble semantic genesis up to its being made a meaningless nickname is a gradual wearing out and fading of meaning, with the sound alone being preserved. Not for nothing do "intelligentsia" parents, i.e., those who have gone so far as complete rationalistic insensitivity toward words, choose names for their children guided by sonority, like parrots; but after all, when the intelligentsia (and now also the people) make a name into something idiotic, this speaks only to their spiritual drying up, and nothing more.

A proper name is precisely such a nickname that has lost its inner form. It is as it were the gesture of a demonstrative pronoun colored by sound, or a counting number or some other mark of distinction, an auxiliary means for our cognitive operations, in the economy of cognitive and verbal means. From this point of view, a proper name is not even a word in the strict sense, just as an algebraic symbol is not a word: it stands on the very bounds of a word, it is a word only according to its sonic covering. Precisely for that reason (here we are crossing over to the other side of the question about a proper name, to the nature of its bearer) it is absolutely individual. Since it expresses nothing and is a concrete demonstrative pronoun or a demonstrative gesture, its naming is an act of the purest arbitrariness, which cannot be generalized or extended beyond the limits of a given case. Any sound, it seems, can be a name, but it must be in its own way singular and unique: only poverty of expression or feebleness of inventiveness prevents names from really becoming absolutely individual and never repeated. In fact, names are repeated, in the language of a given society there is always at one's disposal some quantity of such quasi-words, nicknames, that can be used for proper names. However, one can go further and suggest that a name is not only given arbitrarily but changes on a whim so that there can be as many names as there are whims to change it: in other words, a name is torn from its setting and scattered into individual dust particles.

True, against this, one can refer to utilitarian motives that contradict the multiplicity of names and their transformation by caprice: stability is lost and even social and legal interests are breached that demand the permanence of a name. However, these motives, external and foreign to a word, would be incapable of suppressing the inclination to polyonymy or many names if there were a basis for it in language. And if renaming, generally speaking, represents a rare and exceptional act that must always be sufficiently motivated, this indicates that the situation with a name is not so simple and that a name is not a nickname, or rather, only a nickname.

We have seen that a demonstrative gesture or pronoun is concealed in a name—and in any name. The more forcefully the demonstrative, nominative element comes to light, the more the *proper* character of a name is emphasized in naming; the more energetically a copula is affirmed the more, of course, a name is a nickname. But a name is all the same a word, and as such, it cannot and does not ultimately become a nickname and only a nickname, but it preserves also its nature of predicate. As for naming, however, it affirms the character of judgment, which is naming par excellence, not only as a theoretical judgment but also as a volitional operation, as it were, a command: let there be. In naming in this sense, a certain creative act is hidden, and it would be in vain to reduce it to the whimsical invention of a nickname, which the "intelligentsia parents" now consider the calling of a name to be.

In naming, the one naming says "let there be N." Into some mass that is amorphous in relation to a name the definite seed of a name is sown that will have to sprout and display its vital force. We understand this, of course, of the human being who alone has a name, received in the act of creation; the remaining names either come to light as the names of animals in Adam or are nicknames in which whim and association, enduring and binding anything and everything with its glue, are at work. Until the name is spoken, the subject is not so much indifferent toward the name or hostile to it, anonymous, as only amorphous, potential. This potentiality, this faculty for receiving a name and the vague attraction to a name suggest the absence of a definite name. This means that a human being as a generic being, as the *all-human,* has potentially *all* names and can be called any of them. It does not mean, of course, that in the concrete act of naming, the choice of names is unlimited, which never happens because of external conditions not connected with the potential of naming. It does, however, mean that all names that were at some time applied to a human being or will be applied, *all human* names, belong to the human being not only as an individual but also as a species, or as the first-created Adam who contained in himself the names not only of the lower animal kingdom but also of the entire human race. This is why he put this power into practice with particular acts of naming—his wife *Eve* (Gen 2:23), and later his children.

But as an individual, a human being can have only a definite name, which excludes and pushes away the remaining names: *omnis definitio est negatio.* This idea is quite obvious, so far as naming is a judgment, i.e., the predication of a certain quality, the definition of a subject through a predicate, through an idea. We can call an object by various names, sometimes disposing of hundreds of synonyms;[6] we can express it with an infinite quantity of metaphors, add to it, and thereby name it with all manner of properties, and yet this naming is not a whimsical nickname, rather it brings to light the potential content of a given subject, its cosmic characteristics. Therefore, with any separate act of predication, we push away and remove all the remainders, but this does not mean that we act here by caprice, although without question judgment presumes an act of our intellectual freedom.

Such is the origin of all substantive nouns, or common names. But proper names also have in their prototype a concrete significance, as historical grammar shows, and in this case they do not differ from any other judgment-naming: they belonged to common names that determined their bearer as a permanent predicate: Alexandros, Theodoros, the Terrible, Dobrynia, etc. The strong glue that holds subject and predicate together and the creative act that is included in the calling of a name make them a name: "let it be so."

And yet all the same, when we lose the inner form, forget or lose the meaning of a name owing to the great historical distance [separating us from it], would a name not be converted for us into an empty nickname? It is not true that names that lost their inner form with the passage of time did not have one in each given historical epoch. On the contrary, as they lose their initial inner form their significance and content increase, or better, they acquire the inner form anew, and besides one that is ever changing, is renewed, and grows more complicated. A name lives in history as does any word but not the way a word does because it becomes a symbol of some living essence of a definite quality, a seed or yeast; it always has meaning, and a very heavy-laden one at that. A name is the power, the root of individual being, with respect to which the one being named is the bearer, the earth, the soil, and naming therefore has a fateful, defining character for him. He can succeed or fail as the bearer of his name, but all the same, he will be—bad or good—precisely its exemplar. A name is the idea of a human being, in the Platonic sense of the word.

Here we approach the question of the nature of proper names from the other side, namely from their scope. We have explained that any predicate, anything predicated, expresses an idea, is an idea, neither abstract nor concrete but an idea's definition. But a name, too, so far as it is a predicate, so far as naming is a judgment, likewise must be an idea and consequently have general meaningfulness, a meaning. This idea, a name, is bonded firmly to its given possessor; even more, he becomes the bearer of a name. His name is his ideal core, his "proper" name in comparison with other predicates, but it does not at all follow from this that he is the *sole* possessor of this name, its owner. If his power of possession is satisfied and exhausted by this name, still, by contrast the power of a name is not exhausted in a single bearer but can be poured out on an indefinite number of them. Then all of them are its bearers, but no one of them possesses it exclusively: an idea and a name, by being contained in many, abides in itself without changing, as many shoots can come from one root.

Such in general is Plato's doctrine of ideas, but it is applicable with particular clarity to a doctrine of name. In view of the fact that many are bearers of one name, this name is for them a general, genetic sign. It is no longer a "proper" name but a common one, designating a particular type of human being, distributing the human race by class just as it is distributed by every possible external sign. It is mistaken to think that such an arrangement is connected simply with the actual repetition of names because of the poverty of human imagination, which is incapable of inventing for each individual its proper nonrepeating name. It would be so if a name were simply a sonic nickname not having a meaning, i.e., not a word; and language would not be language but some kind of absurd chirping. A (new) name always has the one or the other initial meaning; it is a word, a predicate, and an idea. Typical here is precisely the conscious, knowing repetition of a name, applicable to new bearers. Here a name wittingly comes forward as an idea, a meaning, a predicate. Since no name is guaranteed against repetition, even were it encountered a single time, this is evidence about its nature as an idea. Thus, the proper nature of a proper

name is included not in the particular nature of the name itself, which as meaning is an idea, a word like any other, but in the stronger bond of the copula and
in the ontological peculiarities from which they spring.

But then, too, when a proper name, in losing its inner form at the same
time loses its initial meaning, it nevertheless never becomes only a nickname
but acquires its special exclusive significance *as a name*. At various times of
its existence a name can also have a different meaning, changing almost to
the opposite, but in each given epoch a name has its definite meaning that
can be recognized with greater or lesser clarity, in large part vaguely, similar
to how the spiritual significance of color or sound is recognized. A name
expresses through itself a spiritual type, a structure, the variety of the human being; the human race is broken into families and groups according to
names, which are its natural classification.

Names can be simple or complex. Usually a name consists of several elements, rolled up or bound as if in a bud (name, patronymic, family—*nomen,
praenomen, cognomen*, etc.), a chord of names; but so as not to complicate the
question, let us take only a single name. It is individual for a given person, but
it is not at all individual in and of itself: as an idea it is realized in many phenomenal exemplars. All Sergeis, through participation *methexis* in the name,
are the idea "Sergei." Among them are different, bad, and good Sergeis,
i.e., those who in expressing the entelechy of their name turned out better or
worse. At the same time, they are also different in the sense that the soil on
which the same seed is cast is individually different. Therefore, there can be
well-turned-out Sergeis in different grafts to different wildings; the diversity
of each name exists, sometimes obscuring its unity.

Names receive not only a changing meaning but also different supplementary definitions that complicate the very impact of a name. In the Christian
calendar, names are given in honor of definite saints: that is, a name is given
not in general but of a definite quality, from different sowings of the same
name. This qualitative nuance of a name does not remain indifferent, quite
the contrary, there are as many types of each name as there are concrete
realizations of it. Here we do not have in mind the significance of the participation of a heavenly patron, "an angel," to whose choir as if to a family
the bearer of a given name belongs, but the action of this very name. Ontologically considered, however, this patronage "of an angel" is a variant of the
reality of a name because this particularizing link that exists between a saint
and his or her like-named is founded not on some kind of special reasons (as
perhaps the special closeness to different saints for these or other reasons)
but precisely owing to homonymy. A common name binds a common fate
no matter how different the separate lots may be.

So, then, a name is a force, a seed, an energy. It forms and determines its bearer from within. It is not the person who bears the name by which he or she is called, but in a certain sense it bears the person, as an inner final cause, an entelechy, by which the acorn develops as an oak tree and the grain as an ear of wheat, although the fates of different oak trees and ears of wheat can vary. A name is not a simple word, "an empty sound" (although generally speaking "an empty sound" entirely impotent and inoperative does not exist). A name is the energy, power, and seed of life. It exists "by itself" or "for itself" independently of whether it is applied, just as an oak tree, the power of an oak tree, exists by itself, apart from separate trees. Yet it exists only in its bearers, as the idea of oak tree exists only in oak trees, as an Aristotelian entelechy. As an object of speculation, a name is an idea; as power, it is an entelechy. The Platonic-Aristotelian definitions here are fully combinable and appropriate: an idea is the ideal basis of entelechy, its essential root; entelechy is the concrete being of an idea, an idea is energy, and entelechy is its hypostatic manifestation.

If this is true, then the answer to a further question of the philosophy of the name follows from it. How ought one to understand the origin of new names—are they invented, as it seems, or do they arise and speak themselves as things speak themselves? Undoubtedly the latter. In constituting the province of real or seeming arbitrariness, only the external covering of names is invented and not what is disclosed in this envelope. "The inner form" of a name, insofar as it is preserved (Leo, Faith, Charity, etc.), gives the theme of a name, points out only the dominating feature but does not at all exhaust its content, exactly as the name "rose" in pointing to a pink flower (and then only initially, in singular instances) says nothing about its structure or its petals or about all that the name "rose" in reality designates. The meaning of a name as some root for a definite type is always wider and deeper than the content that its inner form has. Therefore, one can in essence say that the one who fabricates a name according to some single sign has absolutely no idea what is really happening here, what kind of catch turns up on the hook of the fabricated nickname when it begins to exist as a name.

Here there is a great, qualitative difference between the same word used as a word or as a name: a robin and Robin are completely different things, although a robin enters the composition of Robin as a characteristic of the name that transfers in one way or another onto its bearers.[7] In the invention of completely new nicknames and names, of which some up and die without being born, or turn out to be a husk or a sterile flower, there is an original cunning of reason that uses human powers for its own goals. A name is born through the name giver in the one named, but once born it lives its own life. To an even greater degree one can say this when a name is not discovered anew but is selected from existing ones for these or other motives, at least for "beauty." A name lets itself be taken, but it does not at all obey the stupidity of those who chose it; rather, it lives its own life, going about its own business, and once it has reached a new incarnation, it has seeded new life.

Even a more conscious selection of a name will be myopic because for human beings the secret of one's name and the secret of one's own being are equally difficult to discover. They are frequently guided by illusion or limited visibility, and even if they have a correct intuition of the name, then surely in any case they are blind with respect to what is precisely the ground for the name, i.e., the still unnamed bearer of the name. Nevertheless, the one or other correlation and correspondence between a name and what is named must also determine the results: definite spiritual types ask for a definite name; they need it precisely in order to blossom and vice versa. There can be failures who receive a difficult name for themselves that cannot be fulfilled, and they languish under its weight. Therefore, naming is always more or less blind, and a special dawning of Divine grace is necessary in order to name correctly, i.e., to effect the greatest correspondence of a name and its bearer, to show a name, a human idea in its purity and fullness. It is therefore not in vain that in separate, exceptional cases a name is given by the direct determination of God, even before birth, in the mother's womb, and even before conception.

From this series of instances abundantly attested to in the Old Testament and in hagiography, we will pause only on the two most important gospel instances, specifically the naming of John the Forerunner and the Savior: both the one and the other took place before birth and even before conception. About John, we read that an angel said to Zechariah, "Your wife Elizabeth will bear a son and you will call his name John" (Lk 1:13). When the child was born, "they wanted to call him by the name of his father Zechariah; to this his mother said, 'No, he is to be called John'" (Lk 1:59, 60). Where does Elizabeth have this desire from, clearly going against the natural voice of relatives and custom, which would require that he be called by the name of the father, as this is directly attested in the Gospel? The Gospel does not indicate that Elizabeth was acting here by a direct illumination from above. Is it not more natural to think that in the pure and chaste condition of this righteous woman, the real name, John, more proper to the boy and hence foretold to Zechariah, was born of itself, asked and knocked on her heart? What had been said to Zechariah about the future, as *let there be*, is now already *it was and became*: the child, whose nature yearned for the name John as the one that most corresponded to him, was waiting for his naming. And the feeling of the mother attested to this.

Does this not tell us something about *how* names in general are given, how they arise, at least in a pure uncorrupted human nature? The appellation given by Elizabeth received confirmation from the father, who wrote on a tablet a formula expressive in its conciseness: "His name is John" (Lk 1:63). Let every name fighter become thoughtful. Is it really possible to treat a name so indifferently, to see in it an arbitrary nickname when the Lord, in those cases when the ways of Providence are opened before us and when it is a question of the preparation for the Forerunner of the Lord, reveals the name by a special act of theophany through an angel, by a miraculous intervention? After this they dare to say that a name means nothing, is a simple nickname, so that the Lord is occupied with thinking up nicknames for reasons of convenience, euphony, or I know not what! No, naming is a new birth, the final birth (which is why it happens at circumcision in the Old Testament and at baptism in the New). When it is a matter of birth by divine election, with the logic of internal necessity, it is *naturally* a matter of naming.

The gospel narrative about the giving of the name of the Savior must have significance irrefutable in its uniqueness. (For the time being, we are setting aside the divine significance of this Name and limiting ourselves only to the human naming.) Here this wonderful Name is spoken and foretold twice: first at the appearance of the Archangel of the Annunciation, when he says to the Virgin, "And behold you will conceive a Son, and you will call His Name Jesus" (Lk 1:31). The second time the Angel of the Lord speaks of the same to Joseph, when Mary was already pregnant, appearing to him in a dream: "She will bear a Son and you will call His name Jesus" (Mt 1:21). In telling about the naming itself, the Evangelist once more recalls the connection with the command of the Archangel: "And after eight days have passed, when the boy was to be circumcised, they gave Him the Name Jesus, which had been spoken by the Angel before His conception in the womb" (Lk 2:21).

Calling a name, in certain deliberately significant and solemn instances, is the direct work of God. Thus, it is natural to expect this at the very creation of the human being, for creation is necessarily naming. In fact, we encounter a brief but sufficiently expressive indication in the book of Genesis: "[God] blessed them and called them the name of human being on the day of their creation" (Gen 5:2) (in Slavonic: and he called him the name Adam, on that day he made them). There are cases when God gives names to separate persons or renames them. So it was with Ishmael through the Angel of God: and the Angel of the Lord said (to Hagar): "see, you are pregnant and you will bear a son, and you will call him *Ishmael*, for God has heard your suffer-ings" (Gen 17:19). All three patriarchs, Abraham, Isaac, and Jacob, receive their name directly from God himself, either immediately (Isaac) or through renaming (Abraham and Israel).

(This can also include the solemn prophecy of Isaiah: "behold a Virgin shall conceive in the womb and shall bear a son and they shall call His name Emmanuel" (Isa 7:14), which has a direct parallel with the promise of the Archangel about the name of Jesus at the Annunciation.)

God says to Cyrus in Isaiah, "For the sake of Jacob my servant and Israel, my chosen one, I have called you by name, and honored you although you did not know me" (Isa 45:4). The naming is here a work of special care and of respect, even for a pagan.

We find symbolic calling of names by the direct command of God in the prophets: Isa 8:3—"and I approached the prophetess and she conceived and bore a son. And the Lord said to me: call his name maher-shelal-hash baz" (the spoil hurries, the prey hastens).

God speaks in Isaiah about Israel: "The Lord summoned me from the womb, *from the womb of* my *mother he called my* name" (Isa 49:1). Surely this is not only a rhetorical utterance here, where according to the interpretation of the publishers of the Russian translation of the Bible the Divine Savior is meant (judging from the capital letters in the transcription).

About the "eunuchs" "who keep My Sabbaths and adhere firmly to My covenant, to these I will give in My house and in My walls a place and a name better than to sons and daughters: I will give them *an eternal name which shall not be cut off*" (Isa 56:4–5). "And they will call you by a new name which the mouth of the Lord shall pronounce" (Isa 62:5), says Isaiah about Israel. "No more will they call you "forsaken" and your land they will not call a desert, but they will call you 'My good will towards him,' and your land 'espoused,' for the Lord favors you" (ibid.) "and they will call you a holy people." (12)

For the time being we will not attend to those cases of naming as re-naming that are told about the Savior with respect to his disciples (John—Boanerges, Peter—Simon). Our goal here is to show that the calling of a name is a special creative act that can be executed unerringly only in one definite way. This task admits only one solution, having neither more nor less substantial meaning.

It can seem that a name arises by chance or arbitrarily. In order to be freed from this illusion, one needs to look at the calling of a name in light of general anthropological principles that come to light in human life. One can see random reasons for the emergence of language, and yet language—and scarcely anyone will doubt this—is a faculty of the human being, an inalienable property without which a human could not be a human being. There are faculties for thinking, for science, for engineering, economy, governance that can be understood only anthropologically, no matter how diverse or even accidental they may be in their manifestations. The human being is a *zoon poietikon, politikon* [a creating animal, a political animal], and so on. In a similar way, naming belongs among his basic anthropological definitions: *zoon onomatikon* [a naming animal], a human being *has* and gives *a name*, a race, a nationality.

Names as roots of diversity, as nests of being, are inherent in humanity, although this division by names does not coincide or only partially coincides with humanity's division by other signs, for example, by races. If this characteristic division eludes human inquisitiveness, it is due to the difficulty of establishing this division but likewise because of the general direction of contemporary thought that is inclined to abstraction, and purblind to everything concrete. Names arise not by chance and not arbitrarily; they are not contrived without any internal regularity; they exist in the human being, the many-named first Adam, and are only discovered in naming. Therefore, the naming of a name gets meaning and completeness, the problem of onomastics stands before us in all its breadth.

Still the question again arises: what, then, is a name and what is naming? A name is first of all a sonic word, let's say a phoneme. It can be singular in its class, individual, having no synonyms and foreign to polyonymy, but it can also be polysemantic and abound in synonyms. In a similar manner the words *bark* or *tongue* (indeed the majority of words) in their different meanings, by their sonic uniformity, are in essence quite different words, their phonemes are filled with a different meaning, a sememe. It is the same for names: John, Jesus, Daniel, and the majority of names, by an identical phonation are quite different names. In this way an identical phoneme does not by itself exhaust or determine a word, and only the insufficiency and imprecision of our transcription, though supplied with the general context or meaning, permits us to write different but identically sounding names identically without distinguishing them by any sign. Here we have the case, as it were, of the *metaphor* of a name, similar to how metaphorical meanings of words (bark, tongue) by coalescing with meaning, make them quite different words, and their consonance only recalls the history of the word. Human speech, as in other cases, strives here too toward the greatest economy of means and prefers to make do with old sonorities (phonemes) by connecting a new significance with them. However, a phoneme, or a definite sonority, is a necessary accessory of a name, its most external covering, which is actually taken for the essence of a name by those for whom it is only a nickname, "an empty sound."

Further, a name or phoneme, fused with the familiar meaning of the name as a word, is what is sometimes called the inner form of a word, its original significance. Of course, it has force only in its native language, where it arose; for example, Hebrew names—Hannah, Moses, Jesus, John, and others; Greek names—Andrew, Alexis, Alexander, Irene, Sophia, etc.; Russian names—Iaroslav, Dobrynia, Vladimir, etc. Of course, the meaning of a name points to some general properties of its nature, but in no way does it exhaust them. It is concretized further in the special, particular application of a name corresponding to one of the meanings of a given word (for example, bark): this is the meaning of a name in one or other epoch among a given people. Saints, who give their proper characteristic to the names of like-named people, introduce this concretization of a name into Christian church calendars. In this, of course, the bearers of the same name have an affinity among themselves. A name clusters, sprouts shoots; however, separate branches can diverge far apart (e.g., Paul the apostle and Paul the simpleton). A name in all its concreteness is a certain vital energy that, like all living things, is felt by inner intuition and can only be revealed, spoken of, and felt by the beholder. This corresponds to the sememe of a word, to its significance, fused with the phoneme. Names interbreed, merge, arise, break up, and rise again (renaming, a new name), but every human being is something that has a name. When one gives a name, one frequently reaches only for a phoneme, unconsciously, without a thought for a definite sememe (the beauty of a name). More often, however, although vague or as a means of honoring a saint or hero, a concrete name is given with a view to a sememe. Even independently of this, however, a name operates by its own power, once it is given, has taken root, and begun to seed.

So, what is the role of freedom or arbitrariness here? What kind of power does the one who names receive over the one being named? Yes, it is power, although one needs to consider the nature of this power and freedom carefully. Human beings have the power to enter or not to enter into a marriage, although neither conception nor birth depend on them but only the removal or nonremoval of their possibility through continence. However, to enter into marriage is proper to them, it is the development of their essence, and from an African only an African child, from a Tatar only a Tatar child, is born. In a similar way, they can name one way or another, although they cannot not name because otherwise a surrogate of a name will appear all the same, i.e., an uncommon new name that can be new only for the one who names but not at all in the nature of things. In this is the apparent freedom of choice.

However, this freedom is in actuality only a manifestation of vaguely recognized nominative potencies, of hereditary i.e., of ancestral attraction, of the voice of blood and family, in general of forces not at all individual in the sense of personal but of ancestral arbitrariness. In speaking of the hereditary nature of a name, we do not mean the tendency to repeat and retain at any price one and the same name in a family (although this frequently happens). No, the heredity that we postulate can be very difficult to detect, because it manifests itself in repulsion from some names and attraction to others. And in physiological heredity there can be very colorful combinations of inherited powers.

There is no special significance about the one who gives a name—a father, parents, relatives, or a priest, all the same enter into a rapport with the one being named, and an onomastic current is established. Perhaps too, cases of the most arbitrary, capricious choice of a name (by beauty) attest to the absence of a positive instinct of a name, speaking of the power of heredity as well as degeneracy or outbursts of new talents in a given family. It has only a secondary significance if a name is selected according to these or other scientific, national, or astrological considerations; it determines *how* but not *what*. Thus with conception and pregnancy, parents can behave accordingly to achieve the set goal, but it is attained according to the laws of the wisdom of nature. In naming, the choice of a name with its freedom is only the *how*, the free realization of what has already been preestablished by nature. *Instinct* operates, the name itself. One can admit freedom of choice only in certain limits, between kindred names or their nominal equivalents, of course, not identical, but akin (as synonymous expressions). This freedom of choice must even be allowed, as in all human actions that are intrinsically necessary. But essentially, naming occurs organically, i.e., instinct operates. The further fate of a name, its healthy or sickly development, its power, etc., depends on the soil on which the seed falls and the destinies of this being. A name does not exist non-incarnated as a transcendent idea, it is an entelechy that in name-giving is designated as potentiality, but when spoken it becomes energy, operating like entelechy.

A comparative and mass observation of naming has not been carried out. Probably, it would reveal here its own sort of "statistical regularity," similar to other regularities of the same order (birth rate, mortality, marriages, etc.), the probable expectancy of names would be established, and in general the life of the genus with its regularity of the whole would eliminate the individual's caprice. The general relationship between freedom and necessity in naming would be assimilated to the same relationship in the field of other phenomena of social life, which once so struck Adolphe Quetelet that it made him into a determinist.[8]

In fact, here the question of freedom and necessity does not arise because the one and the other refer to different spheres and there is no conflict between them. Freedom has a place in the life of the individual; it is the manner in which general, ancestral regularity is manifested, which exists for the individual only as an inner stimulating reason for its freedom. Necessity has to do with the life of the genus, although realized only in individuals but never limited by them, for it requires for itself a great number. Individual plurality and free (living) necessity—to such polarization does the question about statistical regularity lead. It is proof that life is deeper than individuality, for it includes a generic essence but at the same time does not diminish the latter. Each human being is simultaneously an individual and a species, freedom and regularity, something and everything, and this paradox comes to light in so-called statistical regularity.

So, then, it seems to us that a mass statistical study of naming, if it was carried according to the nature of the material and the corresponding methods, would reveal here something similar to what it reveals in other fields: super-individual regularity, that very instinct in naming that becomes apparent in individual-free, arbitrary acts of choice. (Of course here the grouping would have to be done more subtly: alongside the commonly used names one would have to combine chance names, given "according to beauty," or whim, etc., into a special group.) It would probably turn out that definite tribes in definite epochs have an inclination toward a certain group of names that express their onomastic characteristic.[9] Just as the structure of a tree or organism exists, so too does the onomastic structure of genus and species exist, although it refers to its ideal structure (ideal in the Platonic sense). Of course, the comparison of the regularity of naming with statistical regularity (representing a polysemantic and not at all self-evident occurrence having an indisputable interpretation) cannot be considered an exhaustive explanation; rather it points to the phenomenology of the occurrence, its *how* and not its *what*. However, the character of onomastic regularity is precisely statistical, i.e., it refers to *aggregates*, whereas individual naming, considered separately, remains fortuitous and free, i.e., irregular in the statistical sense.

In this way, names are the veins, bones, and cartilage, in general, the parts of the onomastic frame of the human being, and naming itself fixes or reveals each of its parts. Until that happens, the human being in the abstract is the possibility of all names, in the more concrete—a definite circle of names, and in the still more concrete—a limited number of names determined by instinctive attraction, which is realized in the parents either as the force of heredity or a kind of decadence. Nevertheless, due to this real and not illusory freedom, when naming takes place, an obscuring and perversion of instinct, of naming, is possible, knowingly untrue and incongruous, an onomastic deformity. Once given, such an alien name becomes its own proper name, the seed that is fated to fecundate soil completely improper to it. The fruit will be strange and deformed in an unfavorable case, but in an auspicious instance, it will yield a variety of names: from a given genus of a name, to this point having only certain features, a new branch divides off, a new meaning of the given name appears, which is to some extent a new name. Every novelty is a deformity, deviating from the path of a given instinct in order to please a higher instinct.

What then do names-seeds represent? Can one express their essence as such? This is very difficult, it requires scrutiny, empathy, a special act of intuition, and besides it is easier in some cases than in others. This difficulty or even actual impossibility (in view of a lack of focus of attention in this direction) ought not to confuse and appear as a fundamental obstacle for onomastics. Does the language of colors, sounds, and natural elements become more muffled because we cannot express all of its meaning in a word? On the contrary, this speaks more to its symbolic nature as one that deepens and is not exhausted by any definition. However, it is ontologically possible to be educated and develop by trying to express the potentiality of a name, to feel one's way into a name.

Of course, a name in the given understanding has the significance of a Platonic idea, *eidos*, which has intelligible being and which organizes and coparticipates in phenomenal being. More particularly, names belong to the idea of a human being and are its powers, potentials, and content. A polyonymous intelligible human is the foundation of historical humanity. As has already been pointed out, a name is individually real in a human being in the sense that it is individual, especially in combination with its given bearer, but at the same time it is ideal, i.e., universal in relation to everything, participatory in it. A name is a word, the word of a human about a human. The human being establishes the regularity of names and of each name, and individuals are concrete exemplars of an idea, of a name, which for them is a theme, a task, and a latent spiritual force.

Nevertheless, the character of the relationship between a name and its bearer is only *methexis*, participation, the natural foundation on which a name falls. It is Platonic matter as *chora* [place], the meonic milieu, malleable matter that cooperates and opposes, that craves but also obscures. Therefore, there is not and cannot be an absolute correspondence between a name and its bearer, or an adequacy of name and matter (except for completely defined exceptions, preestablished acts of naming of a divine character, mentioned above). Otherwise for this, one would have to suppose that the world became transparent in its ideal foundation, in other words, became sophian not in its foundation alone but in its condition, in its being, which is not the case. On the contrary, a name as an organism of names leads to the doctrine of the harmony of the spheres of all that is real, whose foundation is Divine Sophia and the sophian universal human Adam Kadmon, giving everything a name, as finding in itself every name.

Naming is an act of birth; rather it is the moment of birth, of joining name-idea with matter, their *methexis*, the moment when name-idea enters into matter and imprints it. Therefore, *a name is given*, it arrives but is not chosen by the one being named. In a similar way, a human being cannot be born from himself or herself but only from parents who must be capable of birth and who have the will to conceive or consent to it. Of course, the question is not exhausted by this, because one can still ask about the will for incarnation, about the consent of the one being born, and finally about the concrete form of incarnation. One can and must postulate that individuals are not born by chance in a particular environment with certain features of spiritual organization, the way a dull sense of culpability, of responsibility for their character speaks about this. This self-determination and self-willing are found beyond the threshold of empirical being, are perceived only as anamnesis, as remembrance about what was when we were not, and what we were when we still did not exist. How we postulate this will for being, or rather, how it is postulated in us, is similar to how we postulate the will for naming, a dull yearning for a name of one kind or other, for meaning and nuance. Failure or mistake are possible in either case. All the same, the facts are implacable and irreversible, and a name once given becomes like ideal flesh, the form of incarnation of a given spirit that is fated to settle in this name, to live in it, to develop its theme. It recognizes itself as already named; the name is its self-consciousness,[10] with which it finds itself in the world.

However, although it belongs to the very core of individual being, all the same a name represents only the covering, albeit one of the more intrinsic ones. A name defines the being of its bearer, but only in its state, not in its essence. Humans are clothed in a name similar to how they are clothed in flesh. Although they cannot be bodiless or nameless (in the spiritual order this signifies also non-incarnation), their corporeality is not exhausted by the given state of their body, just as their name is not merged indissolubly with their current naming. Faith promises us the transformation of a resurrected body, both our own individual body and the planetary body as a whole (a new heaven and new earth). But it also promises a new name, which we read about in the most joyful, solemn, and tremulous prophecies: "to the one who conquers I will give hidden manna to eat, and I will give him a white stone and written on the stone a new name which no one knows except the one who receives it" (Rev 2:17). The same thing is in Isaiah 65:1. And the Lord even proclaims about Himself: "and I will write on him the Name of My God and the name of the city of My God, the new Jerusalem coming down from heaven from My God, *My new* Name" (Rev 3:12). Even the Lord's Divine Name, announced by the Archangel, is not the single, exhaustive, definitive one, for there is yet to be revealed a New Name, a new revelation of Its Bearer about Himself.

So, is renaming possible, and what does it represent with respect to meaning? If naming is the moment of birth, then renaming is a new birth, suggesting either the death of the old or in any case a spiritual catastrophe, a change not of the theme but of the kind or of the nature of development. Therefore, it is clear that renaming is always a solemn act filled with particular mystical meaningfulness.[11]

Here it is necessary to recall and evaluate in all its depth and significance the solemn and sacred renaming that the Lord Himself carried out when he called His disciples, especially the *three* closest ones. It was Peter, James, and John to whom particular mysteries were revealed; they were the ones on Mount Tabor and in the Garden of Gethsemane; they were born again in name, i.e., in being renamed. "He appointed . . . Simon, having called his name Peter; James the son of Zebedee and John the brother of James, having called their names Boanerges, that is, 'sons of thunder'" (Mk 3:16–17). The initial renaming of Peter is also particularly noted in the Gospel of John (Jn 1:42): "And Jesus, having gazed at him, said—you are Simon son of Jonah; you will be called Cephas, which means rock (Peter)." The renaming of Simon was confirmed with particular solemnity at the most serious moment of his life, at the confession on the road to Caesarea Philippi (Mt 16:16–18): "*Simon Peter* answering said—You are Christ, the Son of the Living God. Then Jesus said to him in reply—blessed are you Simon bar Jonah because flesh and blood did not reveal this to you, but my Father who is in the heavens; and I say to you, you are Peter, and on this rock I will build my church, and the gates of hell will not overcome it." Is it permissible to assume with blasphemous levity that the Lord simply changed a nickname? That he was engaged in inventing pseudonyms? That nothing meaningful took place appropriate to the solemnity of the act? (One should also recall the special renaming of the apostle of the gentiles, Saul, who after the event on the road to Damascus and his Christian rebirth began to be called Paul.)

In their own way no less significant are acts of renaming performed by the Lord Himself in the Old Testament. They occurred at solemn moments, when a spiritual revolution in the fortunes of Israel was determined, upon the patriarchs Abraham and Jacob by the God who calls himself Yahweh. In his ninety-ninth year Abram was renamed Abraham by God after he had shown himself worthy, by a great act of faith and obedience, to become the patriarch of the divinely chosen people, even before the "covenant" between God and humans had been concluded exteriorly through circumcision. And in God's "contract" with a human being, renaming is included organically: "I am—there you have My covenant with you, you will be the father of a multitude of peoples, and you will no longer be called Abram but your name will be Abraham, for I have made you the father of a multitude of peoples" (Gen 17:4–5). This renaming is not limited to Abraham alone, but is extended to his wife as well: "do not call your wife Sarai but her name will be Sarah" (Gen 17:15). The question arises: is God engaged in inventing pseudonyms or more expressive nicknames? Or—and this is the only thing conceivable—do we here have a creative act, the divine *let there be* (let Abram be Abraham)? For God's word is deed, and when God renames, he creates something new.

In a similar manner, after his momentous nocturnal struggle with God, in which human power and human weakness were mysteriously tested, Jacob received a new name together with God's *blessing* on the way to Mesopotamia. "And he said (Jacob's mysterious wrestler), 'Let me go, for dawn has come.' Jacob said, 'I will not let you go until you bless me.' And he said, 'What is your name?' He said, 'Jacob.' And he said to him, 'From now on your name will not be Jacob but Israel, for you fought with God, and you will overcome people.'" (Gen 32:26–28). What then, this solemn renaming, is it only a pseudonym or nickname? Or is it a new birth, a new creation through the power that entered Jacob during the nocturnal struggle? And this new name is once again solemnly confirmed by God after Jacob's return from Mesopotamia to his homeland. "And God appeared to Jacob (in Luz) after his return from Mesopotamia and he blessed him, and God said to him, 'Your name is Jacob; from now on you will not be called Jacob, but your name will be Israel.' And He called his name Israel" (Gen 35:9–10). By a special Divine operation of calling—*and he called*—a new name is given, and afterward the disclosure of the power of this new name follows directly as the confirmation of the promises made to Abraham.

There is a similar case with Solomon: "and Bathsheba bore a son and she called his name *Solomon*. And the Lord loved him and sent the prophet Nathan and he called his name Jedidiah (beloved by God), according to the word of the Lord" (2 Sam 12:24–25). The solemn renaming performed by a human being can be compared with this. Thus "and Moses called Hoshea the son of Nun, Joshua" (Num 13:16). "And from that day he (Joash) began to call Gideon Jerubbaal, because he said, 'Let Baal himself plead against him because he destroyed his altar' " (Judg 6:32). "And she said to him, 'do not call me Naomi (pleasant) but call me Mara (bitter) because the Almighty has sent me great bitterness'" (Ruth 1:20).

On top of this, there are two degrees of absorption of the old by the new. The first is when the old name is preserved and only a nickname is added to it. An accumulation and agglutination of names happens, but in any case, there is no real, complete renaming. The type remains as before, except that it becomes complicated. The second occurs with a complete re-naming and the former name dies away: this happens in monasticism, and in certain mystic, occult consecrations. The Apocalypse speaks about this, only in a much more radical sense, where a new name is promised, written on a white stone. The transfiguration and resurrection too must essentially be such a creative, comprehensive renaming, a revelation of the true name, not one invented by people only tentatively, but one given pre-eternally, by a divine creative act, a Sophian name. For Sophia is the Name of names, the pan-name of the panhuman. Death, on the one hand, is the separation of the name from its bearer (which is why in church, names are remembered as their very bearers).[12] But at the same time, it is the death of the former name, which becomes only the potentiality of the past. Renaming is the transfiguration of a name.

Just as everything has its parody in the prince of this world, that monkey of the Lord God, and as transfiguration has its parody in acting, so too sacred, mystical renaming, the transfiguration of a name, has its parody in pseudonymy, that very characteristic and fundamentally interesting phenomenon of onomastics.

Pseudonymy can have a double character: renaming can be a conventional means for concealing one's true name—objective renaming, or it can refer to the person himself and in that case, it has the character of pseudonymy in the proper sense. As for the first, here we have simply the concealment of a name, and the pseudonym can have purely formal significance, be only a means, although at the same time the soubriquet itself, having a certain inner form, can be accurate and expressive of comparison or metaphor—of a soubriquet. (Such are the many school nicknames and the aliases of criminals, etc.) The distinctive feature here is that this nickname is deliberately not a "proper" but a "common" name, it is a means, a nickname that in case of need is replaced by a number (in prison) or in general some sort of external add-on (e.g., regimental or company numbers). Here we have not so much pseudonymy as divestiture from a name that is not replaced by an equivalent at all but only has something stuck on. In a similar manner, one incarcerated or a patient, on being released from prison or discharged from hospital, takes off his prison or hospital uniform and receives his proper dress together with his name and passport. Thus, the name is preserved here, but for some reason its power is temporarily paralyzed; it is suspended in action.

Exactly the reverse case is possible, viz., that a proper name is doomed to destruction, is predestined for dissolution in the element of someone else's name, patently not belonging to it. We have the classical instance of this in the literature of Hebrew apocrypha and pseudepigrapha, where the authorship of the works was ascribed to one or other historical person. Here a kind of spiritual adoption occurs, in virtue of which a given author regards himself (in the case of a conscientious, naïve forger) as an instrument of the one with whose name it is signed, or as the executor of his testaments, the guardian of his tradition, etc. In this case, some kind of imitator of Pushkin, in the spirit of ancient epigraphy, could sign himself as Pushkin or some follower of Vladimir Soloviev could put Soloviev's name on his own treatise. This situation in particular became even more natural when it was a question of figures with the reputation of a divinely inspired prophet, for example, Moses, Solomon, Enoch, etc. It would go completely against history and psychology to suggest that ordinary vulgar pseudonymy was at work in cases of pseudepigrapha, because this would mean allowing senseless and impudent blasphemy in the very age when it was treated with horror. Even in our corrupted age, would anyone who has kept but a little faith in their soul dare affix to their own composition the name of an apostle or evangelist as its author? Therefore, it is necessary to understand ancient pseudepigrapha as a broad interpretation of a name that lives not only in its bearer or owner but also in all the things that participate in it, that are imprinted with its spirit. By contrast, customary literary pseudonymy has the worst psychological nature: here a "more beautiful" name is fabricated, which is applied like paint or rouge on withered skin. Here we already have a second case of pseudonymy, representing a pure kind of acting in a name.

In naming, a name is given and begins to seed; with renaming, owing to the preceding spiritual catastrophe, a new name is given and new seed begins to be sown. But with the change of a name into a pseudonym (and for onomastics all cases of arbitrary self-renaming are of this kind), a new name is chosen by its bearer himself, and no spiritual catastrophe of renaming occurs; on the contrary, it is simulated. At the basis of pseudonymy, there is thus an objective lie and pretense: the changing of a name here is completely unmotivated; it is arbitrary and fraudulent. Here we have a kind of acting of a name: the actor, as was already said earlier, by simulating a transfiguration, remains himself under this mask and recognizes his pretense. Masquerade here enters into the task itself. The closer his pretense recalls reality, the higher his art is considered, which must tell lies according to the task itself (seeing an actress dying beautifully on stage, the audience sheds tears of pity and admiration, but imagine if it were a real and not a staged death—the whole aesthetic emotion would instantly vanish). Acting finds itself in antagonism with personal life and does not pass unpunished: a mask corrodes the heart, "a role" corrodes the soul, which comes loose on its axle and loses its integrity and density. An actor becomes the more mediumistic the more he "creatively" surrenders to his "art."

Pseudonymity is the acting of a name. Uncorrupted feeling in general experiences pseudonymy as something ambiguous, false, and tasteless. To begin with, it is violence against a proper name, which does not cease to remain the spiritual energy of a person, although distorted and paralyzed. Only when it is performed by others, usually by a legal authority, is renaming not pseudonymy. Current law, which declares the free use of pseudonymy, in essence abolishes the name. If this should penetrate life as the sole norm determining naming (which, of course, will never happen), then all names would be found torn from their settings and an onomastic Babel would move in; people would cease to be individuals and would become actors, pseudonyms of themselves. A pseudonym, further, is thievery, the appropriation of a name that is not one's own, a grimace, a lie, fraud, and self-deception. The latter we have in the crudest form in national disguises by means of a name, which constitutes the most common and widespread motive for contemporary pseudonymy of the likes of Trotsky, Zinoviev, Kamenev, etc. Here there is a twofold transgression: the profanation of the mother—of one's native name and the people who gave it (for national names are given through the intermediary of parents by a whole people, and they are likewise repudiated by a whole people), and the desire to deceive others, if not oneself, by the appropriation of someone else's name. The result of pseudonymity for its bearer is therefore having two or many names: the true name is not extirpated, it preserves its secret power and being, and its owner knows in the depth of the soul that it is his true name and not a stolen one. But at the same time he makes himself the performer of his pseudonym, which leads a vampire-like existence, using the vital juices of another name for itself. There can be no healthy development for a pseudonym, no true greatness and depth with such laxity, denationalization, and pilfering of its spiritual being.

Pseudonymity can have different degrees and completeness. It can touch several elements of a name, especially important and interesting for a given purpose. Thus, in our days it more often concerns surnames that define the family and clan. This is, of course, in practice the most grave and important instance of pseudonymy, a spiritual diaspora and dispersion, an intrusion in someone else's business, and its results are practically and mystically the most repugnant. However, here we are frequently dealing not so much with the mystique of a name as with an impudence that deceives no one, simply a disguise in someone else's clothing, boundless bad taste.

A colorful, partial pseudonymity is possible, a touching up, a simple and sufficiently innocent translation of a name from one language to another, dominant one. Frequently here there are no elements of pseudonymity at all, if renaming was not experienced or did not happen consciously but a new transcription of a name happened because of learning a foreign language. Finally, *full* pseudonymity would be possible in the case of the eradication of *all* elements of a name, but this would be a real renaming, which for pseudonymy is unattainable arbitrarily. The latter differs precisely by the fact that the old name keeps its force even in awareness of pseudonymy itself; although it "plays" someone else's role, it does not itself believe and indeed cannot believe in its masked name, and not for nothing does the genius of language call it false (pseudonym). In this sense, pseudonymy is by way of negation evidence of the nature and power of a name because instead of a renaming, only a pseudonym is obtained here, a mask. *It is just as impossible to change a name in reality as it is to change one's sex, one's race, age, origin, etc.* Renaming occurs with elemental necessity and is accompanied by change in the whole being of the subject, whereas with pseudonymy no change in being occurs. This is why every feeling that has not been darkened turns away from a pseudonym, and if the latter obtains vampire-like being, it finds itself in obvious and fatal discord with its owner.

Therefore, although a name is given in a similar way that a human being is born, a name already given lives its full life, like a child after separation from the umbilical cord. A name is an expression of the essence of a human being, his essential substance. Thus, incidentally, not only good but also evil names exist: "and on his (the beast's) heads are blasphemous names" (Rev 13:1). It is in a certain sense the same as **I**, with the difference that a name is a concrete, qualified, individual **I**, whereas the latter is individual only by the power of a mystical indicative gesture, outside of which it is universal and hence abstract. A name is an invariable predicate for every **I**, its equivalent, a revelation about the person, not in its separate definitions (what predicates accomplish) but in the core: a name is an unconditional subject for all predicates, onto which they are screwed as if onto a barrel. A name is what a human being is, and it signifies and reveals that he is.

Some say that this revelation is vague; it says nothing, and it reveals less than any predicative judgment. Incidentally, although a judgment is also naming, a name is not judgment or naming, exactly in the same way that I, although it is the basis of all the judgments of a subject, itself arose outside judgment, from the depths, apart from predication (the judgment I is I would be imaginary, like a tautology). But a name speaks about being, not about quality: it contains that very ontological gesture, expresses that vision that we have in an implicit demonstrative pronominal gesture in every substantive. Here is not a predicative idea alone but being, an idea that has become reality, a point in the cosmos.

Therefore, a name gives a general, although dull, undifferentiated sensation of being, by listening attentively to which one can hear the logos. Who is it? It is I: question and answer, equally expressive and informative. It is a question not about the *what* (predicate) but about the *who* (subject), and surely *it is* I is a meaningfully defined answer, is it not? Yet it has its depth and concreteness, invariable and inexhaustible by any predicates. But a name can stand here with a "common" I in a completely equal sense. It is obvious that no particular predicative answers will respond to our question; they will not stifle it or assuage it. "Who is it?" "So and so, so and so, so and so . . ." "But who then is it?" "N." There it is! That is how a name is sensed, the trunk of being that has neither flowers or leaves or fruits, but without which they could not grow or be nourished. Therefore, we repeat, an individual is an I, but in the same sense a **he** and a **name**.

But how can one take for an essence what is not even a concept because it cannot be expressed through its attributes? One for whom an idea as the energy of being in the Platonic-Aristotelian sense is something strange and unacceptable will be unable to accommodate the idea of a name as well. For those who understand and accept the ideal roots of being, a name is an ideal concrete, an individuality in its nonrepeatability but hence also inexpressibility through attributes.

Here external, absurd temptations can confuse that, let us hope, are already removed and can appear only on condition of a superficial relationship to word and name. In what is a name? In given sounds? But if there are other sounds in different languages, is a name different? And if sounds of different names are identical, is not the name one and the same? Here one needs to recall what was said about the tripartite structure of a name: sememe, morpheme, and phoneme. Of course, a name is a certain sememe, something concrete, but it is clothed in a phoneme and outside of it, it does not exist, it is continuous with it; but a phoneme too can be changed without a change for the name. It is the same for a morpheme. Under no circumstances is a name only a phoneme and morpheme, which is why their changes and fates have no decisive significance; they cannot hinder the identity of content and are like different photographs that are one and the same in content despite the variety of framings and shots. The difficulty of understanding a name is that it is on the one hand sufficiently independent of its changeable phoneme, and that on the other hand it is connected with it more firmly than any word. It is a word that has a proper sense and meaning, which can be communicated by another word or in another language; it can be described, whereas a name does not have such a meaning and does not admit substitution.

A question thus arises involuntarily. What is the core of a name, its sememe, if we divert our attention from a mobile phoneme? Evidently, there cannot be the same answer here as for every word, and even those cases when a name has an inner form, this latter does not have independent being and significance but is absorbed by the phoneme of the name. "Blessed Man" cannot take the place of "Benedict," i.e., one cannot make a translation of the inner form because the name here is precisely "Benedict." The answer about the inner core of a name can only be this: a name is a power, an energy, an incarnate word. Here the completely particular *ensarkosis* [incarnation] of a word takes place, the mystery of which is incomprehensible as is every mystery of embryonic life, fulfilling the command *let there be*. But the consequences are clear: the word became flesh, the ideal became the real, the idea was converted into energy, yearning for its entelechy, and name entered the cosmos of the names of being.

Let not the convergence of naming with the incarnation of the Word, with the divine incarnation, be taken for something blasphemously or frivolously bold, for our belief in the incarnation of the Word authorizes this audacity for us, which supposes and at the same time postulates the incarnation of words. The source of the word in the world is the Divine Word by which the heavens were made firm. If the Lord was pleased to be incarnated and become a human being, with an individuality and a Name, then this presupposes human individuality and name as the general form of life. The divine incarnation presupposes human name-incarnation. The Lord has two natures, two wills, but one Hypostasis and therefore one Name. His Name does not revoke the general law of name-incarnation but fulfills it, makes use of it. Human naming and name-incarnation exist in the image and likeness of divine God-incarnation and naming (as it is narrated that the Lord was circumcised and received his Name on the eighth day, in keeping with the Law of Moses). In general, the image and likeness of God in the human being, by virtue of which alone the incarnation of God became possible, presupposes a full human Godlikeness, and in particular in what concerns naming as the incarnation of a name. In the sophian order, every human being is an incarnate word, a realized name, for the Lord himself is the incarnate Word and Name.

Therefore it is understandable why in natural self-consciousness a name has as it were independent being, is most stable in a human being, has a life that one needs to restore (Levirate), an honor that one can defend (a duel), and an eternal destiny. Human names are written in the heavens, i.e., not only in existence here and now but also in intelligible eternal existence, about which the Word of God gives direct and irrefutable evidence. "However, do not rejoice that spirits submit to you, but rejoice that your names are written in the heavens" (Lk 10:20).[13] "With Clement and my coworkers whose names are in the book of life" (Phil 4:3). "The one who conquers will be clothed in white garments and I will not blot out his name from the book of life, and I will confess his name before My Father and His Angels" (Rev 3:5).

CHAPTER 6

The Name of God

May It Be Blessed and Glorified Forever

The whole preceding discussion had as its goal to bring us to the correct and clear posing of the great and terrible question that is making the rounds in Orthodox theology with overwhelming force: that of the Name of God, and Its sacred mystery. This question breaks down into two parts: on the one hand, the Name of God is a name to which are proper all the general signs of a name, and on the other hand, singular and exceptional features are inherent in it that are connected with its theophoric nature.

Every judgment is naming, and every judgment is a name, rather, is potentially a name, and can become a name. Every predicate that we ascribe to the Godhead is at the same time a naming of God: Provider, Creator, Good, Eternal, Blessed, Holy, etc. The doctrine of St. Dionysius the Areopagite about the Names of God refers precisely to naming. The ineffable, mysterious, unknowable, transcendent essence of God reveals Itself to humankind in Its properties. These properties are predicates, predicated of the Divine Being, and as predicates, by becoming like a grammatical subject, so to say *pars pro toto*, they become the Names of God—in the plural number. The latter is not accidental but flows from the substance of the matter. Every grammatical subject can have an indefinite plural number of predicates or of predicative names, and the Godhead does not constitute here an exception in the general number of such subjects. If God was revealed to people "many times and in many ways," both in "the shadow" of images and by a more direct path, then these numerous revelations are at the same time also Names of God, the meaning and significance of each of them able to be disclosed more fully and deeply, which is what St. Dionysius the Areopagite does in his treatise. The general nature of predicative value, or attributiveness, does not change here: a substantive noun, the subject, as was demonstrated above, is not in general equal to its predicates; it is disclosed but not exhausted in them and remains transcendent to them in its ontological core. A substantive noun is something transcendent-immanent, thanks to which predicativity concerning it is possible, as its revelation about itself, its immanent disclosure. In a similar manner the grammatical subject of all grammatical subjects, and the grammatical subject par excellence, the foundation of all predicative value, the subject of all predicates, the Godhead, is disclosed as transcendent-immanent; every revelation of God, every theophany is a new predicate, a new name for the ineffable and unnamable.

God reveals himself to humans and in humans, and humans name God, give Him names by analogy with how they give them to their own kind. Of course, God gives himself these names in and through human beings by His own revelation; however, this occurs through religious experience, mystical contemplation, philosophical speculation, scientific comprehension, moral struggle, in a word, through human creativity and life. It can seem (as it seemed to Feuerbach and many before and after him) that humans create God in their own image, as an objective projection of their own self. This illusion is possible precisely because the naming of God takes place in and through human beings; it is their act, the awakening of their theophoric and theophanic potentials, the realization in them of the enclosed image of God, of their primordial theanthropism.[1]

Strictly speaking, in this revelation of itself through another, in its predicative value, the grammatical subject, the Godhead, does not differ from any other subject to which a predicate is joined. For it forces the one pronouncing a judgment to speak about it, and it speaks in us, in anyone who judges or speaks. It is the revelation of the thing in us and through us. Predicativity is ontologically based on this possibility of finding everything in everything, in universality, in the bond of the world. At the same time, no grammatical subject is exhausted by a given predicate because everything, the whole world, is potentially a predicate for it. Predicates are the names of things that have arisen in acts of revelation of the thing about itself, of judgment and naming.

The difference between the Godhead and the world with its things is not in this moment of the transcendent immanence of every subject to its predicates but in a metaphysical hierarchy. The transcendence of the God-head and the transcendence of a thing to its predicates are of a completely different order. The Godhead is transcendent to the world itself, is premun-dane; It exists in Itself and for Itself, is absolutely self-sufficient, and Its revela-tion in the world, which is expressed in the creation of the world, is an act of unconditional love and God's condescension, Its entrance into the creaturely world, the emptying of God. Therefore, we have here the absolute revela-tion of the Principle, beyond the limit of the cosmos, in the cosmos, through the cosmos. Here transcendence, in which the relation of substance to attri-butes, of subject to predicates is expressed, is not inner worldly, not cosmic, but premundane. Here is the relation of "negative" (apophatic) and positive theology: the premundane Godhead, the Absolute, becomes God for the world and is revealed in it. However, this distinction is found beyond the lim-its of the relation of predicativity, which is the basis of naming. The fact that God is the Absolute that does not suffer any definitions, the absolute NOT, negating every naming, this lies beyond the limits of a judgment-sentence that knows only the relation of subject and predicate. The Absolute, having become God, is transcendent-immanent, subject-object, the bearer of the predicative connection.

The revelation of God in the world is the operation of God, the mani-festation of Divine energy: not the essential Godhead itself, transcendent to the world, but Its energy is what we call God. And if the operations of God in the world and in particular in the human being are revealed as divine names, according to the wisdom of Dionysius the Areopagite, then these names are disclosures of the energy of God, which speaks itself, calls itself in the human being through an act of naming. If in general it is not the hu-man being who names things but they that speak themselves through the human being, if the ontologism of a word consists in this, then of course *a fortiori* one must admit that God, in being revealed in the world through the human being, gives evidence about Himself in human consciousness, names Himself, although by means of a human mouth. Naming is the operation of God in the human being, the human response to it, the manifestation of the energy of God.

This manifestation is at once both distinct from this energy and insepara-ble from it. It is distinct from it because it is brought about in the human be-ing and by human means. It is inseparably linked with it because according to the general nature of a word, Divine energy itself speaks about itself in the human being, is revealed in a word, and the word, the naming of God, proves to be its hominization, as it were, its human incarnation. "And the Word be-came flesh" receives here a broad interpretation: the incarnation of the Word is accomplished not only in the divine incarnation of the Lord Jesus Christ but also in the acts of naming that are accomplished by the human being in response to the operation of God. Already by this alone the Names of God cannot be considered as purely human creations, as nicknames invented by a human being. To believe so signifies simultaneously not only an incomprehension of the nature of a name but also the greatest blasphemy. Absolutely characteristic is the helplessness with which the name-fighters endeavor to harmonize their psychological understanding of the nature of word and name with that piety before the Name of God to which their orthodox sentiment for ecclesiastical reality or mere external correctness obliges them. The whole time they get confused between the affirmation on the one hand that the Name of God, as any name, is given by a human being and thus is reduced to letters and sounds but on the other hand that it is sacred and that it befits them to treat it with piety. Not even an attempt is made to elucidate the motive of this latter and the nature of this sacredness.

The question about the Names of God and the meaning of their veneration, in connection with other questions, was already examined once, covertly, at the seventh ecumenical council, where it received the indirect resolution of the universal church. The problem of icons, at least those with a depiction of God, is in many features analogous with the question under discussion. The chief difficulty of the question is that the meaning of icon veneration can waver between two equally false and inadmissible extremes: between an understanding of icons as purely psychological, human signs, images that none the less are worshipped—the sin of iconolatry, levelled against the orthodox by the iconoclasts; and their full divinization, by which the tangible difference between an icon and the Godhead is forfeited—and the same iconolatry results. This is aggravated even more by subversion of the dogma concerning the indivisibility and inconfusability of the two natures in Christ, for here the creaturely and human is absorbed by the Divine. The objective foundation for the resolution of the question about the veneration of icons could only be the same as that about the nature of the Name of God: the doctrine of the divine energy and the incarnation of the word, which has an objective, ontological basis in the image and likeness of God in the human being. This image and likeness is the real basis of any iconic representation brought about by a human being, whether by word or a different way, by paint, chisel, etc. Because the image of God is the image of the human being, and in it and with it of the whole world (for the world is the human being, the macrocosm is the microcosm), an icon is possible on principle as the result of a theophany, of a revelation of God. God could not be revealed to a stone in a stone, but to a human being in and through a human being (and thus also in a stone). The energy of God, operating in the human being, is united with human energy, is incarnated in it, and there results an inseparable and unconfused joining of the power of God and human operation, the latter being, as it were, the bearer for the power of God.

Therefore, an icon is twofold, theanthropic in its particular sense: it cannot be merged or made identical with what is depicted, but it also cannot be separated from it. It is an incarnate antinomy, as is any joining of the divine and the creaturely. It was characteristic and inevitable that in the question about the icon, the question about the name came to be of central importance and the entire dispute carried the concealed, unconscious character of a dispute about names and their meaning. In fact, where can divine energy be manifested indisputably in an icon? In the picture? But this has only an auxiliary character, and it cannot be a question of any portrait-like resemblance (which is even impossible with respect to the unportrayable Godhead of the first and third Hypostases, indeed essentially it is impossible—although by a different impossibility—with respect to the Savior and the Mother of God). Here one only has to observe the requirements of the canon of a pattern, of an iconographic original, which are often conventional. By its expressiveness no painting has ever become an icon, a bearer of divine power; rather, it has remained only a human psychological document.

What makes an icon an icon is its inscription, its name, as the focus of the incarnation of a word, of a revelation of God. The whole icon is a sprawling name, which is clothed not only in the sounds of a word, but also in different auxiliary means—colors, forms, and images. The image in an icon is a hieroglyph of a word, which therefore must be definitely stylized according to an original, and it gets the meaning of the hieroglyphic alphabet of sacred names. The requirements of iconography themselves are understandable in conjunction with this hieroglyphic quality, this possible extinction of the personal and psychological, this premeditated objectification and schematization. By contrast, without names, without an inscription or hieroglyphics an icon would be completely impossible. This is also said in the decision of the seventh ecumenical council: "An icon is similar to the prototype not according to essence but only according to name *kata to onoma* and according to the position of the depicted members" (i.e., according to the hieroglyphic quality, which can use for its purposes not only a schematic image but also consciously allegorical symbolism, such as a fish, a lamb, a shepherd, etc.). This definition implies not only the filling of an icon with Divine power but also its isolation from it, its duality: "A visible icon has communion with the prototype only by name and not by essence (*kata to onoma . . . ou kata ousian*). The true mind does not recognize on an icon anything more than its communication by name, and not by essence with the one depicted on it" (Mansi III, 241, 244, 258). Hence, the iconoclasts even then proved to be name-fighters, *onomatomachoi*, as patriarch Nikephoros calls them (ibid., 178). Of course, it is impossible not to wish for greater precision and intelligibility in these formulas; however, the central meaning of the name in an icon comes out here in bold enough relief. This same question naturally comes up in St. Theodore Studite's theologizing about the veneration of sacred icons, which he connects with the One by the indivisibility of naming (*kata ameres tes kleseos*).[2]

What has been said up to now concerned only icons of the Savior, God the Father, the Holy Spirit, and the Holy Trinity. But the nature of other icons should obviously be understood in a similar way according to the sense of the seventh ecumenical council, first of which are icons of the Mother of God, and then of different saints. The historically conditioned distinctiveness of the iconography of the Theotokos lies in the multitude of types of representation or originals, corresponding to the multiplicity of icons: the different schemas in which these originals appear correspond to various motifs or events in the representation of the Theotokos (so too of the Savior). But here it is not the pictorial quality of the drawing or the portrait-like resemblance (which is obviously impossible) that makes an icon an icon but the act of naming, which is done externally in the form of an inscription. It establishes the unity of the icon with the One Being Depicted, invokes her power. A name is that essence, that energy, that pours itself out on an icon.

Therefore, in a representation, in a drawing for an icon (of course, not for a painting), the schematism of the original has significance so that every icon, in essence, consists of naming, of inscription—hieroglyphic and in letters. At least, this is what is essential; for an icon, everything else, i.e., the artistic quality, is, properly speaking, auxiliary and secondary, it is the human (sometimes too human) in the divine. As an icon, the Sistine Madonna would not differ at all from the most common work of a Vladimir icon-dauber. Its artistic merits, by acting on the human soul, lifting and warming it by means of art, would operate as . . . well, fine singing or the way a church organ operates, although what is decisive is not *how* they play, but *what* they play. Of course, the power of grace can act by regenerating and changing the representation itself, not in an artistic sense, but in the sense of a spiritual face that, generally speaking, iconography, unlike painting, is looking for. (The pictures of the Renaissance, with all their artistic merits, in most cases are quite unfit to be icons.) To find an artistic balance in an icon, to maintain an iconic style without sacrificing the laws of artistry, is one of the most difficult tasks of iconography, resolved only in the happy joining of art and piety.

The same thing has to be said about icons of the saints, the hieroglyphs of which are given by the "original." Here the act of naming, in letters and symbols, has decisive significance, and here too there can be different hieroglyphs corresponding to different aspects of the life of the one represented. This hieroglyphic quality gives scope to the vividness, to the pictorial element in general, which has more room because people are depicted who have acted and lived in a definite historical situation. However, here too the naturalistic element in psychology and history, no matter how artistically it may be expressed, can prove to be excessive and even alien to iconic representation, so far as it draws attention to itself and contradicts the hieroglyphic quality of the image, turning it into a picture. An icon's hieroglyph gives, if only schematically, a representation of spiritual completeness, not of becoming or incompleteness, which inevitably is conveyed in a historical picture. Therefore, from the point of view of historical naturalism, an icon's treatment of a subject is characterized by conventionality, stylization, and even falsity, and vice versa. In St. Theodore Studite's opinions about icons, the question about the Holy Cross is especially singled out, which likewise is examined in the spirit of a general study of icons, i.e., that here too the act of naming has the decisive significance. "The cross, on which Christ was raised, is so named both according to the meaning of the act of naming (*tei semasiai tes prosegorias*) and according to the nature of the life-creating wood. Its representation (*to ektupoma autou*) is called 'cross' only according to the significance of the act of naming but not according to the nature of the life-creating wood, since a representation of the cross can be made out of a different material. But nevertheless, it participates in the name of the prototype and consequently also in the veneration and honor that is rendered to this name." (PG 99, 361 A). Here, evidently, it is not the representation of the cross that is meant, but the crucifixion, which merges for Christians inseparably with the symbol of the cross. For the latter a hieroglyphic inscription, not one in letters, would be sufficient and essential, i.e., the very form of the cross, incarnated in one or other material. Thus a cross is usually shown where it has independent meaning: on churches, walls, in the sign of the cross, in the act of blessing— here the sign alone suffices; by contrast, the cross as crucifixion, except for a corresponding portrayal, requires an inscription, i.e., it already merges fully with an icon.

Thus, if the Name of God is in a certain sense the verbal icon of the Godhead, then vice versa, the real icon of the Godhead is His Name. There are as many of these icons as there are names, and as many names as there are designations. In the Old Testament, we have a whole series of such names of the Lord, received from the acts of naming. Elohim, Sabaoth, Adonai, the Holy One, the Blessed One, the Most High, Creator, the Good: each of these names can be made a predicate for a subject—for the Godhead—and in fact have been so; it is the impress of the Name of God in a word, as is also any icon.

In the issue of icon veneration, the question arose not only about the meaning of any veneration but also about its limits, i.e., about the difference between an icon and a non-icon. Something can be a non-icon simply because it lacks the elements of an icon (in an absolute sense, by the way, this is impossible, and the human being and the whole world through him bear the image of the Godhead, are natural icons, divine symbols, hieroglyphs). In a particular sense, chosen persons or even peoples are an icon. Thus, Israel is frequently called the one bearing the Name of God on its forehead, i.e., His specially chosen icon. A non-icon can also be the result of our having something more than an icon. What, then, is more than an icon? That in which the duality of an icon is overcome, its human and hieroglyphic quality, where we have the realest presence of the Godhead. Such are the Holy Gifts, which are not an icon but more, for they are He Who is portrayed in an icon, the Lord Jesus Himself under the form of bread and wine, with his Divine Body and Blood. Such an absorption of the natural by the divine, i.e., transubstantiation, we do not have in an icon; it is of a different nature with respect to such holiness and always remains so. (The doctrine of the name-fighters that the true icon was the Eucharistic bread and wine was repudiated in this sense: it was explained that here we have not an icon but the true Body and Blood of Christ (Mansi I, p. 260).) But we have a non-icon not only in that singular and exceptional case when it is a question of the Holy Gifts but when we have consecrated and transubstantiated matter: holy water, holy myrrh, holy bread. Here that outpouring of the gifts of the Holy Spirit occurs that does not take place in the consecration of a holy icon; here nature is consecrated. Not a name, or a representation, or a symbolic penetration, but the very flesh or matter here becomes a different nature to itself and belongs to a different world, whereas an icon belongs to this world or, rather, is found at the point of intersection of two worlds. The matter of a holy icon remains itself: the board remains a board, and the paints, paints. Their use for an icon imparts to them a special honor or sacredness, demanding a pious attitude; however, this is a result of the image for which they make room. This image is above them, through them, but not in them: it lies like a thin barely perceptible layer, which however can be separated, although it also sanctifies its bed. Therefore, incidentally, there is a palpable difference in the honor shown various icons, for which of course there can be no analogy with the sacredness of the Holy Gifts or even holy water and the like in various churches.

The Holy Gifts are always equal and invariable, so that the mere thought of their difference would be a sign of impiety. On the contrary, it is clear that each icon is distinctive by its efficacious power and has, so to say, a different intensity, which is expressed in the veneration of esteemed icons, miraculous icons, in the composition of special services for them, etc. Here one can bring an analogy with a living icon—with a human being and the holiness of the saints: one star differs from other stars in glory. If an icon is only a place of the presence of the power of God, and not this power itself, then the possibility of a distinction is natural and on principle intelligible—not only of reverence (which is a subjective result) but also of efficacy itself, of holiness (which is the objective foundation. All icons are holy, and of course, potentially miraculous; however, by the will of God this is effectively brought to light only in definite, predetermined instances).

We have diverged from the immediate question about the Names of God to an aspect of the question about the meaning of icon veneration, but this is not by chance, for it has turned out that in essence it is the same question. For a holy icon is not only a picture, a human article, a photograph, it is rather a bearer of the power of God and a sacred hieroglyph of the Name of God. The Name itself, the Naming of God, is not only a means for designating, chosen in consideration of convenience, it is not a nickname or an empty "symbol" (as they are sometimes expressed, perverting and abasing the idea of a symbol), but it is also a divine icon in word, a sacred symbol whose essence is in the duality of natures. The Name of God is not only a means for designating or invoking the Godhead but is also a verbal icon, and hence it is holy.

So, then, the Names of God are verbal icons of the Godhead, the incarnation of the Divine Energies, theophanies; they bear the stamp of Divine revelation. Here are united indivisibly and without confusion, as in an icon, divine energy and the human power of speech: humans speak, they name, but what they name is given and revealed to them. There this human side in naming gives occasion for skeptical name-fighting to consider the Name of God as a human invention, a moniker or a kind of algebraic sign (and in this sense "a symbol"). But in order to be consistent in this point of view, it is necessary to take it to the end and acknowledge that the content of word-naming is also an entirely human work, an act of human cognition, fully immanent to it. Consequently, this will signify that God is completely immanent to the world and the human being, in other words, that the world and the human being are God—the spirit of Buddhism and contemporary monism, which are turned hostilely against Christianity with its faith in the transcendent Godhead who is revealed to the human being. In such a worldview, the Name of God expresses concepts and judgments as does any other. Between it and other words-names, there is no difference at all, except in content.

One can go still further in this monism and stop at the point of view of skepticism or outright atheism. What can the Name of God signify for an atheist? Obviously, first of all, that it is *not* a revelation having its objective content, for no kind of reality corresponding to the Name of God exists for atheists. For them the Name of God signifies some abstract concept serving to express a certain "transcendental illusion" for which they can have their own theoretical explanations or not. Here in any case the meaning of the Name of God is tied entirely to the subjective human sphere; it is enclosed in and generated by it. With a favorable attitude toward it, this illusion receives an ontological interpretation as the expression of the highest and hidden human essence, of the Godhead in the human being, in the spirit of the religion of Anthropotheism,[3] as Feuerbach and Auguste Comte developed it. With an unfavorable attitude, the significance of this name is reduced to a sort of phantom, like a hallucination, reveries, and "superstitions." In both cases, an identical impotence is ascribed to the Name of God. Objectively we are here dealing with religious insensitivity, blindness, which for various reasons cannot access a sensation of the world. Here, although the word for designating the Godhead remains in the lexicon borrowed from a general wealth of words, strictly speaking, the Name of God is absent; it is only a sound, a nickname completely to the taste of the name-fighters, religious emptiness, and a single sonic husk without a seed.

However, it is necessary to note that we have a similar emptiness only when maintaining religious equilibrium, i.e., in total blindness, indifference, and somnolence. Such a position is so unnatural for humankind that they can be found in it only by exception. Much more frequently, hostile insult and theomachy are hidden under the mask of indifference, and the Name of God is flouted and reviled, as when they smash and destroy an icon not as a simple board but as an icon. In such a case it is no longer possible to speak of emptiness, lethargy, and a deadened state; an evil will exists, namely, malicious abuse combined with unbelief. However contradictory this state may seem, it is psychologically quite routine. Theomachian abuse is not godlessness, but god-contrariness, enmity toward God, and although the Name of God is reviled, in reality it scorches the revilers. For demons, belonging as they do to the spiritual world, do not have the protection of a body and relative blindness, and despite all their hatred for It, the Name of God acts as a flame that they cannot approach.

Let us take another case of immanentism in the use of the Name of God that differs from the foregoing. This is a *philosophical* and not a religious use of the Name, when *the idea* of God is meant. For example, in Aristotle, Spinoza, and Hegel, the philosophical mind, no matter how pious it might be, generally is concerned with this. For philosophical reason all problems are immanent to thinking, and it encounters God only as an object of thought on a field of thought. Strictly speaking, one can speak here only of a revelation in the immanent that is the same as that of every substantive noun or subject (as explained above), and the idea of God, differing from other ideas in content, does not differ from them qualitatively. If the Name of God is also an icon of the Godhead, then it is so only as a natural icon, in the sense that the image of God is in the human being and in the world, and it is identified by philosophizing thought, which however inevitably carries with itself limitation and psychologism. However, even philosophizing reason, in comprehending the Godhead at a certain height, begins to perceive it not only as its own idea or a problem of thought, but as a vital efficacious essence, and for it the Name of God becomes all the more the power of God not only subjectively but also objectively. It is permeated with reverence before it, it becomes for it an icon not made by human hands, though natural. One must not forget the correlation that naturally and inevitably exists between philosophy and religion, where the first is only derivative, a "superstructure" on top of the second and differs not so much by its object as by the special method of examination or treatment.

The next question that arises on this path, and an enticing question at that, is about the Names of God not in philosophy or atheism but in religions, only not in "revealed" but in pagan religions. What do they signify? A philosophical idea? Obviously not, because they arise in religion and have a liturgical, cultic meaning. An illusion, nothing? Likewise, undoubtedly no, as this contradicts everything. First of all because in the many names of gods their naturalistic provenance and meaning shines through with complete clarity,[4] and then it would be a religious absurdity conflicting necessarily with the definite view of the Bible, which does not at all consider the gods to be simple illusions, or their names empty sounds. "Do not recall the name of other gods, and let it not be heard from your lips" (Ex 23:13); "and it shall be on that day, says the Lord Of Hosts, I *shall destroy* the names of idols from this land, and they will not be remembered any more" (Zech 13:2). There is as little basis for this in the biblical outlook as for considering idolatrous sacrifices and the idols themselves as empty space. Besides, it is necessary to take into consideration that in paganism, in the so-called natural religions, which represent enormous differences and nuances, we are dealing precisely with a religious, prayerful, incantatory use of the Name of God or the names of gods. Sacrifices are carried out with them, sacred hymns are replete with them. An answer to this can be given essentially only in connection with what we think about pagan religion, the objective character of its revelation, and the pagan gods (see the corresponding chapter in *Unfading Light*).[5] That pagan gods are not empty space, and hence that their names have some power, is sufficiently attested to by that "jealousy" with which God, the jealous one, treats the constant deviations of the Hebrews on their path of idol worship. The presence of unrevealed religions alongside a revealed religion is a providential mystery that remains undisclosed even until now. But even now it would be folly and blindness to deny the realism of religion outside of Christianity, and if the falling away from Christianity into paganism is the worship of demons, then the abiding in paganism from the beginning, especially when Christianity is unknown, can be natural piety, and more than this, a "natural" revelation of divine powers, of the sophianity of the cosmos. Therefore we cannot say that Zeus, Athena, Apollo, Isis, etc. were simple illusions and fabulous beings, but even less can we say this about the elevated divine worship of the Hindus—Vedanta, or about Islam (although in its relationship with Christianity, there are already antichristian and Christ-fighting elements inherent in it), in general about any concrete religion. The names of gods are here real powers of revelation of these gods: in each particular case, this reality and this revelation can be distinguished qualitatively—from real demonism to elemental naturalism, from orgiastic ecstasy to the lofty divine inspiration of Socrates. The prophet speaks about this with peaceful laconic realism: "all the peoples walk, each in the name of their god, but we shall walk in the name of the Lord our God forever" (Mic 4:5). The ways of God are inscrutable. One thing seems indisputable to us: a name-fighting skeptical attitude is inapplicable even to the names of pagan gods.[6]

According to all the explanations that have been made, such an attitude is blasphemous and senseless when applied to the Name of God in revealed religion, in the Old and New Testaments. Surely if the true God really is revealed to people and these revelations are imprinted in the Names of God, how, then, can one allow the blasphemous thought that the Name of God is only a human fabrication, a nickname? To be consistent, then, the name-fighters must return to iconoclasm and see here, along with the Protestants, only human illustrations of sacred events. Falling down in prayer before these illustrations is for them idolatry. But surely the Name of God is not only a cognitive, theoretical judgment, rather it is a means for summoning God in prayer; it is a ladder uniting heaven and earth: the human being addresses, summons, and God hears His Name in this invocation. In this is the power, holiness, mystery, and tremulous terror of the Name of God, for in calling on Him we stand in the presence of the Godhead, we already have

Him in the very Name, we fashion His icon in sound. If God were far off
and estranged from us, "transcendent," and cold, like the abstract divinity
of the deists, then our word too that names Him, would be theoretical, inef-
fectual, abstract; it would become like our abstractions ending in -**ity** (unity,
quality, plurality, etc.) or -**ence** (patience, confidence, etc.). If the Godhead
were our caprice and illusion, then its name would be powerless. But in the
Name of God, the Very Lord names Himself in us and through us; in it the
thunder sounds and the lightning of Sinai flashes for us; the energy of God
is present that (in accordance with the conclusion of the Constantinopolitan
council apropos the Palamite disputes)[7] is indivisible from the very Godhead,
although it is not identifiable with It. Our sinful indifference, distraction, and
blindness prevent us from being fully aware of the whole magnitude of the
Name of God; when we pronounce it, we seemingly partake of the power of
God. Name-fighting is unconscious, not fully thought through Anthropotheism or godlessness.

Let us return to the question of the sacred Name of God. Until now, in
speaking of it, we had in mind only the Names of God (in the sense of St.
Dionysius the Areopagite), i.e., naming, in which revelations of the Godhead
or of His properties are anchored: predicates that were turned into subjects
that became substantive nouns that acquired substantiality, i.e., the divine
power inescapably inherent to any Name of God. In *this* sense, the *Name
of God* is a general category encompassing many names, from which each
one, however, is in its place a Name. A *name* is the foundation, so to say,
the ontological locus for various acts of naming of predicative provenance.
However, alongside these naming predicates and the predicative names that
flow from them, there can be a "proper" Name of God, at least conceivably,
that, similar to any other "proper name" in keeping with what was explained
above, is not predicative or does not have such a meaning. It is no longer a
crystal of naming but a name as subject, a grammatical subject, a substance
for all other acts of naming. It would be audacious to pose the question
about what kind of name it is or if it is unique. Even when God-pleasing men
who merited divine revelations asked about this Name by misunderstanding
and ignorance, evidently from an undue curiosity, they received the answer:
"Why are you asking about my Name? It is wondrous." The patriarch Israel
the God-contender received such an answer when he questioned the One
fighting with him about His Name (Gen 32:27–28). A similar reply was given
to Manoah by the "Angel of God," who foretold future events for him (Judg
13:17–18). The Divine Name was not communicated to him. The Name of
God in the proper sense of the word, not as a revelation about God but as
the direct Power of God, the energy of God, proceeding from the substantial

essence, cannot be found by a human being in himself, neither in his thought nor in his life, for it is transcendent to it. Every naming of God received as the result of the revelation of the Godhead about Itself, natural or deliberate, is anthropomorphic in the sense that a human being in or through himself, as macrocosm or microcosm, recognizes the essence of God. Therefore, such acts of naming always have a human sense and significance; they are the projection of the human on the divine, or, the other way around, of the divine on the human. This is a legitimate and inevitable anthropomorphism, for the human being has the image and likeness of God, and through the human the divine is revealed to him. This is why all naming of God, written not with uppercase but lowercase letters, is also human naming and can be applied to a human being: such as Lord, Sabaoth, Adonai, Creator, Provider, Father—all of these have also human meanings, and they become names of God only through attribution to the Godhead as to a subject. The agglutinating copulas make them such. By contrast, a proper name, even if it has a verbal, human origin, cannot be a predicate for anything but only a subject. And as the proper name of a human being is his pronoun **I**, so too the Name of God is God's **I**, dread and wondrous. It is completely obvious that *such* a name, the proper Name of God, or perhaps one of the infinite veils of this dread NAME, can be communicated to a human being only by revelation, and by a revelation in the proper sense, a communication of the transcendent in the immanent. The bridge by which the transcendent can be revealed without destroying the immanent, without tearing it to pieces, is the word-name, the logos in the human being. The sonic veil of a word in the given case covers the sun and protects the human being from blinding and scorching: as we look at the sun through darkened glass, so too is the NAME of God concealed for us, but at the same time revealed in a word, in our human, sonic word, which proves to be a certain absolute Icon of the uncontainable, unbearable, transcendent Name, of the very essence of God, the I of God.

Here we must return to the already familiar distinction in a word—of phoneme, morpheme, and sememe. A phoneme corresponds to the paints and board in an icon, the morpheme to the hieroglyphic quality of the "original," which gives the outline of the representation, and the sememe is the name itself, the power of the representation. With respect to the sememe we have in addition a twofold differentiation: the immediate significance of the word as a human word—that which corresponds to the "inner form of the word," (e.g., Yahweh—"Who Is" is the adverbial participial form from the verb "to be" and has a corresponding meaning) and the significance of a regenerated, transubstantiated word, which has become the Name of God. The difference between Names of God and the Name of God as such is connected with the fact that their independent, verbal, predicative meaning lives in them, whereas here it is completely absorbed by the name, it exists only as a name. In both cases the grace and power of God are present, which is why the Name of God always and everywhere is sacred and worthy of being worshipped. But in the first case we have only a gracious hallowing of an element—namely of a word; we have, so to say, a holy word, similar to how we have holy water, holy blessed bread or *prosphora, antidoron,*[8] even holy myrrh. Although here the grace of the Holy Spirit descends, the element nevertheless keeps its proper nature: it is holy *water,* holy *bread,* etc. This element is the natural vessel for receiving the grace of the Holy Spirit, and even more than this, it receives grace precisely by its own nature, as water or bread, etc. In the second case, when we have, as it were, the proper Name of God, God's I, the proper nature of the word, its "inner form," or significance, seemingly evaporates. Yahweh is the Name of God not at all because it signifies *who is,* for the attribute of being still does not express the essence of God in any exclusive sense, it stands here alongside other attributes or names. This word makes the exclusive presence of God's power in it the Name of God. One can assume—of course purely theoretically—that for the Name of God one of the other designations of the Godhead could have been chosen, e.g., Elohim, Sabaoth, Creator, Father, etc. (We understand how impossible this assumption is according to the real essence of the matter in the face of the accomplished revelation of God about His name, but we dwell on this supposition as an auxiliary hypothesis for illustrating our thought.) However, once the revelation has occurred, and the Lord has proclaimed, "I am Yahweh," the independent meaning of the word *who is* completely dissolves and becomes only a verbal form for containing the Name of God, for containing what is a super-word for human language while being a word that humans accommodate. One can say that the proper meaning of the word *who is* no longer has that meaning that it had in the moment of choosing this word for the Name. After this, it becomes transparent glass and only lets the rays through but does not reflect them.

If we return to our comparison, we will have to say that the proper element of the word was not preserved here, as it was preserved in holy water or bread; rather, it was transubstantiated similarly to how bread and wine completely and to the end are transubstantiated only *under the appearance* of bread and wine. That which had its proper materiality and nature now becomes only "under the appearance of," stops being itself and is transubstantiated to the end. And yet, to continue this analogy, from the bread and wine *before* the performance of the sacrament, certain very strictly established qualities are required, which are retained even when they become only their own semblance. So, too, the word that has served as the matter of the Name of God keeps its verbal nature and its meaningfulness. A measureless distance exists between these definite and predetermined qualities of bread and wine and the Body and Blood of Christ, and only a miracle of God's grace can efface this abyss. Similarly, between the meaning of the word "being" in itself—which existed long before and continues to exist in the human lexicon as one of the innumerable words having a definite meaning—and the Name of God **Yahweh**, lies a chasm that is filled up by the Divine will, for us unfathomable, and having the power of an absolute revelation.

We are aware of the whole audacity of arbitrary analogies and approximations with such a sacred thing as the awesome Mysteries of Christ; however, it seems to us that the very essence of the matter compels us to this analogy. In a sacrament, we always have an absolutely indecomposable concretum; therefore, here too it is a question only of analogy, of elucidation by approximation or contrasting of the one miracle of gracious transubstantiation through another. We have in the Name of God that kind of unique *sacrament of the word* not reducible to anything else, its transubstantiation, thanks to which the word, chosen to become the Name, becomes the verbal throne of the Name of God. More than an icon, it becomes the temple, the altar, the shrine, the Holy of Holies, the place for the presence of God and of encounter with God. The Lord ordered a tent to be built, "a tabernacle," and "I shall dwell in their midst" (Ex 25:8). "I shall be revealed to you, and above the lid between the two cherubim that are on top of the ark of revelation, I shall speak about everything whatsoever I may command the sons of Israel through you" (Ex 25:22). This tabernacle of the tent, and later the temple, are built so that the Name of God may dwell there (about which below).

All the seductiveness of the idea of a word-icon and of the transubstantiation of the word in the Name of God disappears when we stop to consider the word as a kind of human artifact that does not even have a natural (I will even say material) character. On the contrary, one must recognize and sense that the human word is an element, natural and original, that is accessible to enlightenment, regeneration, transubstantiation, and transfiguration like any other natural element and any other human power and energy. A word is a symbol—it is appropriate for us to recall here this initial basic formula of ours—and a symbol not in that nihilistic sense of a sign invented by humankind, as the name-fighters and iconoclasts always understand it, but in the sense of the combining of two natures, and hence of power and depth. Not just a word is a symbol; the forces of nature can also be a symbol, as can the elements of nature, which become a receptacle of other content, of other forces. In this sense (but not in the sense of some allegory) divine worship

THE NAME OF GOD

is symbolic and the sacraments are symbolic. And there, in this sense of the co-presence of different natures—which is the sole worthy sense of the idea of symbol—is the most sacred of symbols, the inseparable and unconfused union of God and human being in Jesus Christ, but then the sacred Name of God is the most sacred verbal symbol. It is precisely by setting out from the idea of a symbol and of the symbolic nature of a word that one can grasp the symbolic meaning of the Name of God and the real presence of God's power in it.

This form, this Name spoken in human language, this incarnation of the Name, the verbal incarnation of God in the precise sense of the word, could be only a special operation of God's will, of God's love for humankind and God's condescension, of His voluntary kenosis. Corresponding to the two testaments there were two revelations of the Name of God, the Old Testament **Yahweh** to Moses, and the New Testament **Jesus** to the Virgin Mary, and in her to the whole human race; two images of the Name of the God-head not made by hands. Let us call to mind the features with which this singular and staggering event is described in the Old Testament. "And Moses said to God, here I will approach the sons of Israel and say to them, the God of your fathers has sent me to you. But they will say to me, what is his name? What am I to say to them? God said to Moses, I am the One Who Is, I am who I am. And he said, so shall you say to the sons of Israel, the One Who Is sent me to you" (Ex 3:3–14). "I appeared to Abraham, Isaac and Jacob with my Name 'God Almighty,' but with my Name 'Yahweh' I have not been revealed to them" (Ex 6:3). God communicates His Name as a new revelation, which then is kept like a Dread Secret, a Sanctuary and a Power, being known only to the one high priest, who according to tradition pronounced it on the festival of purification at the entrance to the Holy of Holies for the sprinkling with sacrificial blood.

For every pious or even simply attentive and conscientious reader of the Old Testament it must be clear that the expression "Name of God" occupies here a completely special independent place. To say that it is only a means for expressing the idea of "God" means to say nothing, to manifest only a blasphemously flippant attitude toward the biblical text, amounting to its direct distortion. For even if this verbal equation were true, i.e., "The Name of God = God," then too the question would arise about the meaning and provenance of *precisely* such a descriptive expression. Of course, this sum-mary characterization is incorrect, but it can be understood from the desire to look carefully at the biblical text where the various cases and nuances in the use of the Name of God are completely evident.[9] First, those cases strike one's eyes when the expression *Name of God* can in no way be interpreted simply as a synonym, a descriptive expression that replaces *God*, but designates a particular means of the presence of God, of the power of His name in His Name.

The Name of God is united and converges with the concept of the Glory of God, which cannot be treated as descriptive expressions even by lovers of simplified synonymy (Ex 16:7, 10; Num 16:19; 1 Kings 8:10–11; Ex 35:2, 40:5; Sir 45:3). Ex 33:18, 19: "And he (Moses) said, show me your glory. And he said (the Lord to Moses), I will bring before you my glory and I will proclaim the Name of Yahweh before you, and who is to be shown mercy I will show mercy, and who is to be pitied I will pity"; 34:5: "and the Lord descended in a cloud and stopped there opposite him and proclaimed the Name of Yahweh." Here the manifestation of the Glory of God and the proclamation of the Name Yahweh are compared as two aspects of theophany, as theophanic energies. In this light the commandment receives its meaning, which not only forbids an impious attitude towards the Godhead, realized through the word, but expressly protects the sanctity of the Name of God, similar to how the sanctity of the Glory of God was protected when it appeared in the tent of meeting, as the story of the "protestant" performance of Korah, Dathan, and Abiram indicates: Num 16:31 (the text of the third commandment in the book of Exodus is found precisely in this context where the narrative only just introduced also stands). Ex 20:7: "Do not pronounce the Name of the Lord your God in vain, for the Lord will not leave without punishment the one who pronounces His Name in vain" (parallels in Leviticus 19:12 with another nuance and more narrow content;[10] Deut 5:11; identical to Exodus, Prov 30:9). If we turn our attention to the general context and content of the Decalogue, the specific content of the third commandment becomes even clearer. After the proclamation of belief in one true God and the prohibition of idolatry, veneration of the sacred Name, which had just been solemnly revealed and proclaimed on Sinai, is established in order to go on to the establishment of the sacred seasons (Sabbaths and weekdays) in the fourth commandment. Cf. for example Isa 48:9, "I have set aside my anger for the sake of my Name, and for the sake of my Glory I have restrained myself from eradicating you"; and Dan 3:52, "blessed is the Name of your Glory, holy and praiseworthy and exalted forever."

The expression "Name of God" has a quite particular significance in connection with the temple and the cult in general. Here in no manner can it be a question of *pars pro toto*, of the use of this expression directly instead of *God* (although this, too, as already indicated, would require its clarification not only by means of the theory of Hebrew literature but also theology). No, here the Name of God is taken directly as a real, living force, a Divine energy, which abides at the center of the life of the temple. The temple is the place of habitation of the Name of God; it is constructed for the Name of God. If we recall what is known about the great reverence of the Old Testament Hebrews before the sacred tetragrammaton and about the place that it occupied in divine worship, forming its very heart (as it is pronounced by the high priest in the most solemn and mysterious moment of the whole liturgical life—at the sprinkling of the ark with sacrificial blood), it will become clear for us that for the Hebrews with their religious realism there was not even a possibility of conceiving the temple other than as the place of habitation of the Name of God, as the sacred chronicles bear witness. Already in Deut 12:11, we encounter Moses's testament: "when (after settling in the Promised Land) the Lord your God shall choose the place for his Name to abide, there bring everything that I command you." The first book of Kings tells about the construction of the temple by Solomon. Initially, before this construction, "the people were still offering their sacrifices on the summits, for the house of the Name of God had not been constructed before that time" (1 Kings 3:2). Although David was still thinking about this, it was declared to him through the prophet Nathan that Solomon "will build a house for my Name" (2 Sam 7:13, 1 Chr 17:12, simply "he will build me a house"). When the time came for its construction, Solomon sent to Hiram, the king of Tyre, to say, "You know that David my father could not build *the house of the Name of the Lord* his *God* because of the multitude of wars with the surrounding peoples, until the Lord had subdued them under the soles of his feet. But now the Lord my God has granted me rest on every side: there is no enemy and there are no obstacles. So I intend to build *the house of the Name of the Lord my God*, as the Lord told my father David, saying, 'your son whom I will seat on your throne in place of you, he will build *the house of my Name*'" (1 Kings 5:3–5). The account in the first book of Chronicles is a parallel for this, where David himself speaks about the construction of the temple and in exactly the same expressions as Solomon (1 Chr 22:6–8): "and (David) summoned his son Solomon and bequeathed to him the construction of the house for the Lord God of Israel. And David said to Solomon, my son, I had it in my heart to build a house in the name of the Lord my God, but the word of the Lord came to me and it was said: you have shed much blood and conducted great wars; you shall not build *the house for my Name*." Verse 10: "he (Solomon) shall build the house for my Name." Verse 11: "And now, my son, the Lord be with you so that you may be well consoled and may build a house for the Lord my God as he said about you." In such precise expressions, David speaks of this before the assembly of elders (1 Chr 28:3): "God said to me, do not build *a house for my Name*, because you are a war-faring man and have shed blood." Verse 6: "Solomon your son will build my house and my courts," 2 Chr 2:4—a parallel to the story about the embassy to Hiram: "See I am building *the house of the Name of the Lord my God*, for His consecration so that fragrant incense burns before Him," etc. Further on the liturgical, cultic intentions for this house are defined more precisely, verses 5–6: "The house which I am building, is great because great is our God, higher than all gods. And will anyone have sufficient power to build a house for Him, when the heaven and the heavens of heavens do not contain Him? And who am I that I could build a house for Him except for offerings before his face?"

It is necessary to pause next on the description of the consecration of the temple. When the priests brought the Ark of the Covenant in, the Glory of the Lord filled the temple in the form of a cloud. 1 Kings 8:12–13: "Then Solomon said, 'the Lord said that He favors living in darkness,' and I have constructed the temple as a dwelling for You, a place for You to abide for ever." The history of the construction of the temple goes on: "God said, from that day when I led my people Israel of out Egypt, I did not choose a town in one of the tribes of Israel that a house should be built, in which *my Name* would abide (but I chose Jerusalem *for the abiding in it of my Name*). . . . David my father had it in his heart to build *a temple of the Name of the Lord God of Israel*, but the Lord told David, my father, 'you have in your heart to build a temple *for my Name*; it is good that this lies in your heart, but it is not you who shall build a temple, but your son . . . shall build *the temple for my Name*. And the Lord fulfilled His word which he uttered. I . . . built *the temple of the Lord God of Israel*" (1 Kings 8:16–20).[11] In King Solomon's prayer for the whole nation, we likewise read: "Let your eyes be opened on this temple day and night, on this place about which You said: *my Name shall be there*" (1 Kings 8:29) (parallel, 2 Chr 6:20, "where you promised to place *Your Name*"), and further he asks God to attend to those praying who are coming there and "confessing *Your Name*" (verses 33, 35) (cf. 2 Chr 6:24, 26). "If a foreigner who is not from Your people Israel comes from a distant land because of *Your Name*, for they will hear about Your great Name and about Your powerful hand and about Your outstretched arm . . . hear from heaven . . . that all peoples know Your Name . . . so that they know that this temple which I have built is called *by Your Name*" (2 Chr 8:41–43).[12] (See later in the same prayer, verse 44, "and to the temple which I have built for *Your Name*," and 48). After the consecration of the temple there was a (second) appearance of God to Solomon. God said to him, "I have heard your prayer and your petition, which you have asked me. I have consecrated this temple which you built, so that *my Name* abide *there forever*; and my eyes and my heart shall be there for all days" (1 Kings 9:3; cf. 2 Chr 7:16). Verse 7: "the temple which I consecrated *to my Name*," the same as 2 Chr 7:20. Cf. 2 Kings 21:4, "and (Manasseh) erected an altar in the house of the Lord, about which the Lord said, in Jerusalem *I will place my Name*" (the same as verse 7, "in Jerusalem *I place my Name* . . . forever").

Therefore, the temple is the place of habitation for the Name of God, where it "is placed for the ages." In other writers, we sometimes encounter a definition of the temple as a place over which *the Name of God* is spoken. The text of the prophet Isaiah (Isa 18:17) refers to this: "to the place of *the Name of the Lord of Hosts* on mount Sion." Likewise, for example, in the prophet Jeremiah: "you come and stand before my face in this house, over which *is said the Name of God*, and you say, 'we are saved,' in order to do all these abominations henceforth. Has not this house been made into a den of thieves in your eyes, over which *my Name is said*? . . . Go then to my place in Shiloh, where I previously *designated that my Name would abide*, and look what I have done with it. . . . I shall do the same with this house, over which *my Name* is said" (Jer 7:10–12, 14).[13]

The cited texts themselves are sufficient evidence that the expression *Name of God* in connection with the temple is not at all only a substitute or synonym for the word *God* but has a completely independent meaning, the denial of which would denote an act of violence on the text. It is a question of the deliberate abiding in the temple of the Name of God, alongside the Glory of God, as the power of God, as the energy of God. For the Hebrew religious consciousness there was nothing strange and contradictory in this; this is already clear from the central significance in the cult that belonged to the solemn proclamation of the Name of God. Not only was it proclaimed, but it also existed as a vital energy even outside of this proclamation, having as a place of special abiding the temple as the focus of divine worship. (If the voice of skeptical rationalism is going to say that there cannot be a special place for the abiding of the Name of God, for as an ideal entity it is not connected with a place, one must point out that exactly the same consideration can be applied as well to the temple as a place of the deliberate abiding of the Godhead, the house of God, for the Godhead is not connected with a place. If the condescension of God to humankind, expressed in theophanies and revelations, includes a corresponding anthropomorphism (or anthropologism), then there are no more impediments for seeing in the temple the house of God as well as the place for the abiding of the Name of God.) The deliberate connection of the temple with the Name of God, which for the name-fighters must seem to be some kind of incomprehensible whim of language, in actual fact flows from the connection of cultic ritual and divine worship with the Name of God, which is also a ladder leading up from earth to heaven. It is therefore necessary to treat the evidence of the sacred text with full confidence and realism that the Name of God abided in the temple.

The understanding of the Name of God as a power or energy is manifested also in a series of texts in which the inscription or presence of the Name of God appears as a sign but at the same time as the foundation of a special election and graced state. In this sense, the chosen people of God are called by this spoken Name. "Thus let my Name be summoned upon the sons of Israel, and I (the Lord) will bless them" (Num 6:27). "And all the peoples of the earth will see that the Name of the Lord (your God) is called upon you and they will fear you" (Deut 28:10). "And *my* people will submit, who are *called by my Name*" (2 Chr 7:14). "Each one who *is called by my Name*, whom I made for my glory, formed and arranged" (Isa 43:7). "We were made such over whom You as it were never ruled, and over which Your Name was not named" (Isa 43:9—no such thing). "I was revealed to those not asking about me; those not seeking me found me: here I am, here I am, I said to the people who are not named with my Name" (Isa 65:1). "You o Lord are among us and *Your Name is spoken over us*" (Jer 14:9). "Gaze on the town on which *your Name is spoken*. . . . Do not delay for Your Own sake, my God, for *your Name is spoken on your town and on your people*" (Dan 9:18–19). "*Your Name is spoken on Israel and his race*" (Bar 2:15, cf. 26). (Here also 3 Esd 3:14, "nowhere will Your Name be found except in Israel.") From the New Testament texts, "I will write on him the Name of my God and the name of the city of my God, the New Jerusalem, which comes down from heaven from my God, and my Name is new" (Rev 3:12); also 14:1, "144,000 on whom the Name of His (the Lamb) Father is written on the foreheads."

In a similar sense in the general meaning of the power of God, the expression *Name of God* is used in a series of other texts. "On every place where *I place the memory of my Name*, I will come to you and bless you" (Ex 20:24). "And see I send before you my Angel. . . . He will not pray for your sin, for *my Name is in him*" (Ex 33:20–21). "O Lord Almighty . . . who have closed the abyss and sealed it with your glorious and dread Name" (2 Chr 36, the prayer of Manasseh). "*See the Name of the Lord* comes from afar and His anger burns" (Ex 3:27). "And I will show my Holy Name among my people Israel, and will not let my Name be without glory—and the peoples will learn that I am the Lord, Holy in Israel" (Ezek 39:7); "I will be jealous on account of my Holy Name" (Ezek 39:25); "and the house of Israel will no longer defile my Holy Name" (Ezek 43:7). "From the rising of the sun to its setting they will offer incense to my Name, a pure sacrifice; great will be my Name among the peoples, says the Lord Of Hosts. . . . My Name is dread among the peoples" (Mal 1:11, 14).

Very numerous are the cases when the expression "Name of God" is used in a direct and proper sense, sometimes having immediately in mind the names of the Godhead but sometimes in a patent manner designating the very Godhead itself and being therefore a descriptive expression. It is indisputable that by far not all expressions relate to this case, which the name-fighters consider to be typical, even apart from the above-cited categories, but here too this word usage in and of itself demands and presumes an explanation. Why then in fact does the genius of a language (in this case, Hebrew), and moreover through a divinely inspired writer, permit such a substitution; why precisely does the *name* prove to be such a substitute? A sufficient answer to this question is found in all the foregoing discussions, but here we can only add that precisely this abundant word usage with the substitution of the Godhead by His Name does not in any way provide evidence to the benefit of name-fighting, but quite the opposite, it speaks of the meaningfulness of the name, its weightiness, importance. Therefore, our ultimate opinion concerning these texts is essentially that even where in a patent manner a "name" is only a synonym, by this expression a real nuance in the meaning itself is introduced; contact with the Name of God, with the Godhead in His Name is attested, through the photosphere of the Divine Name. In other words, the Godhead more easily and naturally addresses its venerators, becomes more accessible for them through the holy Name. This is why, for reasons entirely real and ontological, not rhetorical, the expression that interests us is so widespread in biblical language. A series of examples (in no way exhaustive) is given in the notes. The word use of the Bible thus expresses the correlation between the transcendent, incomprehensible, and unnameable Essence of God, the Godhead in Itself and for Itself, and the God of religion and cult, which is in fact precisely the Name of God. Therefore, this expression in essence signifies nothing else than the God who is revered by humankind.

The Names of God, among which is also the sacred tetragrammaton, are only symbolic projections of the transcendent in the immanent, only contacts with the Godhead, illuminating the darkness with flashes of lightning, rays of the sun, blinding and not allowing us to gaze upon it. This is the schematic imprint of the Divine on the human, by which the unconditional abyss separating the Creator from the creature is felt simultaneously with the approach and revelation of the Divine with new force. Therefore, there are many Old Testament names of God, and if there is a preeminent Name, as a proper Name of the Godhead, then the reason for this lies in the incomprehensible will of God. Names of God are means of revelation of God, theophoric theophanies, God's condescension. In a certain sense, *the human being* names the Godhead this, feeling on himself His revelations, answering them with his spirit's power to create names. He gives a name to God, and this even in the case when God directly proclaims His Name Yahweh, for nothing is said to suggest that this is the Name of the Lord Himself, but only His revelation to humankind. "I appeared to Abraham, Isaac and Jacob with the Name of God Almighty, but with my Name Lord (Yahweh) I have not yet been revealed to them" (Ex 6:2–3). The Name of God exists for humankind and in humankind; it is the echo of the Divine in them. Nowhere is this boundary separating God and humankind felt with such clarity and keenness as precisely in the Old Testament, by virtue of the purity and the unobscured quality of its consciousness of God, as a result of the intensity of his transcendence. Thanks to its murkiness and lack of rigor, paganism brings God closer and merges him with the creaturely world and to a very large extent with humankind. Here anthropomorphism becomes the inevitable feature and divine names converge with human names; so too the incarnation of God or the divinization of the human being is accepted rather easily. Hellenic religion, of course, gives the most convincing examples for this. But here there are as many true presentiments and portents as lies and errors, and in any case these well-trodden paths of religious psychologism must now be forever abandoned.

The ladder between earth and heaven is raised by the incarnation of the Son of God from the Most Pure Virgin; Jacob's dream became reality: "from now on you will see heaven opened and the angels of God ascending and descending towards the Son of Man" (Jn 1:51). The Lord Jesus Christ is perfect Human Being and true God: in him were united inseparably and without confusion two natures and two wills in the unity of hypostasis. The unity of hypostasis, among other signs, signifies unity of name, in which is expressed individual being, personality, i.e., precisely hypostaticity. The Name of the Lord Jesus Christ, according to the meaning of the fundamental dogmatic definitions, belongs to both natures; it is the Name of God and of the Human Being in their unity. This means that here this name has a completely different significance from the Old Testament names of God: there they were for the human being, but did not belong to the human being; they had their foundation in the Godhead, but did not belong to God, and were only given to Him by humankind in response to His revelation. Now the Name must belong to and be inherent in the very essence of both God and the Human Being, who are united in the Godman. The Name of the Godman is the Name of God for humankind in a completely particular and *new* sense, for it is the Name also of the Human Being, penetrating to the very depths of his essence, forming his core, and at the same time this very same Name is also the Name of the Godhead, which was incarnated in a human being. Thus, here it is not only a revelation of God to humankind that is deposited by the Name of God in a human being or through a human being; here it is not a symbolic exchange of messages, a question-and-answer session of the transcendent in the immanent but their complete unity and mutual penetration.

How is this possible? It is an incomprehensible mystery of the divine incarnation, which is at the same time the incomprehensible mystery of the Name of the Godman, the unity of hypostasis and unity of name in the two natures and wills, united without separation and without confusion. This is a mystery for the intellect in the sense that it rests here on a certain initial primary fact, not further deducible, which it remains for us to accept as such in all the incomprehensibility of its authenticity. But this mystery of the divine incarnation includes in itself (and up to now this has not been sufficiently brought to light and felt in dogmatic self-consciousness) also the mystery *of the unity of the name*, divine and human, theanthropic, the mystery of this living and true ladder between heaven and earth. The incarnation of God is and necessarily must be and cannot help but be the incarnation of a name—the divinization of the human name and the hominization of the divine. And the sacred, dread, transcendent name Yahweh, the Old Testament revelation, had already become obsolete when the Only-begotten Son, being in the bosom of the Father, "showed" God (Jn 1:18) and gave "power to become children of God to those who received Him, to those who believe in His Name" (Jn 1:12). "Many times and in many ways God spoke to the fathers of old in the prophets, in these last days he spoke to us in the Son, Whom he set as heir of everything, through Whom he made the ages. This one, being the radiance of glory and the image of His hypostasis and holding everything by the word of His power, performed by Himself the purification of our sins, and is seated at the right hand of the throne of majesty on high, being as much the more excellent than the Angels as the more glorious before them is the Name he inherited" (Heb 1:1–4). This "Name is higher than every name, so that before the Name of Jesus every knee must bend of those of heaven, of earth and of those under the earth" (Phil 2:9–10).

The Godman's name associated with the unity of His hypostasis obviously cannot have only a temporary, episodic meaning for earthly existence (it cannot be a sobriquet, almost a nickname, in view of the practical necessity to be called something—which is essentially what the name-fighters think). On the contrary, this divine Name comes to this earthly life and in it accompanies its Possessor, but it also goes beyond its limits into the supratemporal and hyper-temporal, into eternity. The calling of the name *Jesus* was performed not by a human being, but by an angel sent by God, in other words, by God himself (for of course the emissary of heaven uttered this Name not by his own will but by doing the will of God). The Annunciation (and it is necessary to emphasize this dramatically) was the Annunciation not only of the conception of the Divine Child and the approaching incarnation, but also of His Name as the divine incarnation already accomplished. The Annunciation was about the Name of Jesus (and this same announcement was repeated by the angel to Joseph in a dream). And so, the Name of Jesus *preceded* His conception and birth from the Virgin, it was born *before* its Possessor. It is necessary to say more precisely that as divine the Name of Jesus is theanthropic; it was not born but *is in God* pre-eternally, and hence only in the fullness of time does it appear in the earthly incarnation. For the Lord becomes a human being and is incarnated in His Name; His Name is incarnated and around this core of the person there arise a crystallization, a consolidation, and coverings.

This Name accompanies Him in his earthly life and in his death on the cross, on which is indelibly inscribed forever, "It was written: Jesus of Nazareth, King of the Jews" (Jn 19:19), "and there was an inscription above Him, written in Greek, Latin, and Hebrew words: This is the King of the Jews" (Lk 23:38, cf. Mk 15:26), "this is Jesus King of the Jews" (Mt 27:37). If the holy cross, its "incomprehensible divine power," is revealed as the sign of the Son of Man in heaven, as the sign of the end of this age, then the inscription of the divine Name (about which Pilate, not knowing what kind of truth he was speaking, said: "what I have written I have written") is no longer separable from it but has crossed over into the heavens of heavens, the ages of ages. The Lord Jesus rose from the dead with the same Name. More precisely, the same Name passed through the gates of death and life, the gates of the nether regions, being inseparable, one in hypostasis with the one of whom we sing, "o Christ, indescribable one, you were in the grave in the flesh, in hell with a soul as God, in paradise with the thief, and on the throne with the Father and the Spirit filling all things." Just as after the death of their bearers and their departure from this world, names usually share the fate of their bearers (which is expressed in the church's memorialization by names: the name *lives* its own life, experiencing its bearer, and is found with him in an inner, mystical bond, constituting the core of personality as before), so too the holiest of Names remained with its Bearer unseparated, in whom there is no change and who will remain the same always, now and forever, and unto the ages of ages. Therefore the Lord was raised up into heaven in His Name, sitting at the right hand of God the Father, and he will come with glory to judge the living and the dead. "*This Jesus*, who was taken up from you into heaven, will come in the same way as you saw Him ascending into heaven"

(Acts 1:11), therefore it is incumbent "to await His Son from heaven, whom He resurrected from the dead, Jesus" (1 Thess 1:10). Of course this should in no way mean that Jesus is the *sole Name of the Godman*. On the contrary, it is still conceivable to disclose His *new* Name, as the book of Revelation explicitly says. But this second, new Name can in no way remove or weaken the first, similar to how the names "Son of God," "Son of Man," "Son of David," "Teacher," or "Lord," have not altered or made His proper Name, Jesus, powerless. Of course, the disclosure of a new Name must be the supreme religious event, the disclosure of a mystery, a new revelation, but this is how it is depicted in the Apocalypse (Rev 3:12).

Thus, simple attentiveness and faithfulness to the whole Gospel account and Orthodox doctrine in no way permits treating the most sweet Name of Jesus with that blasphemous flippancy displayed by our name-fighters, who see in it only a nickname, *instrumentum vocale* (and in order to be obvious, they trampled and destroyed the writings representing the Name of God).[14] The Name of Jesus written in the heavens lives in heaven and on earth and embraces the destinies of the world and humankind; it is the Name human and divine. So then, in the Name of Jesus—our faith speaks of this to us and the whole of it is in vain without this delightful truth—we have in truth the pre-eternal Name of the Second Hypostasis, the Word of God, the Heart of God. And in keeping with the inseparability and unity of the whole Holy Trinity, this Name inherent in the Son is also inherent in the Father and the Spirit, in the entire Holy Trinity. In contrast to the Names of God as degrees of divine revelation, the Name of Jesus is not one of the Names of God but the Proper Name, God's Name. How then is the great mystery of the Godhead attested? The Nativity of Christ, the Incarnation of God was for people the disclosure of the mystery of the Holy Trinity. The Son showed the Father and called for the Holy Spirit—the Theophany was solemnly accomplished for the first time at the baptism of the Savior, which proved to be evidence also about the other mystery of the Godhead: *it has a Name* (or names), and this Name (or this one of the names) is *Jesus*.

The Name of God, the naming and self-naming of the Godhead is for us, of course, an unknowable mystery, before which we can only keep silent in prayer, and yet this mystery is revealed and attested as the Name of Jesus. God had names in the Old Testament; He revealed His Name Yahweh, and yet this was not the revelation of the mystery about the very Godhead: it was for humanity the operation of the economy of our salvation. *For humankind* it was necessary to name the Godhead just as for humankind the Law was necessary, and although the whole Law is a shadow of future blessings, a shadow of the heavenly image, still this shadow was impenetrable. The very name and naming could be regarded as a human fabrication and invention (as the name-fighters now see it), existing only for the human being and in the human being. The Annunciation of the Archangel about the Name of God, which is also a human name, showed to the world and humanity that the Name of God *exists*, and therefore—it must be further concluded—there is also a human naming, therefore there are also names of God, the daring of naming. The very ability to create names, to name, proves to be ontologically founded; it loses its exclusively psychological aroma but becomes a feature of the image of God in the human being and is ontologically inherent in him. In fact, it becomes clear why it is the human being who is name-bearer and name-creator, why he gives names to everything and everyone and has a name himself. A name (and naming) is elevated to an unattainable ontological height for psychological criticism: it is the Image of God in the human being, it belongs to his ontological composition. Inversely, God's becoming human, which has as a task and a result the divinization of the human being, supposes as a preliminary condition the conformity of the human being to God. And among the many other features that are inherent in a human being—an immortal and free spirit, reason, will, love—the feature interesting us also belongs to him: *the human being has a name* (and hence he gives and names names) as the core of his person.

The whole philosophy of naming and of the name, which up to now was expounded abstractly and theoretically or analytical-anthropologically, now receives objective authentication in fact, in revelation. The Name of Jesus is the foundation stone for a Christian philosophy of the name. It is clear why a human being gives a name and receives a name: because he *has* it as the potential of name-creation. In the same way, naming receives a mysterious, deep, and realistic character. In this statement that the name enters into the image of God in the human being, that it is that image, i.e., belongs to the idea of the human being, to his intellectual essence, is included the ultimate ontological substantiation of naming: thought rests here on the force of fact, before which every *why* ceases and becomes nonsensical. Why does the Lord have a name? But this is the same thing as to ask why God is triune in Persons. It is possible to try without end to understand every meaning of this dogma, to uncover it in all its consequences, to see its seal on the whole of terrestrial and human life, but every *why* here is mad and even irrational. The revealed fact that there is a Divine Name has for thought the same force of a primary foundation. One can find the rays of this Name everywhere, but one can also spare oneself the trouble of substantiating its very existence.

The Name of Jesus is the Name of God, but also a human name. The Lord is the absolute, perfect, heavenly Human Being; in Him, the whole fullness of the Godhead dwells bodily,[15] but also in Him, the whole fullness of humanity is included in a heavenly way. In Him, everything that is proper to the human being as positive power has its foundation and belongs to Him (except sin). It is necessary to understand not allegorically but entirely realistically and ontologically those speeches of the Savior where He identifies Himself with every person. This signifies the union of everyone in Christ, made real in a single communion, and in this sense the Church is the Body of Christ. But this unity is necessarily spread to the name in which the substantial core of personhood is expressed. It would be against nature and incomprehensible if humans, who are united to him in everything, should be separated from Him in this essential thing. In other words, this means that all the diverse endlessly fragmenting names, in their essence, dynamically, form one Name, or rather, are able to enter into it, to partake of it, to become one with it, with its rays existing indivisibly from the sun. If Christ lives, rather, can live and wants to live in each one of the faithful ("behold I stand at the door and knock, that they will open"),[16] this indwelling of the Savior does not signify the depersonalization or dissolution of personhood but its higher, singularly true manifestation in gracious enlightenment. In each of them, the bright Countenance of Christ must be reflected or each of them must find themselves in it and through this see their own countenance. All names meet or proceed substantially and dynamically from the Name of Jesus, for we cannot imagine anything inherent in the human being and lying outside of Christ except the dark region of sin, of non-being, of satanic evil.

The general anthropological and hence Christological principle, namely, to grasp everything human in Christ and through Christ, to see everything in the light of the Son's Hypostasis (the favorite idea of A. M. Bukharev,[17] which he served enthusiastically and consistently) must be extended without fail to the Name of Jesus with respect to human names. The most sweet Name of Jesus also lies inscribed on the whole of humanity through the Son of Man and belongs to all of it. All of us, despite our unworthiness, participate in this great and holy Name; in a certain sense we bear it, we partake of it. Let them not say that this is daring or blasphemy, for is it not a measure of the love and condescension of God? Will the Lord, when he gives His Very Self, His Body and Blood, in the sacrament of the Eucharist, deprive us of the gracious power of His Holy Name? Let it not be so. Since the Lord took on Himself everything human (except sin), which is why each human being can have Him as their personal Savior and Redeemer, so all human names, the essential nuclei of all individualities are united in Him, in His most holy Name, as their center. If the Lord in whom everyone finds themselves is all-individuality, then the Name of Jesus is the *all-name*, the Name of all names.

A hierarchy of names exists (for which the word of God gives direct evidence, Heb 1:4, Phil 2:9–10) that is based on their dynamic correlation. The names of all humanity are only the manifested name of the Heavenly Adam, and the Name of this latter finds itself in its essence, i.e., in God. But true humanity forms the church and is the church. Only such humanity, of course not sinful, temporal, empirical humanity, finds its names in the Name of Jesus, and vice versa. The Name of Jesus as a creative power, as the one human principle, is the Church, i.e., the integral, divine essence of humankind.

It stands to reason that this must be understood not linguistically, which would be simply nonsensical, but mystically. Thus (by using the distinctions established above) it is a question not of the phoneme of a name, and not of the morpheme, but of the mystical sememe, the individual energy inherent in each name and living in it, its core. These forces, these colorful rays, are united into the rainbow of the church and are contained in the white Tabor ray of the Most-radiant Name of Jesus. Such are the ultimate foundations of human names. The name of all names is the Name of Jesus.

But this Name is also a human name, and a concrete human name besides, one of many names, ordinary and widespread among its people: Jesus (perhaps like Ivan among Russians). The mystery of the divine condescension, of kenosis, an unfathomable mystery before which one can only bow reverently, consists in the fact that the most radiant Name of God, by becoming a human name, is clothed in the form of a slave, in the rags of humility. And yet why do they stumble before this, at least those who do not stumble before the appearance of God in the flesh, the divine kenosis? The Lord took on Himself a human body, capable of being mortal and subject to fatigue; it suffered from hunger and cold, was susceptible to wounds; in a word, it was not a phantom, not the mere likeness of a human body, but in truth an ordinary human body that only after the resurrection, indeed in the moment of transfiguration, received and showed a different nature. It is clear that the incarnation of God could not have been accomplished otherwise in order to save and regenerate human nature: the manger, the cave, the wretchedness, the poverty, the homelessness, the sufferings and death—all this lay on the path of the salvation of humankind. But in such a case why, then, are the name-fighters so offended by the fact that the Name of the Godman, which therefore was also the Name of God, was according to human nature a quite ordinary human name? This name—the name-fighters continue to be offended—was widespread; it belonged and even now belongs to many men. The Athonite name-fighters were always pointing their finger at some such monk who had the name Jesus and for this reason, they blasphemed against the sacred Name of Jesus.

But of course, and it goes without saying, an absolutely "proper" name does not exist and cannot exist, as was explained above. All proper names are common, since they are *words*; they therefore express *an idea*, i.e., something general. Even names, which constitute a special aspect according to meaning or designation, do not form an exception, but neither do they forfeit the property of words because of this. Names are qualities of people, the ideas of these qualities, and they can be and inevitably are repeated. There is no power that would establish a monopoly over a name and guarantee its nonrepetition. Nevertheless, a name becomes a proper name only *in concreto*, i.e., on the one hand in combination with all generic cognomens and agnomens, and on the other hand, as a result of that bond that is established between it and its bearer. As for the first, it ought not to be forgotten that the name in its concrete fullness carries only one central core of a name: Jesus, John, etc., but this is in concrete combination with the patronymic, surname, and genealogical tree. Therefore, a personal name, strictly speaking, is always made complex and concrete by the family name, the genealogy, which in this sense is nothing else than an expanded name, a full name, a personal coefficient of a proper name. Thanks to it, a personal name really receives all concreteness and individual nonrepeatability. Thus, the name-fighters, who stumble over the prevalence of the name Jesus, ought to have in mind that this concrete, genealogical definer of a name, which already excludes any repetition and merging, is also given in the Name of Jesus. The "book of the kinship of Jesus" is precisely such a definer, a genealogical book that is given, as is well known, in the gospels of Matthew and Luke according to two different plans.

In Matthew, it appears as "the genealogy of Jesus Christ, Son of David, Son of Abraham." Here in descending order from Abraham is set forth the genealogy of Joseph the Betrothed. In Luke the same genealogy is set forth in ascending order and is traced through the patriarchs to Adam and God Himself. It is clear that all the names of the ancestors in a broad sense are also names of the Son of David and Son of Abraham; they form the photosphere, the outward coverings of the name. (Thus, the impious calumnies and blasphemous doubts of the Athonite and Non-Athonite name-fighters can be rendered powerless by a simple question: does a certain monk Jesus have the corresponding genealogy and, consequently, are the complementary colors of his name identical with the Name of Jesus?) Let them not allege that all this genealogical expertise is usually absent and that a name is taken at face value. The whole genealogy is given potentially in that demonstrative gesture, or agglutination, that unites the name to its given bearer. Therefore—and only therefore—one can say that proper names not being proper but common become individual in the concrete photosphere of the name, of its genealogy. But this connection, which is established between the name and the bearer, fills the name with individual color and scent and gives it a vital force proper to a given person. From the word-predicate or nickname it makes it a name in the authentic sense, to which substance is inherent. In that case the name (even if it were to be abstracted from all discussions concerning its concretization through genealogy), even with full sonic identity in different cases of application, appears and acts as different names. Here one must not forget what was said about the difference between phoneme (and morpheme) and sememe. If a phoneme is the sonic body of a name (in the given case its "inner form" refers to this, i.e., the immediate verbal significance, which is of interest only for its genesis), then its given bearer constitutes the sememe of the name and is inseparably connected with it. Therefore, to take abstractly one sonic form or body of a name without soul and without power, to convert a name into a nickname, as the name-fighters do, means not to understand the essence of a name. The sounds Ivan, Peter, etc., are "proper names" not attributed to anything, they are not names but are words, predicates without subjects, ideas without realization. In general, one cannot pronounce any judgment about them until they become names, i.e., receive a concrete individual sememe. The name-fighters are offended precisely by the abstractly taken phoneme of a name, which, as it turns out, does not present any differences in the various instances of its application. But such would be the fate not only of the name Jesus in view of its ordinariness, but also any other name: Napoleon, Nebuchadnezzar. Indeed one can give a dog that nickname, and Napoleon (the general) and Napoleon (the dog) are simply *different* names, different words; and there are different words, in spite of the identical phoneme and even "inner form," such as the foot referring to a body part and the foot of a hill, or the key for a lock and the key for a piece of music.[18] The inner form is important for the genesis of a word and its historical understanding but does not obliterate the existing difference of the words. Therefore, speaking in general, identical names are not synonyms but have the nature of a species: of families, ideas, tasks in which the life of the bearer of the name elapses. It is a common predicate before various subjects that all in their own way are connected with it.

However, it is necessary to say that this connection, similarity, or identity, can be paralyzed by difference. This takes place also in the case of the sacred and divine Names of the Savior and the Mother of God—Jesus and Mary. The Orthodox Church established that there could be no name days either in relation to the Name of the Savior or the Mother of God; the latter sometimes is practiced as an abuse, but at the same time, the names Jesus and Mary, belonging to different saints, remain in the Orthodox calendar. Nevertheless, the Names of the Savior and of the Mother of God enjoy an especially exceptional position: it is as if they were not identical with their homonyms; they are not the same but are other, singular names, not of a species and an individual, not family names but personal ones. The name day is a secondary indicator in a name: in the general kind—the genus—several families are distinguished by an expressed name, having a common ancestor-saint. This introduces a specification into names: A^1, A^2, A^3, A^4 . . . B^1, B^2, B^3. The names of Jesus and Mary enter their genus according to their phoneme, but still they stand completely apart and do not form any family of those akin and similar to them, obviously because there can be here no question of affinity or similarity. They are like summits, which although belonging to the mountain group, are not found in the chain of mountains but rise above them all. However, this singularity, entirely understandable, does not remove the fact that according to their phoneme these Names belong to their own genus. The Lord truly was incarnated and became human, not disdaining a human name. He was incarnated not only in flesh but also in the Name, which was clothed in a humble, human name, common among pious Hebrews.

So then, the name of the Lord Jesus is the Name of God but also a human name. It is inseparably connected with a human nature and a human name, and being immanent to human nature, it introduces into it the power of God, is the incarnation of God in a Name. Through this, the Name of Jesus has for us a completely singular, exceptional closeness and accessibility. If the Name of God in the Old Testament is dread and wondrous, then the Name of Jesus is sweet, although also mighty; in it we partake of the love of God, taste the grace of the Divine name. If in the names of God, as we have attempted to show, the power of God is present, then in the Name of Jesus it is in a special way palpably close to the human being. As the Divine Name it contains the power of God, is the energy of the Godhead, but it is at the same time the energy of the human nature, it belongs to the Godman. Here there is not that *transcensus*, that break from the immanent to the transcendent, from the world and from humankind—into the not-world and toward the not-human, into the Divine domain. We have something like this in the Old Testament, where only the high priest, protected by all the sacral means—by the solemnity of the liturgical moment, by the vestments, the incense, and the sanctity of the place—entered the Holy of Holies to pronounce the Name of God. On account of the Name of Jesus, we are all called as a royal priesthood, entering the Holy of Holies of our heart, to pronounce and invoke It, and He is present in His Name.

For ancient Judea, the Name of God was like the summit of Mount Sinai, in darkness and lightning, where Moses alone entered, and almost every invocation of the Name of God—except for the ritually and liturgically legitimate—was a sinful use of it in vain. But the Name of Jesus lets itself be invoked "at any time and at any hour" and unceasingly addressed in the heart. It is necessary to recognize and feel this difference in all its force and acuteness, this contrast between the Name of the transcendent Godhead, which was distant and terrible and dwelled only in the temple, and the Name of Jesus, the temple for which is the human heart. Every believer has the priesthood of this temple imprinted with this Name. Of course, it remains terrible and still requires awe for it as the greatest sanctuary, for in truth it is the Name of God. But it became close and accessible and is not separated by the ontological chasm that exists between the Creator and the creature. Across the chasm a bridge is erected, the divine and the human were united already indivisibly and without confusion. We repeat, the majesty of the Name of God was accessible only to the priest or high priest, since he was singled out, transcendent to the world here, and besides in the most transcending moments; but the Name of Jesus is accessible and given to each one "who believes in His Name." In this one thing is already manifested the whole chasm between the two Testaments, the power and salutariness of the incarnation of God. We of course do not want to downplay the difference that exists between the priesthood and the world in the New Testament as well, for the celebration of the sacraments and divine worship here too demand transcending conditions and a basic *transcensus* of personhood— ordination. But the points of this *transcensus* here have shifted. Thus, so far as the Name of Jesus is divine-human, Divine and human, it will accept everyone as its priests, it is accessible to everyone by its human proximity, it is immanent to the human being; but so far as it is divine, it is the Name of God, not in a lesser but even in a paramount sense (as explained above) in comparison with other Names of God. It is the terrible consuming fire of God's presence, the power and glory of God.

Precisely this closeness and accessibility of the most radiant Name confuses and seduces the name-fighters; they are jealous of the goodness of God toward people. It seems to them that God puts Himself at the disposal of the human being who invokes His Name, and the barrier between Him and that human is absent. Yes, it really is so, such is God's love toward people, such is the divine condescension. But why then are the name-fighters so confused only with respect to the Name of God? In any sacrament, and especially in the holy Eucharist, the Lord gives Himself to individuals as they desire: the consent, the Divine readiness is always given, as if it were something self-evident; all that is necessary is the human desire to avail oneself of the grace of the sacrament. In a similar way, that is how it is with the grace of the Name of God, which is given to each one who invokes it with faith and prayer. Here the name-fighters are confused, on the one hand by possible liberties with the Holy Name, which they themselves have shown when they wrote over, tore to pieces, and even trampled on the name Jesus, and on the other hand, by the immeasurable implications that result from invoking the Name of God.

The first doubt is easily resolved on the basis of all the foregoing: a name has a phoneme and a sememe. First, a phoneme differs in different languages: Iisus, Isus,[19] Jesus, Iesous; second, it is not yet a name, but only its shell, its cover. As a word, this phoneme is not yet able to represent a name, it can only be a predicate, not related to the subject, and therefore it is alien to it and unfulfilled. Therefore, the word "savior" or even "Jesus" is not yet the Name of the Lord. From this word, or rather, by using it as a means, a shell or a cover, the Name *is received*, being referred to its Bearer, being filled with His power, receiving the energy of a subject. For this reason, different verbal variations or modes of a given word in different languages are of so little import because the Name, although it has full concreteness, in any given case also has some sort of verbal mode, but this mode, equivalent to any other mode, does not make a name the Name. What does make it the Name is its whole completeness and saturation, the power living in it, like fragrant myrrh in a clay vessel. The vessel can be polished or rough, painted in any color—this does not affect the myrrh; but the vessel will inevitably have *some sort* of concrete form, for without this it cannot fulfill its task—to hold the myrrh contained in it.

The religious lie (and not only a misunderstanding) of the name-fighters is its "psychologism," that here the efficacy of the Name of God is connected exclusively with mood: if someone prays fervently and sincerely, the power of the Name of God will be palpable for them; if they do not, it will not be. The conditions for the perception of grace and the nature of this perception, connected with a subjective moment and personal attitude, they transfer to the objective meaning of what is here taking place. This is entirely similar to how their Protestant precursors rejected the sacrament of the Eucharist in its essence, by imparting to it only a subjective meaning: depending on one's frame of mind, one person receives communion and another does not, as if any mood could give the absent sacrament and compensate for its power. In a similar manner they think that the power of the Name of God is communicated by the mood of the one praying, thanks to which their prayer will or will not be heard, as if it were necessary personally to persuade and invoke God to listen to them. God hears anyone who calls, but not everyone who calls addresses God with their heart and hears this hearing of God. Just as the

Holy Gifts are the Body and Blood of Christ equally for those who partake of them for salvation or for judgment and condemnation so, too, the Name of God is the power of God, no matter how we treat it, reverently or blasphemously. To imagine that the distance between earth and heaven can be traversed only by human good pleasure means to introduce psychologism, anthropomorphism, subjectivism, and ultimately, Anthropotheism, into the very heart of religion, into its holy of holies.

Just as it is impossible to be saved by human power, so is it impossible to pray to God by human power if the Lord is not disposed to this prayer before we have opened our lips, if he is not present in it by His power contained in His Name. Prayer becomes the prayer of God; it receives its objective meaning as the union of a human being with God precisely through God's presence in the prayer itself, the transcendent-immanent abiding of the Name of God in it. The Name of God is the ontological foundation of prayer, its substance, power, and justification. Therefore, in its essence, prayer is the invoked Name of God. But as the Name of God contains divine energy, gives God's presence, then one can say, although with great imprecision, that practically and energetically the Name of God is God. More accurately, God's Power, which is indivisible from the Essence of God and is in this sense God himself, is present in it. Prayer would be impossible, incomprehensible, without this condition.

Every prayer is also a *miracle*, if by miracle one means a breach in the immanent, its penetration by the transcendent: this miracle is the Name of God, which is the Godhead. From this it follows, of course, what folly, blasphemy, and sin our cold distracted prayer is, calling the Name of God in vain, for in it we are always dealing with a fire that scorches us, although we are not aware of this. Prayer becomes a joyful and dread work, but also a boundlessly and exceptionally meaningful one, a standing in the presence of God. What is there to be surprised about if it turns out that the great ascetics' experience of "mental activity," of the Jesus prayer, in particular the experience of so great a practitioner of prayer in our days as Father John of Kronstadt, bears witness to this truth, that "the Name of God is God himself," as an *axiom* and not a debatable *theologoumenon*, a theological opinion or a philosophical idea? It is necessary to read this in the full context of the religious diary of Father John, "My Life in Christ," in order to see how entirely self-evident for him this truth was. It is equally self-evident that if God Himself is present in the Name of God, then in the names of the Theotokos and the saints they themselves are present also.

If this really is what the Name of God means in prayer in general, i.e., in private and personal prayer, then even more so in divine worship, in its cultic use. Strictly speaking, every prayer is a sacrament, so far as it is really prayer, i.e., an address to God and an invocation of Him through the Name of God. It can seem that even for us the decisive sign is the psychological animus, the frame of mind, because outside this a name will not be the Name of God but a simple predicate or simply a word. However, it is not so. The decisive thing here is not at all a psychological but an ontological moment, that mystical intention that makes a subject from a predicate, a substantive noun from a verb. Although this intention has a psychological aspect, its *how*, this does not obliterate its proper nature, does not dissolve its core. Here in this intention, a vital contact with the Godhead takes place, or saying it differently, God Himself is present in the Name of God. Indeed, the simple vocative case contains in itself an especially powerful intention, in it there is not only the presence of the one being named, but a certain spiritual push is given, of course, not psychological alone. This is valid to an immeasurably greater extent in relation to the Spirit, not bound by space, time, and covering. Always and everywhere, where in invoking we name Him, we also have His presence in the Name, and it already depends on us, on the transparency of our soul, how we will feel this presence: here psychologism really does drive us and cripple us.

So it is in private, individual prayer. But in divine worship in general there is no room made for psychologism, here ontology alone operates: what is said is also accomplished, and what is accomplished symbolically here is accomplished in all worlds and reaches the celestial and noetic altar. One must understand the real meaning of divine worship, i.e., its ontological objectivity, in virtue of which there is nothing here only as mood, but everything really happens, everything is symbolic, is illuminated and hallowed by God's presence in the Name of God, which stands at the center of divine worship. One can say that it is all accomplished "in the Name of God"—of the Holy Trinity, of the Lord Jesus Christ, of the Father, of the Holy Spirit, and this is not only a metaphor, as the name-fighters want to assure us, but a mystical reality. Divine worship is an uninterrupted address to the Godhead, which He hears through His Name. And precisely on the strength of this hearing, divine worship is accomplished as a sacred ritual full of real meaning and content, and the sacraments are accomplished—in no way at all by the power of mood or psychological intensity of the celebrants, but by the power of the Name of God in which the Power of God is present. Without this condition of religious realism, divine worship would turn into a theatrical performance on religious themes, into mystery plays performed well or poorly depending on those same "moods." Meanwhile only the measure in which we apprehend, use for ourselves, and assimilate what is happening depends on the mood. If we continue this analogy with a performance, however shocking it may seem, we must say that if the actor playing Napoleon had actually become Napoleon at this time, regardless of his art, but only because of his role, then it would have depended on him and the audience to comprehend his character to some extent. Conversely, without this condition they would all be fakes, even if talented ones, i.e., not Napoleon but only the perception of Napoleon, "a frame of mind" occasioned by him, i.e., an empty nothing. Between the "performance" and the reality of the symbolism of the ritual there exists a chasm—the very same as exists between being and non-being, allegory and reality. And the foundation that fills the sacred ritual of divine worship with reality is, without a doubt, the Name of God, by whose power everything here is accomplished and hallowed, and when it is already hallowed, it becomes complete, authentic, and efficacious.

The Name of God is the foundation of divine worship, its heart, but here in its turn the heart of the heart is the Name of Jesus. For in connection with it and by virtue of it we also have the most holy and splendid Name of the Father and of the Son and of the Holy Spirit, the revelation of the Holy Trinity, the Name of the Mother of God, and of all the saints. If only hypothetically one were to remove this power of the Name of Jesus, the whole of divine worship, the whole sacramental action would crumble. It all grows out of the Name of God, as from its seed. This is why the Lord gives His Name as power and authority to the apostles and in their person to the whole church. "They will drive out demons with my Name, they will speak in new tongues," and so on (Mk 16:17). Cf. Lk 10:17, "Lord, even the demons obey on account of Your Name," and Acts 16:18, "By the Name of Jesus Christ I command you to come out of her." The first miracle of healing that showed the apostles' authority was performed by Peter and John[20] on the lame man: "in the Name of Jesus Christ of Nazareth get up and walk" (Acts 3:6, cf. 4:10), "for there is no other name under heaven given to human beings by which we are to be saved" (Acts 4:12). "And because of faith in His Name, His Name has made this man strong, whom you see and know" (Acts 3:16). This realism was clear for the pagans of Ephesus about whom it is said, "and fear fell on them all and the Name of the Lord Jesus was magnified" (Acts 19:17). Therefore the evangelist also says, "To those believing in His Name he gave authority to become children of God" (Jn 1:12), or "but they were washed, but they were sanctified, but they were justified by the Name of our Lord Jesus Christ and by the Spirit of our God." The practitioners of the Jesus prayer have witnessed from their own experience this same Name as the power of God, as the real presence of the very Lord Jesus. Therefore, we also say with the boldness of faith that our divine worship is not only the service of God but also God's service in which we have Christ the High Priest himself, and the priests consecrated in His Name show the power of His presence. God is present in the church's sacraments and accomplishes them by the power of the Name of God. In general, the sacraments are power and reality that is confirmed by the Name of God.

Is it possible, like those fighting the name, to be led astray by the fact that all of this *is given* to the human being? If I want, I will call the Name of God and I have God Himself, they say. Yes, it is in truth so, such is the love of God and his condescension. Yet, if they have in mind simply a phoneme, an empty verbal husk drained of its content, then of course it is not true. You see, even for performing a sacrament, besides objective conditions, the grace of the priesthood is required, and the animus—the desire to perform the sacrament. So too those desiring to experience the action of the Name of God likewise need to be willing actually to pronounce the Name of God, and not the sounds j-e-s-u-s.

Therefore, let them not be confused and led astray by the closeness and accessibility of God in His Name, when invoked with faith: it cannot be otherwise, for the Lord is near to those who ask of Him. May His Name be blessed always, now and forever and unto the ages of ages!

The Name of God is God—this expression of Fr. John of Kronstadt rang in our days from the Caucasus wilderness to Mount Athos and became the subject of embittered arguments, strife, and the most serious misunderstandings (it seems, most of all the latter). Some, the fanatical "name-glorifiers" even read the formula with this variation: "The Name of God is God *himself*," and evidently they bring the copula *is* close to the sense of full equality: the Name of God = God. But from this, the opposite conclusion also follows, perhaps not fully realized by the "name-glorifiers," made by those led astray by "name-glorifying," i.e., that "God = the Name of God (which is why they call the name-glorifiers "name-divinizers"). First, one has to establish the *irreversibility* of this judgment: the copula *is* in no way at all signifies equality or identity. A judgment is on principle irreversible, for a reversed judgment is a completely new judgment, with a new subject and a new predicate. We have explained in its place that predicativity, the quality of a subject, is connected with an ontological accent. A subject is always a substantive noun, whereas a predicate, even when it has formally the character of a substantive, is dissolved in the copula, becomes an adjective and verb, expresses not *ens*, not *res*, but an idea as a quality and a universal: hence, the irreversibility of a judgment. Those who make a judgment reversible do not reckon with the adjectival quality of a predicate; they are guided by grammatical, etymological signs only formally, ignoring syntax with its inner forms. Therefore, in the expression *the Name of God is God* the word *God* is a predicate (and perhaps, of course, with some approximation of meaning, replaceable, for example, with "divine, divinity"—*theion, theotes*; in Greek, it must stand without an article, so that the entire expression has this form—*to tou theou onoma theos estin,* but **not** *ho theos* [the name of God is divine, but not God]).

Thus, completely inadmissible is the reverse judgment that could sound approximately so: *ho theos to tou theou onoma estin* [God is the name of God]— such a name-divinizing formula would actually signify not only a vicious heresy but also total nonsense. Therefore, the real meaning of the predicate *is God* signifies not substantial identity, existing between the divine essence and its name, but the entrance and abiding of the Name of God in the sphere of divine being, power, and manifestation of that which the fathers of Constantinople called *the energy* of God. In this sense, the Name of God occupies in the ontological hierarchy the same place as the light of Tabor, although, of course, this does not cause Name and Light to become identical in their phoneme, remaining consubstantial in the noumenon. One can calmly compare side by side: "the Name of God is God," and "the Light of Tabor is God" (and one can add to this, "the grace of God which is imparted to people in a sacrament, is God"). In all these cases, the predicate *"is God"* does not in any way at all establish identity with the *hypostatic* being of God but only leads into the sphere of the Divine and marks the quality of Divinity; just as metals or stones passing through fire take on the light and heat of this fire and themselves, and by being in the fire, become fire, and yet all the same are different from the original source fire.

The formula *the Name of God is God* does *not* signify and cannot signify anything more, according to its direct meaning and the very nature of a word and a sentence. Here language, the nature of a word, simply do not allow that name-divinizing raving that frightens and disturbs the name-fighters, and it would be better for the substance of the matter and the peace of the church if this formula did not focus undue and premature attention on itself. In any case, in and of itself, it by no means contains an exhaustive answer to the question or a doctrinal definition. The formula must be developed or completed because "divinity" (is God, *theos estin*) by no means sufficiently defines the specific feature of the case in question and, as we have already indicated, is inherent in other aspects of divine energy, of the self-revelation of the Godhead. It follows that in no case whatever can one consider the formula "the Name of God is God" even as an attempt at a doctrinal definition about the Name of God, for here only a general teaching is given that if properly understood, of course, is correct. (By no means does it provoke those reproaches of name-divinizing that in their own way were even justifiably raised against it.) This general teaching must be completed in the direction of explaining precisely *in what* sense "is God," i.e., divine, the Name of God. Thus, in our understanding and in our interpretation, the formula "the Name of God is God" signifies only that the Name of God is divine and enters into the sphere of the Godhead, His energies. Of course, this does not at all diminish the fact that in the ontological invocation of the Name of God in prayer (in the vocative or nominative case in the sense of subjectivity or substantiality), the Very Lord is present by His power, by His simplicity, by His indivisibility, and the invocation of the Name of God in prayer is an unceasing participation in the Godhead, simple and indivisible. But this presence of the Godhead in His Name, which has compelled someone praying to exclaim in reverent amazement, "The Name of God is God," does not at all signify that God is the Name itself. It does not introduce a fetishism of the Name but shows the eternal and incomprehensible mystery of the incarnation and condescension of God, of the abiding of God in His Name, which is assured in the mystery of prayer.

Post Scriptum to the Essay on the Name of God

A Sophiological Interpretation of the Dogma of the Name of Jesus

I

The Name of God, in conformity with the nature of any "proper name," comes from a naming as a compound sentence, in which a subject (the thing being named) is combined with a predicate (the name) through an implicit copula (*is*) as a logical and verbal agglutination: A (so and so) is B (name). The connection between what is named and naming, agglutination, becomes so strong that the name as meaning (the inner form of a word) loses its significance to a certain degree, partially stops being a sememe, but becomes as it were only a phoneme, a nickname, a pronominal sign, "N," a logical, or more than this, an ontological (and hence also psychological) gesture. It does not always come to the total loss of the semantic significance of "a proper name," due to the solidity of the agglutination or the oblivion, the loss of its primordial verbal meaning; however, it does approach this the more a name becomes "more proper," more saturated by the power of being, more ontic. It approximates vaguely to a pronoun, an inner demonstrative gesture, a wordless word: named-in-place-of. Such is the power of a *proper* name, its nature.

Yet, for all of its "properness," it all the same remains a naming; it does not lose the character of predicative value, at least, in intention, but always keeps it. Since a proper name is twofold, it unites in itself subject and predicate. If as the subject one "pronominally" thinks I, you, he, we, you, they—and this is thought always and inevitably—then in this character of a proper name one can detect not only the nature of a word, as something said about something, but also a form *of hypostatic* being, expressed in every judgment: A (so and so) is B. This is a universal form of being, which is always objective, but it also has its verbal revelation, its word, which is precisely made into an object in a proper name. Such is the *duality* according to significance that is peculiar to a proper name, so far as it remains *a word* as naming but thereby has the significance of a wordless pronominal gesture.

The Name of God does not differ formally from other proper names: it, like they, is a naming that adheres to its subject in a special way and insofar as it is identified with it. This very subject, in the given case the hypostatic essence of God, is nameless because it is beyond name (as pseudo-Dionysius the Areopagite already envisioned). It can be expressed either by a silent mystical gesture, or through the NOT (a-privative) of "negative theology," as a subject; however, here it is also expressed in an undefined series of names, different in their predicative value but equivalent in the intention of their correlation to a single subject. Anonymy is united here with polyonymy— such is the basic thought of pseudo-Dionysian onomastics, which is taken up by Christian dogmatics faced with the same fact in biblical revelation.

However, such polyonymy has its limits even apart from the general anonymy of negative theology. In the Bible (as also in theology), a few of the most important, "great" names, as it were more "proper" than others, are picked out from the general plurality of names of God. There are precisely seven, and among these the most sacred and magnificent of all Old Testament names of God is Yahweh, Who Is, revealed and given by God himself to Moses on Sinai. However, this name too, for all its exclusivity and the solemnity of its revelation, carries in itself the clear features of that twofold character that is inherent to proper names in general. On the one hand, they are words that do not lose their semantic, verbal significance (Who Is), and on the other hand, they have received a "pronominal" use, and insofar as they have forfeited their direct meaning, they have become a phoneme from a sememe. To that extent, one can say that even Yahweh is not a "proper" name of the Godhead, but only a negative name, one of many, although it has become singular in its application. "I appeared to Abraham, Isaac and Jacob with (the name) 'God Almighty' and with the name 'Yahweh' I was not revealed to them" (Ex 6:3). Since its proper, semantic significance is not lost, it resounds, illuminates, and is clearly contained in this name, although it is also a hypostatic name, Who Is, Yahweh. Here the subject is clearly united with the predicate, the grammatical subject with the predicate and (implicit) copula.

One can ask in what kind of relation this revelation of the Name—I, Who Am—stands to the revelation of the Holy Trinity, as I-We, which is already there in the Old Testament as a kind of cryptogram (the narrative about the creation of the world and the human being, about the revelation of God to Abraham, about the confusion of tongues and other texts). Is this I of the divine Tetragrammaton the monohypostatic I—(and if so, then precisely of which hypostasis?)—or the trihypostatic I in its triunity? There are no direct indications for an answer to this question. Where it speaks about the face of God, the Old Testament revelation is applicable in a different context to the different hypostases in conformity with the common meaning; however, this name Yahweh is used only in relation to the hypostatic being of God in general. Does this usage not insist that we refer this sacred Name in general precisely to the triunity of the Divine hypostasis in which the three divine hypostatic lights merge ("oneness in Trinity and Trinity in unity," according to the words of the Great Canon)? Is not "Who Is, I am who I am" contained in the sacred cryptogram of the revelation of the personhood of God, which is revealed in the fullness of Divine being? If this theological-exegetical conjecture is correct, in that case one must understand the scope and content of the revelation of the Name of God Yahweh as simultaneously including in itself the whole fullness of ontological naming. By this, an indication of the sophiological explanation of the Name of God is also given that combines personal character, hypostasis, in indivisible but also unconfused union with the divine essence, *ousia*, in its self-revelation, wisdom, and glory. (The latter becomes clear from that text in which it is said that God, in revealing His Name to Moses, shows him His Glory as well—Ex 33:19—in their bi-unity and ontological indivisibility, identity by difference.) Therefore, Yahweh, Who Is, signifies the divine trihypostasis in its sophianity, in the Wisdom and Glory of God. The Name of God signifies simultaneously both its hypostatic Bearer and Divine Sophia; it expresses by itself not only the hypostatic but also the sophian being of God, although still in the preliminary and unclear contours of the Old Testament. To this, one needs to add that it also has a premundane, transcendent character, although through revelation it becomes immanent to human existence. However, despite this contact and encounter of the transcendent with the immanent, which is inherent in general to any revelation, the latter nevertheless remains addressed more to the premundane character of God than to creaturely being. If one expresses this thought in the terms of Sophiology, then the Name Yahweh refers more to Divine Sophia than to creaturely Sophia.

In the New Testament revelation of the Name of God, the name Yahweh yields its place to the name Jesus, which overshadows and abrogates it, as it were, as an abstract thing is replaced by something concrete. Nevertheless, the former name is presupposed and contained by it, although it already loses the meaning of a "proper name" for the most part. First of all, the question arises as to what kind of hypostatic significance this New Testament name has. Is the one though trihypostatic divine I, the divine triunity, named here as in Yahweh, or is only one hypostasis singled out, namely, the Second, so that the entire Holy Trinity thereby remains nameless or beyond name, and the name Jesus thus belongs only to the Second hypostasis? Or is this not the case? Is the trihypostatic element in the name of Jesus not absorbed by the unity of the immediately named, Second hypostasis, but is it contained in the concrete meaning of this name in a special, corresponding manner? Of course, precisely the latter takes place here. The Name of Jesus belongs immediately to the Second hypostasis, but in it and through it, the entire Holy Trinity is also named, being in this sense analogous and similar in meaning to the name Yahweh, The One Who Is. Such a meaning flows from the personal property of the Second hypostasis, which is also the Word of God, and in this quality the word of the Father and the word of the Holy Spirit, which is announced by Them and reveals Them. The Father-Principle abides in transcendence even in the Holy Trinity itself. He himself is silent, but His word about Himself, His self-naming, is the Word of God pre-eternally begotten by Him, and this Word is not only the word of all words, the all-predicate, but also the proper Name of God, the all-subject; in him is everything about everything. In this sense, as Word of the Father, the name of the Son also names the Father; in the monarchy of the Holy Trinity, it belongs to the Father, although not as a proper name.

The same can be said about the Holy Spirit; not having his own word, the Spirit rests on the Son of the Father and as the Spirit of Truth reveals the word as essential truth. The Name of the Son thus belongs to the Holy Spirit, though not as his "proper" designation. Therefore, the name of Jesus is the single Name of the Holy Trinity in Its unity as concrete, trihypostatic self-consciousness. Just as the Second hypostasis itself is not separated from the triunity of the Holy Trinity through Its hypostatic properties but is only differentiated in it, so too is the Divine Name of the Holy Trinity inherent in the whole triunity, in each of the hypostases in their particular sense. However, there are not three different names, but one. Moreover, it is not even common to the three; it could not be separated as such in parentheses, as a name repeating three times. It is not common in that sense and it is not repeated, but for each hypostasis, it sounds in its own way, in divine triunity: not three completely identical names, $A^1 \ A^2 \ A^3$, but one triune name, the threefold context of the single Divine Name Jesus. It is in this way also the "proper" name of the Son alone, but at the same time also not the "proper" but the "threefold" name of the entire Holy Trinity. In this "improper" but threefold name, each hypostasis manifests its relation to it. The Father is unnameable or beyond all naming as the Principle, the initial hypostasis; the Holy Spirit likewise is unnameable, not having his own word and name, but only that of the Son; and finally, the Son has a name and gives it through Himself to all three hypostases, in triunity. Therefore, it is impossible to reply to the arithmetically formulated question, "How many names does the Holy Trinity have, three or one?" Not three and not one, but triune or unitrine, as are all definitions relating to It.

One must add to this that the three hypostatic designations of the first, second, and third hypostases, Father, Son, Word, Holy Spirit, are **not** proper names, but only designations naming their hypostatic properties or character. They can be used as proper designations of each of the hypostases, and actually, they are used as such alongside other designations that are not so exclusive in their meaning; but this does not make them proper names in the exact sense. Nevertheless, one must also add that in their common character they all the same remain threefold, or triune, they hide the full Trinitarian context of their meaning. The Father is Father of the Son, on Whom also rests the Holy Spirit, proceeding onto the Son; the Son is Son of the Father, begotten by the Father and overshadowed from Him by the Holy Spirit; and finally, the Holy Spirit is from the Father proceeding onto the Son and resting on Him. In this way, each of these hypostatic names can be disclosed as a Trinitarian name, taken only in one sort of initial definition or aspect. Here the triple reciprocity is manifested. However, this is not in the "proper" name of Jesus itself, although in its own meaning it too is disclosed in a threefold aspect, only by proceeding from the already given hypostatic character, by which their reciprocity is established.

II

In the Sophiological interpretation of the Name of God in general, of both the Old Testament name Yahweh and the New Testament name Jesus, the following fundamental question arises. To what does the divine revelation contained in the Name of God refer, to the hypostasis only, the Divine Person, or to the essence, the nature, the "energies," the wisdom and glory, and to Divine Sophia in general? The very first and immediate meaning of the Name of God refers to the Divine hypostasis. A name is a synonym, or power, of the personal pronoun, the hypostatic I, said in a word, and not only an ontological gesture, in essence wordless. As a proper, pronominal name, it is deprived of any verbal content, of predicativity. Nothing is said in it about its bearer who, although he is also the foundation of being, its noumenon, can himself not be expressed in an exhaustive phenomenality. Hence the conclusion that the name as "grammatical subject" or (what is the same) subject is as if external to its own proper sophianity, although it is inseparable from its ontic photosphere. But this leads to the paradoxical and, of course, contradictory conclusion that in the name the Personhood of God is named outside of, without, or apart from the Godhead, that it is non-sophian. At the basis of such a conclusion is obviously a misunderstanding that must be removed.

In Western theology[1] of the eleventh century, in connection with the teaching of Gilbert de Porreta, who was condemned at the council of Reims,[2] the question arose about whether and how (hypostatic) God and the Godhead—*Divinitas*—differed. Gilbert distinguished and contrasted them, whereas the council identified them. It was a question essentially about the correlation of hypostasis and ousia, or self-revelation in God. The question was not brought to complete theological and sophiological clarity and was not so much resolved as rather curtailed and, of course, in the same way barred from discussion, prematurely, of course. It is not possible to agree fully with either side. Hypostasis and ousia, divine personhood and its self-revelation, are distinguished but are not opposed in order to make room for duality in God. God is hypostatic in His being, but being (nature, essence, self-revelation) is always hypostatized and cannot be non-hypostatic. The connection of hypostasis and ousia is such that it is not possible to separate and oppose them, as it is not possible to merge or identify them. There are here two different aspects of the one divine hypostatic being. This difference is expressed in the Trinitarian dogma as the trihypostaticity and consubstantiality of the one and self-identical Godhead. In this way the question does not allow a rational resolution, either-or, but demands the antinomic identity of both definitions, both-and.

In the question about the Name of God, this same distinction and identification is likewise applicable. Name as a mystical gesture or symbol does not name but only points out what is being named, the subject, but it does this predicatively, in the predicate. It is itself a predicate that has become a grammatical subject, the antinomy of identity. This is crystal clear with respect to the Old Testament name: Yahweh, Who Is (so too a whole series of Names of God that express divine "properties," and besides in human language, immanently). They are as much names as they are Designations of a definite content, and consequently of sophian character. But does it not go otherwise with respect to the New Testament name, the name of the

Godman Jesus? Is it not chiefly a proper name? As the name of the Godman, it is simultaneously the Name of God, pre-eternally existing in the heavens and brought to earth from God through the archangel at the incarnation; in this sense, it is transcendent in a particular way. Alongside this, in keeping with its very own character, in the absence of a specific "inner form," of a semantic meaning, its direct significance is so far from corresponding to its uniqueness that it cannot be regarded as adequate to it in any way. Rather, it produces the impression not even of a Name in the exact sense but of a nickname. Therefore, the name Jesus can be perceived chiefly as a proper name, deprived of its special significance or content. By this or some other consideration, the question is posed about its sophian significance. Are *Deus ut deitas* [God as divinity] correlated in it in this way? Is the Name of Jesus sophian, is it the Name of God in general, is it a predicate for the divine subject or not?

It is evident that in the given application of naming as a "concealed" name, we have the coalescence of subject and predicate, of what is named and naming (in an implicit copula). In virtue of this coalescence, the Name of God expresses the unity of the hypostatic subject and sophian predicate or definition in their coalescence and indistinguishability, but simultaneously distinguishability. A name as "proper" expresses hypostasis and has the pronominal significance precisely of a personal pronoun, but likewise a content-rich significance that retains its power as the self-revelation of the hypostatic God. Depending on the context, on the one or other semantic composition, the emphasis in a name is ascribed either to its first or its second significance, that of the subject or predicate. The name itself in the fullness of its significance is not only first or second, but also their duality and indivisibility. Even in the Divine Name of the Holy Trinity this same nuance is manifested, in the names of the three hypostases: the Name of God belongs to the First Hypostasis, the Father's, as "proper" in the precise sense. The Father is the One Being Revealed, the hypostasis par excellence, the subject in the whole threefold self-revelation and self-definition of God. Thus, the logical emphasis lies here on the hypostatic significance of the name. By contrast, the Son, the Father's Word, who reveals, points to, and does the Father's will, is the hypostatized predicate, insofar as He is also named the Word of God and the Wisdom of God. Similarly the Holy Spirit names Divine Being, Life, and Power, likewise hypostatized, but in the primary significance of the connection between Father and Son. In so far it is proper to the Third hypostasis to express also the Glory of God, of the Father in the Son. From this one can understand the Old Testament word usage whereby the Name of God is identified with the Glory of God to such a degree, as we read this in Ex 30:3,

19: "and the Lord said, I shall bring before you all my Glory, and I shall proclaim the Name Yahweh before you."[3] One can therefore say that the proper name, the divine I (= God the Lord) belongs to the First hypostasis, which is revealed; in relation to It the Second and Third hypostases have primarily a "common" Name. They are the ones who reveal the essence of God, divine Wisdom and Glory; in this sense, they are primarily sophian designations, although in a hypostatic application.

Such is the distinction in the threefold naming of the Holy Trinity. But how is it defined in the Name of Jesus, the Godman? It is the one name not only for the Second hypostasis, for the Godman, but the naming of the whole Holy Trinity is concealed in it; it is the Trinity's sacred cryptogram. The essence of the matter does not change even here, in this hiddenness. The twofold significance of the Name of God is fully preserved in the Name of Jesus also, so far as it is also the proper name of the Second hypostasis, of the Godman, and in it and through it the whole Holy Trinity is named in Its threefold reciprocity. At the same time, however, it expresses the power, depth, and self-revelation of the Godhead, revealed in Wisdom and Glory; in a word it is a sophian self-definition. The one meaning, that of a proper hypostatic name, unites indivisibly with the other sophian, ousian meaning, in all the power and fullness of the Godhead. Jesus is Logos, the Word of all words about everything, "through him all things came to be"; he is the univalent and all-containing catholic name; but the name also signifies the Power, Wisdom, and Glory of God. It is as it were the divine Title of all Being, which in the language of the Old Testament reads, "Who Am, I am the One Who Is," but in the New Testament language—Jesus. This is the universal-symbolic name of Divine Sophia, who is pre-eternally in the heavens and is disclosed in creaturely becoming, as *to be, to become who is*, in the emergence out of nothing in creatureliness.

Hence, we make the general conclusion that the Name of God and the Name of Jesus, in heralding the hypostatic being of God, at the same time are also sophian. It must be understood not only Trinitarian-theologically, but also sophiologically, theophanically, anthropologically, and cosmologically, applied to all definitions of divine and creaturely being. This corresponds to the twofold character of the name, on the one hand as the hypostatic subject, the silent "grammatical **subj**ect," and on the other hand, as the sophian self-revelation, existential predicate. It implies in itself "I am who am," "Who Is," but also "in the Beginning (the Godhead, Sophia) was the Word (hypostatic *ho logos*), and the Word was with God (the Father, *ton theon*), and the Word was God (divine, *theos*), and as divine essence, nature, wisdom, glory, being in beauty and essential name." The Names Logos and

Jesus are identical according to their power, as they are self-identical also in their hypostatic correlation.

This identity of meaning of the Name of Jesus can be expressed in the terms of the Chalcedonian dogma about the single divine-human hypostasis and two natures. The Name of Jesus, as hypostatic, is one: of the Son of God and Son of Man, who came down from heaven (Jn 3:13), the Heavenly First Human. But it is proper to two natures, and in this sense it is twofold, belonging simultaneously to His divinity and humanity. In this way, it is single and twofold, in accordance with the entire Chalcedonian definition. But it thereby remains also one, as is the Godman himself.

In conclusion, it is necessary once more to affirm that the "Name of God" is not only a word, a Divine word, in all the depth and inexhaustibility of its meaning, but also Divine power and essence. "The Name of God is God" in the sense of God's presence, of Divine energy. In this essential sense, it must be understood in prayer and in life. It is inscribed on the whole universe, on the whole of humanity, and on the angelic world. All the worlds and their abysses, the heavenly, earthly, and infernal, are not closed for this name. It permeates everything, for "all was through him and without him nothing was which came to be." It is the naming that carries the Name of God in itself.

To him be glory in the ages of ages.

Paris, 1942.

Excursuses

Concerning Certain Cases of the Deliberate Designation of Names in the Bible

The Bible gives us a series of cases when the designation of names is expressly noted. A definite meaning is combined with the name itself, and some sort of explanation is given. In other words, the "inner form" of a name is underscored, its sememe, and in these cases we are present at the emergence of the name itself, which is used for the first time on the given occasion. Sometimes this meaning of the name is especially underscored, e.g., 1 Sam 4:21—(the daughter-in-law of Eli, the wife of Phineas) called the boy Ichabod (without glory), saying "the glory of the Lord has departed from Israel" with the capture of the ark of God and (with the death) of her father-in-law and husband. 1 Sam 25:25—(Abigail said to David), "may my lord not turn his attention to this evil man (Nabal) for as is his name, so is he. Nabal (fool) is his name and folly is with him." Compare Sir 46:2, Eccl 6:10—"what exists has already been given a name, and it is known that this is a human being."

In this way, we have here the designation of a name, with reasons given, justified by its meaning or by its inner form. Usually when no motivation is given, the Bible states briefly "and she gave birth to so and so," and this in the overwhelming majority of cases, which is why the exceptions to general rules always merit particular attention. It is worth noting that except for the early patriarchs, this practice is observed one way or other (in the form either of renaming or of original naming) with respect to the principal patriarchs beginning with Abra(ha)m and ending with the twelve sons of Jacob.

At the head of all naming stands, of course, the designation of the name of the mother of humanity, "and Adam called the name of his wife Eve, for she became the mother of all the living," Gen 3:20. It is not hard to grasp the completely exceptional importance and significance of this naming, which needs no special explanation. From the sons of Adam only the naming of Seth is given a particular reason, "and she (Eve) called his name Seth, because (she said) God placed another seed in me in place of Abel," Gen 4:45, cf. 5:3. "And Seth called his name Enosh; at that time they began to invoke the Lord God," Gen 4:26, though the connection with the name is not fully clear. "Lamech bore a son and called his name Noah, saying 'he will console us in our labor and in the works of our hands in cultivating the earth which the Lord God cursed,'" Gen 5:28–29. "Two sons were born to Eber, the name of one is Peleg, because in his day the earth was divided, and the name of his brother is Joktan," Gen 10:25. "Hagar bore a son for Abram, and Abram called the name of his son which was born from Hagar, Ishmael," Gen 16:15. This example shows that sometimes even when a special meaning of a name is not indicated, the mere fact of its designation is explicitly noted. "And both daughters of Lot became pregnant from their father and the eldest bore a son and called his name Moab, saying 'He is from my father.' He is the father of the Moabites even until now. And the younger one also bore a son and called his name Ben-Ammi, saying, 'He is the son of my clan.' He is the father of the Ammonites even until now," Gen 19:36–38. This entire exceptional case described in the Bible is accompanied by an exceptional naming. Because of this case and similar ones, some may say that here the name clearly receives the character of a mere nickname, connected with a certain reminiscence. But this is not true here either. Here the origin of the name itself is indicated, which is born as it were simultaneously and in tandem with its bearer (which does not happen in simpler and more ordinary cases of naming, when the one being born appears in the world already named in advance, and this is expressed in a brief note: so and so was born). Once it has arisen and been born, a name then leads its life already independently of the inner form of its meaning. All these circumstances, at the very most, can predetermine its meaning, like its horoscope, but having been born, the name acquires its own energy and character, so that the explanation is more typical for naming than for the name itself.

"The children whom God himself gives, he himself also names before birth: 'and you will call his name John.' This happens thus not without reasons. With us a name has broken off relations with the object, names are often empty and even contrary to the objects, but with God, a name designates an object, and the person corresponds to the name. God gives a name beforehand in order to show that He calls 'the things that are not as things that are,' Rom 4:17. Zechariah did not yet have a son; the designation of the name already indicates the authority of those who name over those that are named, as even now they put names to glebes and fields. And besides, a name remains for an entire life, and by its sound it will constantly recall the miracle of naming." Innokentii, archbishop of Kherson and Taurida, *Works*, vol. 11, p. 13.

"And Abram called the name of his son . . . whom Sarah had born him, Isaac," Gen 21:3, obviously in connection with recollection of Sarah's laughter when the birth was foretold to her by the miraculous strangers. "The first (of the twins) came out red, all shaggy like a goat, and she called his name Esau. Then his brother came out, holding Esau by the heel with his hand, and his name was called Jacob," Gen 25:25–26. Reasons are given explicitly for the name of all Jacob's sons who were born from Leah, as well as from Rachel, Walla, and Zilpah. Gen 29:32–35, Reuben, Simeon, Levi, Juda; Gen 30:6–8, Dan, Naphtali; Gen 30:11–13, Gad, Asher; Gen 30:18–21, Issachar; Gen 30:23–24, Zebulun, Dinah, Joseph, Ben-Oni (Benjamin).[1] In Gen 38:3–5, 28–30, especially named are Er, Onan, Shelah, Perez, and Zerah. Particular reasons are given for the name Moses, as one would expect. "And she (pharaoh's daughter) called his name Moses, because (she said) I drew him out of the water," Ex 2:10. Likewise for the names of his sons: "Zipporah bore a son and Moses called his name Gershon, because, he said, I became a stranger in a foreign land." "And she conceived again and born him a second son, and he called his name Eliezer, saying 'the God of my father was a helper for me and delivered me from the hand of Pharaoh,'" Ex 2:22, cf. 18:2–3. Especially noted is the naming of Obed by his neighbors (Ruth 4:17) and of Samuel (1 Sam 20) "for, said Hannah, I have requested him of the Lord (God of Hosts)."

We would have difficulty speaking confidently about the following. First, why are the given names and only those names explicitly explained? About this we can only say that in these cases we are present not only at the birth of individuals but also at the birth of names. Second, why are the relative and even absolute majority of these cases noted in the book of Genesis? About this we must say that the number of explained names comprises a completely insignificant portion of the general number of names mentioned in the Bible. It is worth noting that a similar explanation is given in many cases for geographical names, particularly when the naming or renaming is connected with some religious event, and sometimes a routine event. It is thus that the following names are explained: Zoar (Gen 19:22); the place Yahweh-Yireh (Gen 22:14); the wells Esek and Sitnah and Rehoboth (Gen 26:20–22); the well Shibah and mount Beer-sheba (Gen 26:32–33); the place Bethel, formerly Luz (Gen 28:19); a hill called Jegar-sahadutha by Laban, but Galeed by Jacob, also Mizpah (Gen 31:47–49); Menachaim and Penuel (Gen 32:1–2, 30); El-Bethel (Gen 35:7); Gerem-Gaatad is renamed "lament of the Egyptians," which is near Jordan (Gen 50:11); Succoth (Gen 33:17); Marah (Ex 15:23); Massah and Meribah (Ex 17:7); the altar Yahweh-Nissi (Ex 17:15); Taberah and Kibroth-hatta-avah (Num 11:3, 34); Eschol (Num 13:23); Hormah (Num 21:3, cf. Josh 1:17); a series of towns (Num 32:38–42); Gilgal (Josh 5:9); Ed (Josh 22:34); Luz (Judg 1:26); Bochim (Judg 2:5); Yahweh-Shlom (Judg 6:24), Ramath-lehi (Judg 15:11–19); Selah-Hammachlekoth (1 Sam 23:28); Baal-Perazim (2 Sam 5:20, 1 Chr 14:11).

The Name of the Lord

Gen 13: 4, "Up to the place of the altar, which he made there in the beginning, and there Abram invoked the Name of the Lord." Gen 16:13, "and (Hagar) called the Lord, who spoke with her with this name: You are the God who sees me. For she said, as if I had seen here the one who saw me." Gen 21:33, "and Abraham planted by the grove of Beersheba and invoked there the Name of the Lord, the Eternal God." Ruth 4:14, "And the woman said to Naomi, blessed is the Lord that He did not leave you without an heir. And let His Name be glorious in Israel." 2 Sam 7:23, "And he will acquire him as a people for Himself and he will glorify His Name." 2 Sam 7:26, "and Your Name will be magnified forever."

The Name of God in the Old Testament

Gen 2:19–20, "And God brought them to Adam in order to see how he would call them," *quid vocaret ei, quid nominis imponerent*, designates in Hebrew the same thing as "to give someone a name, *kalein tina ti*" (cf. Gen 26:18, Ruth 4:17, Ps 147:4). Ex 3:13–15, "and Moses said to God: see, I will come to the sons of Israel and say to them, the God of your fathers sent me to you. But they will say to me, what is His name? What am I to say to them? God said to Moses, I am the One who Is. And he said, speak thus to the sons of Israel: The One who Is (Yahweh) sent me to you. And God said again to Moses: speak thus to the sons of Israel, the Lord God of your fathers, the God of Abraham, Isaac and Jacob sent me to you. See, this is my Name forever, and a memorial about Me from generation to generation." Ex 6:2–3,

"God spoke to Moses and said to him: I am the Lord. I appeared to Abraham, Isaac and Jacob with the name 'Almighty God,' but with My Name 'Lord' I was not revealed to them." Ex 9:16, "For this I have preserved you (pharaoh) in order to show My power against you, and so that My Name would be exalted on all the earth." Ex 15:3, "The Lord is a man of battle, Yahweh is His Name" (song of Moses). Ex 22:7, "Do not pronounce the name of the Lord your God in vain, for the Lord will not leave without punishment him who pronounces His Name in vain." (Lev 19:12, Deut 5:11, Prov 30:9). "In each place where I place a memory of My Name, I will come to you and bless you" (Ex 20:24). Ex 23:20–21, "See. I am sending my Angel before you. . . . Do not be stubborn against Him, because He will not forgive your sin, for My Name is in Him." Ex 33:19, "and the Lord said to Moses, 'I will bring before you all my glory and will utter the Name Yahweh before you and who is to be shown mercy, I will show mercy, who to pity, I will pity.'" Lev 18:21, "And do not offer your children in worship of Moloch and do not dishonor the Name of your God. I am the Lord." Deut 6:13, "Fear the Lord your God, and serve Him alone (and stick to him) and swear by his Name." The third commandment, Ex 20:7, Deut 5:11. Cf. Lev 19:12.

1 Kings 3:2, "the people were still bringing sacrifices on the heights, for the house of the Name of the Lord was not yet built until that time." 1 Kings 8:16, "I have not chosen a town in any of the tribes of Israel, that my house be built where My Name would abide." 1 Kings 8:29, "My name will be there (in the temple)." 1 Kings 8:42–43 (with parallels 1 Kings 9:3, 2 Kings 21:4, 1 Kings 9:3), "The temple which you built so that My Name abide there forever," "which I consecrated to My Name" (9) (cf. 2 Kings 23:27; 1 Chron. 22:7–8). 1 Chron. 16:8, 19, "glorify the Lord, proclaim His Name . . . praise his holy Name" (cf. 1 Chron 29:13). 2 Chron. 6:6–9, "But I chose Jerusalem so that there my Name would abide . . . David my father had it in his heart to build a temple to the name of the Lord God of Israel." 2 Chron. 6:20, "let your eyes be opened on this temple by day and by night, on the place where you promised to place Your Name" (cf. 33:7). 2 Chron. 7:14, "This people which is called by my Name." 2 Chron 7:16, "Sanctify this house so that my Name be there forever." (The prayer of Manasseh), "Who closed the abyss and sealed it with *your* terrible and glorious *Name.*" 2 Chron. 6:26, "And they confess your Name." 2 Chron. 6:32, "if also foreigners come from the distant earth for the sake of your Name, for they too will hear about your great Name and your powerful hand." 2 Chron. 6:33, "so that they will know that this temple is called by your Name." 2 Chron. 6:34, "to the temple, which I built to your Name" (cf. 2 Chron. 6:38). 2 Esd 6:12, "And God, whose Name dwells there." Neh 1:11 (his prayer), "who reveres your Name." Tob 3:11

(Sarah's prayer), "Blessed are you, O Lord my God and blessed is your holy and glorious Name forever." Cf. Tob 8:5 (Tobias's prayer), "Blessed are you, Lord God of our fathers and blessed is your holy and glorious Name forever." Tob 11:14 (Tobit's prayer), "Blessed are you, o God, and blessed is your Name forever and blessed are all your holy angels." Tob 12:6, "It is a good work . . . to bless God, to exalt his Name, to preach reverently about his works." Tob 13:11 (Tobit's prayer), "Many nations shall come from afar to the Name of the Lord God with gifts in their hands, with gifts for the King of Heaven." Judith 9:8, "The Lord is your Name, crush their fortress with your power." Judith 16:1, "And Judith said, 'exalt and invoke his Name.'" Job 1:21, "May the Lord's name be blessed."

Ps 5:12, "And they who love Your Name will boast about you." Ps 7:17, "I sing to the Name of the Lord Most High." Ps 8:1, 9, "Lord our God how wonderful is your name through all the earth." Ps 9:2, "I sing to your Name, o most High." Ps 9:10, "may they hope in you who know your Name!" Ps 20:1, "The name of the God of Jacob will defend you." Ps 20:5, 9, "In the name of the God of Jacob he will be exalted, we shall call in the Name of our Lord." Ps 22:22, "I will declare your Name to my brethren." Ps 25:11, "For the sake of your Name, o Lord, cleanse my transgression." Ps 29:2, "bring glory to His Name." Ps 33:21, "And we have hoped in His Holy Name." Ps 45:18, "I will remember your Name in every generation." Ps 48:10, "Like your Name, o God, so is your praise to the ends of the earth." Ps 54:1, 6, "O God, in your Name save me. We confess your Name, Lord, because you are good." Ps 61:8, "thus will I sing to your Name forever." Ps 63:4, "In the Name of the Lord I will lift up my hands." Ps 68:4, "Cry out to God, sing to his Name, extol the one rising in the west, Lord is his Name." Ps 69:30, 36, "I will praise the Name of My God with song . . . and the one loving your Name will dwell in it." Ps 72:17, 19 "His Name will be blessed forever; his Name endures before the sun . . . and blessed is the Name of his Glory forever." Ps 74:10, 21, "the adversary reviles your Name to the end . . . the lowly and poor praises your Name." Ps 75:1, "He will call upon your Name." Ps 76:1, "Great is his Name in Israel." Ps 79:9, "Help us, o God our Savior, for the sake of your Name, o Lord." Ps 83:16, 18, "And they will seek after your Name, Lord . . . and let them know that your Name is Lord." Ps 86:11–12, "let my heart rejoice to fear your name . . . and I will glorify your Name forever." Ps 89:24, "And His horn will be lifted up on account of my Name." Ps 91:14, "Because he has known my Name." Ps 105:1, "Call upon his Name." Ps 106:47, "your Holy Name is to be confessed." Ps 109:21, "work with me, for the sake of your Name." Ps 111:9, "Holy and dread is his Name." Ps 113:1–2, "Praise the name of the Lord . . . blessed be the Name of the Lord forever and ever." Ps 116:4, "I shall call on the Lord's Name." Ps 124:8, "Our help is in the Name of the Lord who made heaven and earth." Ps 129:8, "We have blessed you in the Name of the Lord." Ps 134:3, 4, "Sing to his Name, for it is good . . . o Lord, your Name is forever." Ps 138:2, "We will confess your Name and your mercy and your truth: because you have magnified for all of us your holy Name." Ps 145:1, "Blessed is your Name for ages of ages." Ps 149:5, "let them praise the Lord's name."

Wis 10:20, "The just have cried out your Holy Name, Lord." Wis 14:21, "the people, by submitting either to misfortune or to tyranny applied to stones and trees the Name which cannot be shared." Sir 17:10, "let (the people) glorify his holy Name." Sir 29:9, "Do not turn to the habit of using the Name of the Holy One in an oath, for as a slave constantly subjected to punishment is not delivered from wounds, so too the one who swears constantly by the Name of the Holy One will not be cleansed of sin." Sir 39:19, "Bless the Lord in all your deeds, magnify his Name." Sir 45:19, "(Aaron and his family) served as priests and blessed his people with his Name." Sir 47:20–21, "In the Name of the Lord God, who is called the God of Israel, you (Solomon) gathered gold like bronze." Sir 51:1, 17 "I shall glorify your Name." Sir 51:15, "I will praise your Name."

Isa 9:6, "For a Child is born to us, a Son is given to us, the government is on his shoulders and they call his Name Wonderful, Counsellor, mighty God, Father of eternity, Prince of peace." Isa 12:4, "and you will say on that day, 'glorify the Lord, call upon his Name, proclaim his deeds among the nations, remember that his Name is great.'" Isa 18:7, "to the place of the Name of the Lord of Hosts on mount Zion." Isa 24:15, "Glorify the Lord in the East, on the sea islands—the Name of the Lord God of Israel." Isa 25:1, "I will praise your Name." Isa 26:8, "And on the ways of your judgments, o Lord, we have hoped in you, to your Name and to remembrance of you our soul has hastened." Isa 26:13, "Lord our God, other lords apart from you have reigned over us, but through you alone we glorify your Name." Isa 29:23, "they shall sanctify my Name and they shall sanctify the Holy One of Jacob." Isa 30:27–29, "See the Lord's name comes from afar, his wrath burns and his flame is strong, his mouth is filled with indignation; his tongue is like a consuming fire and his breath like a flowing stream, which rises to the neck, to scatter the nations to the point of exhaustion, and there will be a bridle in the jaws of the nations which directs them to error. But you will have songs as on a night of sacred festival and joy of heart as among those going with pipes to the Lord's mountain, to the stronghold of Israel." Isa 41:20, "they will call upon my Name." Isa 42:8, "I am the Lord. This is my Name." Isa 43:7, "each one who is called by my Name, whom I created for my glory." Isa 47:4, "Our

redeemer is the Lord of Hosts. His Name is the Holy One of Israel." Isa
48:2, "The Lord of Hosts is His Name." Isa 48:9, "For the sake of my Name
I have set aside my wrath, and for the sake of my glory I have restrained
myself from eradicating you." Isa 48:11, "I do this for my sake, for my own
sake, for what would be the censure against my Name. I give my glory to no
other." Isa 50:10, "let him hope in the Lord's name and let him be confirmed
in his God." Isa 51:15, "the Lord of Hosts is his Name." Isa 52:6, "My people
know my Name." Isa 52:56, "every day my Name is dishonored. Therefore,
my people will know my Name . . . that I am the one who said 'see, it is I.'"
Isa 54:5, "The Lord of Hosts is his Name. . . . He will be called God of all the
earth." Isa 56:6, "Those who have been united to the Lord in order to serve
him and to love the Name of the Lord." Isa 57:15, "Holy One is his Name."
Isa 59:19, "And they will fear the Name of the Lord at the setting and his
glory at the rising of the sun." Isa 60:9, "In the Name of the Lord your God
and of the Holy One of Israel, because he has glorified you." Isa 63:13–14,
"In order to make for himself an eternal Name." Isa 63:16, "from the ages
is your Name, our redeemer." Isa 63:19, "we have become like those over
whom you have never reigned, and over whom your Name was not called."
Isa 64:2, "so that your Name be made known to your enemies." Isa 64:7, "and
there is no one who calls upon your Name." Isa 65:1, "I was revealed to those
who were not inquiring about me, those who did not seek me have found
me: see it is I, I spoke to the nation which is not called by my Name."

Jer 3:17, "At that time they will call Jerusalem the throne of the Lord, and
all nations will be gathered in Jerusalem because of the Name of the Lord."
Jer 7:10, 11, 30, 32, 34; 34:15, "This house over which is called my Name."
Jer 7:12, "Come to my place in Shiloh, where I have previously appointed
my Name to abide." Jer 7:14, "I will also do with this house over which my
Name is called." Jer 10:6, "there is none like you, o Lord, you are great, and
your Name is great with might." Jer 10:16, "His Name, the Lord of Hosts."
Jer 10:25, "On the tribes which do not call upon your Name." Jer 14:7, "You,
Lord, do with us for the sake of your Name." Jer 14:9, "You Lord are in
our midst and your Name is called upon us." Jer 14:14–15, "The prophets
prophesy falsehood in my Name." Jer 14:21, "do not reject us for the sake of
your Name." Jer 15:16, "Your Name is called upon me, Lord God of Hosts."
Jer 16:21, "they will know that my Name is Lord." Jer 20:9, "I will speak
no more in his Name." Jer 23:6 (= 33:16), "And see, his Name (offshoot)
with which they will call him: the Lord is our justification." Jer 23:25, "I have
heard how the prophets speak, who prophesy a lie in My Name." Jer 23:27,
"Do they think to lead my people to the point of forgetting my Name by
means of their dreams . . . as their fathers forgot my Name because of Baal?"

Jer 27:15 (= 29:9), "They falsely prophesy in my Name." Jer 33:2, "Lord is his Name." Jer 44:26, "See, I have sworn by my great Name, says the Lord, that my Name will no longer be pronounced in all the land of Egypt by the mouths of anyone of Judah who says, the Lord God lives." Jer 46:18, "I live, says the King whose Name is Lord of Hosts" (= 50:34; 50:19). Bar 2:15, "your Name is called on Israel and his race." Bar 2:26, "You left the house on which your Name is called."

Ezek 20:14, 22, "I acted because of my Name, that it not be defamed before the nations, in the eyes of whom I brought them out." Ezek 20:39, "Do not defile my Holy Name any longer with your gifts." Ezek 36:20–23, "(20) and they have dishonored my holy Name." "(21) and I pitied my holy Name, which the house of Israel dishonored." "(22) Not for you do I do this, house of Israel, but because of my holy Name, which you have dishonored." (And further, the promises, 24–38). Ezek 36:23, "I will sanctify my great Name, profaned among the nations." Ezek 39:7, "And I will show my holy Name among my people Israel and I will not let my holy Name henceforth be defamed." Ezek 39:25, "I will be jealous because of my holy Name." Ezek 43:7, "And the house of Israel will no longer defile my holy Name" (= 43:8). Ezek 48:35, "But the Name for the town from that day will be: The Lord is there."

Dan 2:20, "And Daniel said, 'let the Lord's Name be blessed from age to age.'" Dan 3:34, "Do not betray us forever for the sake of your Name and do not destroy your covenant." Dan 3:43, "Give glory to your Name, o Lord." Dan 3:52, "blessed is the holy Name of your glory and praiseworthy and exalted forever." Dan 9:19, "your Name is called in your city and on your people."

Hos 2:16, "and it will be on that day, says the Lord, you will know me 'my husband,' and you will no more call me Baal (my lord)." Hos 12:5, "The Lord is God of Hosts, the One Who Is (Yahweh)—is his Name." Joel 2:26, "And you will glorify the Name of the Lord your God." Am 4:13, "The Lord God of Hosts is his Name" (= 5:8, 27). Am 6:10, "And he will say, be quiet, for you cannot remember the Lord's Name." Am 9:12, "between which my Name will be proclaimed." Mic 5:4, "And He will stand and he will pasture in the Lord's power, in the great Name of the Lord his God." Zech 13:9: They shall call upon my Name, and I will hear them and say, this is my people, and they will say, the Lord is my God." Mal 1:11, "From the rising of the sun to its setting great will be my Name among the nations, and in every place they will offer incense to my Name, a pure sacrifice, great will be my Name among the nations." Mal 1:14, "I am the great King, and my Name is dreadful among the peoples." Mal 2:2, "So that glory be returned to my Name." Mal 2:5, "He was reverent before my Name." Mal 3:16, "those who honor My Name."

Zech 13:9, "And they will call upon my Name." 3 Esd 3:34, "Nowhere will my Name be found but in Israel."

The Name of God in the New Testament

Mk 16:17, "By my Name they will cast out demons." Lk 9:48, "Whoever receives a child in my Name receives me." 1 Cor. 6:11, "But you were washed, you were sanctified, you were justified by the Name of our Lord Jesus Christ and by the Spirit of our God." Phil. 2:9–10, "Therefore God exalted him and gave him the Name above every Name so that the every knee of those in heaven, on earth and under the earth should bend before the Name of Jesus." Heb 1:4, "being as much superior to angels as the Name he inherited is more glorious than theirs." Rev. 2: 13, "you (the angel of the church of Pergamum) hold fast to my Name." Rev. 3:8, "and did not deny my Name." Rev. 3:12, "and I will write on him the Name of my God and the name of the city of my God, the new Jerusalem which comes down from heaven from my God, and my new Name." Rev. 14:1, "the 144,000 who have the Name of his Father (of the Lamb) written on their foreheads." Rev. 16:9, "they blasphemed the Name of God." Rev. 19:12–13, "He had a Name written which no one knew except him alone, his Name: the Word of God."

The Glory of God

Ex 16:7, 10; Num 16:19; 1 Kings 8:10–11; Isa 35:2; 40:5.

The Name of Other Gods

Ex 23:13, "do not recall the name of other gods; let it not be heard from your mouth." Zech 13:2, "and it will be on that day, says the Lord of Hosts, I shall exterminate the names of idols from this earth, and they shall be remembered no more." 2 Sam 7:26, "and let your Name be magnified forever."

Appellations Given by God (or by an Angel)

Gen 2:5, "(God) blessed them and called their name 'human being' on the day of their creation." Gen 16:11, "And the Lord's angel said to her (Hagar): see, you are pregnant and will bear a son, and you will call his name Ishmael, for God heard your suffering." Gen 17:5, "And you shall no longer be called Abram, but your name shall be Abraham, for I have made you the father of a multitude of peoples." Gen 17:15, "Do not call your wife Sarai but let her name be Sarah." Gen 17:19, "Sarah your wife will bear you a son and you will call his name Isaac, and I shall make my covenant with him." Gen 32:29, "Jacob asked, saying, 'tell me your name.' And He said, why are you inquiring after my name? It is wonderful." Gen 35:10, "and God said to him, your name is Jacob, henceforth you shall not be called Jacob, but your name shall be Israel." Judg 13:17–18, "And Manoah said to the Angel of God, 'what is your name?' so that we may glorify you when your word is fulfilled. The Angel of the Lord said to him, 'why do you inquire after my name?' 'It is wonderful.'" Isa 65:15–16, "You will leave your name to my chosen ones for a curse, and the Lord God will kill you, but he will call his servants by a different name; whoever shall bless himself with it on earth shall be blessed by the God of truth, and whoever shall be cursed on earth shall be cursed by the God of truth." Rev 2:17, "I will give to the one who conquers the hidden manna to taste, and I will give him a white stone and on the stone a new name is written, which no one knows except him who receives."

Texts of the Bible Concerning Naming

Gen 3:20, "And Adam called the name of his wife Eve, for she became the mother of all the living." Gen 4:25; cf. Gen 5:3, "And she (Eve) called his name Seth, because (she said) God placed another seed in me in place of Abel." Gen 4:26, "And Seth called his son's name Enosh; at that time they began to invoke the Lord." Gen 5:28–29, "Lamech bore a son and called his name Noah, having said, 'he will console us in our labor and in the works of our hands when cultivating the earth which the Lord (God) cursed.'" Gen 10:25, "With Eber two sons were born: the name of one was Peleg, because in his days the earth was divided, the name of his brother was Joktan." Gen 16:15, "Hagar bore a son for Abram and (Abram) called his son's name, which was born by Hagar, Ishmael." Gen 19:36–38, "And both daughters of Lot became pregnant from their father, and the elder bore a son and she called his name Moab (saying, he is from my father). He is the father of the Moabites until now. And the younger one likewise bore a son and she called his name Ben-Ammi (saying, he is the son of my clan). He is the father of the Ammonites until now." Gen 21:3, "And Abraham called his son's name, born of him, whom his wife Sarah bore him, Isaac." Gen 25:25–26, "The first (of the twins) came out red, entirely hairy, like a hide, and they called his name Esau. Then his brother came out, holding Esau's heel with his hand, and his name was called Jacob." Gen 29:32–35, "Leah conceived and bore (Jacob) a son and she called his name Reuben, because she said, 'the Lord looked on my poverty (and gave me a son); for my husband will love me.'

And (Leah) conceived again and bore Jacob a (second) son, and she said, 'the Lord heard that I was unloved, and he gave this one to me.' And she called his name Simeon. And she conceived again and bore a son and said, 'now my husband will adhere to me, for I have born him three sons.' Because of this, his name was called Levi. And again she conceived and bore a son and said, 'now I exalt the Lord.' Therefore, she called his name Judah. And she ceased giving birth." Gen 30:6–8, "And Rachel said, 'God has judged me, and he heard my voice and gave me a son' (N.B. the son of her serving girl Walla). Therefore, she called his name Dan. And again Walla the serving girl of Rachel conceived and bore another son for Jacob. And Rachel said, 'I have fought a powerful fight with my sister and overcome.' And she called his name Naphtali." Gen 30:11–13, "And Leah said 'it has increased'[2] (N.B., the son is from the serving girl Zilpah). And she called his name Gad. (And again) Zilpah conceived, Leah's serving girl, and she bore another son for Jacob. And Leah said, 'it is to my good, for women shall call me blessed.' And she called his name Asher." Gen 30:18–21, "And Leah said, God gave a recompense to me because I surrendered my serving girl to my husband. And Leah conceived again and bore Jacob a sixth son. And Leah said, 'God gave me a beautiful gift; now my husband will live with me for I bore him six sons,' and she called his name Zebulon. Then she bore a daughter and called her name Dinah." Gen 30:23–24, "Rachel conceived and bore Jacob a son and said, 'God has taken away my shame.' And she called his name Joseph, having said, the Lord will give me another son." Gen 35:18, "And when her soul was departing from her (Rachel), for she was dying, she called his name (a son) Benoni. But his father called him Benjamin." Gen 38:3–5, "She (the daughter Shua from Judah) conceived and bore a son and he called his name Er. And she conceived again and bore a son and she called his name Onan. And again she bore a (third) son and called his name Shelah." Gen 38:28–30, "And she (the midwife) said, 'how have you broken the barrier for yourself?' And his name was called Perez. Then his brother came out with a red thread in his hand, and his name was called Zerah." Ex 2:10, "and she (pharaoh's daughter) called his name Moses, because, she said, I drew him out of the water." Ex 2:22, "Zipporah (conceived and) bore a son and (Moses) called his name Gershom, because he said I became a stranger in a foreign land. (And having conceived, she bore another son and he called his name Eleazar, having said 'the God of my father was a helper for me and delivered me from the hand of Pharaoh')" (cf. Ex 18:2–3). Num 13:17, "Here are the names of the men whom Moses sent to spy out the land. And Moses called Hoshea, son of Nun, Joshua." Judg 6:32, "And he began to call him Jerubbaal from that day, because he said, 'let Baal himself be judged with him because he destroyed his altar.'" Judg 13:24, "And his wife bore a son and she called his name Samson" (cf. Isa 9:6). Ruth 1:20, "She said to them, 'do not call me Naomi (pleasant) but call me Mara (bitter), because the Almighty has sent me great bitterness.'" Ruth 4:17, "the neighbors called his name and said, 'by Naomi a son has been born' and they called his name Obed." 1 Sam 1:20, "Hannah conceived and bore a son and gave him the name Samuel, for (she said) I asked for him from the Lord (God Of Hosts)." 1 Sam 4:21, "(The daughter-in-law of Eli, wife of Phineas) called the boy Ichabod (without glory) having said, 'the glory has departed from Israel'—with the capture of the ark of God and (with the death of) her father-in-law and husband." 1 Sam 25:25, "(Abigail says to David) let my lord not turn attention on that evil man, on Nabal, for as his name, so is he. Nabal (foolish) is his name, and folly is with him." 2 Sam 12:24–25, "And (Bathsheba) bore a son and called his name Solomon. And the Lord loved him and sent the prophet Nathan, and he called his name Jedidiah (beloved of God), according to the Lord's word." Sir 46:2, "corresponding to his name Joshua son of Nun was great in the salvation of God's chosen." Eccl 6:10, "What exists, is already given a name, and it is known that this is a human being." Isa 60:14: And they will call you the city of the Lord, Zion of Holy Israel." Isa 61:6, "They shall call you the ministers of our God" (cf. 62:2–12). Jer 33:9, "And Jerusalem shall be for me a joyful name, the praise and honor before all the nations of the earth who hear about all the good things which I have done for him." Rev 21:1–2, "on the gates are written the names of the twelve tribes of Israel."

Names of God in the Books of the Old Testament

I.   *God*—Gen 1:1; Deut 32:15; Ps 50:2, 3; Lev 3:3. *Living*—1 Sam 17:26; Dan 5:27; Jer 10:10; *Everlasting*—Dan 6:26. *First, Last*—Isa 44:6; 48:12. *Ancient*—Deut 33:27. *Ancient of Days*—Dan 7:9, 22. *Eternal*—Isa 40:28. *Eternally living*—Isa 57:15. *Always the same*—Isa 44:5; Ps 102:27; 1 Chr 17:26. Neh 9:6–7; Isa 48:10, 13; 48:12. *Hidden*—Isa 45:15.

II.   *Mind*—Deut 8:14. *All-knowing*—1 Sam 2:3. *Light*—Ps 27:1; Ps 36:9. *Sun*—Ps 74:12. *Great in counsel*—Jer 32:19. *Knowing the secrets of the heart*—Ps 44:21. *Testing heart and kidneys*—Ps 7:9. *Wise in heart*—Job 9:4.

III. *God*—Ex 15:2; Num 12:13. *Sturdy*—Deut 10:17; Ps 147:1, 7, 12; Neh 9:32. *Strong*—Deut 10:17; Ps 24:8; Jer 32:18; Neh 9:32. *Mighty one*—Gen 49:24; Ps 132:2; Isa 1:24. *Mighty*—Ps 89:8. *Mighty in power*—Job 9:4. *Greatly mighty*—Ps 147:5. *All-powerful*—Isa 40:26. *Sovereign*—Ps 24:8; Deut 10:17. *Almighty*—Gen 17:1; Num 24:4; Job 5:17; Ps 91:1. *Good*—Ps 25:8; Ps 86:5; Ps 100:5; Ps 147:1; 2 Chron. 30:18. *Beneficent*—Ps 119:68. *Merciful*—Ps 119:68. *Sparing, Generous*—Ps 86:15; Ps 145:8. *Beneficial, charitable*—Ps 145:17. *Long-suffering, slow* to anger—Ps 103:8. *Much-merciful*—Ps 7:10; Ps 112:4; Ps 145:17; Neh 9:33. *Righteous*—Ps 7:10; Ps 145:17; Neh 9:33. *Truthful*—Deut 32:4; Ps 92:15. *True*—Isa 65:16. *Faithful*—Deut 7:9. *God of truth*—Ps 31:5.

IV. *Creator*—Isa 40:28. *Maker*—Ps 149:2. *Savior*—Ps 7:10; Isa 45:15. *Deliverer*—Ps 18:2; Ps 70:6. *Redeemer*—Ps 19:14; Isa 63:16. *Shepherd*—Ps 80:1. *Preserver, guard*—Job 7:20; Ps 31:2. *Helper*—Ps 30:10. *Intercessor*—1 Sam 24:16; Ps 68:5. *Shield*—Gen 15:1; Deut 33:29; Ps 3:3; Ps 18:30; Ps 84:9. *Protection, protector*—Ps 32:7; Ps 119:114. *Stronghold, fortress*—Deut 3:24; 1 Sam 2:2; Ps 140:8. *Haven*—Ps 94:22. *Refuge*—Ps 14[?]; Ps 46:1. *Shelter*—Ps 90:1. *Peace*—Judg 6:24. *Near*—Ps 34:18; Ps 145:18. *Distant*—Prov 15:29. *Judge*—Gen 18:25; Judg 11:27; Ps 7:11; Ps 9:4; Ps 75:7. *Rewarding*—Ps 31:23; Jer 32:18. *Punishing faults*—Ex 20:5. *Jealous*—Ex 20:5; 34:15. *Avenger*—Ps 99:8. *Consuming fire*—Deut 4:24. *Chastiser, striking*—Ez 7:9. *Crushing*—Deut 32:39; Ps 68:21. *Healing*—Ex 15:26; Deut 32:39. *Exalting, humbling*—1 Sam 2:7. *Killing*—1 Sam 2:6; Deut 32:39. *Quickening*—1 Sam 2:6; Neh 9:6; Deut 32:39. *Impoverishing*—1 Sam 2:7. *Enriching*—ibid. *Benefiting*—Ex 20:6; Jer 32:18. *Patient*—Ps 99:8 [?]. *Gentle*—Ps 86:5 [?]. *Father*—Deut 32:6; Ps 103:13; Isa 43:16; 44:8; Mal. 16 (conditionally).

V. *Lord Adonai*—Gen 15:2; Ex 23:17; Ps 113:1; Isa 1:24. *Adonai*—Ex 34:9; Num 14:17. *Master*—Job 34:22; Dan 2:47; 5:23. *King*—Ps 5:2; Ps 24:7–10; Ps 145:1.

VI. *Glory*—Ps 106:20. *Great*—Ps 48:1; Ps 145:3; Neh 9:32; Jer 32:18. *Majestic*—Ps 8:1; Ex 15:11. *High*—48:2; Ps 99:2; Isa 57:15. *Exalted*—Ps 46:10. *Highest*—Job 35:25; 37:23. *Most High*—Gen 14:18; Ps 57:2; Ps 9:2; Ps 21:7. *Wonderful, dread*—Deut 10:17; Ps 68:36; Ps 76:12; Neh 9:32. *Extolled*—Ps 57:11. *Blessed*—Ps 18:46; Ps 68:35. *Most-glorious, worshipful*—Ps 18:3; Ps 48:1. *Holy*—Lev 11:44–45; Ps 22:3; Ps 99:3, 5, 9; Isa 1:4; 5, 16; 40:25; 57:15.

VII. *Only one*—Deut 6: 4.

Names of God in the Gospels or in Other Books of the New Testament

I. God is: *Spirit,* Jn 4:24; *Living,* Acts 14:15; 1 Tim 3:15; 4:17; Heb 9:14. *From the beginning,* 1 Jn 2:13, 14. *Living forever,* Rev 4:10. *The Sole, having immortality,* Tim 6:16. *Incorruptible,* Rom 1:2–3; 1 Tim 1:17. *Invisible,* 1 Tim 1:17; 6:16; Jn 1:18; 6:48. *Dwelling in unapproachable light,* 1 Tim 6:16.

II.   *Light*, 1 Jn 1:5. *Knower of hearts*, Acts 1:24; 15:8. *Wise*, 1 Tim 1:17;
Jude 25. *Powerful*, Lk 1:49.

III.   *Mighty*, 1 Tim 6:15. *Quickening all things*, 1 Tim 6:13. *Father of
spirits*, Heb 12:9. *Master*, Acts 4:24. *King of the ages*, 1 Tim 1:17. *Lord*,
Acts 4:24; 1:24. *Lord of heaven and earth*, Mt 9:25. *King of kings*, *Lord
of lords*, 1 Tim 6:15. *Pantocrator*, Rev 1:8.

IV.   *Lawgiver*, Jas 4:12. *Judge*, 1 Pet 2:23, 2 Tim 4:12. *Avenger*, 1 Thess
4:46. *Righteous*, Jn 17:25; 1 Jn 1:9. *Pure*, 1 Jn 3:3. *True*, Rom 3:4; Jn
17:3; 1 Thess 1:9. *Truthful*, Tim 1:2. *Faithful*, 1 Thess 5:24; 1 Jn 1:9.

V.   *Good*, Mt 19:17; Mk 10:18. *Compassionate*, Jas 5:11. *Deliverer*, Rom
11:26. *Savior*, Lk 1:47; Jude 25; 1 Tim 2:3; 4:10. *Guardian, shepherd*,
1 Pet 2:25. *Father*, Matt. 5:48; 6:9. *Merciful, God of consolation*, 2 Cor.
1:3. *God of peace*, Rom 15:32; 16:20; Heb 13:20; 2 Thess 3:16. *Love*, 1
Jn 4:48; 2 Cor. 13:11.

VI.   *Great*, 1 Tim 2:13. *Most High*, Lk 1:32, 76. *Rich*, Eph 2:4. *Perfect*, Mt
5:48; *Blessed*, 1 Tim 6:15. *Blessed forever*, 2 Cor. 11:31. *Holy*, Jn 17:3; 1
Tim 1:17.

VII.   *One*, 1 Cor 8:5; Gal 3:20; 1 Tim 2:5. *The one true God*, Jn 17:3; 1 Tim
1:17 (Sablukov, 21–23).

The Naming of Places

Gen 22:14, "And Abraham called the name of that place Yahweh-Yireh. Thus
even now it is said, on Yahweh's mountain he will watch for." Gen 26:20–22,
"And the shepherds of Gerar quarreled with the shepherds of Isaac saying,
it is our water. And they called the name of the well Esek, because they
quarreled with him. (When Isaac moved from there) they dug out another
well, and likewise they quarreled over it; and he called its name Sitnah. And
he moved from there and dug out another well about which they no longer
quarreled and he called its name Rehoboth, for, he said, now the Lord has
given us a spacious place, and we will multiply on the earth." Gen 26:32–33,
"On that day the servants of Jacob came and informed him about the well,
which they had dug, and they said to him, we found water. And he called
it Shibah. Therefore, the name of that town is Beersheba until the present
day." Gen 28:19, "And (Jacob) called the name of that place Bethel, but the
former name of that town was Luz." Gen 31:47–49, "And Laban called it
(a stony hill) Jegar-sahadutha, but Jacob called it Galeed. And Laban said to
Jacob: today this hill (and the monument which I have set up) is witness between me and you. Therefore, its name was called Galeed, likewise Mizpah,
because Laban had said, may the Lord oversee me and you, when we hide

from one another." Gen 32:1–2, "And the angels of God met him. Jacob, seeing them, said, it is God's host. And he called the name of that place Mahanaim." Gen 32:30, "And Jacob called the name of that place Penuel, for (he said) I saw God face to face and my soul was preserved." Gen 35:7, "Jacob set up an altar there (in Bethel) and called this place El-Bethel, for there God himself appeared to him when he ran from the face of his brother (Esau)." Gen 50:11, "And the inhabitants of that land, Canaan, saw mourning in Goren-ha-Atad and said, great is the mourning among the Egyptians. Therefore, the name of that place is called Abel-mizraim, it is beyond the Jordan." Ex 15:23, "They came to Marah and they could not drink the water in Marah, for it was bitter, which is why the name of that place is called Marah (bitterness)." Ex 17:7, "And he called the name of that place Massah and Meribah (temptation and reproach) because of the reproach of the sons of Israel, and because they tested the Lord, saying, is the Lord in our midst or not?" Ex 17:15, "And Moses set up an altar (to the Lord) and he called its name Yahweh Nissi (the Lord my banner)." Num 11:3, "And he called the name of that place Taberah (burning), because the fire of the Lord was enflamed among them." Num 11:34, "And they called the name of that place Kibroth-hatta-avah (graves of craving) for there they buried the craving people." Num 13:25, "This place they called the valley of Eshcol, because of the grape cluster which the sons of Israel cut there." Num 21:3, "The Lord heard the voice of Israel and handed the Canaanites into his hands, and he laid a curse on them and on their towns and called the name of that place Hormah (curse)" (cf. Josh 1:17; Num 32:38–42 (the renaming of towns)). Josh 5:9, "And the Lord said to Joshua: now I have removed from you the disgrace of Egypt. Therefore, this place is called Gilgal even to this day." Josh 22:34, "And the sons of Reuben and the sons of Gad (and half the tribe of Manasseh) called the altar Ed (witness), because (they said) he is a witness between us that the Lord is our God." Judg 1:26, "This man came to the land of the Hittites and built there a town and called its name Luz (N. B. instead of 'the destroyed': 23–25). This is its name to this day." Judg 2:3, "From this the place is called Bochim (mourners)." Judg 5:24, "And Gideon set up there an altar to the Lord and called it Yahweh Shalom (Lord of peace)." Judg 15:17, "Samson threw the jawbone from his hands and called this place Ramath-lehi (thrown jawbone)." Judg 15:19, "Samson drank (from the spring) and his spirit returned, and he lived: for this reason the name of this place is called spring of the one appealing, which is in Lehi to this day." 1 Sam 23:28, "And Saul returned from pursuing David and went to meet the Philistines, therefore, they called this place Selah-Hammachlekoth (rock of division)." 2 Sam 5:20, "And David went to Baal-perazim and struck them there and David said, the Lord has scattered my enemies before me, as water is scattered. Therefore, the name was given to that place Baal-perazim" (1 Chron. 14:10).

Names of God in Liturgical Prayers

I.   Everlasting (Oktoechos, tone 5, ode 9). Self-existent, Invisible, Ineffable, Unknowable, Incomprehensible (Chrysostom liturgy, it is worthy). Uncaused (2nd canon of Pentecost, ode 4, irmos). Without beginning, Untraceable, Uncontainable (Oktoechos, tone 5, ode 9). Immaterial (canon for Nativity of Christ, ode 4, irmos). Immeasurable, Incorruptible, Unchangeable (canon for the Visitation, ode 5, irmos). All-hymned, Perfect (2nd prayer at approaching sleep). Unlimited, Uncircumscribed, Pre-eternal, Existing everywhere, Eternal.

II. Strong, All-powerful (Trinity troparion 1 for morning prayer). Invincible, Master, Creator, Maker, All-maker, Preserver (prayer 5 at approaching sleep). Deliverer, Savior, Benefactor (2nd canon for Pentecost, ode 9). Physician of souls and bodies, King of peace (Oktoechos, tone 4, ode 5, irmos, tone 3, ode 5). Peace, Giver of life, Treasury of goods.

III. Source of light (Oktoechos tone 2, ode 5, irmos). Wise, Knower of hearts (in the Ode at Great Vespers).

IV. Good, Gracious, Great-endowed, Generous, Philanthropic (prayer of St. Macarius the Great 4 at approaching sleep). Not malicious, much-merciful, sympathetic (2nd prayer for Vespers on Pentecost day). Hospitable, long-suffering, all-merciful (step 8 tone ant 2). Meek, kind, well-wishing (Litany at the Lity[3] at the All-night Vigil).

V.   Unblemished, most pure, wonderful (Oktoechos, tone 8, ode 1, irmos). Dread (prayer of the priest at Chrysostom liturgy). Most High, Great, blessed, super-glorified, Adored.

VI. One in essence (Canon of St Andrew of Crete, 9th ode on Thursday of week 1 of Great Lent).

The Book of Needs. The Name of God

Prayer in which a newborn child is signed with the name on the eighth day.[4] "And grant, o Lord that your ineffable, holy Name abide on him, being united in time to your beneficent holy church and perfected by the dread mysteries of your Christ."

Prayers after forty days for a woman who gave birth. "Reckon her to your holy flock of rational sheep who are called by the Name of your Christ."

Prayer for making a catechumen. "In your Name, Lord God of truth and of your consubstantial Son and Holy Spirit, I lay my hand on your servant whom you have made worthy to find refuge in your Holy Name. . . . May your Holy Name be glorified in him . . . may he confess your Name by worshipping and praising your great and most-high Name." Second injunction, "By us His unworthy servants he commands you (the devil) and all your assisting powers to depart from the one newly sealed with the Name of our Lord Jesus Christ, our true God."

Ritual of holy baptism (or consecration of water). "Let those who slander your creation flee from it (water), because I have invoked your Name, o Lord, that is wonderful, glorious and dreadful to the enemy."

Ritual for unction. "And where we offer this oil in your great Name."

St. Basil's Prayer of exorcism over one suffering from demons. "Grant that my exorcism, performed in your dread Name, be terrible to him, the master of wickedness."

Order at the founding of a church. Litany. "Look kindly upon this place for the foundation on it of a church, to the glory of his most holy Name chosen . . . and propitiously lay a beginning to the glory of Your Name." From the prayer, "Deign to have on earth a temple for yourself to the perpetual praise of your most holy name."

The order of prayer at the erection of a cross on the top corners of a newly built church. From the prayer, "that in this temple built to your Name."

Concerning Baptismal Naming (Aleksandr Ivanovich Almazov. *Istoriia chinoposledovaniia kreshcheniia i miropomazaniia.* Kazan', 1884 VII, 136–151.)

The custom of giving new names to those entering Christianity has been noticed since the third century. Before that time the previous pagan names were retained (sometimes borrowed from occupations: Agricolus, Pastor, Nauticus; from colors: Candidus, Rubens; from animals: Aquila, Capreolus, Leo; from numbers: Primus, Secundus, Septimus; from countries and cities: Africanus, Macedonia, Roma; from deities: Apollo, Apollinaris, Phaebus, Bacchus, Dionysius, Ceres, Cerealis, Demetra, Mercurina, Saturnus, Saturnina, etc.). Only from the fourth century does the custom of giving a name at baptism come into use everywhere. The names of apostles and holy martyrs were given, and from abstract concepts of a dogmatic or ethical nature: Redemptus, Renatus, Pius, Pistis (Faith), Elpis (Hope), Agape (Love);

self-effacing names: Servus, Singuriosis, Calamniosus, Importunus, etc. The new name was announced in church publicly before the day of baptism (when the institution of the catechumenate was in force); simultaneously it is entered into the diptychs, and there were cases where the name was given at baptism too.

Concerning the practice of the Russian church (cf. A. Dmitrievskii, *Bogosluzhenie v russkoi tserkvi v XVI veke*. Part 1. *Sluzhby kruga sed'michnogo i godichnogo i chinoposledovaniia tainstv*. Kazan', 1881, 256–264), one must say that here, too, a Christian name was given in honor of one of the saints venerated in the Russian church. In fact, however, up to the reform of Peter the Great many Russians, in addition to Christian names, still had national, pagan names by which they were entered in the common registry and cadasters. So, too, Russian princes frequently had two names: Vladimir-Vasilii, Iaroslav-Georgii, Iziaslav-Dimitrii, in the twelfth century Mikhail-Sviatopolk, Vasilii-Vladimir, David-Vseslavich, Mikhail-Oleg, Pankratii-Iaroslav Sviatoslavich, Andrei-Mstislav Vsevolodovich, Boris-Vseslavich, Gleb Mirskii. Examples from commoners: in Vyshegorod at the time of Iaroslav there was the elder of gardeners who "was called Zhdan in the world, Mikula in baptism"; in Kiev in 1199 there was an artisan architect "among his own with the name Miloneg, and Peter in baptism." Boyars are mentioned in the chronicles with such names as Zhiroslav, Zhiriata, Nesdima, Sudimir, Iavolod, etc. In acts at the time of Ivan the Terrible, we continually encounter Slavonic-pagan names: Bulgak Vasil'ev, Chernets Gavrilov, Putila Serkov, Istoma Cheglokov, Zloba Fedukov; cf. such names as Dobrynia, Neriadets, Snovid, Goriuk, Slavn, Dorozhai, etc. Although the Russian clergy censured twofold naming, considering it a Latin custom, this too is encountered: in "the response of Nifont" Luka-Evdokim is mentioned, in the *Nikonian Chronicle*,[5] "the son Timofei, but they called his name Ivan," and Gavriil-Vasilii, tsarevich Dmitrii is called Uar.

Here are some of the opinions of Fr. John of Kronstadt. "Worshipper! Let the name of the Lord or the Theotokos, the name of an angel or a saint be for you in place of the Lord Himself, or the Theotokos or a saint. . . . The Name of the Lord is the Lord himself, the name of an angel, the angel, of a saint, the saint. How is this so? We do not understand. It is like this: let us say that you are called Ivan Il'ich. If they call you by this name, you surely recognize yourself among them and respond to them (that means, you agree that your name is you yourself with soul and body). So too the saints: when you call on their name, you call on them themselves. But, you will say, they don't have a body. What of it? The body is only a material covering for the soul, its house, but the person, their essence or the inner person is the soul. When they call you by your name, it is not only your body that answers, but your soul, by means of the body's organ. And so, the Name of God and of the saints is God himself and his saints (*Moia zhizn' vo Khriste*, p. 628). "The Divine Name is God himself. Therefore, it is said, 'do not take the name of the Lord your God in vain' (Ex 20:7, Deut 5:11) or 'if you bring my soul out of the dungeon, I must confess your Name' (Ps 142:7). As the Lord is the simplest Being, the simplest Spirit, so He is in one word, in one idea—all things entirely at the same time everywhere—in every creature. Therefore, only call on the Name of the Lord: if you call on the Lord Savior of believers, you will be saved. Everyone who calls on the Name of the Lord will be saved (Acts 2: 21). 'Call on me—my name—in the day of your sorrow, and I will deliver you, and you will glorify me' (Ps 50:15)" (Ibid. 692).

"Naming the name on an icon means a great deal for the believer. This name acts as if in place of the soul. Call upon the name of a saint with all your soul: he will hear you and will show his wonder-working power in the icon. The name of the Savior, called upon with faith, works miracles: it expels demons, extinguishes passions, and heals disease; by the grace of God, saints too who are called upon by name with faith likewise work miracles" (720). "You read a prayer, and He is wholly in each word, like Holy Fire, he penetrates each word; everyone can experience this for themselves if they pray sincerely, zealously, with faith and love. But especially in the names belonging to Him He is wholly there: Father, Son and Holy Spirit, or Trinity, or Lord, or Lord God, Lord of Hosts, or Lord Jesus Christ, Son of God, or Holy Spirit, Heavenly King, Consoler, Spirit of Truth . . . and the other names of Angels and saints. They are as close to us in their names as their names and our faith in them are close to our hearts" (177). "What is firmer, steadier, and mightier than the word? By a word the world is made and stands (Heb 1:3) and yet how flippantly and negligently we sinners treat words. . . . We do not understand that by a word proceeding from a believing and loving heart we can perform miracles for our soul and the souls of others, e.g., in prayer, at divine worship, in sermons, in the celebration of sacraments . . . besides, a word is the principle of life. The Word must still be respected firmly because in a single word the one and undivided Lord who is everywhere and fills all things is present. It is said 'you shall not take the Name of the Lord your God in vain' (Ex 20:7) because in the one name is the Lord himself, the simple Being, the eternally worshipful Unity" (234–235). Cf. 530, 531, "When for yourself you speak or pronounce in your heart the name of God, of the Lord or the Most Holy Trinity, of the Lord of Hosts, or the Lord Jesus Christ, in this name you have the whole being of the Lord; in it is His endless goodness, limitless wisdom, unapproachable light, omnipotence, immutability.

With the fear of God, with faith and love, touch lightly on this all-creating, all-directing Name with thoughts and heart." Cf. 636, 637, 638. Incidentally, this opinion is also interesting: "The very name "man" and then the name given him at baptism or at the rite of bestowal of a name, is proof that he came from the word of God. As long as the man lives, he will be called by this name and he will answer to it, because he is precisely this, he is wholly included in his name. Finally, when he dies and his corrupted remains are buried in the earth, his name alone remains in the memory as evidence of his origin from the Word of God—this is his and our possession, immaterial and eternal like the soul" (638).

Philo's Doctrine of the Name of God

Philo teaches that the completely unknowable God naturally does not have a name in the proper sense. No matter how many names for God we have adopted, not one of them is an exact designation for Him—(de sacrificiis Abelis et Caini, 147). This is why, when to the question about his name God replies, "I am who exists," he teaches us by this that in contrast to what does not exist, it belongs to him alone to exist but not to be named, because God does not have a name in the proper sense (de vita Moysis, 614; also de somniis 1, 599; Quod deterius potiori insidiari, soleat, 184; de mutatione nominum, 1045). God in his essence does not have a name and is unknowable, whereas the Logos is the archangel having many names; he is beginning and word and even the very name of God (de confusione linguarum, 341).

Word-Logos

In conformity with his general (metaphysical) realism, Anselm of Canterbury establishes a connection between objects and words (locutio rerum). "Who will deny that supreme wisdom, when it knows itself in creation, creates its own likeness (similitudinem), i.e., a word? Even if this word, as a result of the eminence of the object, cannot be called precise and fully adequate, it all the same can be recognized in a not fully inappropriate manner, as a comparison, a figure, or as its description. But this word, by which supreme wisdom speaks, creates consciousness, and by the same token it is not at all a word of this created being, because it is not the representation of this latter, but a primordial essence. From this it follows, in this way, that supreme wisdom (speaks) creates a creature not by a word of the creature itself. But in what way does this wisdom speak it (the creature) if it creates (speaks) it not by its word? For what it (wisdom) says with the help of a word it speaks (creates), but a word is a word about something, i.e., a representation. If then it speaks something other as its own self or an entity created by it (supreme wisdom), then it can speak only either by its own word or by the word of the creature. But if it says nothing by the word of the creature, then it says everything that it says with the help of its own word. In this way with one and the same word supreme wisdom expresses (speaks) its very self and all that it has created" (cited from prof. A. L. Pogodin, *Iazyk kak tvorchestvo. Proiskhozhdenie iazyka*, Kharkov', 1913, 381 = *Voprosy teorii i psikhologii tvorchestva*, t. IV). (Here Anselm of Canterbury is groping about for the difference between Divine and creaturely Sophia, the pre-eternal transformation of the creature and its creaturely being in becoming, which is established in Sophiology.)

G. Sablukov. *Collation of the Muslim Doctrine of the Names of God with the Christian Doctrine about It.* Kazan', 1872.

In believing in God, Muslims divide their concepts about Him into two categories: into names of God and into properties of God, which is evident from the following words of a confession of faith, "I believe in God as He is with his names and his properties" (1). The names of God are known under the title "beautiful names of God," and there is one particular name that they call "the great name of God."

"God has beautiful names. With these call on Him and leave aside those who quarrel about His names" (*Koran* 7: 179). There are ninety-nine beautiful names of God, which is confirmed by Mohammed. However, some who are not satisfied with this, increase the number of beautiful names to 1001, and there were contemplative ascetics who increased this number to 4000 (p. 314). Here is a list of the ninety-nine beautiful names as this is laid out in chapter 66 of the book *Mishkiat-ul'—musabir* (The niche for lamps), written in Arabic by Ed-din Mohammed ben-Abdulla of Tabriz, who lived in the thirteenth century:

> God, apart from whom there is none worthy of veneration, is: 1) Merciful, 2) Kind, 3) King, 4) Holy, 5) Reconciler, 6) Faithful, 7) Defender, 8) Sovereign, 9) Strong, 10) Exalted, 11) Builder, 12) Creator, 13) Educator, 14) Readily forgiving, 15) Subduer, 16) Granter, 17) Furnisher, 18) Revealer, 19) Knower, 20) Fleeing, 21) Allotting, 22) Humbling, 23) Exalting, 24) Magnifying, 25) Destroying, 26) Listening, 27) Seeing, 28) Judge, 29) Just, 30) Showing mercy, 31) Knowing, 32) Meek, 33) Supreme, 34) Forgiving, 35) Benefactor, 36) Most High, 37) Great, 38) Observing, 39) Overseeing, 40) Protector, 41) Majestic, 42) Generous, 43) Guard, 44)

Attending, 45) Embracing, 46) Wise, 47) Loving, 48) Glorious, 49) The one who resurrects, 50) Witness, 51) True, 52) Guardian, 53) Powerful, 54) Unshakeable, 55) Helper, 56) Praiseworthy, 57) Knowing all without exception, 58) Renewer, 59) Returner, 60) Enlivener, 61) Killing, 62) Living, 63) Everlasting, 64) Finding, 65) Honorable, 66) Solitary, 67) Sole, 68) Uncorrupted, 69) Mighty, 70) Potent, 71) Converting, 72) Postponing, 73) First, 74) Last, 75) External, 76) Internal, 77) Ruler, 78) Lauded, 79) Beneficent, 80) Favorably disposed toward the penitent, 81) Avenger, 82) Pardoning, 83) Good, 84) King, Kingdom, 85) Master of glory and greatness, 86) Righteous, 87) Gathering, 88) Rich, 89) Enriching, 90) Retaining, 91) Harmful, 92) Useful, 93) Light, 94) Directly leading, 95) Fashioner, 96) Eternal, 97) Welcoming in inheritance, 98) Shower of the right path, 99) Patient.

These names are produced from the *Koran*, although not all of them are found directly in it (Sablukov, 51–57). The invocation of different names of God in prayer often has spiritual consequences (e.g., "whoever pronounces the name 'All-knowing' every evening, will easily keep his knowledge and will not forget what he knew." "Whoever pronounces the name 'Holy' one hundred times will have his heart purified of sadness and darkness," etc. (95–97)). Alternatively, it takes on the character of vulgar magic (as a means against thieves, fever, etc.).

The Great Name of God, in the opinion of Muslims, is his hundredth name. The miracles that were performed by the prophets and emissaries of God were accomplished by pronouncing the Great Name. The Great Name of God was revealed by God in each of the books: in the Law, the Psalter, the Gospel; it is also in the Koran, but which of the names of God transmitted by it is the Great Name, the Koran did not indicate. Therefore, some Muslims consider that the Great Name is known to no one, others believe that they have grasped the Great Name of God; some accept for it the Arabic name Allah (examples of findings, see page 135–144). The Great Name gives knowledge of the mysteries of nature and free instruction by them, healing the sick and raising the dead (it would seem that Christ performed his miracles with this name); in general it gives knowledge of mysteries and power.

The Great Name of God among the Jews (Sablukov, op. cit. 144)

The Jews, in reverencing the Great Name of God, from a certain time stopped pronouncing it in their community, in Divine worship, when reading Sacred

Scripture, and they indicate it with other names of God. One proposes the
epoch after the Babylonian captivity, which ended in 516 BC, as the time for
this development, although even after the Babylonian captivity the prophets
(Haggai, Zechariah, Malachi, Esdras, Nehemiah) wrote it. After more than
a century had passed after Nehemiah, namely during the high priesthood of
Simon I the Righteous, the tenth high priest after the Babylonian captivity,
they stopped using the Great Name of God, as the Babylonian Talmud attests. In the Septuagint translation (some 270 years before the birth of Christ)
the Great Name is indicated as *kurios* Lord. In the translation of Sacred Scripture into Chaldean (Targum), the Great Name is designated by two letters.
The Masoretic redaction of the text (from the fourth to the sixth century),
in place of the Great Name YHWH pronounces Adonai, Lord. When in the
text of the Bible Adonai stands alongside the Great Name, in place of
the Great Name we read Elohim—God and for this the Masoretes wrote
the vowels of that name above the letters of the Great Name. Thus in the
book of Gen 15:2; Deut 3:24, YHWH Adonai the Jews read Adonai Elohim,
cf. Ps 109:21; 2 Sam 7:18, 28; Ps 71:16; Ps 141:8; Jer 2:22; 8:20; Ezek 5:5; 7:8;
13:8. The Jews of the present day also do not say the great Name of God,
but when reading Scripture where it is encountered, they indicate it with the
name Adonai.

When the Epistles and Gospels recorded the words of the Old Testament
prophets translated into Greek, in which the Gospel teaching was transmitted, they indicated the Great Name of God as had the seventy interpreters,
with the word *kurios* Lord (p. 182). In almost all Christian churches, incidentally especially those in Jerusalem, Antioch, Persia, and Arabia where the
churches were originally composed of Jews, the Jewish custom of not pronouncing the real Hebrew name revealed by God to Moses was preserved for
a long time. Because of this, we do not hear the sounds of the Great Name
in the translations of Sacred Scripture composed in the first centuries of the
Christian era for the Gentiles who entered the Church of Christ. It started
to come into use in the Christian churches of Europe from the time when
the study of theology was connected with the study of the Hebrew text of
the Bible.

In Indian religion, the word, and precisely the word of prayer, is given
the meaning of the beginning of the world, uniting in itself the heavenly
and earthly. Such is the concept of Brahman, in which the barrier between
humanity and the Godhead is removed (cf. Deussen, *Allgemeine Geschichte
der Philosophie*, 1. Bd. 1. Abtl. Leipzig, 1894, p. 239. See A. I. Vvedenskii, *Religioznoe soznanie iazychestva*, p. 426f; Bart, *Religii Indii*, pp. 46–47). The focus
of prayer is the great and incomprehensible *Om*. "By recognizing this, said

Rishi, what was and shall be, that do I extol, o Brahman, who consist of but a single syllable, so great and only from one syllable—for in this syllable all the gods and all beings enter." Therefore, the formula of Indian name-glorifying runs, "Syllable Om is Brahman, syllable Om is the whole world" (Deussen, I, pr. 257). In the final books of cosmology Satapatha is explained as Brahman (Deussen, p. 259–260), "Brahman was truly the beginning of this world. He created the gods (Agni, Vayu, and Surya). . . . He himself entered the other world and when he got there, he asked 'How can I penetrate these worlds?' And he penetrated them through the form (hand) and the name (nâman). Because there is always a name for a thing, this is also his name, and if some kind of thing has no name they recognize such a thing according to the form and say, if this is the form (image) then he is its form. For this world extends only as far as form and name extend. . . . The one and the other are two great manifestations (yaksha) of Brahman."

Names among Indigenous Peoples

"Among indigenous peoples a mysterious link is perceived between the name and its bearer. One can harm a human by means of a name and therefore the names of kings are kept in deep mystery. To pronounce a name means to unsettle the person to whom it is attached. Therefore, African indigenous avoid pronouncing the names of the deceased and names in general, whereas they conceal their own name" (L. Lévy-Bruhl, *Les fonctions mentales dans les sociétés inférieures*, 46–47; cited in Karl Tiander, "O nachalakh misticheskogo mirovozreniia," *Voprosy teorii i psikhologii tvorchestva*, vol. 5 (Khar'kov, 1914): 424). "The choice of a name for a child becomes predetermined by custom. Sometimes when it is necessary to give a name to a child, they look for signs on his body, and according to this sign, they give him the name of a dead person, who had such a mark. Or they rhyme off a series of names in the presence of a child; that name is given at which the child sneezes, coughs, or simply gives a shout. In India such a custom exists: a priest pours rice into a bowl with water and for each kernel he pronounces the name of some ancestor; the priest chooses the name by the way the rice circles about in the water" (p. 433).

Plato's *Cratylus*

383A. The question concerns *orthotes onomatos*—not the correct name, but the correctness of a name, i.e., its ontological root, where Cratylus's opinion is that "for each thing there is a name naturally appropriate for it." Therefore,

Cratylus proposes that at the basis of different dialects and sonorities "for both Hellenes and Barbarians" there exists the same *orthotes* of a word: "and a name is not whatever people agree to call a thing, a portion of their own voice joined to a thing, but there is a certain correctness of names by nature, which is the same for Greeks and Barbarians." So, then, it is a question of the word of words (or, what is the same thing, the language of languages). But then in Hermogenes's question the clarity is lost because he immediately moves on to the correspondence or noncorrespondence of proper names with their bearers (Socrates, Cratylus, Hermogenes), i.e., about the correctness of appellations, whereas the questions about name and naming, i.e., about the giving of a name, are different questions that one must not confuse and straightaway muddle. Hermogenes half-ironically, half-seriously calls Cratylus's speech "an oracle" (*sumballein ten kratulou manteian*).

Further on, an antithesis is established through the mouth of Hermogenes. The true foundation of a name lies in convention or harmony; every name that is given is correct in its own way, and if it happens that another name is given to it, the second is not less correct than the first. No object gets its name from nature but from use and the habit of those who use it (384D).

At first, Hermogenes's instrumental-subjective theory is discussed, that a human being gives names and that different appellations are equal and indifferent in their own way. Against this relativism, Socrates raises the question of the nature of error, and consequently, falsely used words or appellations (385B–E). In so doing, he compels Hermogenes—not without anxiety—to repeat once more his expressed idea without deepening it: things can be called as one pleases, whence arise the differences in appellations of one and the same object among different people or nations. Thus, the question revolves around the problem of the inner word in its relation to the word-sound.

Then, with his leading question pointing precisely to **such a** meaning of the discussion, Socrates deepens it even further and asks about the nature of truth itself that is expressed through a word. Does he extend his skeptical realism of the type of Protagoras ("the human being is the measure of things") even to things themselves? Is the essence of things particular for each individual, or do things have something permanent in themselves and in their essence (386A)? Hermogenes rejects Protagorean skepticism, and Socrates, in developing his thought that objects have their own essence, says in addition that they have their own action, conformed to their nature. This pertains to speech also, one of whose particular manifestations is naming [387C]. Hence naming is a certain action—*praxis*—having as a result its own proper nature—*idian phusin*. Therefore, naming should be consistent with the nature of things and not with previous conventions. A name is the instrument (*organon*) of naming; it is defined more closely as an instructive and distinctive instrument relative to essence (388C). "Names are transmitted from the hands of some 'lawgiver,' an artisan of names (*onomatourgou*)—which is a difficult work and rare gift." Further, a rather obscure exposition, though clear enough from its content, follows: the distinction between the inner word and the linguistic means, especially "of appellations," i.e., **of the word** and words, "on what the lawgiver fixes his gaze when he gives names." Just as different instruments, such as a shuttle or an auger, are divided "by looking at the form" and "setting it in a corresponding material," i.e., they have an idea and a palpable embodiment, a form, so, too, a name corresponding to a thing according to nature must be expressed in letters and words (389D). In a similar manner, the lawgiver here or among barbarians, i.e., in different languages, imprints the form of a name, its idea (*to eidos tou onomatou*), the inner word, in corresponding words (390A). Those who will make use of a word, wordsmiths such as dialecticians (understood in the Platonic sense, i.e., in opposition to the Sophists), are obligated to define and judge how this work of the lawgiver is performed. (Obviously, here this concept is taken entirely conditionally, and not at all in the sense of an idea about the origin of language through convention, *thesei*.) This is why Socrates once more seemingly goes along with the opposing thesis of Cratylus that "things receive their names from nature, and not everyone is a maker of words, but only the one who gazes at the real natural name of each thing and can propose its idea in words and sounds" (390E). Then a variation follows—an excursus on different ways of producing words relating to linguistic schools of the day, full of irony, but again stimulating the development of the thought (391–97E).

Then comes a lengthy philological and onomatological excursus taking up the greater part of the dialogue, where Socrates sets forth different word formations, evidently having in mind contemporary Sophist doctrines and ridiculing them. This part does not have a fundamental meaning for the general question about the nature of a name and does not advance the discussion, but it makes the general plan or intention of the *Cratylus* unclear. Is it imagined as a critique of Sophist philology, and the general introduction is only an assault, or the reverse, is the philological excursus an excessively extended episode that destroys and obscures the plan? In any case, in the *Cratylus* we have an inchoate or incomplete work by Plato that lacks the usually inherent symmetry. The result of the lengthy and semi-ironic discussion is that the interlocutor arrives at the conclusion that incomprehensible parts of words must be taken for barbaric if they cannot be tracked down in the ancients; however, an ancient language is scarcely distinguished from a present-day barbarian one (421D). In the end, if the one inquiring about the words that make up a name starts to direct his questions to what the words are made of and does not wish to curtail his questions, the respondent will be compelled to give up and remain silent; but by rights (*dikaios*) he would do this when he had arrived at the primary elements of the word, which are not further decomposable. Plato calls this "the elements of words," *stoicheia* (422A). But where are these elements to be sought? Are they not in a certain sense what has been subjected to analysis up to now? Or, more likely are such primary elements primary sounds, i.e., letters? "Imagine that we had neither voice nor tongue but wanted to let others know about things—would we not start to make signs with our hands as deaf mutes do now, with the head and other parts of the body, imitating the things by motion?" (423E). But such an imitation is accomplished precisely by the voice, and one must understand this not in the sense of external imitation (e.g., the baaing of sheep) but of imitations of essence, for "each thing has its own voice and form, and many have their own color." In other words, it is necessary from the start to examine the letters, both vowels and consonants, from which words are formed, similar to the colors mixed by a painter in a definite proportion to make one or other complex paint. The question is posed, in this way, not in the sense of a crude and superficial onomatopoetic but of the inner correspondence of a word and a sound; in other words, the very fabric of a verbal body (some of the investigations of Andrei Bely refer to this, for example—the occultism of a word). Then follows a series of examples of the meanings of separate letters—*rho, iota, phi, psi, sigma, zeta*—in which Plato, evidently again having in mind some investigations contemporary to him, speaks half-jokingly, half-seriously, with clear irony. For that reason, we will leave these excursuses out of consideration.

Thus far (until 428) Hermogenes's thesis that words arose according to convention was subjected to lethal criticism. Now the difficulties of the thesis defended by Cratylus, that words correspond to the nature of things, are brought to light; and the chief difficulty here is the question about the correctness or incorrectness of naming, or of the nature of a mistake in a word. Socrates forces Cratylus to acknowledge that similar to laws that are better or worse (429), words too are of different correctness. For a name is all the same not the very thing, just as a representation of Cratylus is not Cratylus. "Ludicrous things would arise, Cratylus, from the names of those to which these names refer, if names were like them in everything. Then everything would become double—*ditta*—and it would be impossible to say about anything what it is itself and what its name is" (432 D).

By his dissection of the question, Socrates sets before the consciousness not only the **unity** of thing and name, which Cratylus defends, but also their distinction or bifurcation. This is obviously the fundamental question of the metaphysics of word—the relation between the logical and the a- or anti- or super-logical principle of being. Having acknowledged a certain autonomy and distinctive life of a word, Socrates thereby considers as demonstrated its different states, in particular approximations and errors, which initially Cratylus had expressly denied. "And so boldly admit that one name is applied well, another is not, and do not require all such letters in order to obtain a full correspondence of the name with the object, but make room for a letter that may be unsuitable. But if you bring in a noncorresponding letter, then do the same for a name in speech (*onoma en logoi*); and if an unsuitable phrase is brought into it, nevertheless the object (*pragma*) will be no worse because it is named and expressed in a word while the type (*tupos*) of object in question is preserved" (432E).

Essentially Socrates is expressing here the idea that a name-word is in essence more or less an imperfect cast from a certain "type," the creation of an arbitrary fiction by convention. But having established a distinction between a word and a thing and by rejecting their complete mutual alienation, which is found in explaining words from convention—*xuntheke* (433A, 434A), the interlocutors again return to the question about the nature of the connection between a word and a thing, and the question about letters, or sounds, as proto-elements (*stoicheia*) of a word returns as well. "Names would never have been likened to anything if that from which they were assembled did not have some original likeness to that for which the names are imitations" (434B). After a fleeting return again to the character of individual letters, Socrates detects in their application within words (e.g., the word is pronounced *sklerotes* among Athenians, among Eritreans *skleroter*, etc.) elements of convention or arbitrariness, which he considers it necessary to accommodate in his composition. "Although it pleases me that names are as similar to things as possible, it is necessary for the correctness of names to use this crude means of convention (*tei xunthekei*) also, so that this investigation of similarity not be too obtrusive (435 C); however, it would be the most beautiful speech possible if it had been expressed entirely or for the most part with the greatest number of similar, i.e., appropriate *proskenousin* words."

Here Socrates makes a final and decisive turn in the argument and approaches the fundamental question of the metaphysics of word, and the nature of word itself in relation to knowledge, i.e., the nature of ideas. The question is posed rather unexpectedly. "After this, answer for me also this question: what power do words have with us and what good, ostensibly, do they do?" (435D). Cratylus answers in the sense that names teach about things: whoever knows the names knows the things too. Socrates points to the danger of being mistaken by following untrue names, and Cratylus forgetting his own initial point of view refers to the supernatural wisdom of the composer of a name. When Socrates poses the question of how then the lawgiver could know things before he applied names, he points to the difficulty that arises as a result of the contradiction of names referring to motion or rest. "Apart from these names it is necessary to search for something different, evidently, that even without names it is revealed to us which of them are true, i.e., show the truth of things" (438E), "therefore, things too must be studied and investigated not from names but from their very selves much more so than from names" (439B). In that case, once the discussion has been set on that ground, the question is inevitably put forward about where to look for the thing identical to itself that remains in Heraclitus's stream *panta rhei* [everything flows]. "Is it possible to express correctly what always is departing, to express, first of all, that this is the same (*ekeino*) and then that it possesses such and such properties (*toiouton*)? In what manner could something be that *ekeino* which it never was (*medepote hosautos echei*)? If it were such, then evidently it could not change at the same time, but if it were always such and identical to itself (*to auto estin*), then how could it change or move without separating from its own idea to some degree? Then it would be known by no one, for as soon as you moved with the intention of knowing it, it would become other and alien (*allon kai alloion*) (440A). In all fairness, Cratylus, it is impossible to point to knowledge[6] where all things change and nothing stands. Surely, if this is the same knowledge of that which does not change, then knowledge always remains and is always knowledge. If, however, the character (*eidos*) itself of knowledge changes and besides passes over to another form (*eidos*) of knowledge, it would no longer be knowledge. Where perpetual changeableness is, there is no knowledge; from this it follows that there is neither knowledge nor the known" (440B); "if however, on the contrary, it is always knowing, then it is knowable, and it is both beautiful and good, it is the being of each separate thing that exists,"[7] "*esti de hen hekaston ton onton*" (440B). Socrates invites Cratylus to consider who is right, the followers of Heraclitus or their opponents; at this point, the conversation unexpectedly breaks off.

The question now arises about the general meaning of this difficult, rather confused, and even disheveled dialogue, which by its form does not belong to the number of exemplary works of Plato, although it does give a full sense of the power of his dialectical muscles. It is entitled "*he peri onomaton orthotetos logikos* [On the Correctness of Names],"[8] and it actually begins with this question, but it ends with a theory of ideas, and the serious question arises as to what the real theme of the dialogue is. Does he want to dismiss Sophistic philology, by ruffling their thesis and antithesis, *phusei* and *thesei* [*nature* and *convention*] with sophistic methods in order to clear the field for his own theory of knowledge through ideas? In such a case, Plato's own attitude to words remains skeptical: cognition happens above and apart from words, through ideas, by metalogical contemplation. Then, too, the whole dialogue pursues a destructive purpose by means of irony and sophistry. At least, based on the text it is possible to understand *Cratylus* that way. However, a different meaning of the whole argument presents itself to us, and the transition to the question about ideas is in essence an expressive gesture indicating where one must begin the problem and where to look for its unifying center. Plato exposes the difficulties of one and other aspect of the alternative, the doctrine of the origin of words from the nature of things and from convention, but thereby their relative correctness is revealed, and even their mutual necessity. It is not at all the case that Plato here eclectically joined antagonistic points of view or playfully ridiculed both. He wants to find the supreme, fundamental point of view on the question, by which the incompleteness would be clarified, and therefore also the limitation of the prevailing doctrines. The latter, however, can be accepted only when they are put in their proper place and when they cease to be "abstract principles." Plato clearly wants to connect a theory of words with a theory of ideas, and by removing the question from vacillating phenomenology, where the relativists had held it, onto the soil of ontology that is clearer and more fundamental than the defenders of the fullness of words, he wants to reexamine it all over again. In this sense, *Cratylus* is only a first, perhaps critical-historical part, an introduction after which should follow a systematic, positive reconsideration of the question. It was either not written or has not come down to us.

Thus, Plato connects the question about the nature of words with a general doctrine of the verbal artistry of human beings, with all its mistakes, and yet not about ideas at all. It is then possible to continue Plato's thought in his own spirit—words can be understood not as such but as vessels of ideas. As the world of ideas in general grounds by itself the world of phenomena, but at the same time is replaced by it, so too words have their roots in ideas, but in their phenomenal historical being they bear on themselves the stamp of human subjectivism, psychologism, and historical becoming, in general. Obviously, it is impossible to accept the skeptical thesis of Hermogenes that words arose by convention, because this would mean in essence to abrogate entirely the nature of a word, reducing it to auxiliary "economic" means. But it is also impossible to take a word as the power of things, not to mention that they bear on themselves the obvious stamp of the historical and conditional, since one would have to reexamine them as a duplication of the things themselves, which is clearly absurd. Otherwise, one would have to pose the following question: in what sense do words express the nature of things? But this leads us directly to the theory of ideas as the basis of objective knowledge. Since the world of ideas shines through and is perceived in knowledge, so, too, words have roots in the nature of things, i.e., they contain ideas in their aspect expressed by word and thought. "Since this world consists of being and non-being, ideas and meonal matter, so too words are a human institution, representation and so on, and the human being is the measure of things."

It is remarkable that in his dialogue Plato touched on all the most important aspects of a philosophy of the word, even if only casually. He is equally concerned with the question of the inner nature of a word, or the word of a word, as he is about the body of a word, i.e., the sound, and he wants to push through the labyrinth of the history of words and of semasiology to the proto-elements of words, letters, i.e., he offers his hand to the mystics of the Cabbala. Plato's dialogue does not satisfy, but this is not because of its incompleteness but as a result of the limitation of the task proposed in it, for in it he is talking about the problems of a word and not of these or other solutions. And in this area, as in others, an unfading freshness and sharpness belong to Plato; his questions remain unsurpassed even today, despite the enormous successes of the science of language.

An outline of the dialogue. It presents itself as a two-membered and thus bipartite work corresponding to the thesis being considered—that of Cratylus, and the antithesis—that of Hermogenes, whereas in the last, third and concluding part, the author distances himself entirely from the alternatives. Each of these parts, especially the first, less so the second, has an introduction and episodic digressions. The style of leading questions, examples, and dissection of concepts, especially in the first part of the dialogue, brings to mind in fact the early Socratic dialogues sparkling with youthfulness and a certain naïveté, although its entire content is undoubtedly deeper and does not permit us to attribute it to that era when Plato was not yet inwardly ready for a theory of ideas. Inasmuch as one can judge by its content, *Cratylus* belongs to the mature period. It has one more exceptional trait: the manner, whether deliberate or by chance (owing to its incompleteness), of exposition. Here the favorite Platonic myths are entirely absent, and *Cratylus* comes close to the business-like and dry cycle of the *Sophist*, *Parmenides*, and *Theaetetus*; here the soil is most favorable for them. There is also no artistic introduction so common in many dialogues and forming a kind of artistic vignette.

A. First Part

Cratylus, supported by Socrates against Hermogenes (383–391). Through a series of questions, in the spirit of the early dialogues, Hermogenes is forced to agree with Socrates (390E–391).

The largest part by dimensions.

Episode I: historical-philological (391B–422C). Of enormous dimensions and variegated with respect to content: proper names of kings and heroes, gods, natural elements, luminaries, seasons, abstract concepts, and spiritual qualities, a whole dictionary and encyclopedia.

Episode II: on the proto-elements of a word, on sounds and letters (422C–442). Introductory argument: onomatological theory—a name is an imitation (422C–425); the characteristics of letters: (426C–428).

B. Second Part

Socrates against Cratylus (428E–439B). With a series of questions, he forces Cratylus to reject his thesis.

The episode about letters and words (434C–435; 437).

C. Conclusion

Transition to the theory of ideas and the interruption of the discussion (435C–440E).

Plato in the *Sophist* on Words and Speech

Here this question is broached on the way to a lengthy series of doctrines and then is quickly abandoned, but in a few words Plato succeeded in expressing some substantial thoughts that give evidence of how he pondered over the problem of word, for example.

It is a question of the general decomposition of concepts, which is evidence of someone's alienation from both the muses and philosophy (259E). The removal of every word from everyone is the most radical means of destroying all speech (*panton logon*), for speech proceeds from the interweaving of ideas (259E). "Having been deprived of speech, we would be deprived of philosophy also." "We would be speechless if we allowed that nothing is connected with anything in anyone" (260B).

Here the ontological basis of discourse is briefly noted—in ideas and the connection of ideas, in what we have called the ontological communism of being.

Further, having made a few zigzags, the conversation again turns to discourse. A question about the concreteness of speech arises or about the nature of the connection that exists between words. A distinction is made between two types of combinations, those that agree when they are combined and those that do not (261E). Here a very important fundamental question of the philosophy of grammar is provoked, about the difference between nouns and verbs, *onomata* and *rhemata* (i.e., subject and object function). "Statements of action we call a verb, whereas a sign of the voice, accompanying the one who produces the action, is a noun; but discourse never arises from individual nouns pronounced one after the other, or from verbs[9] pronounced separately from nouns . . . for example: *goes, runs, sleeps* and the like are verbs that designate action; even if someone puts them in order, they do not constitute discourse of any kind. . . . In a similar way if one says *lion, deer, horse*—and no matter how many nouns that produce actions—by bringing them together no discourse is constituted because neither in the former nor the latter case can what is pronounced express any action or inaction, any essence of an existent or nonexistent, until someone mingles nouns with verbs; then they come to agreement and their first combination immediately becomes discourse." "An example might be this phrase: 'a man learns.' The one who said this would express his thought relative to the existent, what is, what has been and what shall be; he would not only name something, but by connecting a verb with words, he would have limited the one or the other." Therefore, "as some things agree among themselves and others do not, so too with the signs of the voice: some do not come into agreement, others do, and they compose speech" (262E). Plato here is groping about for the nature of the copula and sees the unity of speech in a judgment, the connection of subject and predicate that can be realized in a judgment correctly or incorrectly—and sometimes directly parodied. This follows from a comparison of two examples of sentences, "Theaetetus is sitting" and "Theaetetus, with whom I am now conversing, is flying."[10] Of these sentences, the true one says what exists as it is, but the false one says what does not exist is what exists, i.e., "from what exists he ascribes to you what does not exist." For indeed we have posited that with respect "to each thing there is much that exists and much that does not exist" (263B). "And so, if we say about you 'the other' as 'the same' and 'the nonexistent' as 'the existent' (*peri de sou legomena mentoi thatera hos ta auta kai me onta hos onta*), it seems that when such a combination (*sunthesis*) of verbs and nouns is formed, it becomes truly and really false discourse" (263D). Thus, Plato brings the inner structure of discourse into connection with the distinction between *dianoia, doxa,* and *phantasia,* reasoning, opinion, and fantasy. Complete affinity is established between *dianoia* and *logos* so that it is said "reasoning and discourse are the same thing, and the inner dialog of the soul with itself, occurring without voice, we call reasoning" (263E), i.e., Plato again (as in *Cratylus*) approaches the problem of the inner word.

From these fleeting observations, one can see how tenaciously Plato's thought clutched at the very roots of the philosophy of grammar and how considered were the separate aspects of the problem. However, here this question has only an auxiliary role, and having played with it, he abandons it. In general, *Sophist*, in accordance with its title, belongs to a number of business-like and prosaic works of Plato, being at the same time more sophistical in style (deliberately, in accordance with the purpose). It would be a mistake to expect more here than such a treatment of the myth about words. However, it would be wrong to pass by the flashes of Plato's judgment about word, even those dropped in passing.

Humboldt on Language

"It is impossible to teach language in the proper sense; one can only stir it up in the soul: one only needs to release for it a thread along which it will develop by itself. In this way, one can consider languages the creation of peoples, and at the same time they remain the creation of individuals, because they can occur only in individuals, and again only where each person expects to be understood by everyone and where they all justify this expectation in fact" (Wilhelm von Humboldt, *O razlichii organismov chelovecheskogo iazyka i o vliianii ètogo razlichiia na umstvennoe razvitie chelovecheskogo roda* (St. Petersburg, 1857), 34). "Language is an operation (*energeia*), and not a finished work (*ergon*)" (40). Language and cognition: "The striving of the mind for the objective world flows out into the external world through the mouth, and the result of this striving—a word—returns again to the subject through the ear. This is possible only by means of language, and without this passage into subjectivity and return to the subject, which takes place even when thinking happens in silence, the formation of a concept is impossible, but so too is thinking itself. Therefore, far from touching the need for communication between people, language would be the necessary condition of thinking for a person even in their perpetual solitude" (51). "Every human being carries language in their soul in all its scope, i.e., in each person there is the aspiration and capability to produce and understand language in all its limitlessness, little by little, in measure with external and internal factors, by their own power, and to give to it a particular character in conformity with his or her individuality" (52).

NOTES

Introduction

1. Bulgakov never fully abandoned philosophy even when his writing was entirely devoted to theological themes. See V. V. Zenkovsky, *A History of Russian Philosophy*, trans. George Kline (London: Routledge & Kegan Paul Ltd., 1953), 2: 895–96.

2. S. N. Bulgakov, "Na piru bogov. Pro i contra. Sovremennye dialogi," in *Iz glubiny* (Moscow, 1918), 111–69. Translation: "At the Feast of the Gods. Contemporary Dialogues," trans. A. G. Pashkov, *Russian and East European Review*, 1/1 (June 1922), 172–183, 1/2 (Dec 1922), 391–400, 1/3 (Mar 1923), 604–22.

3. S. N. Bulgakov, "U sten Khersonesa," *Simvol* 25 (1991), 169–334. Reprint in S. N. Bulgakov, *Trudy po sotsiologii i teologii* (Moscow: Nauka, 1997), 2: 351–500. S. N. Bulgakov [Père Serge Boulgakov], *Sous les remparts de Chersonèse,* trans. Bernard Marchadier (Geneva: Ad Solem, 1999).

4. S. N. Bulgakov, "Tragediia filosofii," in *Sergii Bulgakov. Sochineniia v dvukh tomakh,* ed. S. S. Khoruzhii (Moscow: Nauka, 1993), 1: 311–518. S. N. Bulgakov [Sergij Bulgakov], *Tragedy of Philosophy (Philosophy & Dogma)*, trans. Stephen Churchyard (Brooklyn, NY: Angelico Press, 2020).

5. This neglect has been slowly changing. See the following studies: N. K. Bonetskaia, "O filologicheskii shkole P. A. Florenskogo: 'Filosofiia imeni' A. F. Loseva i 'Filosofiia imeni' S. A. Bulgakova," *Studia Slavica Academiae Scientiarum Hungaricae* 37 nos. 1–4 (1991), 113–189; Antoine Nivières, "La Philosophie du Nom dans l'oeuvre du père Serge Boulgakov," *Le Messager Orthodoxe* 124, no. 1 (Paris, 1994–1995), 39–42; Maryse Dennes, "Les Glorificateurs du Nom: une rencontre de l'hésychasme et de la philosophie au debut du XXième siècle, en Russie," *Slavia occitania* 8 (1999), 143–71; N. K. Bonetskaia, "The Struggle for Logos in Russia in the Twentieth Century," *Russian Studies in Philosophy* 40, no. 4 (Spring 2002), 6–39; Antoine Arjakovsky, "La glorification du Nom et la grammaire de la Sagesse (Serge Boulgakov et Jean-Marc Ferry)," in *Essai sur le père Serge Boulgakov*, 199–214 (Paris: Parole et Silence, 2006); Denis Ioffe, "Passivnoe protivostoianie diamatu na puti k ontologii i fenomenologii: Imiaslavie i kriticheskoe neogumbol'dtianstvo: russkie religioznye filosofy i Gustav Shpet," *Russian Literature* 63, nos. 2–4 (2008), 293–366; Zh. L. Okeanskaia, *Iazyk i kosmos: "Filosofiia imeni" ottsa Sergiia Bulgakova v kontekste poèticheskoi metafiziki kontsa Novogo vremeni (prolegomeny k problematike filosofskogo imiaslaviia)* (Moscow: Bibleisko-bogoslovskii institut sv. Apostola Andreia, 2008); N. A. Vaganova, *Sofiologiia protoiereia Sergiia Bulgakova* (Moscow: Izd. PSTGU, 2011), 307–12; Anna Reznichenko, *O smyslakh imen. Bulgakov, Losev, Florenskii, Frank et dii minores* (Moscow: Regnum, 2012); N. K. Bonetskaia, *Russkii Faust XX veka* (St. Petersburg: Rostok, 2015), 234–47.

6. S. N. Bulgakov [Sergius Bulgakow], *Die Tragödie der Philosophie*, trans. Alexander Kresling (Darmstadt: Otto Reichl Verlag, 1927).

7. S. N. Bulgakov, *Filosofiia imeni* (KaIr, 1997, Inapress / Iskusstvo, 1999, 2008).

8. "Was ist das Wort" appeared in *Festschrift Th. G. Masaryk zum 80. Geburtstag* (Bonn, 1930). S. N. Bulgakov [Père Serge Boulgakov], *La philosophie du verbe et du nom*, trans. Constantin Andronikof (Lausanne: Éditions L'Âge d'Homme, 1991). S. N. Bulgakov, "The Name of God" in S. N. Bulgakov [Sergius Bulgakov], *Icons and the Name of God*, trans. Boris Jakim (Grand Rapids, MI: Wm. B. Eerdmans Publishing Company, 2012), 115–77.

9. Heyman Steinthal, a philologist and philosopher, served as a university lecturer for philology and mythology (1850) and from 1872 as assistant professor at the University of Berlin. He edited Humboldt's *Sprachwissenschaftliche Werke* in 1894 besides composing numerous works on language and psychology.

10. Aleksandr Afanas'evich Potebnia (or Oleksandr Opanasovich Potebnia) was a linguist, philosopher, and Panslavist who held the position of professor of linguistics at Kharkov / Kharkiv University. While his most famous work was *Thought and Language*, he wrote influential studies on Slavic folk poetry, historical phonetics of East Slavic languages, and the theory of literature.

11. Famous for his work on phoneme and phonetic alternations, he elaborated a distinction between language as an abstract group of elements and speech as its implementation by speakers, similar to Ferdinand de Saussure's distinction between *langue* and *parole*. He was the editor of the third and fourth editions of Vladimir Dal's *Explanatory Dictionary of the Living Great Russian Language*.

12. Regarded as the founder of modern semantics.

13. See chap. 7.

14. For a brief but insightful discussion of his criticism, see I. V. Rodnianskaia. "Skhvatka S. N. Bulgakova s Immanuilom Kantom na stranitsakh 'Filosofii imeni,'" in S. N. Bulgakov [Sergei Bulgakov], *Pervoobraz i obraz*, vol. 2. *Filosofiia imeni. Ikona i ikonopochitanie*, 7–12 (Moscow: Iskusstvo, 1999).

15. Bonetskaia, *Russkii Faust XX veka*, 234–47.

16. For example, A. F. Losev, *Bytie. Imia. Kosmos* (Moscow: Mysl', 1993), and Losev, *Imia: izbrannye raboty, perevody, besedy, issledovaniia, arkhivnye materialy*, ed. A. A. Takhogodi (St. Petersburg: Aleteiia, 1997).

17. Sophiology is a complex system elaborated by Bulgakov, inspired by Vladimir Soloviev (1853–1900) and Pavel Florenskii, as a way to recast traditional Orthodox doctrine about the Trinity, Christology, creation, and the relation of God and humankind. An accessible introduction to sophiology is Bulgakov's own book, *Sophia: The Wisdom of God*, trans. Rev. Patrick Thompson et al. (New York, NY: Paisley Press, 1937, rev. ed., Hudson, NY: Lindisfarne Press, 1993).

18. S. N. Bulgakov [Sergei Bulgakov], *Philosophy of Economy. The World as Household*, trans. Catherine Evtuhov (New Haven, CT: Yale University Press, 2000), 130–31.

19. Bulgakov, *Philosophy of Economy*, 145.

20. See chap. 2.

21. From his diary entry for November 30, 1934. The full text in S. N. Bulgakov, *Tikhie dumy, Ètika, kul'tura, sofiologiia* (St. Petersburg: Izd-vo. Olega Abyshko, 2008), 511–13.

22. See chap. 4 for both references.

23. See chap. 1.

24. See chap. 1.

25. See chap. 1 for both references.

26. See chap. 6.

27. "Words have ceased to be words; they have weakened and wilted, passing through all the mists of non-being and shrouds of subjectivism or psychologism. Now a word is only an instrument of communication, 'a tongue' and not the voice of the world. The imperative mood (or exclamatory judgment) is applied only from human to human: now only a human hears a word and obeys (or does not obey) it. This only shows how deep is the sickness of the word together with the sickness of being itself, which has become visible only in reflections, schemas, and caricatures. Where once there were full-weight grains, now a husk is left, swept away by the wind" (chap. 4).

28. See chap. 4.

29. See chap. 2.

30. See chap. 2.

31. See chap. 2.

32. See chap. 2.

33. See chap. 2.

34. See chap. 2.

35. See chap. 5.

36. See chap. 2.

37. For an overview of the historical development of the controversy, with a very helpful bibliography, see Scott M. Kenworthy, "The Name-Glorifiers (*Imiaslavie*) Controversy," in *The Oxford Handbook of Russian Religious Thought*, ed. Caryl Emerson, George Pattison, and Randall A. Poole, 327–42 (Oxford: Oxford University Press, 2020). Also see Tom Dykstra, *Hallowed Be Thy Name: The Name-Glorifying Dispute in the Russian Orthodox Church and on Mt. Athos, 1912–1914* (St. Paul, MN: OCABS Press, 2013); G. M. Hamburg, "The Origins of 'Heresy' on Mount Athos: Ilarion's Na Gorakh Kavkaza (1907)," *Occasional Papers on Religion in Eastern Europe*, 23, no. 2 (2003), 1–34. Konstantinos Papoulidis, *Oi Rosoi onomatolatrai tou Agiou Orous* (Thessaloniki: Institute of Balkan Studies, 1977). An early appraisal of the controversy, especially focusing on Bulgakov's involvement in it, is offered by Catherine Evtuhov, *The Cross and the Sickle. Sergei Bulgakov and the Father of Russian Religious Philosophy, 1890–1920* (Ithaca, NY: Cornell University Press, 1997), 210–18. See also Nel Grillaert, "What's in God's Name: Literary Forerunners and Philosophical Allies of the *Imjaslavie* Debate," *Studies in East European Thought* 64 (2012), 163–81. Hilarion Alfeyev, "L'onomatodoxie." après la controverse onomatodoxe," *Cahiers saint Silouane* 10 (2004), 139–171. For a theological treatment of the controversy and its importance for modern Orthodox theology, see Ilarion (Alfeev), *Sviashchennaia taina tserkvi: vvedenie v istoriiu i problematiku imiaslavskikh sporov* (St. Petersburg: Aleteiia, 2002), and Paul Ladouceur, *Modern Orthodox Theology* (London: T&T Clark, 2019), 361–77.

38. Ilarion (Schemamonk), *Na Gorakh Kavkaza. Beseda dvukh startsev o vnutren-nem edinenii s Gospodom nashikh serdets chrez molitvu Iisus Khristovu—ili—Dukhovnaia deiatel'nost' sovremennykh pustynnikov* [On the mountains of the Caucasus. Conversations between two elders on the inner union with the Lord of our hearts through the Prayer of Jesus Christ, or the Spiritual activity of contemporary hermits] (Batalpashinsk, 1907). It was reprinted in 1910 and 1912. French translation: *Sur les monts*

du Caucase: Dialogues de deux solitaires sur la prière de Jésus, trans. André Louf (Paris: Éditions des Syrtes, 2016).

39. Hamburg, "Origins of 'Heresy,'" 6–10.

40. Dykstra, *Hallowed Be Thy Name,* 23–24, citing Ilarion (Schemamonk), *Na gorakh Kavkaza.*

41. Ladouceur, *Modern Orthodox Theology,* 362.

42. Dykstra, *Hallowed Be Thy Name,* 25.

43. Kenworthy, "Name-Glorifiers (*Imiaslavie*) Controversy," 329.

44. Details in Dykstra, *Hallowed Be Thy Name,* 35–41.

45. Dykstra, 45.

46. The Theological School of Halki, founded in 1844 on the island of Halki in the Princes' Islands, was the main institute of higher theological studies for the Ecumenical Patriarchate.

47. Dykstra, *Hallowed Be Thy Name,* 75–78. Kenworthy, "Name-Glorifiers (*Imiaslavie*) Controversy," 330.

48. Antonii Bulatovich, *Apologiia very vo imia Bozhie i vo imia Iisus* is reprinted in *Imiaslavie: Antologiia,* ed. E. S. Polishchuk, 9–160 (Moscow: Faktorial Press, 2002). Ilarion (Alfeev), *Sviashchennaia taina tserkvi,* 405–67.

49. Kenworthy, "Name-Glorifiers (*Imiaslavie*) Controversy," 329. Dykstra, *Hallowed Be Thy Name,* 62–64, 66–68.

50. What follows is a summary of Scott M. Kenworthy, "Archbishop Nikon (Rozhdestvenskii) and Pavel Florenskii on Spiritual Experience, Theology, and the Name-Glorifiers Dispute," in *Thinking Orthodox in Modern Russia. Culture, History, Context,* ed. Patrick Lally Michelson et al., 90–100 (Madison: University of Wisconsin Press, 2014).

51. Interestingly, Bulgakov will address the question of teaching authority in the church in his article "The Athos Affair." See note 63.

52. Kenworthy, "Archbishop Nikon," 102.

53. Ivan Nikolaevich Stragorodsky (1867–1944), in monastic life Sergei, became acting Patriarchal locum tenens in 1927. That year he issued the *Declaration* in which he promised the loyalty of the Russian Orthodox Church to the Soviet Union. Publication of the *Declaration* led many members of the church, including several highly respected bishops, to break communion with the patriarchate. He continued efforts to appease the Soviet government, but only after the Germans invaded in 1941 was there a change of direction by the state. In 1943 Stalin granted the church some important concessions, including the reopening of the Moscow Theological Academy. Archbishop Sergei was elected Patriarch in September 1943 by a council of bishops.

54. Kenworthy, "Name-Glorifiers (*Imiaslavie*) Controversy," 330–33. See Dykstra, *Hallowed Be Thy Name,* 109–33 for a fuller description of the Church's actions.

55. Dykstra, *Hallowed Be Thy Name,* 13–14, 138–55, gives a compelling account of the deportation and its effects on the monks.

56. The Hundred Chapters Council (Stoglav) was organized by Metropolitan Makarii of Moscow during the reign of Ivan IV Vasilievich to regulate church and civic life along Orthodox principles with a decidedly Muscovite hue. See Jack E. Kollman, "The Moscow *Stoglav* (Hundred Chapters) Church Council of 1551" (PhD diss., University of Michigan, 1978); E. B. Emchenko, *Stoglav: issledovanie i tekst* (Moscow: Izd-vo "Indrik," 2000). David B. Miller, "The Orthodox Church"

in *The Cambridge History of Russia. Volume 1. From Early Rus' to 1689*, 355–57 (Cambridge University Press, 2006). Patriarch Nikon undertook wide-ranging liturgical and disciplinary reforms in the church, often at variance with the decisions of the Hundred Chapters Council. Initially supported by Tsar Aleksei Mikhailovich, he fell out of favor and was deposed. The reforms sparked violent protests at times among laity and clergy alike and led to a schism and the creation of a separate ecclesial reality, the "Old Belief," which suffered much persecution from the state until after the Bolshevik Revolution. See Nikon, *Trudy* (Moscow: Izd-vo Moskovskogo universiteta, 2004). Paul Meyendorff, *Russia, Ritual and Reform*: The Liturgical Reforms of Nikon in the 17th Century (Crestwood, NY: St. Vladimir's Seminary Press, 1991). Boris A. Uspensky, "The Schism and Cultural Conflict in the Seventeenth Century," in *Seeking God: The Recovery of Religious Identity in Orthodox Russia, Ukraine, and Georgia*, ed. Stephen K. Batalden, 106–141 (DeKalb: Northern Illinois University Press, 1993).

57. On this point, see Scott M. Kenworthy, "Debating the Theology of the Name in Post-Soviet Russia: Metropolitan Ilarion Alfeev and Sergei Khoruzhii," in *Orthodox Paradoxes. Heterogeneities and Complexities in Contemporary Russian Orthodoxy*, ed. Katya Tolstaya, 250–64 (Leiden: Brill, 2014).

58. Berdiaev excoriated the moribund state of the official church and its use of coercive force to quash the Name-glorifiers on Mount Athos in N. A. Berdiaev, "Gasiteli dukha," *Russkaia molva* (August 5, 1913).

59. Florenskii wrote an important study, "Imiaslavie kak filosofskaia predposylka." *Materialy k sporu o pochitanii Imeni Bozhiia* [Name-glorifying as a philosophical premise. Materials for the controversy about worship of the Name of God] (Moscow, 1913).

60. Aleksei Fedorovich Losev (1893–1988) wrote philosophical studies on a variety of topics, including aesthetics, music, mathematics, and language. He ardently supported the Name-glorifiers, penning *Filosofiia imeni* in 1927. Of particular interest to him throughout his lengthy career was the issue of symbol. See Sr. Teresa Obolevitch, "Alexei Losev: 'The Last Russian Philosopher' of the Silver Age," in *The Oxford Handbook of Russian Religious Thought*, ed. Caryl Emerson, George Pattison, and Randall A. Poole, 565–79 (Oxford: Oxford University Press, 2020).

61. Mikhail Aleksandrovich Novoselov (1864–1938) was active in a number of groups promoting a religious transformation of society, hosting one such circle in his Moscow home that Bulgakov frequented. His *Pis'ma k druziam* offered spiritual and theological commentary on current topics affecting church life. In 1931 he was arrested and sentenced to eight years in the labor camps and was subsequently executed in 1938.

62. See Kenworthy, "Name-Glorifiers (*Imiaslavie*) Controversy," 333–38, and Ladouceur, *Modern Orthodox Theology*, 366–73 for an exposition of their ideas.

63. S. N. Bulgakov [S. Bulgakov], "Afonskoe delo," *Russkaia mysl'* 9 (1913): 37–46.

64. S. V. Troitskii, *Ob imenakh Bozhiikh i imiabozhnikakh* (St. Petersburg, 1914).

65. S. N. Bulgakov [S. Bulgakov], "Smysl uchenie sv. Grigoriia Nisskogo ob imenakh," *Itogi zhizni*, 12–13 (1914): 15–21.

66. Evtuhov, *Cross and Sickle*, 213.

67. For an in-depth study of Russian Symbolism, see Avril Pyman, *A History of Russian Symbolism* (Cambridge University Press, 1994); for Andrei Bely, 198–211.

68. Russian Futurism was an early form of the avant-garde in Russian literature, coming to prominence in the first two decades of the twentieth century. Poets and theorists focused on the poetic power of sounds, experimenting with jarring juxtapositions of words and nonsensical syllables, among other techniques. Chief representatives of the futurist poets were Velimir Khlebnikov (1885–1922) and Aleksei Kruchenykh (1886–1968). See "The Poetics of Language" in *A History of Russian Literature*, ed. Andrew Kahn et al., 611–24 (Oxford: Oxford University Press, 2018).

69. For an English translation, see Saint Augustine, *Teaching Christianity*, trans. Edmund Hill, O. P. (Hyde Park, NY: New City Press, 1996).

70. Vaganova, *Sofiologiia*, 310.

71. S. N. Bulgakov [S. Bulgakov], *Dva grada. Issledovaniia o prirode obshchestvennykh idealov*, 2 vols. (Moscow: Put', 1911). Both volumes have Latin epigraphs drawn from the *City of God*, book 14, chap. 4.

72. See Myroslaw Tataryn, *Augustine and Russian Orthodoxy. Russian Orthodox Theologians and Augustine of Hippo: A Twentieth-Century Dialogue* (Lanham, MD: International Scholars Publications, 2000).

73. John Milbank, "Foreword" in S. N. Bulgakov [Sergij Bulgakov], *The Tragedy of Philosophy (Philosophy & Dogma)*, trans. Stephen Churchyard, xiii–xxvi (Brooklyn, NY: Angelico Press).

74. See Edward N. Zalta, "Gottlob Frege" in *The Stanford Encyclopedia of Philosophy*, ed. Edward N. Zalta (Fall 2020), https://plato.stanford.edu/archives/fall2020/entries/frege/; Roger Scruton, *A Short History of Modern Philosophy* (London: Routledge, 1995), 241–54.

75. See New World Encyclopedia contributors, "Ferdinand de Saussure," in *New World Encyclopedia*, https://www.newworldencyclopedia.org/p/index.php?title=Ferdinand_de_Saussure&oldid=997805 (accessed May 31, 2021). Burch, "Charles Sanders Peirce" in *The Stanford Encyclopedia of Philosophy*, ed. Edward N. Zalta (Spring 2021), https://plato.stanford.edu/archives/spr2021/entries/peirce/.

76. S. N. Bulgakov [Sergius Bulgakov], *The Holy Grail & the Eucharist*, trans. Boris Jakim (Hudson NY: Lindisfarne Books, 1997), 63–138. "The Icon and Its Veneration (A Dogmatic Essay)" in S. N. Bulgakov [Sergius Bulgakov], *Icons and the Name of God*, trans. Boris Jakim (Grand Rapids, MI: Wm B. Eerdmans, 2012), 1–114.

77. See chap. 1.

Chapter 1. What Is a Word?

1. Definitions of a word in linguistics treatises are usually absent or are replaced by a definition of language. Here are a few examples: Georg von der Gabelentz, *Die Sprachwissenschaft: Ihre Aufgabe, Methoden und bisherigen Ergebnisse* (Leipzig, 1891), 3: "Human speech is the organized expression of thought through sounds." (Cf. D. N. Kudriavskii, *Vvedenie v iazykoznanie*, 2nd ed. (Iur'ev, 1913), 14, where Gabelentz's definition is simply repeated). F. I. Buslaev, *Istoricheskaia grammatika russkogo iazyka* (Moscow, 1881), 115, I: "Language is the expression of thought with the help of articulated sounds." In the extensive articles of Professor Baudouin de Courtenay, "Iazyk," "Iazykoznanie," (see Kudriavskii, 19), in *Èntsiklopedicheskii slovar' Brokgauz-Efron*, 1st ed., vol. 81, an independent definition of language and word is characteristically

absent. Professor A. I. Tomson limits himself to a preliminary definition of language as "the means of communicating articulated thought by means of the sounds of speech." See his *Obshchee iazykovedenie*, 2nd ed. (Odessa, 1910), 4–5. Professor S. I. Bulich, in the lithographed "Kurs lektsii po russkomu iazyku," 3rd ed. (1902), defines language as a "means for communicating our thoughts to other people" (13), but "a word is only a symbol of a certain idea or concept" (25). Later on, it becomes clear that "the connection between a word and a certain concept is purely external, and the concept of word and the concept of object, meeting side by side in our brain, are associated only by frequent use on the basis of the psychological law of association by contiguity. In this way a word becomes the sign of an object or concept" (27). A. Potebnia pondered most deeply over this central question of the philosophy of language. Because of his feeble philosophical abilities, he was in no position to give his thought the proper clarity and fell into psychologism; however, he reflected concertedly on the problem of word as the proto-element of thought. See in particular chapter 8, "Word as an instrument of apperception," and chapter 9, "Representation, judgment, concept," in *Mysl' i iazyk*, 2nd ed. (Kharkov, 1892). We will have to return later more than once to the treatise of the Kharkov linguist.

2. From Goethe's *Faust Part One*, study scene, line 1995. [Translator]

3. From Wilhelm von Humboldt, *Über die Verschiedenheit des menschlichen Sprachbaues und ihren Einfluss auf die Entwickelung des Menschengeschlechtes* (1836), section 2, 35. [Translator]

4. The Stoics actually called the voice the body. Plutarch, *De placitis philosophorum*, IV, 20. See G. Gerber, *Die Sprache und das Erkennen* (Berlin 1885), 55, note 1.

5. *The language of gestures*. Gestures are a type of surrogate for language the basis of which is nevertheless the inner word, even though this is not brought to such a degree of deployment and perfection as in a vocal or written word. On this is based the intelligibility of gestures, or what is formed from them, a language, i.e., a system of ideograms of words in which an outline is shown by movement. But thanks to this, one can understand the comparative inaccessibility of this language, connected not only with its intelligibility but also its elementary nature, as follows from a series of examples. "According to the words of Müller, Native Americans easily make themselves understood by deaf mutes. When in 1873 various tribes of Indigenous inspected an institution for deaf mutes in Pennsylvania, they understood the gestures of the deaf mutes more quickly and easily than the latter understood the deaf-mute gestures of the Indigenous, which in their turn were distinguished by great pantomime effect. No less striking is the coincidence of gestures of other peoples with the gesticulation of deaf mutes. Taylor recounts how an indigenous man of the Hawaiian Islands, after arriving in an American institution for deaf mutes, immediately conducted a quite animated conversation with children by means of gestures, telling them about his travels and homeland. A Chinese man who did not have anyone with whom he could speak fell into despair but revived as soon as they brought him to an institution for deaf mutes where he was able to converse to his heart's content by means of gestures. Mallery recounts how a teacher from an institution for deaf mutes, on encountering natives of North America, was able to make himself understood by each of them, without understanding a word of their language," Prof. V. I. Shertzl', *Osnovnye èlementy iazyka i nachala ego razvitiia* (Voronezh, 1889), 40–41. This

remarkable fact, which resembles how Chinese characters, although to a superior degree, are intelligible when there is a difference in idioms and words, is connected with the elementary nature and "visual quality" of this Volapük of gestures. But he too presumes an inner field of language, a unity of the inner word that the Babel event did not touch. Strictly speaking, our language is always realized not only by words, but also by gestures that play an auxiliary role in speech; we speak not only with the tongue but also with the whole body. However, this universality and elementary nature of gesture, which appears in a human being prior to an articulated word, does not permit one to explain or derive words from gestures (as do Wundt and Shertzl'). The incomplete and underdeveloped can be understood only from the whole and the manifested, and not the other way around as is usually done by the partisans of evolutionism and generic explanations, forgetting that *ex nihilo nihil fit* [out of nothing, nothing comes].

Sound and word. "By the power of the soul, a human being draws from his organs an articulated sound, that basis of speech and the material instrument of the gift of word. Animals would also be able to do this, if they had a soulish impulse for it. Thus, already in its very first and necessary element, language entirely and exclusively answers to the spiritual side of the human being in such a way that the mere action of the latter is necessary in order to turn the cries of an animal into an articulated sound; but then the action of the soul is utterly essential for this transformation. Because the purpose and capability of sounds is to be meaningful, and not merely in the sense determined by the details of the represented thought, only this purpose constitutes the essence of articulated sound. In order to distinguish it from an animal cry on the one hand and from a musical tone on the other hand, it is impossible to point to anything else but this purpose." Wilhelm von Humboldt, *O razlichii organismov chelovecheskogo iazyka i o vliianii ètogo razlichiia na umstvennoe razvitie chelovecheskogo roda*, trans. V. Biliarskii (St. Petersburg, 1859), 69.

Pronoun. Humboldt refers to his monograph *Über die Verwandschaft der Ortsadverbien mit den Pronomen in einigen Sprachen,* Abhandlungen der historischen philologischen Classe der Berliner Akademie der Wissenschaften (1829), 107–108, where he showed that "personal words in any language without fail must be primary," and that "the pronoun is incorrectly taken as a later part of speech. . . . For the one speaking, the very first thing, without a doubt, is his own person: he is ceaselessly and uninterruptedly in contact with nature, and naturally cannot make do in language without another person, a you, etc."

6. Telepathic communication is also possible through immediate mutual influence, without the aid of words, and of course, it has its natural explanation as well as an occult one. But even in this case what sounds in the soul is what is given to it and what is usually clothed in a linguistic form; the whole difference here is reduced to the fact that this content, instead of being perceived as something communicated by another, is felt as one's own, completely independent of this external transmission.

7. If it refers to the language of deaf mutes and to various cases of aphasia, then these exceptions do not at all refute the general rule but on the contrary confirm it. That deficiency of form which deaf muteness is hinders the expression of the whole fullness of humanness; as a result, in order to attain this goal, it is necessary to use not direct and appropriate ways but surrogates and equivalents. Because of this, the

form of a word (i.e., correlation, rhythm, and sign) gets its expression in the forms not of hearing and vision, but touch. Here too as everywhere, however, a word remains form and meaning.

8. Of course, genetically words and ideas do not appear fully distinct and broken down. They are subject to further crystallization, specialization, and subdivision, and this life of a word is expressed in various semasiological manifestations. One of the interesting and paradoxical manifestations is the use of the same word with different shades of meaning; it can sometimes have the character of something directly opposite, the same word receives two directly opposite and mutually exclusive meanings, the so-called enantiosemy. Professor V. I. Shertzl' dedicated his interesting essay to this question: "O slovakh c protivopolozhnymi znacheniiami (ili o tak naz. ènantiosemii)" (Voronezh, 1884). Shertzl' sees the principal cause for the emergence of such a phenomenon in the fact that "by way of further differentiation more concrete nuances of the basic meaning are singled out from the general sphere of a given concept, and these gradually cross over to the region of words that are opposite each other" (4). A vague, amorphous idea, in becoming concrete, receives additional features that are mutually exclusive (e.g., "to go" as motion in general can mean both "to come" and "to depart," "odor" as smell in general can mean in the concrete "fragrance" and "stench," etc.). See Shertzl', "O slovakh," for numerous examples from different areas. In a similar manner, different colors are often designated by one word, as the same Shertzl' shows in detail in his interesting monograph, *Nazvanie tsvetov i simvolicheskoe znachenie ikh* (Voronezh, 1884).

9. In works dealing with linguistics, the definitions of a word as the proto-element of thought, as idea, usually have the pitiable character of a confusion of different points of view and different logical moments. As examples we bring two or three such opinions: "Each word designates a general notion, or concept of an object but not the object itself. This abstractness of a word presumes the multiple repetition of homogeneous perceptions that the human being has learned to identify. A general concept can be made only when a person has already learned each new perception, for example, of a given tree, to find what is common with all previous perceptions of other trees. The general concept here is the conscious or unconscious deduction from a whole genus of homogeneous perceptions. This all points with certainty to the fact that 1) lengthy experience and 2) the classifying work of the mind precede the building of a word. Actually, thanks to words that designate general concepts, the whole world of phenomena is already analyzed to a certain degree for every person who possesses language, broken into more or less large groups. In this manner, one can already see from these considerations that the rudiments of a kind of scientific thought are reflected in a word for the first time." Kudriavskii, *Vvedenie v iazykoznanie*, 36–37. Here, obviously, a word is defined in logical and psychological terms as the result of conceptual work that, of course, can be accomplished only in words and already supposes them. Therefore, here we have an irrelevant conclusion; the author explains how words of a certain general meaning, of the character of terms, can arise but not words in general. It follows that it is a question about the use of a word and not about the word itself, not about its birth. What the author calls the abstractness of a word, having in mind its meaning, its idea, he explains as the logical operation of abstraction. By the way, language that in this sense is logical is already assumed

by logic; it may be explained from the logical requirements in its use, but not at all in its origin, in its *fieri* [becoming], but not in its *esse* [being].

Here is another example of the same confusion of points of view and various aspects of the problem, thanks to which a characterization of word in terms of concepts is obtained. "From the point of view of language (!), the meaning of a word, composed of a general concept, is called an abstract meaning. 'Hand washes hand' and 'a low chair is uncomfortable'—all the words have an abstract meaning. The concrete meaning of a word is something presented as really existing in the bounds of space and time, i.e., an individual notion or concept. In 'this chair is low' and 'the taking of Kazan' by Ivan' turn your attention to this relationship—all the words have a concrete meaning. According to its content, the concrete meaning can remain not differentiated from an abstract meaning; in consciousness, the same unclear, accidental, fragmentary elements, which constitute the psychic content (!) of a general concept, can come to the surface. The awareness accompanying the concrete notion that some such phenomenon here or there is intended is the essential difference between a concrete and an abstract meaning. Here the quality of judgment is ascribed to words, the content of thought, and the author himself sees that 'according to its content, the concrete may not differ from the abstract,' or speaking more precisely, the words *chair* or *hands* are exactly the same thing, both in one use and in another, and the distinction does not at all apply to the words." Tomson, *Obshchee iazykoznanie*, 278–279.

Potebnia comes closer to the problem by forcing his way through the thick of psychologisms but in the end does not break free of them. He recognizes that in a word there is something prototypal and indissoluble: "as the core of a plant is not the leaf, the flower, the fruit, but all of this taken together, so in the beginning a word is still deprived of any formal definitions and is neither a noun, an adjective nor a verb." Potebnia, *Mysl' i iazyk*, 147. "The significance of a word is not that it has a definite meaning in general" (186). "A word is a means of forming a concept, and is not external, as are the means invented by humankind to write, to chop firewood etc., but is suggested by the very nature and is irreplaceable. The clarity (divisibility of signs) which characterizes a concept, the relation of substance to attribute, the necessity of their union, the striving of a concept to occupy a place in a system—all of this is primordially attained in a word and is transformed by it just as a hand transforms all possible machines" (166). "A word belongs equally to the one speaking and the one listening, and thus its significance is not that it has a definite meaning for the speaker, but that it has a meaning in general" (186). "One cannot look at a word as the expression of a prepared thought. . . . On the contrary, a word is the expression of a thought only in as much as it serves as the means for its creation" (188). "Finding that a work of art is a synthesis of three moments (of external form, inner form and content), and seeing in it the same signs as are in a word, and, the reverse, uncovering in a word the ideal and the whole, which are proper to art, we conclude that a word too is art, namely poetry" (198). "A word is the organ of thought and the unfailing condition of all later development of and understanding of the world and itself only because it originally is a symbol, an ideal and has all the properties of a work of art. But over the course of time a word must lose these properties, just as a poetic work, if it is given such a prolonged life as a word is, ends by ceasing to be itself" (205). Potebnia wants to say that a word is first of all a word, an incarnate form, an idea, which has its own being, similar to a work of art, and that it is not at all "abstractness," the abstract or the concrete, etc.

10. As is known, this is the opinion of W. Wundt, *Völkerpsychologie*, vol. 1, *Die Sprache, I–II*, 2nd ed. (Berlin, 1901). Wundt does not acknowledge an independent meaning for roots; they exist only in abstraction. A word is composed of *Grundelemente* [roots] and *Beziehungselemente* [relational elements] (I, 599). But words themselves are not the primary elements of speech, they enter the composition of a sentence, *Satz*, which corresponds to *Gesammtvorstellung, Einzelvorstellung* [a comprehensive conception, a particular conception], and a word is singled out only by way of isolation. Cf. also B. Delbrück, *Grundfragen der Sprachforschung* (Strassburg, 1901), V. Kap., 115–120. On the contrary, others consider the root period in the history of language as certain (e.g., M. Müller, *Lektsii po nauke o iazyke,* 272). From the earlier Pott (cf. A. Giesswein, *Die Hauptprobleme der Sprachwissenschaft* (Freiburg i. Br., 1892), 216–217).

11. M. Müller gives a satisfactory analysis of the theory of onomatopoeia (bow-wow theory) and interjection (pooh-pooh theory), *Lektsii po nauke o iazyke*, lecture IX. Cf. also Giesswein, *Die Hauptprobleme der Sprachwissenschaft*, part 2. See also the detailed analysis in Potebnia, *Mysl' i iazyk*, 9f. Also in Kudriavskii, *Vvedenie v iazykoznanie*, 53.

12. See note 11.

13. Wundt's idea about the origin of words from sound metaphors [*Lautmetaphern*] applies here, which in their turn are connected with sound gestures [*Lautgebärde*]: "The organs and actions which are related to the formation of speech sounds very frequently are named with words in whose articulation the same organs and actions cooperated" (I, 34). Natural "sound metaphors" are those "which have arisen via natural speech development and at the same time show the connection with the mediating emotional tone of the sound and its meaning" (377). According to Wundt, these sound metaphors are also a bridge toward the building of a language.

14. This term is attributed to Ernst Haeckel (1834–1919), a German zoologist, who proposed the existence of a speechless ape-human derivative of pithecanthropus. [Translator]

15. This point of view is characteristic of a few linguists, for example, Müller who says, "Language and thought, though distinguishable, are inseparable; no one truly thinks who does not speak, and no one truly speaks who does not think. . . . Both philosophy and philology had established the fact that language . . . is thought and thought is language." Müller, *Science of Thought*, 63, 82, cited in Giesswein, *Die Hauptprobleme der Sprachwissenschaft*, 159. However, this opinion is far from being generally accepted among psychologists of language and linguists, and one can consider the opposite opinion to be much more widespread. See Giesswein, *Die Hauptprobleme der Sprachwissenschaft*, 159.

16. Steinthal, as usual, introduces here the most annoying though typical mishmash. His own point of view is expressed in the following confused words: "the alleged inseparability of thought and speech is an exaggeration; a human being does not think in sounds and through sounds, but . . . accompanied by sounds." Heymann Steinthal, *Einleitung in der Psychologie und Sprachwissenschaft*, 2nd ed. (Berlin, 1881),

52. Several of his arguments are interesting for characterizing the grandiose obscurity and mishmash in his thought. First: "an animal thinks without speaking" (48) proves that an animal thinks in the same sense as a human being. As this is what it is all about, he considers it even superfluous to prove it. Further there follows a reference to deaf mutes, for whom inner speech is alien. Then something even better: "we dream, and dreaming is indeed a thought"—without words besides (48–49). Next comes a reference to the silent contemplation of a work of art, of technique, and so on, and finally comes the solemn reference to "strictly scientific, logical thinking, mathematical, with the help of ciphers and signs or drafts." "Geometric thinking is speechless, intuitive thinking." "All such formulas are not spoken, they are seen and thought" (51). What this means is unclear, but if this is said of an elaborated automatism, which builds the path of thought, then the elaboration preceded it and the earlier completed work of thought is already included in it. In this hopeless confusion of the psychological mechanism of thought and word, of abbreviations, conventions, and then interruptions in thinking, when thought is not yet born, but only being born, it is of course difficult even to recognize the essence of the problem of word-thought. Giesswein, who praises Steinthal, adduces the testimony of an engineer, that plans and inventions are made without any words. Likewise added to this is a reference to the creative process for a work of art, which is nurtured and is created without any words. This is all true, but what relation does it have to thought? For a work of art is not a thought but an incarnate image, which awakens a thought, and then this is expressed in a word, but of course this is not its element. An even greater lack of clarity occurs, for example, when Preyer, who likewise denies the link between word and thought, suddenly asserts, "Thinking is indeed inner speaking, but there is also a speaking without words" (!), William T. Preyer, *Die Seele des Kindes* (Leipzig, 1895), 273. Cf. the discussion of Giesswein himself (*Die Hauptprobleme der Sprachwissenschaft*). Generally speaking, chaos reigns in this question, because they have not carefully examined word as such, and each is speaking about their own things, and the whole time there is a blatant *quaternio terminorum* [quadrupling the terms].

17. See Humboldt, *Über die Verschiedenheit des menschlichen Sprachbaues*, § 2. [Translator]

18. Humboldt, *Über die Verschiedenheit des menschlichen Sprachbaues*, § 8. [Translator]

19. This may be an allusion to a work by Jacob Boehme, *De signatura rerum*, 1621. [Translator]

20. Gabelentz, *Die Sprachwissenschaft*, 289.

21. So, for example, Giesswein, *Die Hauptprobleme der Sprachwissenschaft*, 217: "Nevertheless, one cannot imagine the primeval character of this language other than that it consisted of pure roots." For example, Pott proposes that "one should not think that roots are historically before speech and are present unalloyed in a language, but that they have already entered into connections," Giesswein, *Die Hauptprobleme der Sprachwissenschaft*, 210. Delbrück considers it a universally recognized opinion that roots were originally words. Delbrück, *Einleitung in der Sprachstudium*, 73. Likewise Müller, Steinthal, Curtis, Whitney, cf. Gerber, *Die Sprache und das Erkennen*, 77, note 6.

22. The rich lexicon of English, which counts up to 100,000 words (excluding a small percentage of foreign words) is derived from no more than 461 Indo-Germanic roots. Chinese, with its 400 sound groups, which thanks to various accents yield around 1,200 basic words, has more than 40,000 words. Giesswein, *Die Hauptprobleme der Sprachwissenschaft*, 219, 221.

23. Gerber's fundamental idea, which he develops in this work on the nature of language, *Die Sprache und das Erkennen* (Berlin, 1884)—a work that in any case deserves serious attention—is diametrically opposed to our point of view. For he considers language to be the result of human creativity and symbols to be subjective signs. From our point of view, a theory like this destroys language. Objectively, the ontological nature of language in no way contradicts the fact that in its realization, in each of its concrete manifestations, language is art (as Gerber also considers it).

24. Müller expresses a related thought in a naïve form in his *Lektsii po nauke o iazyke*, 294–295: "How can sound express thought? How do roots become signs of general concepts? I will attempt to respond as briefly as possible. The 400 or 500 roots that constitute the basic parts in languages of various families are not interjections or imitations of sound. They are sound types, produced by the power inherent in human nature. They exist, as Plato put it, by nature; but in saying "by nature" with Plato, we must add that under this we understand "by Divine providence." A law exists, common for almost all natures, according to which everything existing has its sound. Every essence has its particular sound. We can judge about the more or less perfect structure of metals by their sonic vibrations. Gold sounds different from lead, wood different from stone, different sounds are produced in conformity with the nature of each percussive tap. It was the same with humans, the most perfect of organisms. In their original and perfect state humans were endowed, among other things, with the faculty for imparting more articulate expressions to the rational representations of their intellect; they did not create this faculty in themselves. It was an instinct, an instinct of their intellect, as involuntary as any other. Language belongs as much to the kingdom of nature as it is the product of instinct." With these comparisons, Müller muddles once and for all his already unclear idea, and importantly, he does not recognize its ontological significance; nevertheless, the idea about the non-arbitrary pronouncing of a word as some kind of natural phonation, is correct.

25. "In certain periods the vitality of the inner form gives thought the possibility of penetrating into the limpid depth of language. For example, the word designating the old age of a human being, by its affinity with words for trees, points to the myth of the origin of people from trees. In its own way it connects the human being and nature, it introduces, consequently, something conceivable by the word *old age* into the original system which does not correspond to a scientific system but which is supposed by it." Potebnia, *Mysl' i iazyk*, 165–166.

26. Plato considered the opinion that language originated by divine will but did not accept it, at least not entirely. *Cratylus*, 438C.

27. The definite negation of the *homo alalus* on the part of Ernest Renan, *De l'origine du langage* (Paris, 1848), merits attention. He remarks, "To invent language would have been as impossible as to invent a faculty." "It is a dream to imagine a first state where humans do not speak, followed by another state where they conquer the use of the word. Humans naturally speak and naturally think, and it is scarcely

philosophical to assign a willed beginning either to language or to thought." Cf. Giesswein, *Die Hauptprobleme der Sprachwissenschaft*, 143, 3, 5.

28. St. Gregory of Nyssa expresses corresponding opinions in his polemic with Eunomius. "Eunomius attributes to God a language composed of noun, verb and conjugations as something grand, ignoring that God is not said to produce all our operations separately, although He gave our nature a working aptitude. Although He gave this aptitude to our nature, still a house, a bench, a sword, a plough and the other necessities of life are manufactured by us. The same holds for each separate work of ours, although it too must be traced back to our Creator, so far as He created our nature capable of every art. In the same manner, although the aptitude for speech is the work of the one who arranged our nature, the acquisition of separate words is accomplished according to the need to name what is present and must proceed from it. . . . From our proper will things have arisen, but not names. Therefore, an existing thing is a work of creative power, and the sounds that have meaning for the existing thing, through which language brings all particular things to precise and clear knowledge, are works and inventions of the conceptual aptitude. This same aptitude of our speech, like nature, is the work of God." Gregory of Nyssa, *Contra Eunomium*.

29. Faced with the well-known garrulity and confusion of thought in Steinthal, it is a hopeless task to impose any refinement on it. Here are some examples of his opinion about the "theory" of the origin of language. "Language is a reflex motion to the same degree as is any other motion. For first of all we know that each intentional motion rests on a reflex; and then, if someone visualizes the pleasure of swimming, in whatever situation he may find himself, he can no doubt make the motions of swimming either fully or partially. We may say in a wholly particular sense that a human speaks in the way a hedge rustles. Air that carries tones and odors, ether and the rays of the sun and the breath of the spirit, pass over the human body and it intones." Steinthal, *Abriss der Sprachwissenshaft*, part I, *Einleitung in die Psychologie und die Sprachwissenschaft* (Berlin, 1871), 361, 366.

30. For Wundt's opinion on "innere Lautmetapher," see above. He establishes *Klanggebärde* on analogy with other gestures; sound gestures form the foundation of language, which is obtained when they are used with the intention of communicating their representations and feelings.

31. According to Diodorus, "the first people would have led an erratic animal life, they would have walked alone on the meadow where they would be nourished with tasty grass and the fruits of wild trees. But being always threatened by the attack of wild animals, they were forced to support one another, and out of fear society was formed. Gradually they began to attain understanding of the things surrounding them. In the beginning they uttered only indistinct sounds having no meaning, but gradually they learned to utter articulated words and gave thereafter names to things, until they arrived in the end at expressing all of their thoughts with language." Diodorus Siculus, *Bibliotheca Historica*, I. 8, in Giesswein, *Die Hauptprobleme der Sprachwissenschaft*, 148. According to Vitruvius, fear united people who originally had been living alone. When the first human society arose, from those different sounds that the people produced, they created words by means of constant use (*vocabula*). Since they designated certain things by this, they began by chance to speak and in this way

created among themselves speech (*sermones procreaverunt*). Vitruvius, *De architectura* II, 1, in Giesswein, *Die Hauptprobleme der Sprachwissenschaft*, 149.

32. Lucretius, in *De rerum natura*, imagines the origin of language in the following lines:

"But Nature incited them to utter the varied sounds of the tongue, and usefulness formed the names of things; by a not so different reason it seems that the very infancy of their tongue draws children toward gesture, and it causes them to point with their finger to whatever is before them. 1028–1032

Likewise, to imagine that some person then distributed names to things, and from then on people learned their first words, is silly. For why would this one person have been able to mark out everything with sounds and utter the varied noises of the tongue, when at the same time others cannot be imagined to do the same? 1041–1045

Finally, what in this regard is so remarkable if the human race, whose voice and tongue thrive, should mark out by sound varied things for the sake of varied feeling? When dumb cattle, when even wild beasts are in the habit of uttering distinctive and varied sounds when they are in fear or pain or when joys are blazing up? 1056–1061

If varied feelings, therefore, force animals, dumb though they are, to utter varied sounds, how much more reasonable it is that mortals at that time could use one and another sound for different things. 1087–1090

Thus the age draws up gradually every little thing, and reason lifts it into the regions of light." 1387–1388

I have corrected the erroneous line numbers given by Bulgakov. [Translator]

33. In speaking of the difficulty of this task, Gabelentz wants to impose a general tax on specialists. "Each person must try to describe as realistically as possible the language of which they have the best command as they themselves feel it." Gabelentz, *Die Sprachwissenschaft*, 458–459.

34. Whitney finds that "no human language exits completely deprived of the expression of forms. You cannot speak in favor [of this] if only certain languages are called 'languages of forms,' except when this expression should be understood in the sense that they possess this property in a special and exceptional degree, but at the same time in fact share it with all others." Giesswein, *Die Hauptprobleme der Sprachwissenschaft*, 193. Similarly, "strictly speaking there are neither perfect nor imperfect languages. No language in and of itself can give precise expression to thought in every respect and under all circumstances." Giesswein, *Die Hauptprobleme der Sprachwissenschaft*, 192.

35. These classifications are set forth in general and special works on linguistics. At the present time they distinguish the Indo-Germanic group of languages, the Semitic, Finno-Ugric, Turco-Tatar, the Bantu family, and others.

36. The fundamental thought with respect to the nature of language that Gerber developed in his worthwhile treatise *Die Sprache und das Erkennen* (Berlin, 1884), is completely opposed to our own because he understands language as our creation and symbols as subjective signs. "And precisely the fact that sound images derive from us, that they are created by us, makes them the bearers of our knowing; for it is only through this that we are capable of feeling them as something objective that belongs to us. The possibility that the many come together in their imagining and thinking rests on their form-determined solidity, that the concept of truth is recognized as

one that is valid for the genus. Language is created from the soul of the individual, and as a result of language the soul of the genus becomes powerful in the soul of the individual" (5). In our opinion, such a point of view negates language. The objective-ontological nature of language does not contradict the fact that in its realization, in each separate case of a concrete language, it is art, according to the definition of the same Gerber.

37. "The laws of language form an organic system among themselves that we call the spirit of language. The spirit of language determines the way the language material is shaped—the word-form and sentence formation; in this respect it is the principle of formation or the inner form of language." Gabelentz, *Die Sprachwissenschaft*, 63. "Every language represents certain thinking habits on which it rests and that are propagated by the genus. The external form corresponds to the so-called inner form. This grasps something double in itself: first, the way in which the individual representations are portrayed with the aids on hand, e.g., moon, *men* as what measures, and *luna* as what shines,—and second, the way in which the representations are ordered, separated and attached to structured thoughts." Gabelentz, *Die Sprachwissenschaft*, 160.

38. Rudolf Steiner (1861–1925), an Austrian philosopher and spiritualist, developed with Marie von Sivers a type of performance art known as eurythmy, or "harmonious movement." Bulgakov refers to its application to the spoken word; eurythmy associates specific gestures and movements with the sounds and rhythms of speech to make speech visible. [Translator]

39. The adjectival form of zaum [заум], a term for experimental poetic language of indeterminate meaning, coined by the futurist Aleksei Kruchenykh (1886–1968). It is built from the Russian preposition/prefix "za" "beyond, behind," and the noun "um" "mind," i.e., "beyond or behind mind." I have chosen to render it "surrational," in imitation of "surreal." [Translator]

40. "Flatus vocis," literally "breath of the voice," meaning a mere word, a sound without meaning, was used by Nominalists to describe universals. [Translator]

Chapter 2. Speech and Word

1. "Of course, specifically human speech lives first in the sentence; this is its first organic self-existing unit, and its parts receive their particular value from that whole. They would, however, not receive that value, indeed, the whole would not be able to arise at all, if the assembling spirit, even only obscurely or unconsciously, had the universal meaning of the parts in mind." Gabelentz, *Die Sprachwissenschaft*, 210.

2. In the opinion of Humboldt, which in this part is shared by Potebnia, "as the seed of a plant is not a leaf, a flower, a fruit or all of this taken together, so a word in the beginning is still deprived of all formal definitions and is neither a noun, an adjective nor a verb." "The activities lying at the basis of nouns, Steinthal says, are not verbs but adjectives, the names of signs. A sign is an attribute, by means of which instinctive self-consciousness understands a sensible image as a unit and represents this image. As our intellect does not comprehend an object in its essence, so too language does not have proper, primordial nouns, and as the composition of signs is received by us as the object itself, so too in language there is only the name of

signs." . . . "A word in the beginning of the development of thought does not yet have for thought the significance of a quality and can be only an indication of a sensible object, in which there is neither motion nor quality, nor object, taken separately, but all of this in an indissoluble union. It is impossible, for example, to see motion, rest, whiteness in themselves, because they are represented only in objects, in a bird which is flying or sitting, in a white stone, etc.; precisely just as it is impossible to see an object without certain signs. The formation of a verb, a noun, etc. is already such a decomposition and modification of the sensible image, which supposes other simpler (?) phenomena, following on the making of a word. Thus, for example, parts of speech are possible only in a sentence, in a composition of words, which we do not assume (?!) at the beginning of language. The existence of adjective and verb is possible only after the consciousness separates from accidental attributes that unalterable kernel of the thing, that essence or substance that a person thinks to see behind the combination of signs and which is not given by this combination." Potebnia, *Iazyk i mysl'* (1878), 147–148. Schleicher also advances the correlation of parts of speech, i.e., a purely grammatical view of them in *Compendium der vergleichenden Grammatik*, 2nd ed. (Weimar, 1866), 513: "Because *verbum* and name stand in correlation to each other, since they are to be considered as more specific qualifications of earlier undetermined speech elements, one cannot appear without the other. A language either separates *nomina* and *verba* by form or it has neither of them. Hence one cannot speak of a priority of one or the other; *nomen* and verbum both arose at the same time." Cited by Gerber, *Die Sprache und das Erkennen*, 78, note 7. Cf. Steinthal, *Typen der Sprache* (Berlin, 1893), 285. Gerber's opinion is typical: "The difference between *nomen* and *verbum* is found only syntactically, i.e., through the sentence relation, and we have to speak about *nomen* and *verbum* initially only in the sense that they are subject and predicate in a sentence." Gerber, *Die Sprache und das Erkennen*, 69.

3. Gerber, *Die Sprache und das Erkennen*, 81: "There is sunshine, and one states 'the sun shines,' 'sol lucet.' In the beginning, the single root would have sufficed for the depiction: (Skt.) *ruk, luk* (*luchnos, lux, luna,* ahd. *lioht*), also probably (following Curtius, *Grundzüge der griechischen Etymologie* (Leipzig, 1858–66), 551): (Skt.) *svar* (*seir, selas, selene; serenus, sol;* (Goth.), *savil,* (altn.) *sôl*). Later, *luk*, an element that would have already been formed, was singled out from the perception image, and 'sol' was added to 'lucere' as the subject, 'sun' as the subject to 'to shine.' "

4. "Every appellation is a putting in order, subordinating the particular to the general; all that we know by way of experience or theory, we know only by means of general concepts." Müller, *Lektsii po nauke o iazyke*, 290. Here is an example of such a judgment: "Each word designates a general representation or concept of an object, and not (?) the object itself. Preceding (!) the making of a word are the following: 1) long experience, and 2) the classifying work of the intellect. In fact, thanks to words that designate general concepts, the whole world of phenomena is already analyzed to a certain degree, broken into more or less large groups, by every human being who possesses a language." Kudriavskii, *Vvedenie v iazykoznanie*, 36–37.

5. "It is to be regarded as an astonishing lack of observation that nowhere in *Logic* can one find the fact that a sentence such as 'the individual is the universal' is addressed in every judgment," G.W.F. Hegel, *Encyclopädie der philosophischen Wissenschaften in Grundrisse* (Heidelberg, 1817, 1830), 166. He does not find proof of the

philosophical depth of language in the fact that language in general can designate only the universal even when it understands the individual. G.W.F. Hegel, *Phänomenologie des Geistes* (Jena, 1807), 83.

6. Steinthal distinguishes a twofold type of root: a qualitative and a demonstrative one. Bonn called these demonstrative roots pronouns. In later phases of the life of a language, the boundary between the one and the other sometimes combines into one. See S. Bulich, "Mestoimenie," *Èntsiklopedicheskii slovar' Brokgauza-Efrona*, vol. 39, 326.

7. "The type of word which must be distinguished first from all the others is, in our opinion, the pronoun. I believe this category to be more primitive than that of the substantive, because it is more instructive, more easily commented on by gesture. One must therefore not allow oneself to be misled by the denomination of 'pronoun' (*pro nomine*) which comes to us from the Latins who translated the Greek *antonumia*. The error has lasted until our own day. Pronouns are, on the contrary, I believe, the most ancient part of a language. How could *I* ever have lacked an expression for designating itself?" M. Bréal, *Essai de sémantique* (Paris, 1897), 207. Concerning demonstrative roots, which form the basis of pronouns, although they are not numerous and show little variety in their external form (some vowels, *a, i, u*; or consonants with *a*, such as *ka, ta, ma*), Fick notes that it is utterly pointless to consider them only as substitutes for other words—as *pronomina*. It is pointless "to recognize in them precisely the true old *Urnomina*, so that conversely *nomina* could be called the multiplied and strengthened representatives of *pronomina* around the verbal concept, whereas the so-called *pronomina* show the nominal concept in a pure way, without verbal mixing and expansion," and so on. August Fick, *Wörterbuch der indogermanischen Sprache*, vol. 4–5 (Göttingen, 1870), 9f. See Gerber, *Die Sprache und das Erkennen*, 321, note 2.

8. In synthetic languages, the syntactic relations between parts of a sentence are established by inflection, i.e., the addition of morphemes to a root word that provide grammatical properties. A second type of synthetic language is agglutinating, where two or more morphemes are combined to form one word. Isolating languages have no inflectional morphology and show a morpheme per word ratio of one. Russian is a synthetic inflectional language, Turkish is a synthetic agglutinating language, and Vietnamese is an isolating language. [Translator]

9. The phrase is taken from Baruch Spinoza, *The Ethics*, part 1. [Translator]

10. "We notice in language the use of the law of perspective, or egocentrism. According to this "law," as the distance from the place in which we find ourselves increases, the distinction between objects diminishes and disappears more and more, so that what is more distant is assimilated and absorbed by what is nearer. Whence arises a group composed only of one, the first person (I), where the other persons, a second (you) and a third (he, she) are perceived as the first person plural (we); a group consisting only of one second person (you) in combination with many third persons is perceived as a second-person plural (you). Having designated with the help of 'p' the coefficient of any arbitrary recurrence, we can express this in the following formulas: we = I + p, you + p, he (she) + p; you = you + p, he (she) + p." Baudouin de Courtenay, "Iazyk," *Èntsiklopedicheskii slovar' Brokgauza-Efrona*, vol. 81, 536.

11. This is a striking image. Primiparous [*pervorodiashchaia*] refers to a woman who gives birth for the first time, and while the Russian could be translated as

"primordial," this would erase the image that I believe Bulgakov wanted to convey by choosing this particular word. [Translator]

12. Cf. Gerber, *Die Sprache und das Erkennen*, 82, 91, note 2.

13. Cf. Delbrück, *Grundfragen der Sprachforschung*, 144–145.

14. "Cases designate the relation of an object to an action, as the one producing the action *agens* (subject—nominative case, *nominativus*), as the object to which the action is immediately directed, *patiens* (direct object—accusative case, *accusativus*), as the object in benefit of which or in relation to which the action happens (object in the dative case, *dativus*), as the object in association with which (*sociativus*) or by means of which (*instrumentalis*) the action is produced (genitive case), or as the object in which the action occurs (locative case, *locativus*). The relation of one object to another is designated more often by a form of the genitive case, but also the dative case, etc. In various languages, still other case forms, constituting formal categories, or cases, with such meanings, are designated by prepositions, e.g., in the following combinations: from town (the setting aside case, ablatives), in the town (*ilativus*), on the town (*superessivus*), against the town (*sublativus*), out of the town (*elativus*), by the town (*adessivus*), etc." Tomson, *Obshchee iazykovedenie*, 321. Professor Baudouin de Courtenay distinguishes cases that are spatial-temporal, or local-chronological, as this: *locativus* in general, ablatives, *elativus, allativus, inessivus, superessivus, subessivus, sublativus, superlativus, adessivus, instrumentalis*, etc. Cases of social origin are the *genitivus, dativus, accusativus*, etc. Baudouin de Courtenay, *Ėntsiklopedicheskii slovar' Brokgauza*-Efrona, vol. 81, 536.

15. In Gerber's study, we come across interesting discussions about the nature of the substantive noun and subject in a sentence. He psychologizes this in the sense that in the selection of the subject he sees a repetition of the human I: from the general indetermination of knowledge arises an act of cognition, which is realized by the person. "In fact, in forming substantive words the human being emerged from the circle of what was given by the universe, what was known. If he separated and individualized the same from the phonetic structure of roots, which he himself shaped, he created a something to which no other external or internal reality is due than the one based on this creation, no meaning therefore than the one set by him lying in his delimitation (definition) of the phonetic image. Thus, the substantive means nothing for itself but precisely this phonetic image in which it has been realized, and it would not mean anything real at all if the human himself were not still within the universe in his creating, in the exercise of his individual imagination. Nothing real outside us corresponds to the meaning of the word *serpens* (snake), but only through the real have we come to the vocal image *serpens*, and the sound *serp* points to the sound of the perception that caused him to form it." Gerber, *Die Sprache und das Erkennen*, 73. "The substantive-subject holds that position in the sentence, which [in the consciousness I occupies; in the act of consciousness the content that it encloses corresponds to the predicate of the sentence].* . . . Every subject would become thus a personification of the I, in every predicate would live an analogue of the motion of the soul as the I causes and directs" (80–81). These ideas are connected with Gerber's general epistemological conceptions, which differ significantly from ours. It is Gerber's merit to have attempted to introduce epistemological consciousness into basic language function, whereas the inadequacy of his whole conception is the ambiguous meaning of I and its role in judgment. Is it here a question of an

ill-fated "psychological" explanation, which appears everywhere in linguistics where it ought to and ought not to, or is I understood here as epistemological or, finally, metaphysical? The dreary idea about the difference between *Kennen* and *Erkennen* as two degrees of cognition, the first in cosmic indeterminacy, the second overcoming that amorphousness by the reflection of a subject, is the basis of the whole construct, by the way, of an epistemologically antiquated theory of cognition, going back to the era of earlier neo-Kantianism with its over refinement in this field. *Correcting Bulgakov's otherwise unintelligible citation. [Translator]

16. This judgment of naming, which is the basis of any substantive noun, the subject being a pronoun—a gesture, and the predicate a name, usually is not noticed in linguistics, not even in philosophical linguistics. For example, the same Gerber, while linking perfectly correctly the difference between a noun and a verb with a syntactic correlation, thanks to which the root word is defined in its being, stops helplessly before substantives in isolation, although such, of course, exist even outside a sentence and represent a riddle demanding a solution. He is forced simply to deny it. "As long as the root alone preceded the sentence, it could only have sounded either as the interjection of satisfied astonishment, as a pleasing work of language art, an apt phonetic image, created for its own sake: *sar (sarp—serpens) ta* crawling (of that) there—or it would signify, when it entered the service of communication, a tautological sentence: crawling (that) crawls there." Gerber, *Die Sprache und das Erkennen*, 69. It is only later on when the given word develops in meaning: "*sar ta agh (anguis)* crawling (of that) strangles (twines around) there; that which crawls, which is crawling, is now a crawling thing which strangles. One and the same thing is based in two different processes in the same way as, under certain circumstances, it can be based unchanged on many others. It is the concept of substance as opposed to accidents" (70). Gerber misses a third possibility in his judgment, distinct both from an interjective meaning of a word and from a tautology, namely that *serpens* as a noun is *already* a judgment—"this is *serpens*." Without a preliminary judgment that converts an idea-word into a noun, its further development into the subject of a judgment is impossible: *sar ta agh—serpens—anguis*. The matter is presented still more simply by Gabelentz, who lets this judgment fall in passing: "A human being calls things after some sort of prominent quality, which means, he replaces the subject (!) with the predicate." Gabelentz, *Die Sprachwissenschaft*, 336.

17. Here it is appropriate to recall the judgment of W. von Humboldt that "language can arise in no other way but at once," and that "in every moment of its existence, it must possess that thing which makes it into a whole." Humboldt, *Über das vergleichende Sprachstudium in Beziehung auf die verschiedenen Epochen der Sprachentwicklung*, in *Gesammelte Werke*, vol. 111, 243, cited by Gerber, *Die Sprache und das Erkennen*, 6.

18. Potebnia looks at it differently. "The sensible form of a sound, of a color, is in itself a contradiction, because we see not a color alone but a colored object, and even a sound, whose actual source can be concealed from us, we fix to that object from which it is heard. The naming of several colors even now plainly indicates sensible forms, from which they are deduced (!?). Blue is the color of a dove (why not the reverse), light bay, the color of a nightingale, Polish niebieski—the color of the sky, so too green—initially it was not conceived separately as a quality but in a sensible

form which embraced the object, action and quality." Potebnia, *Mysl' i iazyk*, 158. Kudriavskii argues in a similar manner and repeats the same example of the dove. "Evidently, the naming of all colors occurred by the same path as the naming of the color blue. Thus 'rose' comes from the word 'rose' and designates the original color of a flower, 'crimson' [malinovyi] comes from 'raspberry' [malina], 'brown' [korichnevyi] from 'cinnamon' [koritsa], etc. The names 'violet' [fioletovyi] and 'orange' [oranzhevyi], which Russian borrows from the French 'violette,' 'orange,' according to their original meaning indicate the color of a violet flower [fialka] and an orange fruit [apel'sin]." Kudriavsky, *Vvedenie v iazykoznanie*, 41–42.

19. Cf. Müller, *Lektsii po nauke o iazyke*, 210, counts 600 necessary roots in Gothic and 250 in contemporary German. A. F. Pott proposes that each language has around 1000 roots. *Etymologische Forschungen auf dem Gebiet der indogermanischen Sprachen* II (1833), 73. According to Grimm, the Germanic languages have 462 verbal roots (Potebnia, *Mysl' i iazyk*, 19). "Having at its disposal 400–500 predicative roots, a language would have no difficulty in coining names for all objects that are presented to our knowledge: language is a thrifty landlord. If each root gave 50 produced words, then we would have 25,000 words. But we know from reliable authority, the village priest, that some workers in his parish have no more than 300 words in their dictionary. Cuneiform inscriptions in Persia contain not more than 379 words, of which 131 are proper nouns. The dictionary of ancient Egyptian sages, so far as it is known from hieroglyphic inscriptions, contains around 658 words. The libretto of some Italian opera rarely displays greater variety. A well-educated person in England rarely uses more than 3000 or 4000 words in conversation. Shakespeare, who probably presents a greater variety than any other writer in any language at all, composed his dramas from approximately 15,000 words, in Milton, there are all of 8000 words, in the Old Testament are encountered not more than 5,642 words." Müller, *Lektsii po nauke o iazyke*, 202–203.

20. Leibnitz, *De arte combinatoria*, Opp. 11, 387–388, ed. Dutens. Quoties situs litterarum in alphabeto sit variabilis [whenever the position of letters in the alphabet is variable]: twenty-three letters in Latin permit 25,852,016,738,884,976,640,000 combinations; twenty-four letters in German permit 620,448,701,733,239,739,360,00 0. Müller, *Lektsii po nauke o iazyke*, 201–202.

21. Potebnia explains the inner form of a word thus: "A word itself expresses not the whole thought taken as its content, but only one attribute of it. The form of a table can have many attributes, but the word *table* [*stol*] means only that which is spread (the root *stl* is the same as the verb *stlat'*). By the word *window* we usually understand a frame with panes of glass, whereas judging by its resemblance with the word 'eye,' it means 'where they look.' In a word, consequently, there are two contents: the one, which we above called objective but now can call the proximate etymological meaning of the word, always includes one attribute, the other—subjective content, in which equally there can be a multitude of them. The first is a sign, a symbol, replacing the second for us. . . . The inner form of a word is the relationship of content to creation, it shows how its own thought is presented to the human being . . . in a series of words of one root that consistently flow out one from the other, every preceding one can be called the inner form of the last one." Potebnia, *Mysl' i iazyk*, 101–102. Kudriavskii distinguishes: "1) the phonetic form, i.e., a certain

combination of sounds, 2) the symbol, i.e., the preceding meaning of a word used as a sign for another meaning, and finally, 3) the very meaning of the word, i.e., the representation or concept united with it. Especially important in the development of a word is the symbol, which is the vital, connecting link between the sonorous composition of a word and its meaning. Sometimes this element of a word is called the inner form of a word."

22. Bulgakov's reference is difficult to decipher. He may be referring to the six-volume edition of Jacobi's works, *Friedrich Heinrich Jacobi's Werke*, ed. J. F. Köppen and C.J.F. Roth, vols. 1–6 (Leipzig: Gerhard Fleischer, 1812–1825). [Translator]

23. "One fact that dominates the whole matter is that our languages, by a necessity the reasons for which we shall see, are condemned to a perpetual lack of proportion between the word and the thing. The expression is one time too broad, another time too narrow. We are not aware of this lack of precision because for the one speaking, the expression itself is proportionate to the thing, thanks to the ensemble of circumstances, thanks to the place, the moment, and the visible intention of the discourse. It is also because for the listener, who is half in any language, the attention going straight to the thought without stopping at the literal scope of the word, restricts it or extends it according to the intention of the speaker." Bréal, *Essai de sémantique*, 134, note 1.

24. "In language there are no proper expressions, and the more we subject a word to precise analysis, the more affinities it will display with symbolic expressions of later folk poetry." Potebnia, *Mysl' i iazyk*, 158.

25. According to the remark of Quintilian (VIII, 6), apparently, thanks to metaphor every object has for itself a word in language. Bréal, *Essai de sémantique*, 134, note 1.

26. Examples of synecdoche [Bulgakov has "anecdote"]: we have as a generalization of a concept, for example, in the Latin *aedes*—dwelling, building, which is derived from the root *idh*—to burn; originally it designated the place of the hearth. From the Latin *pavimentum*—trampled down earth (from *pavis*)—the Romanian *pâmentu*, designating the whole terrestrial globe. In a similar manner, the German *Erde* (root *ar*) signified originally plowed earth. Proper names can receive a generalized meaning: from Caesar came *Kaiser, kesar, tsar*, from Karl—Slavic and Hungarian *kral, kiraly*—nation. Much more often is a specification of meaning, in which the genus is used in place of the species. Thus, for example, *alogon* in New Greek signifies horse. The German word *Fohlen, Füllen*, standing in connection with the Greek *polos*, and Latin *pullus*, designated originally "young animal," in German use it means young horse or even young ass. *Poulain*, which comes from this—"young animal," as in a similar German word, now designates a young horse. Giesswein, *Die Hauptprobleme der Sprachwissenschaft*, 110–111.

27. Examples of metonymy: the meaning of *Sonne* (*sol, helios*)—sun and *luna* (*luc-na*) moon were originally only "shining," *Mana, Mensch*—thinking, *femina* (woman)—nourishing, *filius, filia*—son, daughter, suckling, *argentum, aurum*, Gold—gold, silver—sparkling, *terra*—dry land, *Rost*, Rose, Latin *rubus* (strawberry)—red, Hebrew *lebanâ*, Arabic *aquar* (fox)—red, Arabic *laban* (milk), Hebrew *Lbânâ* (month), *lebânâ* (tile), Arabic *gamar* (month), French *aube* (dawn), Latin *alba* (pearl), Hebrew *hôri* (wheat bread), German *Weizen*—wheat—white, German *Galle*, Greek *chole*, Latin *fel*—bile—yellow, *Bär* (bear)—brown—*ovis der Braune*; Latin *ovis*—sheep—humble, tender, German *Wolf*—wolf—ripper, German *Hahn*—rooster—singing,

Latin *galus*—rooster—crying, German *Gerste*, Latin *hordeum*, Hebrew *Secôrâ*—chopping, *Himmel und Hemd*—covering, *equus, aqua*—quick, *cervus Hirsch*—hoofed, *sus, Schwein*—birthing, *bos, Kuh, bu-te-o, bu-of*—crying (root *gu*—to cry), *corvus, cornix, Krähe* (crow)—cawing, *Gras*—growing, etc. Giesswein, *Die Hauptprobleme der Sprachwissenschaft*, 111.

28. "Metaphor changes the meaning of words, creates new expressions suddenly. The momentary life of a similarity between two objects, two actions, causes it to arise. It will be adopted if it is sound, or picturesque, or simply if it fills a lacuna in vocabulary. But metaphor only remains such at the beginning; soon the mind becomes accustomed to it; its success causes it to fade, it becomes a reflection of the idea scarcely more colorful than the proper word." (Bréal, *Essai de sémantique*, 135). Here are some examples of metaphor: "from similarities in external form—'eye' of a needle, 'vein' of marble, 'dandelion,' a flower, pastry 'straws,' 'vint,' a card game, 'crest' of a rooster or a mountain, 'leg' of a table, etc. From similarities of functions—'skates,' 'head' of a town, 'sister' (nurse) of mercy, he is his 'right hand,' etc. Similarities of position:—'neck and head' of a bottle, 'wing' of an army, a 'windmill,' etc. Tomson, *Obshchee iazykovedenie*, 297.

29. In an earlier time "the legitimacy of a word and its connection with the object itself were felt much more vividly. And in actual fact, in language and poetry there is positive testimony that according to the beliefs of all Indo-European peoples, a word is a thought, a word is truth, and justice, wisdom, and poetry." Potebnia, *Mysl' i iazyk*, 176. "The creation of language, beginning with its first element, is a synthetic activity in the strict sense of this word, namely in the sense according to which a synthesis creates something that is not included in the composed parts taken separately." Potebnia, *Mysl' i iazyk*, 184, citing Humboldt, *Über die Verschiedenheit des menschlichen Sprachbaues*, 104.

30. Bréal imparts paramount significance to the participation of the will in language: "One would have to close one's eyes to the evidence in order not to see that an obscure but persistent will presides over changes to language. How ought this will be represented? I believe that it must be represented under the form of thousands, millions and billions of attempts by trial and error, most often unsuccessful, sometimes followed by a modicum of success, a partial success, and which thus guided, thus corrected, thus perfected, would have taken shape in a certain direction. The aim with respect to language is to be understood. The child spends months training the tongue to bring forth vowels, to articulate consonants: how many miscarriages before it arrives at pronouncing one syllable clearly! Grammatical innovations are of the same type with this difference: an entire people collaborates in them. How many clumsy, incorrect, unclear constructions before finding the one that will be not the adequate expression (there are none) but at least a sufficient one for thought! Throughout this long labor there is nothing that does not come from the will." Bréal, *Essai de sémantique*, 7–8.

31. Concerning Stilpo, see in Plutarch, *adversus Colotem*, 22, cited by Gerber, *Die Sprache und das Erkennen*, 79, note 11: "Life is abolished by him who says that one thing cannot be predicated of another. For how shall we live if we cannot call a man good . . . but must separately call a man a man, good good, etc." Bulgakov erroneously refers to Aristotle, *Metaphysics* IV, 29. He correctly refers to Plato, *Sophist*, but the pertinent section is 251ABC. [Translator]

Gerber handles this question, which has serious philosophical significance, in a simple and rather naïve manner. "In order to find our way correctly we must pay attention to the fact that the conception that is to be expressed does not receive its expression in the words but in the sentence, and that the words can only come into consideration and be correct as members of a unity that encloses them. In every sentence, the word members receive a special determination, one can say, an individualization of their meaning through the relation in which they stand to each other. There is no crawling in general, about which we are speaking in our sentence, but one that strangles, and it is not stated about some arbitrary strangling but about that of a crawling thing. Thus, we are not to pose the question this way: how can the strangling of this crawling thing be expressed about a crawling thing? You can see that the identical judgment that Antisthenes and Stilpo demanded does not need to be missing in the sentence." Gerber, *Die Sprache und das Erkennen*, 70–71. Gerber's attempt to avoid the question only leads to its transference. The very same question arises in the form: How is judgment possible? How is it possible to obtain not simply *Würgen* but *Würgen des Kriechenden*, with what can one glue these two words together? Gerber is not aware of the actual urgency of the question.

32. "If we stop to consider the oldest designation for *name*, we find in Sanskrit *nâman*, in Latin *nomen*, in Gothic *namo*. This *nâman* stands instead of *gnaman*, in Latin it was kept as *cognomen*. The letter 'g' disappeared, as for example in the word *natus*—son, instead of *gnatus*. *Nâman*, name, arose from the root to **know** and originally signified that by which we know things." Müller, *Lektsii po nauke o iazyke*, 289.

33. From the introduction to "Transcendental Logic," in *Critique of Pure Reason*. [Translator]

34. The reference given by Bulgakov does not seem to fit the context, as it comes from a section in *Timaeus* dealing with smells and sounds. [Translator]

35. "I indeed believe that words were created to have full meaning in themselves and not to serve a syntax as yet not existing." Bréal, *Essai de sémantique*, 210.

36. "A language that consisted only of pronouns would resemble the wail of a child or the gesticulation of a deaf mute. The need for another element from which the substantive, adjective and verb would be formed, is thus evident. But it is no less true that the pronoun comes to be placed at the base and origin of languages: it is no doubt that in coming to be affixed to other kinds of words the pronoun caused the beginning of the distinction of grammatical categories." Bréal, *Essai de sémantique*, 207–208.

37. Bréal, *Essai de sémantique*, 228.

38. Cf. Gerber, *Die Sprache und das Erkennen*, 120. See Bulich, "Imia chislitel'noe," *Èntsiklopedicheskii slovar' Brokgaus-Efrona*, vol. 76, 861–863.

39. "One of the most recent is the adverb, words such as *oikoi, pedoi, chamai, eu, kakos, houtos, humi, domi, recte, valde, primum, rursum, hic, illic* are regularly inflected substantives, adjectives or pronouns. But when a word has ceased to be in a direct and necessary relation with the rest of the phrase, when it serves to determine better some other term without being indispensable, it is ready to assume the value of an adverb." Bréal, *Essai de sémantique*, 200.

40. "A time came for all our idioms where the cases of declension, in not seeming clear enough or precise enough in themselves, were accompanied additionally by an adverb. . . . But the custom of seeing them joined to a certain case suggested the idea of a causal relation: this little word, which was a simple accompaniment of the

accusative or ablative, seemed to rule them. Since then it has ruled them in fact: from an adverb it became a preposition." Bréal, *Essai de sémantique*, 202.

41. The example Bulgakov gives is a strictly Russian manner of expression—*my s nim idem*—we [i.e., I with him] are going. "With him" is just as much the subject of the sentence as is "we/I." This is clear, he says, because "with him" can be replaced by the nominative case, so that the sentence would read "he and I are going." [Translator]

42. "The subject necessarily must be in the nominative case of the noun. That this is really so can be seen from the fact that every word that plays the role of subject is unfailingly recognized by us as the nominative case. If in many cases when this word is invariable, we cannot prove this, nevertheless there are cases when the category of nominative case takes on completely clear forms. Thus in Pushkin's "*daleche grianulo ura*" [hurrah burst forth from afar] it is not clear that "*ura*" is recognized as the nominative case, although the word "grianulo" partially points to this; but in a sentence such as "*akhi da okhi delu ne pomogut*," [ohs and ahs don't help] interjections took even the ending of the nominative case plural, corresponding to that role of the subject that they play in the sentence. Undoubtedly, a subject must likewise be a substantive noun. If sometimes the role of the subject can be played by an adjective, then in such a case it is always turned into a substantive," etc. Kudriavskii, *Vvedenie v iazykoznanie*, 109–110.

43. To the question what is a subject, school grammar replies: a subject is the object spoken about in a sentence. Potebnia best of all refutes the correctness of this definition by the following exemplary lesson: "Do not be concerned about tomorrow." What is being spoken about here? About tomorrow. No, not that. What is the main subject of the saying? That we not be concerned. No, the subject that is spoken about here is you, the second person. But indeed here nothing is said about us." Potebnia, *Iz zapisok po russkoi grammatike*, 187 f. The sentence "they fell with an axe" is about an axe, but the word "axe" is not at all the subject; the sentence "it is dark in the cave" is about a cave, but the words "in the cave" likewise are not the subject." Kudriavskii, *Vvedenie v iazykoznanie*, 109.

44. An attribute can consist of both an adjective and a substantive in the nominative case (apposition): Tsar Peter, or in the genitive case: the property of my father, the war of the Greeks and the Persians. However, for a pure attribute, these proper nouns do not have an ontological accent, and according to meaning, they are adjectives or predicates, which is demonstrated by their substitution with adjectives: "of parents—parental," "of the Greeks and Persians—Greco-Persian," "of Alexandria—Alexandrian," etc. Substantive nouns as attributes generally are equal to adjectives, so too in all cases when the substantive noun is a predicate, and signify quality, not being, property, not existence.

45. Kudriavskii, *Vvedenie v iazykoznanie*, 119.

Chapter 3. Toward a Philosophy of Grammar

1. This observation was made by Kant's closest contemporaries, Johann Georg Hamann [1730–1788], Friedrich Heinrich Jacobi [1743–1819], and Johann Gottfried Herder* [1744–1803], although later on it was lost. Hamann remarks in *Metakritik über den Purismum der reinen Vernunft* (Schriften, vol. 7, 5): "The first purification of philosophy consisted in the attempt to make reason independent from all tradition

and belief in it. The second (Kant) is more transcendent and boils down to nothing less than independence from experience. The third highest and at the same time empirical purity concerns therefore language, the sole, first, and last organon and criterion of reason." Jacobi says, "There was still missing a critique of language, which would be a metacritique of reason." (*Allwills Briefsammlung. Zugabe*, 109). Herder says in *Eine Metakritik zur Kritik der reinen Vernunft*, vol. 1, 451: "The building of human language from the ground up fundamentally destroys the mechanism of an abstract reason *a priori*." Gerber, from whom we are taking these comments, remarks in turn, "Kant did not subject language to a critique. Thus, he does not speak at all about sentences, but only about judgments. Judgments, however, presuppose a finished language, and he also knows no words as elements of a perception sentence, but only a word concept." Gerber, *Die Sprache und das Erkennen*, 190–191, 194. *Reading Herder for Gustav Gerber (1820–1901). [Translator]

2. Regnaud poses the question differently in *Origine et philosophie du langage* (Paris, 1887), 239. According to him, on the contrary, *nihil in dictu, quod non fuerit prius in intellectu* [there is nothing in a word that has not previously been in the intellect]. Strictly speaking, there is neither *prius* nor *posterius* here.

3. We encounter even in such a serious thinker as Hermann Lotze, *Logik* (Leipzig, 1874), 540, an example of a surprisingly superficial attitude toward the question of language. "The expression of our thoughts is accustomed to language, and its inner course has long been accustomed to the reproduction of words; perceptions, memories, and expectations hardly have full clarity until we find exhaustive expressions for them in the sentences of language. The advantage thereby gained does not really depend on the language and its sounds but on an inner work of analysis and grappling that remains the same even when it uses other forms of communication. In fact, however, after language arose for this purpose, the form and facility of thought movements is dependent on the means that it offers, and therefore even nationally different after diverse causes have been bound together, to make the structure and disposition of different languages heterogeneous. In itself, therefore, what we logically mean is independent of the manner by which we linguistically express it in actual practice, but all human thinking is forced to produce intellectual thought through separations, connections, and reformulations of the content of the imagination,* which language has consolidated in its words." Cited in Gerber, *Die Sprache und das Erkennen*, 59. *Reading *Vorstellungsinhalte* for *Verstellungsinhalte*. [Translator]

4. "Although all parts of experience are empirical, i.e., they have their ground in the immediate perception of the senses, yet conversely it is not the case that all empirical judgments on that account are parts of experience. Rather, it is the case that over the empirical and especially over what is given by sense perception, particular concepts must still be added that have their origin entirely *a priori* in pure understanding under which every perception must be first of all subsumed, and then by means of the same they can be changed into experience. Empirical judgments, as far as they have objective validity, are experience judgments; those however that are only subjectively valid I call simple perception judgments. The latter require no pure concept of the mind but only the logical linking of perceptions in the thinking subject. The former, however, beyond the representations of sensual perception, always require special concepts originally produced in the mind, which cause the judgment of experience to be objectively valid." Kant, *Prolegomena*, 78.

5. It should be noted that the fundamental Kantian distinction of analytic and synthetic judgments, on which the entire structure of the *Critique of Pure Reason* rests, itself does not stand up to criticism and on principle has no meaning. Every judgment is synthetic as a naming, as the joining of an idea-predicate with a subject; therein lies the essence of a judgment, completely irremovable, without which there is no judgment. Even the complete tautology "A is A," taken in all the seriousness of a judgment, signifies such a synthesis: a connection is established precisely between the existential centers, the ontological point A and the idea A. The tautology here consists in the fact that this synthesis is already produced once in the naming of A through A. This name now as it were loses its power, is played out, and merges with a pronoun as a demonstrative gesture; it becomes a sign or number. In a predicate, on the contrary, a word preserves its power (thus, perhaps, if the significance of a name, as the result of antiquity or excessive use becomes obsolete, it will be necessary to rejuvenate it). But such a pure tautology is, of course, a rare exception and does not at all constitute the type of "analytic" judgments in which the one or other feature is apportioned in a predicate and becomes the object of a particular cognitive act or apperception. Kant defines analytic and synthetic judgments thus: "Judgments either simply clarify (?!) and do not add anything (?) to the content of cognition (thus, they are entirely without content, but then what kind of judgments are they and in what sense can one call them clarifying?), or they are expansive and increase a given cognition. The first can be called an analytic, the second a synthetic judgment." Kant, *Prolegomena*, trans. V. Soloviev, 2nd ed., 17. Kant's example of a would-be analytic judgment is "a body is something extended." But this is completely unsuccessful, for, evidently, he replaces body as subject, as a noun, designating something, with the concept of body, with its definition, in which various signs are calculated, and among them is extension, so that an analytic judgment would be reduced to a tautology: "extended extensively." In fact, this is, of course, not so. Besides this, evidently, factual knowledge according to Kant is required, which makes a judgment analytic, otherwise it will be synthetic. So his own example of a synthetic judgment—"this street is 676 meters long," or "today it is plus 2° C"—can be a perfect example of an analytic judgment, no less than "a body is extended," if the length of the street is known with certainty by all and is introduced physically into the concept of this street. The same holds for today's temperature. But, although on the one hand Kant's division into analytic and synthetic judgments does not stand up to criticism, and in the precise sense all judgments are synthetic, at the same time the opposite can be correct, i.e., that under certain conditions all judgments can be synthetic, if the predicate, as something already known, is introduced into a concept. On this is based logical deduction and all mathematics. It is a question there of the synthetic judgments *a priori*, which Kant searches for: they are not tautological judgments, in which it is possible to develop the definition hidden in a given intuition. Now, he considers space and time to be such an intuition, but here, of course, there are no grounds to agree with him. The axiom of discourse and thinking is an ontological communism: everything is in everything and through everything. In this ultimate sense all judgments are analytic, for any subject, any point of the world, can lead to all the rest, can join to itself any predicate. "Analytic judgments (Kant continues here) express in a predicate only that which was already effectively conceivable in the concept of the subject, although not as clearly and not with the same consciousness."

One can say precisely the same about the thought of Kant. "When I say, 'all bodies are extended,' I in no way expand my concept of body, but only break it down, since extension was in reality conceivable about this concept even before judgment (?! What is this concept before judgment?); although it was not clearly expressed (and therefore not conceived?), this judgment is in this way analytic. On the contrary, the postulate 'some bodies have weight,' contains in the predicate something that in the general concept of body really is not yet conceived. (Why, then, is it not conceived if it already came to this, if only as a possibility?) In this way this postulate increases my understanding, by adding something new to my concept, and therefore it must be called a synthetic judgment." What vagueness Kant introduced into this question is evident. On the one hand, there are some sort of concepts before judgment and independent of judgment; on the other hand, a *quaestio facti* [question of fact] evidently appears by including or not including this or that sign in the actual composition. Thus, it is impossible to distinguish beforehand by the content of analytic and synthetic judgments, for every judgment can become analytic; that which is analytic for the teacher proves on the contrary to be synthetic for the student. Kant has not considered that with a pronominal subject, which corresponds to the absence of any concept and expresses only a demonstrative gesture, every judgment is synthetic.

6. "Only two cases are possible: either logic exercises full dominion over language because it is itself the creative impulse in language, the idea being embodied in it; or with respect to logic, language is a peculiar creation, that is, one using particular powers. In the first case, language cannot deviate from logic even by a hair's breadth; there can be no grammar, only logic." Steinthal, *Einleitung in die Psychologie und Sprachwissenschaft*, 2nd ed. (Berlin, 1881), 66–67. "Therefore, either logic swallows grammar or grammar frees itself entirely from logic" (68). Steinthal admits a connection between logic and grammar only within the same limits as for the remaining sciences. "Like nature and the natural sciences, so too language and linguistics are logical and not logical, that is, their object with its conditions is peculiar to them. But while this object and these conditions are being thought, the logician observes that the linguist acts according to logical laws and that in the process of language to form its elements and assemble them according to inherent laws, logical considerations and laws have unconsciously prevailed. These logical laws, which language and linguist, chemist, physicist, and nature follow, are the common logical laws whose explanation the linguist and natural scientist presuppose, which they do not examine, and which are not their particular subject matter" (70). Cf. the description of Steinthal's views in V. V. Zenkovskii, *K voprosu o funktsii skazuemogo* (Kiev, 1908).

7. Wilhelm Windelband (1848–1915) and his student Heinrich Rikkert (1863–1936) were representatives of the Baden or Southwest school of neo-Kantianism, which like the Marburg school promoted a nonpsychological interpretation of Kant's philosophy. [Translator]

8. The Russian has "vorota, gate," a plural noun. [Translator]

9. Gabelentz, *Die Sprachwissenschaft*, 417.

10. *Critique of Pure Reason*, trans. Vladislavlev, 52–53, 2nd part, Transcendental Logic. Introduction 1.

11. Kant, *Prolegomena*, 2nd ed., 75–76.

12. Hermann Cohen (1842–1918) was a philosopher at the University of Marburg and headed the Marburg school of neo-Kantianism. He wrote numerous influential studies of Kant's philosophy, especially *Kant's Theory of Experience* (1871), which became a classic expression of neo-Kantianism. His work is a significant building block for the development of phenomenology and logical positivism in the twentieth century. He was also an influential religious philosopher, writing extensively on Judaism. [Translator]

13. That is, in potential or relative nothingness. [Translator]

14. Kant, *Prolegomena*, 103.

15. Kant, *Prolegomena*, 103.

16. "Es tritt jemand an eine runde Tafel und spricht: diese runde Tafel ist viereckig; so schweigt der Grammatiker (some grammarian!). Der Logiker aber ruft, Unsinn! Jener spricht, dieser Tafel sind rund, oder hic tabulum sunt rotundum. Der Logiker an sich (a new sort of homo sapiens) versteht weder Deutsch noch Latein und schweigt, der Grammatiker tadelt." [Someone steps up to a round table and says, this table has four corners; the grammarian is silent. But the logician cries, nonsense! He says, this table are round, or hic tabulum sunt rotundum. The logician-in-himself understands neither German nor Latin and is silent; the grammarian scolds.] Steinthal, *Einleitung in die Psychologie und Sprachwissenschaft*, 70. This example recalls the anecdote about two Germans, one of whom said, "I have been shorn," and the other corrected, "I was being clipped." The persuasiveness of the example lies in the exemplary dull-wittedness of the grammarian-in-himself, who does not understand the meaning, and the logician-in-himself, who does not know the language. With such "specialists" one cannot expect anything good either for logic or grammar, whatever their "autonomy."

17. A reference to Plato's *Apology of Socrates*, 31CD, where Socrates mentions having a *daimonion,* something like an inner voice, that always warns him against certain actions but does not tell him what to do. [Translator]

18. His argument is as follows: "If language were logical, and its form the organic imprint of the logical form of human thinking, what would be the result? It would follow . . . with undeniable necessity that it must be impossible to express in grammatically correct language a logical error, that is, something thought illogically, in a logically false manner. In the ability to express a thought in language we would therefore have a touchstone for the correctness of this thought. When for example two contrary concepts cannot be connected with each other as subject and predicate in a judgment, when the judgment 'the circle has four corners,' or 'a four-cornered circle' is unthinkable, logically wrong, then the same thing must be inexpressible in the language. As often as someone insists that he should let himself be carried away by a logical error of thought to think falsely, that is in fact, not to think, the use of language would have to abandon him. He would have to be in a predicament over the word or the grammatical form; at the very least, every error of thought irredeemably and unavoidably would have to be connected with an error of language, every transgression against logic with a corresponding one against grammar. However, that is not at all the case, but the wildest nonsense can be expressed correctly and even in a fine sentence structure." Steinthal, *Einleitung in die Psychologie und Sprachwissenschaft*, 55. It is obvious for everyone that you cannot consciously think "a square circle" any

more than you can consciously say "square circle," and you cannot call every piece of verbiage "speech." The notion that language should not allow logical errors, as far as logic does not allow and does not notice it, is clearly absurd, not meriting analysis. Here in essence is one and the same philosophical question about the nature of error in both thought and speech. And here in his discussion of the question about the relation between logic and grammar, he only hit on a preposterous misunderstanding.

19. So far as one can acknowledge together with Steinthal "the wonderful autonomy of language" and even agree that "the power of its autonomy is the objective measure for the superiority of language," it is also correct that "just as there are chemical, physical and psychological categories, so too there are grammatical ones, e.g., substantive, verb, attribute"; and that "linguistic and logical categories are disparate concepts (?) that exist peacefully side by side." Steinthal, *Einleitung in die Psychologie und Sprachwissenschaft*, 68, 72.

20. Potebnia, *Mysl' i iazyk*, 176: "According to the beliefs of all Indo-European peoples, 'a word is the thing itself, and this is demonstrated not so much by the philological connection of words, which designate *word and thing*, as by the belief extended to all words that they designate the essence of phenomena. A word as the essence of a thing in prayer and occupation gains power over nature. Verba . . . quae mare turbatum, quae concita flumina sistant [words . . . which check the swollen sea and stop the rapid rivers] (Ovid, *Metamorphoses* VII, 150, 204, et al. [Actually, lines 153–154. Translator]). These words have such power not only in exorcism but also in poetry ("to starina, to i deian'e, kak by sinemu moriu na utishen'e" [at one moment olden times, at another, a deed, as if to the blue sea for comfort]), *Drevnie rossiiskie stikhotvoreniia*) because poetry too is knowledge. The power of the word was the result neither of the moral force of the speaker (this would suggest the separation of word from thought, but there was no such separation), nor of the rituals accompanying it. The independence of a word is visible already in the fact that no matter how mighty the outbursts of the one praying may be, he must know precisely which word is to be used in order to produce what is desired. The mysterious connection of a word with the essence of an object is not limited to the consecrated words of incantations alone: it remains in the words of ordinary speech as well. Not only should you not invoke evil ("don't call evil, it can only be a spell," cf. Proverb 199), but even with the most innocent intention, in the calmest conversation, you should not mention certain beings or, if speech cannot make do without them, you should at least replace their usual and lawful names with other arbitrary ones that do not have that power. Even today, a Ukrainian peasant who spoke one of these words without thinking, carefully makes a reservation: 'may it not appear, may it not be dreamt.' A Serb says 'do not be applied' when in conversation he compares the fortunate with the unfortunate, the living with the dead, etc. (cf. Proverb 195). It is difficult to determine here where customary courtesy ends and serious danger for the life and fortune of your interlocutor begins. If someone who does not know the language does not utter the word that the thought requires, then the thought of the speaker is not fulfilled, but there is only a word. For example, when a Serbian soothsayer wants to fly, he smears himself with a certain ointment (like our witch) under his armpits and says, 'Not into a blackthorn bush, nor into a low-lying oak tree (or thorny shrubs), but rather into a swept granary.' They report that one woman, having smeared herself with that ointment, being ignorant, instead of 'not into a blackthorn bush' and the rest, said 'first fly into a blackthorn bush'—and having taken flight got torn up on the bushes."

Chapter 4. Language and Thought

1. A concept is "purely and simply that which operates, and not as a cause with the appearance of effecting something other, but the operating being itself." Hegel, *Encyclopädie der philosophischen Wissenschaften*, §163. "This realization of the concept is the object." Ibid. §193.

2. On this question, Bulgakov refers the reader to his *Tragödie der Philosophie*, Darmstadt, Reichlverlag, 1927. Here and in the following paragraph, Bulgakov used a neologism, "genohypostasnost'" or "henohypostaticity," which I have translated here as "the one hypostaticity." He seems to be relying on a distinction in Greek between two ways of indicating "one" as a prefix, mono- and heno-, and likely had in mind the distinction between "monotheism" and "henotheism" that had become current in the study of world religions. Monotheism recognizes one sole God, while henotheism focuses on one God in particular but accepts the possibility of many Gods. Bulgakov analogously uses his neologism to express Hegel's focus on the hypostasis of the Logos at the expense of the other two persons of the Trinity. The word appears again in Bulgakov's *Glavy o troichnosti* (Paris, 1928–1930). [Translator]

3. In 1: 1, 3. Bulgakov also gave the Greek text. [Translator]

4. Taken from Goethe's *Faust*, part 1, in Faust's study, 1227–1228. Bulgakov slightly alters the word order of the sentence, which in the original reads "Ich kann das Wort so hoch unmöglich schätzen, ich muss es anders übersetzen." [Translator]

5. The Russian is "logizm." [Translator]

6. An excerpt from the 1840 poem by Mikhail Lermontov, "Est' rechi— znachen'e." [Translator]

7. The famous brothel in Pompeii. [Translator]

8. It is Wagner who refers to this aphorism, in German translation, in *Faust*, part one, l. 558–559. [Translator]

9. From a poem by Aleksei Tolstoi, "Menia vo mrake i pyli [me in gloom and dust]," 1851. [Translator]

10. Herbert Spencer (1820–1903), an English philosopher, biologist, anthropologist, and sociologist produced a ten-volume *System of Synthetic Philosophy* in which he sought to demonstrate his belief in the universality of natural law that was applicable to all spheres of organic and inorganic life, to humans and the rest of creation. He also argued for the inevitability of progress. He was inspired by the work of the French philosopher and writer Auguste Comte (1798–1857) who developed the doctrine of positivism and the new science of sociology. [Translator]

11. For "sobornyi," often rendered "collegial," "conciliar." [Translator]

12. "All words are phonetic images and as to their meaning they are in themselves and from the beginning tropes. As the origin of value was an artistic one, so it also substantially changes its meaning through artistic intuition. Actual values, i.e., prose, do not exist in language." Gerber, *Die Sprache als Kunst*, vol. 1, 2nd ed. (Berlin, 1885), 309. Cf. Giesswein, *Die Hauptprobleme der Sprachwissenschaft*, 119–121.

13. Here is an example of this rationalism in a contemporary philologist. "The less significance a word has for us, the more nebulous is the inner form and vice versa. The most precise words are those in which the inner form is entirely forgotten. Often one can hear regret over the loss of the original picturesqueness of an old or folk language. Here one must add that in losing the old picturesqueness, language always creates a new one: we have seen that without inner form it is impossible to

change the meaning of a word, therefore this process continues into the present time. It is hardly possible to assert that in a new language there are fewer images than in an old one. But the question nonetheless is changed significantly. One can say with certainty that a word overwhelmed primitive naïve humankind with its images. It summoned in them a superstitious dread and submission to its power. Belief in the power of exorcisms and curses and the certainty that the sorcerer "knows the word" is based on this. The contemporary cultured person masters a word and begins to understand that a word is their own creation (?!). This liberation of the person from the overwhelming meaning of their own word must necessarily be accompanied by the loss of the old inner form of the word, which is the main bearer of images. The old picturesqueness of language, of course, is forfeited, and language becomes more sober. But one should remember that the person is liberated from the spell of witchcraft of their own word." Kudriavskii, *Vvedenie v iazykoznanie*, 44.

14. "The fact that a word lacks content is very important: it makes a word a powerful instrument of thought. In order to make this still clearer, let us turn our attention to mathematics, which has brought the precision of its conclusions to an unusually high level. Mathematics attained this thanks to its special language of signs. Letter designations of magnitudes are completely without content and arbitrary in and of themselves, but at the same time, precisely thanks to this convention and lack of content, they allow us to deposit in them an entirely definite content. Language, of course, cannot reach such a state, but in it we notice the same dependence: language becomes more precise the more meaningless words themselves become, losing their inner form, the closer they approach simple language, a symbol." Kudravskii, *Vvedenie v iazykoznanie*, 43. Bréal evaluates the verbal bungle somewhat differently: "do words created by scholars and the well-read have greater precision? One should not count on it. In the seventeenth century, Van Helmont, remembering more or less vividly the Dutch *gest* (spirit), calls *gaz* bodies that are neither solid nor liquid. This is just as vague and incomplete as *spiritus* in Latin and *psuche* in Greek. In the spirit of patriotism, a French chemist, on discovering a new metal, named it gallium; a German scholar, no less a patriot, answers back with germanium. Designations that teach us just as little about the substance of things as the names Mercury and Jupiter given to planets, or those of ampere and volt recently given to quantities in electricity." Bréal, *Essai de sémantique*, 195. In general, by coming too close to rationalism, even Bréal proposes, "The further a word is detached from its origins, the more it stands in service to thought: it retreats or stretches out, becomes specific or general. It accompanies the object for which it serves as label across the events of history, rising in dignity or falling in opinion, and passing sometimes to the opposite of the initial meaning: the more suitable for these different roles, the more fully a sign it has become. Phonetic alteration, far from harming it, is favorable to it in that it hides the connections it had with other words that remained closer to the original meaning or that went off in different directions. But even though phonetic alteration has not intervened, the actual and present value of the word exerts such power on the spirit that it strips from us the sentiment of the etymological signification. The derivatives can withdraw with impunity from their primitive meaning and on the other hand the primitive can change meaning without the derivatives being affected." Bréal, *Essai de sémantique*, 196–197.

15. "Every language must be learned, no language is offered to us, not even our mother tongue. At most one can surmise that like other aptitudes, it too can be

bequeathed to a certain language form, that an Iroquois child, for instance, which comes to French foster parents, has more difficulty learning French than it would have learning Iroquoian from its physical parents. Every normally developed human being who has left the time for language learning behind, handles their mother tongue free of error as long as it is not spoiled for them through foreign influences. The accurate handling of one's mother tongue happens without thinking, without the one speaking taking account of the linguistic laws that determine their speech. . . . Linguistic laws form an organic system, which we call the spirit of language." Gabelentz, *Die Sprachwissenschaft*, 61–63.

16. The first line of Alexander Pushkin's 1825 love poem addressed to Anna Petrovna Kern, with whom he had a brief affair. [Translator]

17. A general term encompassing a particular manner of reading and interpreting texts, particularly biblical texts, that was developed by Clement of Alexandria (c. 150–c. 215 CE) and especially Origen of Alexandria (c. 185–c. 254 CE) and their followers. [Translator]

18. An allusion to the post-resurrection appearance of Christ to two disciples on the road to Emmaus, Luke 24: 27. [Translator]

19. After an invocation, the prayers are the "Glory to you, o God," "Heavenly King," "Holy is God," "Our Father," typically ending with a threefold "Come let us worship." [Translator]

Chapter 5. The "Proper" Name

1. One can agree with Gerber up to a point that "proper names (*onomata kuria, nomina propria*) are just as much originally generic names (*onomata prosegoreka, nomina appellativa*) as these themselves. If in the communication of humans among themselves one used them in order to designate individual, specific living entities, this only created a special type of their use, by means of which they marked an individual thing through a word in order to be able to keep it as this specific thing." Gerber, *Die Sprache und das Erkennen*, 105. By ascribing properties of a particular kind to them, Apollonius (*De constructione orationis* 103, 13) already says that proper names designate a general quality,* but in separate objects: *"he onomaton thesis epenoethe eis poioteta koinas e idias, hos anthropos, platon* [the setting of names was contrived for common or particular qualities, such as man, Plato]." The designation of a proper name as *onoma kurion (proprium)*, that is, dominant, agrees with this. Cf. Gabelentz, *Die Sprachwissenschaft*, 366: "The human names things according to some prominent property, that is, he replaces the subject with the predicate." Bréal's opinion likewise merits attention: "one can say that between proper names and common names there is only a difference of degree. They are so to say signs to the second power. If the etymological sense counts for nothing, we have just seen that it is no different with ordinary substantives for which progress consists precisely in freeing themselves from their starting point. If they pass from one language to another without being translated, they have this particularity in common with many nouns of dignity, functions, uses, inventions, clothes, etc." Bréal, *Essai de sémantique*, 197–198. *reading "kachestvo" instead of "kolichestvo, quantity" because of the context. [Translator]

2. "All nouns initially express one of many attributes of an object, and this attribute, whether it expresses a quality or an action, is without fail a general concept. A word that has been formed in this manner was applied initially to one object,

although it almost immediately was extended onto an entire class of objects similar to the initial one. When the word *rivus*, 'river,' was formed for the first time, it referred without a doubt to one well-known river, and this river was called *rivus*, from the root *ri* or *sru*, 'to run, flow,' by reason of its running waters. Often a word that signified 'river' or 'runner' remained the proper name of a river without ever becoming common. Thus, for example, *Rhenus*, Rhein, means 'river' or 'flowing,' but it referred to one river and could not be used as the common name of other rivers. Ganges, in Sanskrit *Ganga*, is an appellation entirely corresponding to a majestic river, but in Sanskrit it referred only to that holy river. *Ind*, in Sanskrit *Sindhu*, means 'irrigator,' from *Syand*, 'to irrigate,' however in this case the word did not remain a proper name but was used also as the common name of all great streams." Müller, *Lektsii po nauke o iazyke*, 288–289.

3. "All proper (personal or geographical) names arose from ancestral or common designations that in the beginning received primary use in a certain sense. It is especially easy to follow this formation in geographical names. For example, New town—Novgorod (cf. German Neustadt, Neuburg, Neuchatel, Villeneuve, English Newcastle, etc.); the German Berg, Burg, Hof, Münster, Hochburg, Neukirch, the Russian Chistopol', Krasnyi Iar, Novgorod, Krutoi Vrag, Krutogorki, Belaia gora, Ozersk, Ostrovki, kliuch Gremiachi, kliuch Sosnovoi, ruch'ia Rzhavets, Berezovyi, etc. Frequently families have a similar origin: Bespalov, Shestopalov, Griaznov, Smirnov, Zviagii (from *sviaga*—bawler, shouter), Anokhin (*anokha*—ninny), Boldyrev (*boldyr'*—mongrel), Krivonosov, Lomonosov, Bulychev (*bulyk*—naked, shameless person, knave), Bulygin (*bulyga*—large stone, cudgel, blockhead). Families of the type Annin, Mar'iashkin, Tat'ianchikov, Katerinin, Sof'in, Marinkin, Marfin, Mashkin, etc. point to an origin from illegitimate children, etc." S. I. Bulich, "Sobstvennye imena," *Ėntsiklopedicheskii Slovar' Granata i Efrona*, vol. 60, 1st ed., 667.

4. A line from "Ode on the day of the ascension to the All-Russian throne of her Majesty Empress Elizaveta Petrovna in 1747" by Mikhail Lomonosov. [Translator]

5. Khlestakov is the main character in Nikolai Gogol's satirical play "The Inspector General," who is mistaken for a high-ranking civil servant by corrupt town officials. He personifies irresponsibility, impudence, hypocrisy, and dissoluteness, captured by the noun "khlestakovshchina [khlestakovism]" [Translator]

6. "The wealth of synonyms reached an improbable level in Arabic. They say that an Arab philologist composed an entire book about the names for "lion" (around 500), a second about the names for "snake" (around 200). They likewise say that Firouzabadi, the author of Kapus, compiled a book about the names of bronze and having counted more than 80 acknowledges that his list is far from complete. The same author certifies that there exist at least 1000 words for designating "sword"; others have found 400 words for expressing the concept of misfortune. Hammer counted Arabic words that refer to camel and found 5,744 of them. The Lapp language reckons around 30 words for designating deer according to its sex, age, coloration, etc. Ancient Anglo-Saxon had more than 15 words for designating sea." E. Renan, *Proiskhozhdenie iazyka. Sobranie sochinenii*, VI: 47.

7. Bulgakov uses "lev" [lion] and "Lev" [Leo] to illustrate this point. [Translator]

8. Adolphe Quetelet (1796–1874) was a Belgian astronomer, mathematician, sociologist, and statistician who developed the theory of the "average man" and

applied statistics and probability to the analysis of social phenomena, particularly as indicators for the propensity of some people to commit antisocial and criminal acts. [Translator]

9. "This inclination can be manifested from outside and in firmly established laws or customs, although it is not exhausted by them, indeed in general it is expressed much more forcefully in an indistinct and confused attraction for naming. As examples of such customs are very numerous, here are a few: the same name is given uninterruptedly to all the sons in remembrance of a famous ancestor (Heinrich in the Norwegian family Reiss). Or, beginning with some famous date, the eldest son always receives a certain name (e.g., in the family Schmoller the name Gustav Adolph, beginning with the battle of Lützen) etc." M. Schlesinger, *Geschichte des Symbols* (Berlin: 1912), 423.

10. In linguistic literature, references to the speech of children are quite widespread, which is why it will be appropriate here to name one such example from the onomastic field. One little girl at an early age resolutely and stubbornly refused to use the first person pronoun, replacing it with her name, so that instead of "I want" she said "M-a want." It is impossible not to say that here was manifested a true onomastic instinct, thanks to which she equated her name with its bearer.

11. P. A. Florenskii has gathered material relating to this in his handwritten work on renaming (both secular and sacred). [Now published: Pavel Florenskii, *Maloe sobranie sochinenii. Imena* (Moscow: Kupina, 1993). Translator]

12. Expressive are the words of the priestly prayer in the liturgy of St. Basil the Great (at the "It is worthy"): "and those we have not remembered, by ignorance or forgetfulness, or multitude of names, do you, O God, yourself remember, who know the age and name of each one, who know each one from their mother's womb."

13. Corrected from Mt 10:80. [Translator]

Chapter 6. The Name of God

1. For "bogochelovechestvo," often translated "divine humanity" or "Godmanhood."[Translator]

2. "In the definitions (*horos*) of the iconoclast council of 753, we encounter judgments that are surprisingly parallel to the reasoning of the current namefighters. Here is an example. 'A painter has made an icon and called it Christ, but the name Christ is the name of God and of a man. Therefore, the icon is an icon of God and of a man, for he depicted together (*sumperiegrapse*), as it seemed to his weak mind, the indescribable divinity by his depiction of created flesh, or he merged the union without confusion and fell into the impious error of merging. He permitted in this way two blasphemies with respect to the Godhead: its circumscription and its mixture (*perigraphe te kai sugchusis*). And whoever worships icons falls under the same blasphemies'" (Mansi 13, 252). Fr. N. Gross, *Prep. Feodor Studit, ego vremia, zhizn' i tvoreniia* (Kiev, 1907), 170.

Here are some opinions of St. Theodore Studite: "Christ is one thing, an icon of Christ is another by nature (*kata phusin*), although there is also a unity between them by the indivisibility of their appellation (*kata ameres tes kleseos*). Thus when we gaze at the nature (*phusin*) of an icon, we cannot call what is contemplated either Christ or an icon of Christ, for the nature of an icon is constituted by wood, paint, gold, silver, or some other material. But when we observe what is obtained in it through the likening of the prototype, then we call it both Christ and an icon of Christ. But it is only Christ according to the identity of the Name (*kata to onomunon*), whereas it is an icon of Christ on the basis of its relation (*kata to pros ti*), since an image (*to paragonon*) supposes a prototype, precisely as the identity of name supposes the name itself of the one who is called by it" (PG 99, 341), cited by Gross, *Prep. Feodor Studit*, 181. Cf. *Tvoreniia prep. Feodora Studita*, vol. 1 (St. Petersburg, 1907), 127. In the same "First Refutation of the Iconoclasts," we read the following retort: "A Heretic—Should one venerate the inscription or only the representation, the name of which is inscribed? And in any case, one of them but not two? And which one namely? An Orthodox—This question is like asking if one should venerate the Gospel or the name written on it, the image of the cross or what is written on it. I would add with respect to people (should one honor) a certain person or their name, e.g., Peter and Paul, and each of the individual objects of one and the same kind. . . . What of that which is seen by the eyes lacks a name? In what manner can that which is named (by a certain name) be separated from its proper appellation, so that we would repay one of them with veneration but the other we would deprive (of veneration)? These things suppose each other; a name is the name of that which is named by it and as it were is a kind of natural image of the object, which bears this name. In them the unity of veneration is inseparable." *Tvoreniia prep. Feodora Studita*, vol. 1, 129. Cf. also 140, 142. Cf. the completely analogous discussions in the holy patriarch Nikephoros and his *Antirrheticus* I, *adversus Constantinum Copronymum* (PG 100, 318; *Antirrheticus* III, 432). "An icon of Christ is called by His name according to the significance of appellation; therefore, it is worthy of equal honor and veneration with It" (PG 99, 361A, Gross, *Tvoreniia prep. Feodora Studita*, vol. 1, 183). As proof in defense of holy icons, he pointed out that "the Savior is called not only by a common name but also by the proper name Jesus, which means that He can be depicted according to his humanity" (PG 99, 397A, Gross, *Prep. Feodor Studit*, 185). Here iconology is brought into connection with onomastics (and in essence with name-glorifying).

3. For "chelovekobozhie," often translated "mangodhood, human divinity." [Translator]

4. In Indo-European idioms, the name of the Godhead is borrowed for the most part from the names of the forces of nature. "The primitive appellation of the heaven is the basis of the name for the mighty national God in four mythologies. The names, in Sanskrit *dyuas* "heaven, god of heaven," Greek Zeus, Latin Jupiter, German *Tiu*, Zio (the root is dive "to shine"), in the most precise sense are identical. That this divinity is a force of nature, the word *dyuas* in the Vedas already shows fully clearly, "heaven" and "god of heaven" already completely merge in it. . . . One of the names for heaven was "what envelops" Sanskrit "*varuna*," Greek *ouranos*, "heaven," from the root *var* "to envelop." Another epithet of heaven, *bhaga*, from the root *bhaj* "to provide" could have already in primitive time the sense of "provider of boons" because "every good thing comes down from above." In the *Vedas* this is a particular epithet of the gods, in the *Avesta* in the form *bhaga*, this word directly means "god." Among the Frigians there was *Vagaios*, according to Hesychios = Zeus. The old Slavic "*bog*" is the basic name of God in all Slavic languages." Otto Schrader, *Sravnitel'noe iazykovedenie i pervobytnaia istoriia. Lingvisticheski-istoricheskie materialy dlia issledovanie i indogermanskoi drevnosti* (St. Petersburg, 1886), 458–459, 460. Thus,

a rationalistic decadent skepticism wafts from the appeal to Aeschylus, which Professor Zelinskii by some kind of misunderstanding welcomes so fervently. "Zeus, whoever you might be—if it is agreeable to you that we call you with *this* name—we call you indeed with this name." F. Zelinskii, *Drevnegrecheskiia religiia* (Moscow, 1918), 56. This *if* is of course skeptical name-fighting. It is for other, much more profound motives that Eastern monism is hostile toward any name, i.e., to a concrete, formed being, with its doctrine of the *maya* of all that is: "the main idea of the Vedanta is that everything that has name and form is transitory. The earth is transitory because it has name and form. Eternal heaven would be a contradiction in words, as would "eternal earth" because everything that has name and form must begin in time, continue in time, and end in time." Swami Vivekananda, *Dzhnani Ioga*, trans. Ia. K. Popov (St. Petersburg, 1914), 292–293. "In the Upanishads it is declared that these heavens where people live with their ancestors cannot be eternal, since all that has name and form must die." Swami Vivekananda, *Dzhnani Ioga*, 293–294.

5. Bulgakov spoke of pagan religions throughout *Unfading Light*, but he may have in mind the chapter "The First Adam." See Sergius Bulgakov, *Unfading Light: Contemplations and Speculations*, translated, edited, and introduced by Thomas Allan Smith (Grand Rapids, MI, 2012), 285–342. [Translator]

6. Here, for example, is a summary about the Name of God that we find in the handbook Rudolf Smend, *Lehrbuch der alttestamentlichen Religionsgeschichte*, 2nd ed. (Freiburg, 1899), 277, note 1: "The name of a thing in Hebrew often enough means its essence: what exists. That the name is already given and what a human being is, is already known (in advance) (Eccl 6:10, cf. Gen 2:18ff). More often in the Old Testament, it is a question of the name Yahweh as the core of his essence, especially of his power and glory: 'Yahweh is his name,' or 'Yahweh Sabaoth is his Name,' (Ex 15:3, Isa 47:3). Yahweh makes his name known when he demonstrates his greatness in the liberation and glorification of his people (Isa 52:6; 64:1). The name of Yahweh is often also equivalent to his honor, which has been desecrated through Israel's sins (Lev 17:21), which is to be feared and hallowed (Ps 86:11; 102:15; Mal 16) and praised (Ps 102:22). Besides, the name of Yahweh is as much his honoring and his cult that culminates in the solemn invocation of his name. In this sense, it means that the false prophets cause Judah to forget his name (Jer 23:27). To love Yahweh's name means to love his service (Isa 56:6). Further, the name of Yahweh is also as much as the invoked God. 'May the name of the God of Jacob help you' (Ps 20:1–2). 'Those boast of wagons and these of horses, but we boast of the name of Yahweh our God' (Ps 20:7). 'Through you we push down our foes, through your name we trample on our enemies' (Ps 44:5). 'You come against me with sword and lance and spear, but I come against you with the name of Yahweh' (1 Sam 17:45). Hence, the listening God even seems to call the name of Yahweh 'your name is kind' (Ps 52:9; 54:6; 135:3). Without question, the passage Ex 22:24 belongs here: 'on all the places where I will establish the veneration of my name.' So, too, Isa 18:7 calls Jerusalem the place of Yahweh's name, and in a similar way one should interpret the phraseology of the deuteronomical texts where Yahweh has set his name in Jerusalem (1 Kings 9:3), lets it reside there, or that his name is present there (1 Kings 8:16, 29). Everywhere the name of Yahweh is God who is present for the cult" (cf. 1 Kings 8:29).

7. Gregory of Palamas's teaching on the distinction between the divine essence and the divine energies in God, and that we know God not in the divine essence, which is forever transcendent and unknowable, but in the divine energies, was

debated and finally accepted as Orthodox doctrine at a series of six councils held in Constantinople between 1341 and 1351. [Translator]

8. The first refers to the small loaves of bread used in the Divine Liturgy, the second, to blessed bread that is distributed after communion. [Translator]

9. Lev 19:12. "Do not swear falsely in my Name and do not dishonor the Name of your God" (this is not in the Decalogue but from a general exposition of the demands of holiness). Pagans sometimes avoided speaking the names of the gods, likewise for reasons of reverence toward them. "For example, in Rome the exact names of the gods were considered taboo because revealing them made it possible 'to summon' them. For that reason, we know above all the epithets that replace the divine names. Even the city of Rome had a secret name, which was used only during the most solemn addresses. Its mystery was so well guarded that it has remained unknown to us." Solomon Reinak, *Orfei. Vseobshchaia istoriia religii* (Paris, 1910), 121.

10. Parallel to this is the narrative of 2 Chr 6:5–10. "Since the day that I brought my people out of the land of Egypt, I have not chosen a city among any of the tribes of Israel for the building of a house, in which my Name would abide, but I chose Jerusalem so that my Name would abide there. And it lay on the heart of David, my father, to build a house for the Name of the Lord God of Israel. But the Lord said to David, my father: you have in your heart to build a house for the Lord's Name; what you have in your heart is good. However, you shall not build the temple, but your son, who will come from your loins, shall build a temple for my Name. And the Lord set his word, which he uttered: I . . . have built a temple to my Name."

11. Parallel in 2 Chr 6:32–33. "Even the foreigner, who is not from your people Israel, when he comes from a distant land on account of your great Name and your mighty hand and your outstretched arm, he will come and pray in this temple, and you will hear from heaven, from the place of your dwelling, that all nations may know your Name, and that they fear you, as do your people Israel, and know that this house which I have built is called by your Name."

12. Here one can refer to Jer 32:34 as a parallel. "And in this house, over which is spoken my Name, they have put their abominations, desecrating it." And Jer 34:15–16. "And they concluded a covenant before me in the house over which my Name is spoken, but afterwards they reconsidered and dishonored my Name." This thought is expressed less definitely by the prophet Ezekiel in his description of the temple of Jerusalem. After the glory of God enters the temple, a voice is heard from there: "Son of man! This is the place of my throne and the place for my footstool, where I will live among the sons of Israel forever; and the house of Israel will no longer desecrate my holy Name. . . . When they placed their threshold by my threshold and their doorpost beside my door, so that there was a single wall between me and them, and they desecrated my name with their abominations" Ezek 43:7–8.

13. Here on the one hand one needs to single out divine appellations given for diverse instances: "And Hagar called the Lord, who spoke to her with this sign: You are the God who sees me, for she said, I saw you exactly in the vestige of the one seeing me" (Gen 16:13). "The Lord is a man of battles; Yahweh is the name of God" (Ex 15:3). "Lord is your name; crush them with your power" (Jdt 9:8). "A child is born to us, a Son is given us, the government is on his shoulders, and they will call him Wonderful, Counsellor, mighty God, Father of eternity, Prince of peace" (Isa 9:8). "I am

the Lord, this is my name" (Isa 42:8). "Our redeemer the Lord of Hosts is his name, the Holy one of Israel" (Isa 47:14). "The Lord of Hosts is his name" (Isa 48:2). "The Lord of Hosts is his name . . . he will be called God of all the earth" (Isa 56:6, 51:15). "Holy is his name" (Isa 57:15). "Forever is your name: our Redeemer" (Isa 63:16). "His name is the Lord of Hosts" (Jer 10:25). "They will know that my name is Lord" (Jer 16:21). "And here is His Name with which they shall call him: the Lord is our Justification" (Jer 23:6 = Jer 33:16). "Lord is his name" (Jer 33:2). "I live, says the King, whose name is Lord of Hosts" (Jer 46:18 = Jer 50:34 = Jer 51:19). "And it will be from that day, says the Lord of Hosts, you will call me my husband and you will no longer call me Baal (my master)" (Hos 12:16). On the other hand, it is necessary to mention those extremely numerous cases where the expression "Name of God" is used both in its proper sense and replaces the divinity itself. "Abram summoned the Name of the Lord" (Gen 13:4, cf. 21:33). "To acquire it for Himself among the people and to glorify his name" (2 Sam 7:23, 26). "In every place where I place a memorial to my name, I will come to you and bless you" (Ex 20:24). "Fear the Lord your God, serve Him alone," "swear by his name" (Deut 6:13, cf. 10:20). "And do not surrender your children to Moloch in worship and do not dishonor my name. I am the Lord" (Lev 18:21). "Glorify the Lord, proclaim his name . . . be praised. Let them call my name over the sons of Israel and I will bless them" (Num 6:27). "By his holy name" (1 Chr 16:8, 10, cf. 29:13). "Show reverence before your name" (Neh 1:11). "Blessed are you, Lord my God, and praiseworthy and glorious is your name forever" (Tob 3:11, cf. 8:5, 10:13). "It is a good deed to bless God, to exalt his name and reverently proclaim his works" (Tob 12:6). "Many peoples from afar will come to the name of the Lord God with gifts in their hands for the King of Heaven" (Tob 13:11). "And Judith said, lift up and invoke his name" (Jdt 9:8). "May the name of the Lord be blessed" (Job 11:12). "The just ones cried out your name, o Lord" (Wis 10:20). "May they shine his holy name" (Sir 7:8). "Magnify his name" (Sir 39:19; cf. 33:9, 45:19, 47:20–21, 51:1, 15, 17). "And you will say on that day, praise the Lord, invoke his name, tell among the peoples his works, remember that his name is great" (Isa 12:4). "Praise the Lord in the east, on the islands of the sea the name of the lord of Israel" (Isa 24:15). "My soul has yearned for your name and for a remembrance of you" (Isa 26:8). "Through you alone do we praise your name" (Isa 26:13). "You will invoke my name" (Isa 41:25). "May he hope in the name of the lord and be strengthened in his God" (Isa 50: 10). "Every day my name is disrespected. Therefore my people will know my name . . . that I am the one who said here I am" (Isa 52:5–6). "To love the Lord's name" (Isa 56:6). "And they will fear the Lord's name in the west, and his glory at the rising of the sun" (Isa 59:19). Further, cf. Isa 60:9, 63:12–14, 16, 64:2, 64:7. "At that time they will call Jerusalem the Lord's throne and all peoples for the sake of the name of the Lord will be gathered in Jerusalem" (Jer 3:17). "There is no one like you Lord, you are great and your name is great in might" (Jer 10:17). "You, Lord, do with us for the sake of your Name" (Jer 14:7). "You, Lord, are among us, your name is called upon us" (Jer 14:9). Cf. Jer 14: 14–15, 21, 20:9, 23:25, 27; 27:15 (= Jer 29:9), 44:26; Lam 3:55. "I have acted for the sake of my name so that it not be abused before the nations, in the eyes of whom I led them out" (Ezek 20:14). "Do not sully my name with your gifts any longer" (Ezek 20:39). Cf. Ezek 20:14, 39; 36:21 (= 36:22–23); 39:7, 25; 43:7–8). "And Daniel said may the Name of the Lord be blessed now and forever"

(Dan 2:20). Cf. Dan 3:34, 43, 52; Joel 2:26; Am 6:10. "And he shall stand and pasture his flock in the strength of the Lord, in the majesty of the Name of the Lord his God" (Mic 5:4). Zech 13:9. "From the rising of the sun to its setting great will be my name among the peoples, and in every place they will offer incense to my name, a pure sacrifice; great will be my name among the peoples. . . . My name is dreadful among the peoples" (Mal 1:11–14). Cf. Mal 2:2, 5; 3:6; Zech 13:9.

The most frequent use of the expression "Name of God" is in the Psalter as a book of worship. Since it serves no purpose to give a full list of corresponding places, we will bring forward a few: Ps 5:12; 8:2–10; 9:2, 10; 20:2–8; 22:22; 29:2; 33:21; 45:17; 48:10; 54:1, 6; 63:4; 66:2–4; 68:4; 69:30; 72:17–19; 74:21; 75:1; 76:1; 79:9; 83:16–18; 86:9, 11–12; 89:24; 91:14; 105:1; 106:47; 109:21; 111:9; 113:1–2; 116:4; 124:13; 129:8; 138:2; 145:1–2; 148:5. See Hieromonk Antony (Bulatovich), *Apologia*, for a list of places from the Psalter with mention of the Sacred Name of God.

14. An allusion to the violent destruction of religious objects, including icons and books, in the aftermath of the 1917 Revolution and the promotion of militant atheism in the newly founded Soviet Union. [Translator]

15. Cf. Col 2:9. [Translator]

16. Rev 3:20. [Translator]

17. Aleksandr Matveevich Bukharev (1824–1871) was a significant theological voice in nineteenth-century Russia, writing principally in the field of biblical studies and the spiritual life. See Paul Valliere, *Modern Russian Theology. Bukharev, Soloviev, Bulgakov. Orthodox Theology in a New Key* (Grand Rapids, MI: 2000), 19–106. [Translator]

18. I have changed this example to make sense in English; Bulgakov used po-doshva = sole of the foot or foot of a hill, and kliuch = key for a lock, and kliuch = spring of water. [Translator]

19. Bulgakov references the different spellings for Jesus used by the Russian Orthodox Church and the Old-Believers, respectively. [Translator]

20. Replacing "Paul." [Translator]

Post Scriptum to the Essay on the Name of God

1. See "Glava o Troichnost', chast' 1, èkskursy." *Pravoslavnaia Mysl'*, 1. [Original publication—S. Bulgakov, "Glavy o troichnosti. Èkskurs. Uchenie ob ipostasi i sushchnosti v vostochnom i zapadnom bogoslovii," *Trudy Pravoslavnogo bogoslovskogo instituta*, sections 1–10 and excursus, Vyp. 1 (Paris, 1928), 31–88, sections 11–13, Vyp. 2 (Paris, 1930), 57–85. [Translator]

2. Gilbert was tried in Reims in 1148, in a consistory held directly after the council had finished its business, but was not formally condemned. [Translator]

3. And then the same connection of the Glory (in the form of a cloud) and the Name is revealed in the following text: "and the Lord came down in a cloud and stopped there near him and proclaimed the Name of Yahweh" (Ex 34:5).

Excursuses

1. He is named in Gen 35:18. [Translator]

2. As in the Russian bible, but most other versions read "good fortune." [Translator]

3. Literally, prayer or entreaty, this is a solemn procession with intercessions on the eve of certain great feasts of the church year. [Translator]

4. The *Book of Needs* or *Trebnik* is the Slavonic version of the *Small Euchologion* and contains the prayers needed by the priest to celebrate the sacraments, except for the Eucharist, and other services performed in a parish. [Translator]

5. The *Nikonian Chronicle* is a compilation and edition of earlier east Slavic chronicles produced during the reign of Ivan IV in the mid-sixteenth century. It is available in an English translation: Serge Zenkovsky (ed.), *The Nikonian Chronicle*, 5 volumes (Princeton, NJ, 1984–1989). [Translator]

6. Correcting for Bulgakov's "naming, title." [Translator]

7. Correcting Bulgakov's Greek, and his translation, which originally read "the being of each separate thing in what exists, *esti de en hekaston ton onomaton.*" [Translator]

8. The standard title of the dialogue is *Kratulos, e peri onomaton orthotetos.* [Translator]

9. The Russian has "words" but that is a misunderstanding of the Greek *rhema* which means "verb" in a grammatical context, though its base meaning is "that which is said, a word." The quotation is from *Sophist 262A: oud' hau rhematon choris onomaton lechthenton.* [Translator]

10. The Greek for this sentence reads: "Theaitetos, hoi nun ego dialegomai, petetai." *Sophist,* 263A. The Russian has "lezhit" or "is lying down," which is a misreading of "letit," "is flying," the correct translation of *petetai.* [Translator]

BULGAKOV'S SOURCES

Classical and Premodern Authors

Apollonius Dyscolus. *De constructione orationis libri quatuor* [Four books on the construction of speech]. Edited by Immanuel Bekker. Berlin, 1817.

Aristotle. *Metaphysics*.

Diodorus Siculus. *Bibliotheca historica* [Historical library].

Gregory of Nyssa. *Contra Eunomium* [Against Eunomius].

Lucretius. *De natura rerum* [On the nature of things].

Nikephoros I, Patriarch. *Antirrheticus* I and III. PG 100.

Philo of Alexandria. *De sacrificiis Abelis et Caini, De vita Moysis, De somniis, De mutatione nominum, De confusione linguarum, Quod deterius potiori insidiari soleat* [On the sacrifices of Abel and Cain, On the life of Moses, On dreams, On the change of names, On the confusion of tongues, That the worse tends to plot against the better].

Plato. *Cratylus*.

——. *Sophist*.

Plutarch. *Adversus Colotem* [Against Colotes].

——. *De placitis philosophorum* [On the tenets of the philosophers].

Theodore Studite. *Opera omnia* [Works]. PG 99.

——. *Sochineniia sv. Feodora Studiiskogo* [Works of St. Theodore Studite]. Vol. 1. St. Petersburg, 1907.

Vitruvius. *De architectura, libri decem* [Ten books on architecture].

Modern Authors

Almazov, Aleksandr Ivanovich. *Istoriia chinoposledovaniia kreshcheniia i miropomazaniia* [A history of the order of service for baptism and chrismation]. Kazan', 1884.

Bart, A. *Religii Indii* [Religions of India]. Moscow, 1897.

Baudouin de Courtenay, Jan Niecislaw Ignacy. "Iazyk [Language]," "Iazykoznanie [Linguistics]." *Èntsiklopedicheskii slovar' Brokgauza-Efrona* [Encyclopedic dictionary Brockhaus-Efron]. 1st ed. Vol. 81. St. Petersburg, 1890–1907.

Bréal, Michel. *Essai de sémantique* [An essay on semantics]. Paris, 1897.

Bulgakov, Sergei. "Glavy o troichnosti. Èkskurs. Uchenie ob ipostasi i sushchnosti v vostochnom i zapadnom bogoslovii [Chapters on Trinitarity. Excursus. The doctrine of hypostasis and essence in Eastern and Western theology]." *Trudy Pravoslavnogo bogoslovskogo instituta*. I, Paris, 1928, 31–88; II, Paris, 1930, 57–85.

Bulich, S. I. "Imia chislitel'noe [Numeral]." *Èntsiklopedicheskii slovar' Brokgauza-Efrona.* Vol. 76, 861–863.

——. "Kurs lektsii po russkomu iazyku" [A course of lectures on the Russian language]. Lithographic edition, 1902–1903.

——. "Mestoimenie" [Pronoun]. *Èntsiklopedicheskii slovar' Brokgauza-Efrona.* Vol. 39, 326.

——. "Sobstvennye imena" [Proper names]. *Èntsiklopedicheskii Slovar' Granata i Efrona,* 1st ed. Vol. 60, 667.

Buslaev, F. I. *Istoricheskaia grammatika russkogo iazyka* [Historical grammar of the Russian language]. Moscow, 1881.

Curtius, Georg. *Grundzüge der griechischen Etymologie* [Fundamentals of Greek etymology]. Leipzig, 1858–1866, 5th ed. 1879.

Delbrück, Berthold. *Einleitung in der Sprachstudium* [Introduction to the study of language]. Leipzig, 1893.

——. *Grundfragen der Sprachforschung* [Basic questions of linguistic research]. Strasbourg, 1901.

Deussen, Paul. *Allgemeine Geschichte der Philosophie* [A general history of philosophy]. Leipzig, 1894.

Dmitrievskii, A. *Bogosluzhenie v russkoi tserkvi v XVI veke* [Liturgy in the Russian church in the 16th century]. Part 1. *Sluzhby kruga sed'michnogo i godichnogo i chinoposledovaniia tainstv* [The services of the weekly and annual cycle and the orders of service for the sacraments]. Kazan', 1881.

Drevnie rossiiskie stikhotvoreniia [Old Russian verse]. Compiled by Kirsha Danilov. 1804.

Fick, August. *Vergleichendes Wörterbuch der indogermanischen Sprachen* [Comparative dictionary of Indo-Germanic languages]. Göttingen, 1870.

Florenskii, Pavel. *Maloe sobranie sochinenii. Imena* [Small collection of works. Names]. Moscow: Kupina, 1993.

Gabelentz, Georg von der. *Die Sprachwissenschaft: Ihre Aufgabe, Methoden und bisherigen Ergebnisse* [Philology: its task, methods and hitherto existing results]. Leipzig, 1891.

Gerber, Gustav. *Die Sprache als Kunst.* Vol. 1 [Language as art]. 2nd ed. Berlin: R. Gaertners Verlagsbuchhandlung Hermann Heyfelder, 1885.

——. *Die Sprache und das Erkennen* [Language and cognition]. Berlin, 1884.

Giesswein, A. *Die Hauptprobleme der Sprachwissenschaft* [The chief problems of philology]. Freiburg i. Br., 1892.

Grossu, Nikolai. *Prepodobnyi Feodor Studit. Ego vremia, zhizn' i tvoreniia* [St. Theodore Studite, his time, life and works]. Kiev, 1907.

Hamann, Johann Georg. *Metakritik über den Purismus der reinen Vernunft* [A metacritique about the purism of pure reason]. 1784.

Hegel, Georg Wilhelm Friedrich. *Encyclopädie der philosophischen Wissenschaften im Grundrisse* [Encyclopedia of the philosophical sciences in outline]. 1817, 1830.

——. *Phänomenologie des Geistes* [Phenomenology of spirit]. 1807. Rev. ed. Leipzig, 1907.

Herder, Johann Gottfried. *Eine Metakritik zur Kritik der reinen Vernunft* [A metacritique on the Critique of Pure Reason]. 1799.

Hieromonk Antony (Bulatovich). *Opravdanie very v nepobedimoe, nepostizhimoe, bozhestvennoe imia gospoda nashego Iisusa Khrista* [Justification of faith in the invincible, incomprehensible, divine name of our Lord Jesus Christ]. Petrograd, 1917.

Humboldt, Wilhelm von. *O razlichii organismov chelovecheskogo iazyka i o vliianii ètogo razlichiia na umstvennoe razvitie chelovecheskogo roda* [On the difference of the organisms of human language and on the influence of this difference on the mental development of the human race]. Translated from the German by V. Biliarskii. St. Petersburg, 1857.

——. *Über das vergleichende Sprachstudium in Beziehung auf die verschiedenen Epochen der Sprachentwicklung* [On comparative language studies with regard to the different epochs of language development]. 1820.

——. *Über die Verschiedenheit des menschlichen Sprachbaues und ihren Einfluss auf die Entwickelung des Menschengeschlechtes* [On diversity in human language construction and its influence on the development of the human race]. 1836.

——. *Über die Verwandschaft der Ortsadverbien mit den Pronomen in einigen Sprachen* [On the relationship of adverbs of place with pronouns in some languages]. Abhandlungen der historischen philologischen Classe der Berliner Akademie der Wissenschaften. 1829.

Innokentii, Archbishop of Kherson and Taurida. *Sochineniia* [Works]. Moscow, 1872?

Jacobi, Friedrich Heinrich. *Eduard Allwills Briefsammlung. Mit einer Zugabe von eigenen Briefen* [Eduard Allwills's collection of correspondence with an appendix of his own letters]. Königsberg, 1792.

Friedrich Heinrich Jacobi's Werke. Edited by J. F. Köppen and C.J.F. Roth. 6 vols. Leipzig: Gerhard Fleischer, 1812–1825.

John of Kronstadt. *Moia zhizn' vo Khriste* [My life in Christ]. 1894.

Kant, Immanuel. *Kritika chistogo razuma* [Critique of Pure Reason]. Russian translation by M. Vladislavlev. St. Petersburg, 1867.

——. *Prolegomeny ko vsiakoi budushchei metafizike* [Prolegomena to any future metaphysics]. Translated by Vladimir Soloviev. n.d.

Kudriavskii, D. N. *Vvedenie v iazykoznanie* [Introduction to linguistics]. 2nd ed. Iur'ev, 1913.

Leibniz, Gottfried Wilhelm. *De arte combinatoria*. [On the combinatorial art]. Leipzig, 1666. Bulgakov used the edition by Louis Dutens of 1768.

Lévy-Bruhl, L. *Les fonctions mentales dans les sociétés inférieures* [Mental functions in primitive societies]. Paris, 1910.

Lotze, Hermann. *System der Philosophie. 1. Logik* [System of philosophy. 1. Logic]. Leipzig: S. Hirzel, 1874.

Müller, Max. *Lektsii po nauke o iazyke chitannyia v korolevskom britanskom institute v Aprile, Mae i Iiune 1861 g.* [Lectures on the science of language. Delivered at the Royal Institution of Great Britain in April, May, and June of 1861]. St. Petersburg: Izdanie redaktsii "Vivlioteki dlia chteniia," 1865.

——. *The Science of Thought*. London, 1887.

Pogodin, A. L. *Iazyk kak tvorchestvo. Proiskhozhdenie iazyka* [Language as creativity. The origin of language]. Kharkov', 1913.

Potebnia, A. *Iz zapisok po russkoi grammatike* [From notes on Russian grammar]. Bulgakov likely used vol. 4, *Glagol, mestoimenie, chislitel'noe, predlog* [The verb, the pronoun, the numeral, the preposition]—published posthumously in 1941 by Akademiia Nauk SSSR.

——. *Mysl' i iazyk* [Thought and language]. Kharkov, 2nd ed. 1892.

Pott, August Friedrich. *Etymologische Forschungen auf dem Gebiet der indogermanischen Sprachen* [Etymological research in the field of the Indo-Germanic languages]. Lemgo, 1833.

Preyer, William T. *Die Seele des Kindes* [The soul of the child]. 4th ed. Leipzig: Th. Grieben, 1895.

Regnaud, Paul. *Origine et philosophie du langage* [The origin and philosophy of language]. Paris, 1887.

Reinach, Salomon. *Orpheus. Histoire générale des religions* [Orpheus. A general history of religions]. Paris: Alcide Picard, 1909. Bulgakov cited the Russian translation, Solomon Reinak, *Vseobshchaia istoriia religii*. Paris: Alcide Picard, 1910.

Renan, Ernest. *De l'origine du langage* [On the origin of language]. Paris, 1848.

——. "Proiskhozhdenie iazyka [The origin of language]." *Sobranie sochinenii*. Vol. 6. Kiev: Izdanie B. K. Fuksa, 1902.

Sablukov, G. *Slichenie magommedanskogo ucheniia o Imenakh Bozhiikh s khristianskim o Nem ucheniem* [Collation of the Muslim doctrine of the Names of God with the Christian doctrine about it]. Kazan', 1872.

Schleicher, August. *Compendium der vergleichenden Grammatik der indogermanischen Sprachen* [A Compendium of comparative grammar of Indo-Germanic languages]. 2nd ed. Weimar: H. Böhlau, 1866.

Schlesinger, Max. *Geschichte des Symbols. Ein Versuch* [The history of symbol: An Essay]. Berlin, 1912.

Schrader, Otto. *Sprachvergleichung und Urgeschichte. Linguistisch-historische Beiträge zur Erforschung des indogermanischen Altertums* [Comparative linguistics and primitive history. Linguistic-historical materials for the study of Indo-Germanic antiquity]. 1st ed. Jena, 1883. Bulgakov cites the Russian translation, *Sravnitel'noe iazykovedenie i pervobytnaia istoriia. Lingvisticheski-istoricheskie materialy dlia issledovanie i indogermanskoi drevnosti*. St. Petersburg, 1886.

Shertzl', V. I. "Nazvanie tsvetov i simvolicheskoe znachenie ikh" [The naming of colors and their symbolic meaning]. *Filologicheskie zapiski*. Voronezh, 1884.

——. "O slovakh c protivopolozhnymi znacheniiami (ili o tak naz. ènantiosemii)" [About words with opposite meanings (or the so-called enantiosemy)]. *Filologicheskie zapiski*. Voronezh, 1884.

——. "Osnovnye èlementy iazyka i nachala ego razvitiia" [Foundational elements of language and the principles of its development]. *Filologicheskie zapiski*. Voronezh, 1886–1889.

Smend, Rudolf. *Lehrbuch der alttestamentlichen Religionsgeschichte* [Textbook of the history of Old Testament religion]. 2nd ed. Freiburg, 1899.

Steinthal, Heymann. *Abriss der Sprachwissenschaft. Einleitung in die Psychologie und Sprachwissenschaft* [A compendium of philology. Introduction to psychology and philology]. Berlin: F. Dümmlers Verlagsbuchhandlung, Harrwitz & Gossman, 1871.

——. *Abriss der Sprachwissenschaft*. Vol. 2. *Characteristik der hauptsächlichsten Typen des Sprachbaues. Neubearbeitung des Werkes von Prof. H. Steinthal (1861) von Franz Misteli* [A compendium of philology. Vol. 2. Characteristics of the principal types of language structure. Revised edition of Prof. H. Steinthal's 1861 work by Franz Misteli]. Berlin: F. Dümmlers Verlagsbuchhandlung, Harrwitz &

Gossman, 1893. This may correspond to *Typen der Sprachen* cited by Bulgakov in chapter 2, note 2.

Swami Vivekananda. *Dzhnani Ioga* [Jnani Yoga]. Russian translation by Ia. K. Popov. St. Petersburg, 1914.

Tiander, Karl F. "O nachalakh misticheskogo mirovozreniia." *Voprosy teorii i psikhologii tvorchestva* [On the principles of a mystical worldview. Questions of the theory and psychology of creativity]. Vol. 5 (Khar'kov, 1914): 417–478.

Tomson, A. I. *Obshchee iazykovedenie* [General linguistics]. 2nd ed. Odessa, 1910.

Vvedenskii, Aleksei Ivanovich. *Religioznoe soznanie iazychestva* [The religious consciousness of paganism]. Moscow, 1902.

Wundt, Wilhelm. *Völkerpsychologie* [Psychology of peoples]. Berlin, 1901.

Zelinskii, F. F. [Tadeusz Zieliński]. *Drevnegrecheskaia religiia* [Ancient Greek religion]. Moscow, 1918.

Zenkovskii, V. V. *K voprosu o funktsii skazuemogo* [Toward the question of the function of the predicate]. Kiev, 1908.

Works Cited

Alfeyev, Hilarion. "L'onomatodoxie après la controverse onomatodoxe." *Cahiers saint Silouane* 10 (2004): 139–71.

Arjakovsky, Antoine. "La glorification du Nom et la grammaire de la Sagesse (Serge Boulgakov et Jean-Marc Ferry)." In *Essai sur le père Serge Boulgakov*, 199–214. Paris: Parole et Silence, 2006.

Augustine, Saint. *Teaching Christianity*. Translated by Edmund Hill, O. P. Hyde Park, NY: New City Press, 1996.

Berdiaev, N. A. "Gasiteli dukha." *Russkaia molva* (August 5, 1913).

Bonetskaia, N. K. "O filologicheskii shkole P. A. Florenskogo: 'Filosofiia imeni' A. F. Loseva i 'Filosofiia imeni' S. A. Bulgakova." *Studia Slavica Academiae Scientiarum Hungaricae*, 37, nos. 1–4 (1991), 113–89.

———. *Russkii Faust XX veka*. St. Petersburg: Rostok, 2015.

———. "The Struggle for Logos in Russia in the Twentieth Century." *Russian Studies in Philosophy* 40, no. 4 (Spring 2002), 6–39.

Bulatovich, Antonii (ieroskhemamonakh). *Apologiia very vo imia Bozhie i vo imia Iisus*. Reprinted in *Imiaslavie: Antologiia*. Edited by E. S. Polishchuk, 9–160. Moscow: Faktorial Press, 2002.

Bulgakov, S. N. [Bulgakov, S]. "Afonskoe delo." *Russkaia mysl'* 9 (1913): 37–46.

Bulgakov, S. N. "At the feast of the gods. Contemporary Dialogues." Translated by A. G. Pashkov. *Russian and East European Review*, 1922–1925, vol. 1/1, 172–83, vol. 1/2, 391–400, vol. 1/3, 604–22.

Bulgakov, S. N. [Bulgakov, S]. *Dva grada. Issledovaniia o prirode obshchestvennykh idealov*. 2 vols. Moscow: Put', 1911.

Bulgakov, S. N. *Filosofiia imeni*. KaIr, 1997, Inapress/Iskusstvo, 1999, 2008.

Bulgakov, S. N. [Bulgakov, Sergius]. *The Holy Grail and the Eucharist*. Translated by Boris Jakim. Hudson NY: Lindisfarne Books, 1997.

Bulgakov, S. N. [Bulgakov, Sergius]. *Icons and the Name of God*. Translated by Boris Jakim. Grand Rapids, MI: Wm. B. Eerdmans, 2012.

Bulgakov, S. N. "The Name of God." In Sergius Bulgakov, *Icons and the Name of God*. Translated by Boris Jakim, 115–77. Grand Rapids, MI: Wm. B. Eerdmans, 2012.

Bulgakov, S. N. "Na piru bogov. Pro i contra. Sovremennye dialogi." *Iz glubiny* (Moscow, 1918), 111–69.

Bulgakov, S. N. [Boulgakov, Père Serge]. *La philosophie du verbe et du nom*. Translated by Constantin Andronikof. Lausanne: Éditions L'Âge d'Homme, 1991.

Bulgakov, S. N. [Bulgakov, Sergei]. *Philosophy of Economy. The World as Household*. Translated by Catherine Evtuhov. New Haven, CT: Yale University Press, 2000.

Bulgakov, S. N. [Bulgakov, S]. "Smysl uchenie sv. Grigoriia Nisskogo ob imenakh." *Itogi zhizni*, nos. 12–13 (1914): 15–21.

Bulgakov, S. N. [Boulgakov, Père Serge]. *Sous les remparts de Chersonèse*. Translated by Bernard Marchadier. Geneva: Ad Solem, 1999.

Bulgakov, S. N. *Tikhie dumy, Ètika, kul'tura, sofiologiia*. St. Petersburg: Izd-vo Olega Abyshko, 2008.

Bulgakov, S. N. *Tragediia filosofii*. In *Sergii Bulgakov. Sochineniia v dvukh tomakh*, 1: 311–518. Edited by S. S. Khoruzhii. Moscow: Nauka, 1993.

Bulgakov, S. N. [Bulgakov, Sergij]. *The Tragedy of Philosophy (Philosophy & Dogma)*. Translated by Stephen Churchyard. Brooklyn, NY: Angelico Press, 2020.

Bulgakov, S. N. [Bulgakow, Sergius]. *Die Tragödie der Philosophie*. Translated by Alexander Kresling. Darmstadt: Otto Reichl Verlag, 1927.

Bulgakov, S. N. "U sten Khersonesa." *Simvol* no. 25 (1991), 169–334. Reprinted in S. N. Bulgakov, *Trudy po sotsiologii i teologii*, 2: 351–500. Moscow: Nauka, 1997.

Bulgakov, S. N. "Was ist das Wort." In *Festschrift Th. G. Masaryk zum 80. Geburtstag*, 25–46. Bonn, 1930.

Bulgakov, S. N. *Sophia: The Wisdom of God*. Translated by Rev. Patrick Thompson et al. New York: Paisley Press, 1937, rev'd ed., Hudson, NY: Lindisfarne Press, 1993.

Burch, Robert. "Charles Sanders Peirce." In *The Stanford Encyclopedia of Philosophy*, edited by Edward N. Zalta. Spring 2021. https://plato.stanford.edu/archives/spr2021/entries/peirce/.

Dal', Vladimir. *Tolkovyi slovar' zhivogo velikorusskogo iazyka*. 4th ed. 4 vols. Moscow, 1912–14.

Dennes, Maryse. "Les Glorificateurs du Nom: une recontre de l'hésychasme et de la philosophie au debut du XXème siècle, en Russie." *Slavia occitania* 8 (1999): 143–71.

Domratchev, Hilarion (Hiéromoine). *Sur les monts du Caucase: Dialogues de deux solitaires sur la prière de Jésus*. Translated by André Louf. Paris: Éditions des Syrtes, 2016.

Dykstra, Tom. *Hallowed Be Thy Name: The Name-Glorifying Dispute in the Russian Orthodox Church and on Mt. Athos, 1912–1914*. St. Paul, MN: OCABS Press, 2013.

Emchenko, E. B., ed. *Stoglav: issledovanie i tekst*. Moscow: Izd-vo "Indrik," 2000.

Evtuhov, Catherine. *The Cross and the Sickle: Sergei Bulgakov and the Father of Russian Religious Philosophy, 1890–1920*. Ithaca, NY: Cornell University Press, 1997.

Florenskii, Pavel. "Imiaslavie kak filosofskaia predposylka." *Materialy k sporu o pochitanii Imeni Bozhiia*. Moscow, 1913.

Grillaert, Nel. "What's in God's Name: Literary Forerunners and Philosophical Allies of the *Imjaslavie* Debate." *Studies in East European Thought* 64 (2012): 163–81.

Hamburg, G. M. "The Origins of 'Heresy' on Mount Athos: Ilarion's *Na Gorakh Kavkaza* (1907)." *Occasional Papers on Religion in Eastern Europe*, 23, no. 2 (2003): 1–34.

Ilarion (Alfeev). *Sviashchennaia taina tserkvi: vvedenie v istoriiu i problematiku imiaslavskikh sporov*. St. Petersburg: Aleteiia, 2002.

Ilarion (Schemamonk). *Na Gorakh Kavkaza. Beseda dvukh startsev o vnutrennem edinenii s Gospodom nashikh serdets chrez molitvu Iisus Khristovu—ili—Dukhovnaia deiatel'nost' sovremennykh pustynnikov*. Batalpashinsk, 1907. French translation, *Sur les monts du Caucase: Dialogues de deux solitaires sur la prière de Jésus*. Translated by André Louf. Paris: Éditions des Syrtes, 2016.

Ioffe, Denis. "Passivnoe protivostoianie diamatu na puti k ontologii i fenomenologii: Imiaslavie i kriticheskoe neogumbol'dtianstvo: russkie religioznye filosofy i Gustav Shpet." *Russian Literature* 63, nos. 2–4 (2008): 293–366.

Kenworthy, Scott M. "Archbishop Nikon (Rozhdestvenskii) and Pavel Florenskii on Spiritual Experience, Theology, and the Name-Glorifiers Dispute." In *Thinking Orthodox in Modern Russia: Culture, History, Context*, edited by Patrick Lally Michelson et al., 90–100. Madison: University of Wisconsin Press, 2014.

——. "Debating the Theology of the Name in Post-Soviet Russia: Metropolitan Ilarion Alfeev and Sergei Khoruzhii." In *Orthodox Paradoxes: Heterogeneities and Complexities in Contemporary Russian Orthodoxy*, edited by Katya Tolstaya, 250–64. Leiden: Brill, 2014.

——. "The Name-Glorifiers (*Imiaslavie*) Controversy." In *The Oxford Handbook of Russian Religious Thought*, edited by Caryl Emerson, George Pattison, and Randall A. Poole, 327–42. Oxford: Oxford University Press, 2020.

Kollmann, Jack E., Jr. "The Moscow *Stoglav* (Hundred Chapters) Church Council of 1551." PhD diss., University of Michigan, 1978.

Ladouceur, Paul. *Modern Orthodox Theology*. London: T&T Clark, 2019.

Losev, A. F. *Bytie. Imia. Kosmos.* Moscow: Mysl', 1993.

——. *Imia: izbrannye raboty, perevody, besedy, issledovaniia, arkhivnye materialy.* Edited by A. A. Takhogodi. St. Petersburg: Aleteiia, 1997.

Meyendorff, Paul. *Russia, Ritual and Reform: The Liturgical Reforms of Nikon in the 17th Century*. Crestwood, NY: St. Vladimir's Seminary Press, 1991.

Milbank, John. "Foreword." In Sergij Bulgakov, *The Tragedy of Philosophy (Philosophy & Dogma)*, translated by Stephen Churchyard, xiii–xxvi. Brooklyn, NY: Angelico Press, 2020.

Miller, David B. "The Orthodox Church." In *The Cambridge History of Russia. Vol. 1: From Early Rus' to 1689*, 355–57. Cambridge University Press, 2006.

Nikon, Patriarkh. *Trudy*. Moscow: Izd-vo Moskovskogo universiteta, 2004.

Nivières, Antoine. "La Philosophie du Nom dans l'oeuvre du père Serge Boulgakov." *Le Messager Orthodoxe* 124, no. 1 (Paris, 1994–1995): 39–42.

Obolevitch, Sr. Teresa. "Alexei Losev: 'The Last Russian Philosopher' of the Silver Age." In *The Oxford Handbook of Russian Religious Thought*, edited by Caryl Emerson, George Pattison, and Randall A. Poole, 565–79. Oxford: Oxford University Press, 2020.

Okeanskaia, Zh. L. *Iazyk i kosmos: "Filosofiia imeni" ottsa Sergiia Bulgakova v kontekste poèticheskoi metafiziki kontsa Novogo vremeni (prolegomeny k problematike filosofskogo imiaslaviia)*. Moscow: Bibleisko-bogoslovskii institut sv. Apostola Andreia, 2008.

Papoulidis, Konstantinos. *Oi Rosoi onomatolatrai tou Agiou Orous*. Thessaloniki: Institute of Balkan Studies, 1977.

"The Poetics of Language." In *A History of Russian Literature*, edited by Andrew Kahn, Mark Lipovetsky, Irina Reyfman, and Stephanie Sandler, 611–24. Oxford: Oxford University Press, 2018.

Pyman, Avril. *A History of Russian Symbolism*. Cambridge: Cambridge University Press, 1994.

Reznichenko, Anna. *O smyslakh imen. Bulgakov, Losev, Florenskii, Frank et dii minores*. Moscow: Regnum, 2012.

Rodnianskaia, I. V. "Skhvatka S. N. Bulgakova s Immanuilom Kantom na stranitsakh 'Filosofii imeni.'" In Sergei Bulgakov, *Pervoobraz i obraz*, vol. 2. *Filosofiia imeni. Ikona i ikonopochitanie*, 7–12. Moscow: Iskusstvo, 1999.

Scruton, Roger. *A Short History of Modern Philosophy*, 1981. Reprinted London: Routledge, 1995, 241–54.

Tataryn, Myroslaw. *Augustine and Russian Orthodoxy. Russian Orthodox Theologians and Augustine of Hippo: A Twentieth-Century Dialogue*. Lanham, MD: International Scholars Publications, 2000.

Troitskii, S. V. *Ob imenakh Bozhiikh i imiabozhnikakh*. St. Petersburg, 1914.

Uspensky, Boris A. "The Schism and Cultural Conflict in the Seventeenth Century." In *Seeking God: The Recovery of Religious Identity in Orthodox Russia, Ukraine, and Georgia*, edited by Stephen K. Batalden, 106–41. DeKalb: Northern Illinois University Press, 1993.

Vaganova, N. A. *Sofiologiia protoiereia Sergiia Bulgakova*. Moscow: Izd. PSTGU, 2011).

Valliere, Paul. *Modern Russian Theology: Bukharev, Soloviev, Bulgakov: Orthodox Theology in a New Key*. Grand Rapids, MI, 2000.

Zalta, Edward N. "Gottlob Frege." In *The Stanford Encyclopedia of Philosophy*, edited by Edward N. Zalta. Fall 2020. https://plato.stanford.edu/archives/fall2020/entries/frege/.

Zenkovsky, Serge, ed. *The Nikonian Chronicle*. 5 vol. Princeton NJ, 1984–1989.

Zenkovsky, V. V. *A History of Russian Philosophy*. Translated by George Kline. 2 vols. London: Routledge & Kegan Paul, 1953.

INDEX

Adam (biblical figure), and act of naming, 4–5, 37, 46, 166, 174, 175
adjective(s): attributes as, 307n44; verbs compared to, 73, 93
adverb(s), 94, 95, 306n39
adverbial modifier(s), 92, 95, 101–2, 109–10
agglutinative languages, 63, 92, 300n8
Aleksei Mikhailovich (Tsar of Russia), 14, 287n56
Alexandria, school of, 168, 315n17
algebraic metaphor, 80–81
algebraic symbols, pronouns compared to, 71
all-unity, doctrine of, 17, 90–91
Almazov, Aleksandr Ivanovich, 264
analytic languages, 109
Anselm of Canterbury, 267–68
Antisthenes, on judgment, 86, 306n31
Antonii (Bulatovich), Hieromonk, 11–12, 14
Antonii (Khrapovitskii), Archbishop, 12
Apollonius, on proper names, 315n1
Arabic language: metonymy in, 304n27; Name of God in, 269; synonyms in, 316n6
Aristotle: categories of, 126; God as object of thought in, 207
art: as incarnation of intention-form, 23; thought as verbal work of, 155–56; word/language as, 24, 295n23
aspect, temporality expressed through, 110
Athos, Mount, Name-glorifying controversy on, 10–11, 13
"The Athos Affair" (Bulgakov), 14, 15
"At the Feast of the Gods" (Bulgakov), 1
At the Walls of Chersonesus (Bulgakov), 1
attribute(s), 92, 95, 98–99, 307n44
Augustine of Hippo, 15
auxiliary words, 25
avant-garde, Russian, 15, 288n68

Babel-like confusion of languages: explanation for, 17, 35, 37, 48, 49–50, 58, 148; science and, 148
baptismal naming, 264–65, 267

Basil the Great, St., prayer of, 317n12
Baudouin de Courtenay, Jan, 2, 284n11, 288n1, 300n10, 301n14
Bely, Andrei, 15, 163, 274
ben-Abdulla, Ed-din Mohammed, 268
Berdiaev, Nikolai, 14, 287n58
Bible: divine inspiration of, 169–70; Glory of God in, 256; on idol worship, 207, 208; as monument of written language, 168; names/naming in, 247–50, 256, 257–59; place names in, 249–50, 261–63; renaming in, 187–90, 256–57; symbolic nature of, 169. See also New Testament; Old Testament
Bonetskaia, Natalia, 3
Brahman, concept of, 270–71
Bréal, Michel, 2, 41, 284n12; on adverb, 306n39; on derivatives of words, 314n14; on language's lack of precision, 304n23; on metaphor, 305n28; on preposition, 306n40; on pronouns, 300n7; on proper vs. common names, 315n1
Brianchaninov, Ignatii, 10
Buddhism, sacred books of, 168
Buffon, Comte de, 153
Bukharev, A. M., 225, 322n17
Bulgakov, Sergii Nikolaevich: At the Walls of Chersonesus, 1; "The Athos Affair," 14, 15; "At the Feast of the Gods," 1; careers of, 1; Evkharisticheskii dogmat, 17; Ikona i ikonopochitanie, 17; influences on, 2, 3; Name-glorifying controversy and, 14, 15, 16–17; Philosophy of Economy, 3; Philosophy of the Name, 1, 2; Sophia: The Wisdom of God, 284n17; The Tragedy of Philosophy, 1–2, 3; Two Cities, 15; Unfading Light, 3
Bulich, S. I., 289n1, 316n3
Buslaev, F. I., 288n1

Cabbala, 53, 54, 55, 57, 278
case(s), 72–73, 109, 301n14; instrumental, 126; nominative, 96, 111, 126, 307n42; spatiality expressed through, 109

Gabelentz, Georg von der, 2; on grammar as reflection of habits of thought, 119; on human speech, 288n1; on inner form of language, 298n37; on native language, 314n15; on predicative value, 302n16; on proper names, 315n1; on roots of words, 40; on sentence, 298n1; on specialists' use of language, 297n33

gender: absence in Kantian categories, 126–27; grammatical, 64–65, 127

Genesis, book of: Logos and creation in, 140; naming in, 4–5, 37, 46, 166, 174, 175, 180–81, 257–58; renaming in, 189; on unity of language, 49–50

Gerber, Gustav, 2; on human creativity and language, 295n23, 297n36; on judgment, 306n31; on Kant's neglect of language, 308n1; on parts of speech, 299nn2–3; on personal pronoun "I," 301n15; on proper names, 315n1; on root words, 302n16; on words as tropes, 313n12

German language: cases in, 109; names of gods in, 318n4; philosophical, 49; roots in, 303n19

gesture(s), language of, 21, 22, 289n5

Giesswein, A., 294n16, 294n21, 297n34

Gilbert de Porreta, 243, 322n2

Glory of God: biblical references to, 256; Name of God and, 214, 216, 217, 219, 240, 244–45

God: image of, as image of human being, 200; Logos as, 4, 140; revelation to human beings, 200–201; sacraments and, 230, 235. See also Name(s) of God

Goethe, Johann Wolfgang von, 139, 147

Gogol, Nikolai, 316n5

Gospel(s): genealogy of Jesus in, 10, 227; names written in heavens in, 196; naming in, 179–81; renaming in, 188–90

Gospel of John: on primacy of logos, 139–40, 142; renaming in, 188; two ideas about Logos in, 4, 140–41

grammar: comparative study of, 132; and epistemology, 105, 106, 120–29; Kant's failure to consider, 3, 21, 64, 84, 104, 105–8, 111, 113–20, 123–25, 307n1; and logic, 105, 106, 124, 129–32, 133, 310n6, 311n16; philosophy of, Bulgakov's, 7, 119–33; philosophy of, Plato's Sophist and, 3, 280–81; spatiality expressed through, 108–10, 113; and supplementary meaning of words, 25; temporality expressed through, 108–9, 110–11, 113

Greek language: conjugation in, 110; grammar in, 129, 132

Greek religion, names of gods in, 208, 318n4

Gregory of Nyssa, St., 14, 15; on origins of language, 47, 296n28

Gregory of Palamas, on divine essence vs. divine energies, 11–12, 319n7

Haeckel, Ernst, 293n14

Halki, Theological School of, 11, 286n46

Hamann, Johann Georg, 307n1

Hartmann, Eduard von, 36, 136

Hebrew language: Cabbalists on, 54, 55, 57–58; conjugation in, 110; "consonantism" of, 55, 58; grammatical gender in, 65; as one true primeval language, hypothesis regarding, 33, 57; root words in, 77

Hegel, Georg Wilhelm Friedrich: failure to pay attention to language, 21, 105, 134; on general meaning of words, 62, 299n5; God as object of thought in, 207; on hypostaticity of logos, 136–37, 313n2; on primacy of reason, 139

Heraclitus, 276

Herder, Johann Gottfried, 307n1

hieroglyph(s): icons and, 6, 201, 202, 203, 204; morpheme compared to, 210; words as, 6, 40. See also symbol(s)

Holy Gifts, 204–5, 232

Holy Spirit: and gift of tongues, 50; Name of God and, 241–42, 244

Holy Trinity: names of three hypostases in, 241–42, 244–45; revelation of, 240

homo alalus (speechless human), 293n14; and invention of language, theory of, 29, 31; Renan on, 295n27

human being(s): and articulation of cosmic word-symbols, 4, 5, 6–7, 8, 36, 37–38, 39, 43–44, 48, 74, 134–35; as bearers of world logos, 4, 21, 139–40, 141; created as image of Divine Logos, 4, 5, 136; and divine, union in Jesus Christ, 5, 10, 220–21, 222; free will in, 82; language as inalienable faculty of, 181–82; Name of God in relation to, 198, 220; Name of Jesus and closeness to, 229–31; and naming, 8, 182, 224

Humboldt, Wilhelm von, 2, 15; on language, origins of, 33, 302n17, 305n29; on language and thought, 21, 281; on language as energia, 36; on pronouns, 290n5; on root words, 298n2; on sound and word, 290n5

Hundred Chapters Council of 1551 (Stoglav), 14, 286n56

hypnotism, magical quality of words and, 6, 145–46